GERMAN S-BOATS IN ACTION

GERMAN S-BOATS IN ACTION

in the Second World War

Hans Frank

TRANSLATED BY
GEOFFREY BROOKS

First published in Great Britain in 2007 by
Seaforth Publishing,
Pen & Sword Books Ltd,
47 Church Street,
Barnsley S70 2AS

British Library Cataloguing in Publication Data
A catalogue record for this book is available from the British Library

ISBN 978 1 84415 716 7

First published in 2006 as
Die deutschen Schnellboote im Einsatz
by Verlag E. S. Mittler & Sohn GmbH

Translated Geoffrey Brooks
Designed and typeset by Sally Geeve
Printed in China through Printworks Int. Ltd.

Contents

Foreword

Before the First World War, fast motor launches were an extravagance available only to the wealthy few. When steam reciprocating machinery was still a novelty in ships, there were already international competitions for speedboats. When war came, they were found employment from early on as weapons carriers. The most impressive demonstration of what they could achieve was the sinking of the Austro-Hungarian battleship *Szent István* by an Italian motor torpedo boat in 1918.

A volunteer Motor Boat Corps was formed in Germany, but despite the Kaiser's patronage, was never integrated into the naval organisation. Designated LM-boats, the craft were equipped with powerful airship engines and used to remove anti-submarine nets laid by the Royal Navy across the channels used by U-boats leaving their Belgian bases.

On the eve of the Second World War, the S-boats of the Kriegsmarine (designated for uncertain reasons 'E-boats' by the British) were already an obsolescent breed, being the produce of early clandestine moves by individual officers and shipyards to circumvent the Versailles Treaty. Their strategic and tactical role was considered to be that of naval auxiliaries. The new arm of the service, poorly prepared, now took its place in the great confrontation. As with all German units, from the outset too much was expected from too few boats. In the long run, despite outstanding technical improvements and the wiles of their experienced crews, the S-boat Arm was unable to hold its own against Allied defences, whose sheer advantage in numbers, superior electronics and continual aerial bombardment demanded of it too high a levy.

In this fascinating historical account, the author describes the missions, operations and finally the collapse of the German S-boat Arm. The impressive story of human achievement in all theatres is a chronicle of success and failure. The vain hopes of a political leadership vested in the S-boat Arm to the very end could not be, and were not, met.

Professor Peter Tamm
Wissenschaftliches Institut für Schiffahrts- und Marinegeschichte, Hamburg

1
Development and First Operations
From the Beginnings to March 1940

Three basic factors made the creation of the S-boat Arm possible. First was the torpedo as a self-contained weapon of devastating effect; second, the operational advantage, already recognised by the Torpedo Boat Arm, of high speeds; and third, new engines, allowing the construction of smaller boats.

Germany had played a major role in the development of small, fast boats before World War I, the leader being Lürssen with his round-frame racer *Donnerwetter* (1905–9) and the Lürssen-Daimler boat with which he won the 1911 'Championship of the Seas' at Monaco. The real developments in the fighting role, in which the craft was equipped with torpedoes, were made principally by Italy and Great Britain. Both used small motor torpedo boats successfully in operations. The Italian MAS-boats (*Motobarca Armata Svano*) achieved a string of successes in the Adriatic against the Austro-Hungarian navy, an example being the sinking of the battleship *Szent István* by MAS-boats on 10 June 1918. British MTBs were often in action in the Channel against German units. Their successes were few, however, for they had to discharge the torpedo over the stern tail-first. This required high speed to prevent the torpedo 'catching up'. A surprise approach and a sure aim were therefore difficult. In July 1919, however, they proved their effectiveness by sinking the Russian cruiser *Oleg* at Kronstadt.[1]

The German development followed a different path. Not until the summer of 1916 were small, fast motor launches required, when their task was to clear British anti-submarine nets at Zeebrugge and Ostend and so allow U-boats safe access and departure at these ports. A mix of boats was needed, some to work at the nets, the others to keep the lurking British destroyers and torpedo boats at a safe distance. These guard boats therefore had torpedo armament. In the autumn of 1916 the C-in-C Baltic requested small torpedo carriers for use against Russian naval forces in the Baltic Islands region.

Two net boats and a guard boat (right).

The first six boats were built in 1917 at the Lürssen, Naglo and Oertz yards. They displaced around seven tonnes, were sixteen metres long and with their three Zeppelin airship engines could make thirty knots. Designated LM 1 to LM 6 (LM standing for *Luftschiff-*

Motor), the first four boats were equipped with net cutters; the other two each had a torpedo tube.

After inclusion in the Motor Launch Division, the boats were attached to Naval Corps Flanders. Several skirmishes off the coast of Flanders resulted in only a single success. Later in the Baltic, on 24 August 1917, the 1,200-gross-ton Russian minelayer *Penelope* was sunk by them in the Irben Strait off the Baltic Islands.[2]

Experiments were run with LM-boats off the Belgian coast using remote control, but these craft were never used operationally. Another fourteen LM-boats were built in 1918 as torpedo carriers; others ordered remained incomplete at the war's end.[3]

Reichsmarine

After the drastic reduction of the fleet by the terms of the Versailles Treaty, Germany was allowed to have six battleships not exceeding 10,000 tonnes, six 6,000-tonne cruisers, twelve 800-tonne destroyers and twelve 200-tonne torpedo boats. German Naval Command directed its efforts to keeping the predominantly old ships in commission and kept a stern watch on the permitted standing force of 15,000 men, bearing in mind the revolutionary confusion of the time.

The Navy had continuing interest in small torpedo carriers, primarily for coastal defence work. For fear that these boats might be considered 'torpedo boats' within the meaning of the Versailles Treaty, the development was kept secret. For this purpose Kapitän zur See Lohmann, head of the Naval Transport Department at the German Admiralty, founded TRAYAG (Travemünder Yachthafen AG), HANSA (the High Seas Sporting League), the Neustädter Slip GmbH and the NAVIS shipping company. From unofficial special budgets, partly from the Ruhr Fund and the 'funds for war purposes', boats completed during or shortly after the war were bought through NAVIS for extensive trials. In the autumn of 1919, HANSA sailing instructors with military training took over the TRAYAG boats and carried out nautical and tactical exercises, often with naval units.

At the termination of this training, a kind of master's certificate was awarded.[4] The experience gained coincided extensively with the knowledge gained by the end of the war and emphasised the following requirements:

development of light motors, particularly diesels, to reduce the risk of fire;
displacement hulls (instead of planing hulls) for better sea-keeping, but at the expense of very high speeds;
two bow torpedo tubes with one reload each tube for maximum weapons efficiency.[5]

Despite these very concrete specifications, open contracts were distributed to various yards. Abeking and Rasmussen came up with the experi-mental boat *K*, a stepped planing boat, Lürssen the experimental boat *Lür*, a displacement boat, and the Caspar Werft at Travemünde a large planing boat, the *Narwal*. The boats were delivered in 1926, and in tests over the next three years the advantage of the displacement boat as a good sea-keeper was clearly demonstrated.

The results provided adequate grounds for the formation of a small-boat arm. The available boats were taken over by the Reichsmarine and attached to

TRAYAG LM-boat.

Four UZ-boats of the Baltic Mining Squadron.

the Baltic Mining Squadron (*Ostseesperrverband*) in April 1929. The seven former LM-boats and the three new prototypes were given the designation UZ-boats (anti-submarine destroyers). At the conclusion of all trials, the *Lür* repeatedly proving its worth, in November 1929 the Lürssen yard received orders for the first boat to be supplied directly to the Reichsmarine.

Designated UZ16(S), the boat was commissioned on 7 August 1930 ('S' corresponding to '*Schnellboot*', or speedboat). The Baltic Mining Squadron was renamed UZ(S) Experimental Group at the same time. The prototype was reclassified *Wachboot* (guard boat) W 1 at the end of March 1931, and *Schnellboot* S 1 on 16 March 1932. In this way, the term '*Schnellboot*', used hitherto as a cover, became an official type of vessel of the German Navy. Twenty-seven metres in length, displacing fifty-one tonnes and with a speed of thirty-four knots, it was already climbing towards the specifications for the future wartime S-boats. At this stage, marine diesels were not available and petrol engines provided the propulsion.[6]

After the introduction of the classification 'S-boat' in March 1932, the UZ(S) Experimental Group (commanded by Kapitänleutnant Bey) was renamed 1.Schnellbootshalbflottille (S-boat half-flotilla). Despite the name, the function of the boats as torpedo carriers was kept secret initially and the torpedo tubes were only mounted on boats for tests and torpedo practice, 'since it is not intended to count the S-boats as part of the fleet of torpedo carriers we are permitted to have'.[7] The half-flotilla was allotted the tender *Nordsee*, which dated from the time of the Imperial Navy.

At the end of 1933, S 6 entered the unit as the first diesel-driven boat (MAN seven-cylinder four-stroke). Other boats followed in 1934 and 1935.

The long-term expansion of the S-boat Arm was delayed at first by the personnel question. The German Admiralty ruled in May 1933 that the commissioning of further S-boats would not be possible until 1936 at the earliest, having regard to the shortage of officers coming through training.[8] A decision on diesels was also awaited, since the S-boat half-flotilla had argued for petrol motors on account of the higher speeds they provided.[9]

1st S-boat Half Flotilla.

When the Reichsmarine was renamed 'Kriegsmarine' on 21 March 1935, the older boats had already been decommissioned, so that the half-flotilla was composed of the seven boats numbered S 2 to S 8. When S 9 was commissioned on 12 June 1935, the unit was redesignated 1.Schnellbootsflottille (S-boat flotilla), abbreviated to '1.SFltl'. The new depot ship

1 S-boat Flotilla.

Tsingtau was allotted in March 1936. S 10 to S 13, already ordered, were delivered in the second half of 1936.[10] In these boats, the MAN diesels had been replaced by the Daimler-Benz MB502 sixteen-cylinder four-stroke diesel, which was substantially less troublesome than the MAN engines.

To prove the point, in May 1937 the boats fitted with the Daimler-Benz engines made a trouble-free endurance voyage from Heligoland to Kiel round the north of Denmark at twenty-five knots, while the MAN-boats were plagued by breakdown. The DB engine – with improvements – then became the standard engine of the S-boat Arm.

Because of the difficulties in supplying these motors, the next group of boats, S 14 to S 17, were fitted with a MAN one-cylinder version. They arrived in 1936–8 and joined 2.SFltl., formed on 1 August 1938 with depot ship *Tanga*.[11] By now, the petrol boats had been stricken from the active list so that in 1938 the two flotillas had six diesel boats each, one or two old, decommissioned boats in reserve and a modern depot ship.

As to the further expansion of the S-boat Arm, there were now major differences. Fleet commander Admiral Carls demanded a halt to S-boat construction on the grounds that the boats were too dependent on fair weather and the type itself was close to the limits of its possibilities.[12] After long discussions, to which earlier flotilla chiefs Korvettenkapitän Bey, Korvettenkapitän von Conrady and Korvettenkapitän Schubert were invited, *Seekriegsleitung* (Naval War Directorate, abbreviated to 'SKL') decided to proceed with the building programme set out in the Z-Plan. This predicted forty-eight S-boats by 1943, with a final goal of seventy-five boats by 1947.[13] This would provide eight flotillas (North Sea and Baltic four flotillas each), with eight boats each on active service, the rest in reserve.[14] Accordingly, further boats were built and commissioned, so that by the outbreak of war in 1939 there were fifteen boats in all. The Daimler-Benz boats were concentrated in 1.SFltl., while 2.SFltl. had the vulnerable MAN-boats.

First Baltic Operations

At the outbreak of war on 1 September 1939, 1.SFltl. (Kapitänleutnant Sturm) was in the Baltic while 2.SFltl. (Kapitänleutnant Petersen) operated from Heligo-land. The naval force of destroyers, mine-sweepers and S-boats assembled in the Bay of Danzig against Poland were controlled by Naval Commander

Even on exercise things can go wrong. S 10 after a collision with the light cruiser *Königsberg*.

Leaving port on operations.

East, Konteradmiral Lütjens. It was planned for 1.SFltl. to lay mines near Gotenhafen port, but after the Polish navy did the job for them, the S-boat flotilla was detached to watch over assumed gaps in the minefields and to intercept and inspect ships leaving. A small Polish vessel was gunned and sunk. Afterwards 1.SFltl. withdrew and transferred into the North Sea, remaining there until November 1939 as protection for the force of light cruisers and mineships laying the Westwall minefield complex in the eastern North Sea.[15] The operations were hampered by heavy weather, which de-monstrated the unsuitability of the small boats for the allotted task. At the beginning of December, the flotilla retired to the Baltic for a refit lasting until the beginning of March 1940.

As its first mission in war, 2.SFltl. scouted around Heligoland. In heavy seas, S 17 was so seriously damaged that repairs were abandoned and the boat decommissioned. The flotilla then transferred into the Baltic, initially to patrol the Sound, to prevent the escape from the Baltic of the Polish submarine *Orzel*, to search for British submarines in the western Baltic and Belt and to transport depth charges to German patrol boats in the Kattegat. On the orders of Vizeadmiral Mootz, Commander, Baltic Naval Defences (BSO), to whom S-boats were subordinated at this time, for a period they congregated in the Kattegat to serve in the armed support role for Baltic operations. No contact was made with enemy forces and the flotilla was recalled for training to the western Baltic. This was soon abandoned when the sea froze, the flotilla then passing through the Kiel Canal to the North Sea to refit at Wilhelmshaven until March.

In this opening phase of the war, both flotillas had been used in a manner completely foreign to their intended purpose and, despite carrying depth charges, they were never involved in anti-submarine duties. The low height of the bridge for vision did not allow the early detection of a periscope or the bubble trail of a torpedo, while the boats themselves were betrayed to submarines early on by their engine noise.

When the boats were operating as part of the escort force protecting large vessels, the low speed required was possible only by using the central engine alone. This placed an unfair burden on the engine and led to early deterioration, overhauls and replacements. It was therefore set down in the Commerce Warfare Directions S-boat Tactics: 'Anti-submarine work is a secondary task for S-boats,'[16] and it went on to say: 'S-boats are unsuitable for anti-submarine protection with Fleet units.'[17] Naval Staffs were bemused by these instructions, for they gave no positive indication as to what the true role was. What remained clear was the fact that knowledge regarding operational uses and the necessary conditions to be applied to S-boat deployment was scanty, and the naval leadership had still not given much thought as to what S-boats were *for*.

2
Weserübung
March–May 1940

How the unwanted and, in their view, probably unwinnable war against Great Britain was to be conducted dominated the naval strategic considerations of the Kriegsmarine. The experiences of the First World War, in which the High Seas Fleet had been condemned to inactivity in the dead North Sea, led to early ideas of securing the Nordic region for the battle against British supply lines. In October 1939, Kriegsmarine C-in-C Admiral Raeder consulted Hitler on the subject for the first time. Hitler was in favour of delay. Not until December 1939, when the signs appeared that the British were intending to occupy Norway, did Hitler recognise the threat to his indispensable iron-ore transports, which loaded at the ice-free port of Narvik. From Narvik, a later direct British attack on the mines in Sweden would be a possibility. Thus arose the need to take countermeasures. In January 1940, on Hitler's order, a Special Staff for the Planned Occupation of Norway and Denmark1 was formed. Both countries would be occupied suddenly, and without warning. Denmark could be taken principally across the land frontier, supported by transport ships and a few old battleships, such as *Schleswig-Holstein*. For Norway, the necessary Army invasion force would have to be shipped aboard warship groups.

Hitler's instruction *Fall Weserübung* of 1 March 1940 set up the concrete planning based on the earlier thinking, the decisive element being that 'our measures will come as a surprise to the Nordic states as well as our western enemy'.[2] In the further operational planning, SKL foresaw five warship groups for the invasion of Norway:

Group 1: Narvik – ten destroyers protected by the battleships *Scharnhorst* and *Gneisenau*
Group 2: Trondheim – heavy cruiser *Admiral Hipper* and four destroyers
Group 3: Bergen – two light cruisers, two torpedo boats, one gunnery training ship, one S-flotilla
Group 4: Kristiansand – one light cruiser, three torpedo boats, one S-flotilla, one minesweeping flotilla
Group 5: Oslo – heavy cruisers *Blücher* and *Lützow*, one light cruiser, three torpedo boats and one R-boat flotilla (motor minesweepers)[3]

The final decision to invade had not been taken, because the Army wanted France defeated first, while SKL feared that the venture involved too high a risk: major fleet units might be lost, and these would then not be available for the offensive against British merchant traffic.[4] The *Altmark* affair showed, however, that Norway could not, or would not, enforce its obligations under the laws of neutrality,[5] while additionally reports from Norway warned of a growing tendency to fall in with the British.[6] Accordingly, the decision was taken to invade quickly, and on 2 April 1940 Hitler gave the order to begin the landings on 9 April (*Wesertag*) at 0515 hrs (*Weserzeit*).[7]

On account of the strict secrecy ordered, the two S-boat flotillas, as well as the other groups, were not informed as to the true purpose of the operation for which they had been ordered into the North Sea. Both flotillas had just begun the working-up phase after the long dockyard lay-up, which included changes in commanders and crews and the introduction of new boats to replace those decommissioned for age or wear and tear.[8]

On 7 April 1940 the ships of Groups 1 and 2 sailed with troops, passed the Shetland–Bergen Narrows

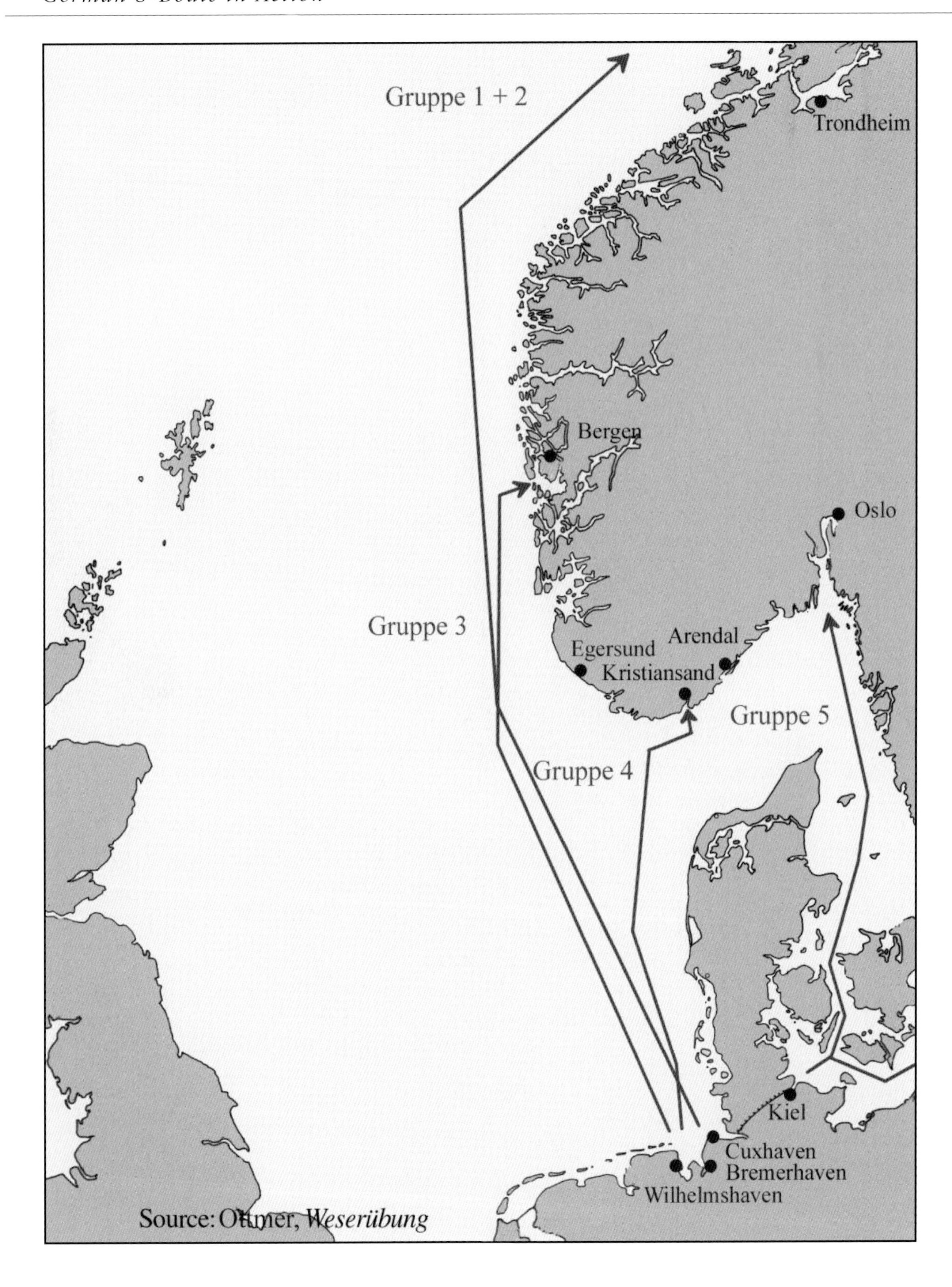

Source: Ottmer, *Weserübung*

that night and fought their way northwards in worsening weather. Here they encountered Home Fleet units covering British minelaying operations actually inside Norwegian territorial waters, while cruisers and destroyers waited in Scottish ports with invasion troops aboard.[9]

The remaining German warship groups left harbour on the night of 7 April 1940, after the heavier units had shipped troops under cover of darkness. Group 3 for Bergen consisted of the light cruisers *Köln* and *Königsberg*, the gunnery training ship *Bremse* from Wilhelmshaven, and the torpedo boats *Leopard* and *Wolf* with the S-boat depot ship *Carl Peters*[10] from Cuxhaven. The 1st S-boat Flotilla (Kapitänleutnant Birnbacher) left Heligoland with six S-boats, of which four met up with the main Group 3 force off the Norwegian coast on the evening of 8 April. On the way north along the Danish west coast, two boats of the flotilla collided and were forced to return to Wilhelmshaven. Another two boats collided in rough seas after joining Group 3 but continued after receiving assistance from the torpedo boat *Wolf*.

The units of Group 4 for Kristiansand had all been at Bremerhaven (then known as Wesermünde) but had set out in four convoys: the light cruiser *Karlsruhe* and torpedo boats *Luchs* and *Seeadler*; S-boat depot ship *Tsingtau* and torpedo boat *Greif*; the 2nd S-boat Flotilla (Kapitänleutnant Petersen) with seven S-boats; and the 2nd Minesweeping Flotilla, which headed directly for Egersund, while *Greif* was detached to occupy Arendal once the group had assembled. Kapitän zur See Bütow was aboard *Luchs* but not as C-in-C Torpedo Boats; he was taking notes for his future role as C-in-C Naval Security Forces.

Occupation of Bergen

The Norwegians had been alerted by the activities of the British and German fleets but were unclear which side was on their coast. When Group 3 approached the entry channel to Bergen, the coastal lights had been extinguished since midnight, guardships were on station and some of the coastal fortifications were at

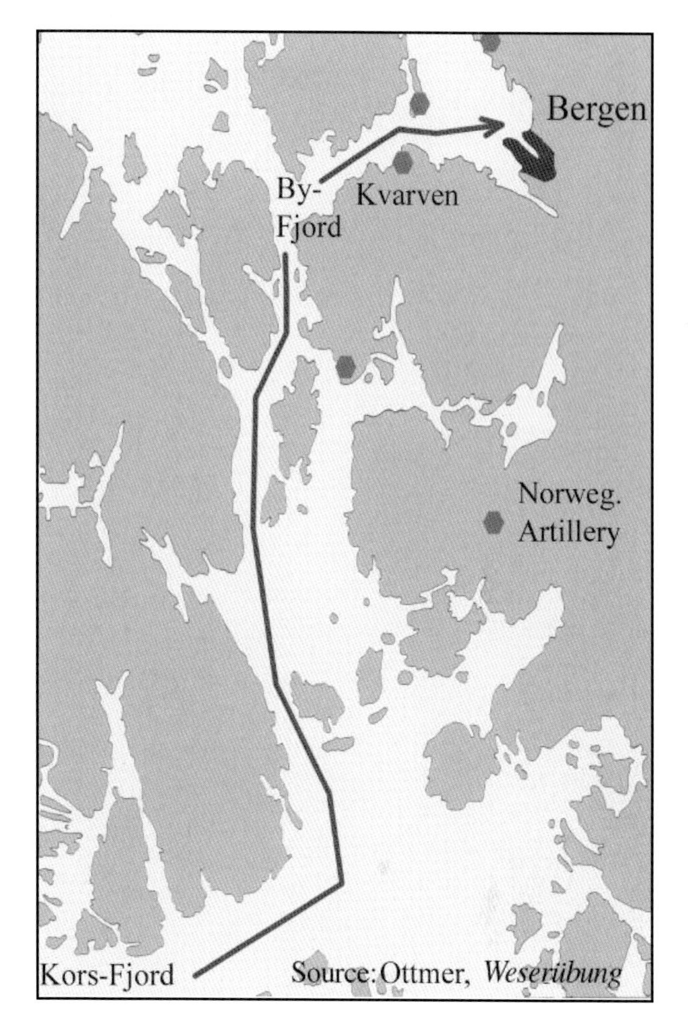

readiness. Despite this, the warships entered Kors Fjord as planned and announced themselves to the Norwegian guardships as British. They were allowed to reach By Fjord unimpeded and transferred a part of the Army troops to S-boats, from which they were disembarked below the Kvarven batteries.

Meanwhile, the torpedo boats had run on at high speed to land their troops directly at Bergen. The ships that followed received fire from the Kvarven batteries and some were hit, the light cruiser *Königsberg* receiving serious damage. Once the S-boats had landed their troops, they also ran into Bergen and helped bring ashore the Army units still aboard the cruisers *Köln*, *Königsberg* and the S-boat depot ship *Carl Peters*. By 1000 hrs next morning, Bergen and its batteries were in German hands.

Capture of Kristiansand

The situation at Kristiansand was more critical. The batteries at Odderöy took the cruiser *Karlsruhe* under fire at seven kilometres' range as she entered the fjord, forcing the group to break off the attack. Air support was requested and came, but failed to silence the batteries. *Karlsruhe* made repeated attempts to force her way into the fjord but was repulsed each time by very accurate Norwegian artillery fire. The Army troops were transferred to 2.SFltl. in the outer fjord and brought into the inner fjord at very high speed to be disembarked while the cruiser kept the land batteries occupied. The torpedo boats then followed and also landed their invasion troops. Shortly afterwards, Norwegian resistance collapsed.[11] The ports of Arendal and Egersund were captured as per timetable, no problems being encountered.

After Groups 1 to 4 had reached their destinations and disembarked troops, the navigable ships sailed immediately for home waters to avoid contact with the incoming British naval forces. Only Group 5 for Oslo, where the heavy cruiser *Blücher* was lost to torpedo hits from the shore batteries, fought on into the next day. The feared losses now occurred. At Narvik, all ten destroyers were sunk; at Bergen, the damaged cruiser *Königsberg* sank in harbour after being dive-bombed, and the cruiser *Karlsruhe* of the Kristiansand group was torpedoed by a British submarine after leaving the fjord and had to be scuttled. Another victim to a torpedo was the heavy cruiser *Lützow* returning from Oslo; though seriously damaged, she was towed safely to Kiel.

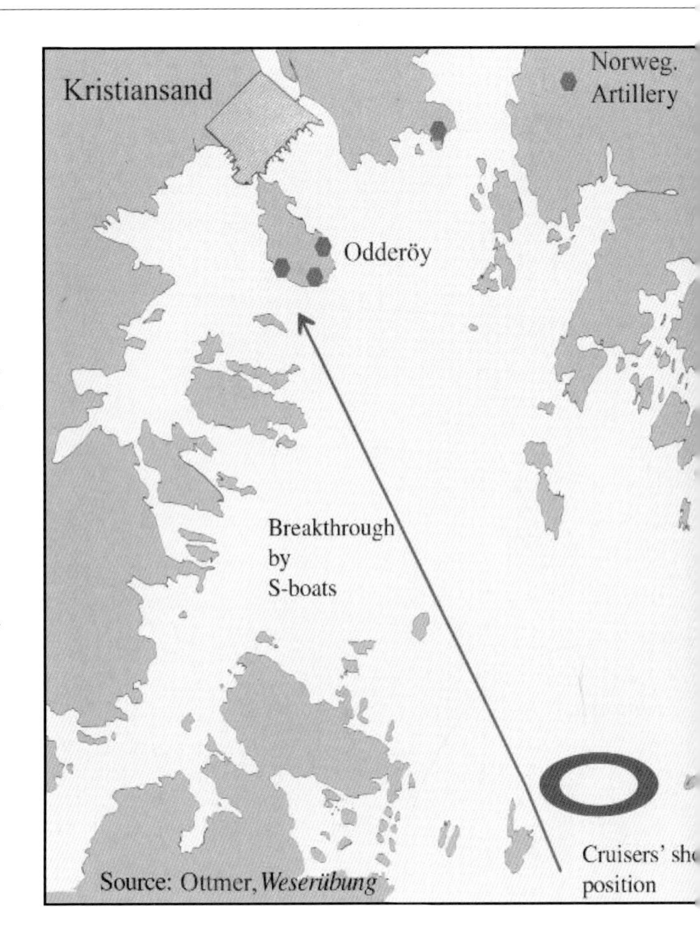

Source: Ottmer, *Weserübung*

Security Duties

Together with a number of torpedo boats and R-boats, the two S-flotillas remained in Norway to secure the captured ports and safeguard supply. The 1st S-boat Flotilla was placed under Admiral West Coast, Admiral von Schrader, with headquarters at Bergen. In the coming weeks, the flotilla operated in the Sonje–Hardanger Fjords region, searching for scuttled or concealed Norwegian shipping and putting ashore German troops in locations where Norwegians inland were still offering resistance. During this mission, they sank a Norwegian torpedo boat in Hardanger Fjord and captured various vessels, including the Norwegian minelayer *Gor*.

Under Vizeadmiral Mootz, C-in-C Naval Security Forces, Baltic, 2.SFltl. integrated with torpedo boats and R-boats escorting transports that were bringing troops and equipment to Norway. Initially Bütow, the FdT, was subordinated to Mootz to command the small craft, but since he never had more than two or three torpedo boats at his disposal because of engine breakdowns, he suggested that Mootz direct the flotillas personally. Group East accepted the idea and on 14 April 1940 released Bütow so that he might devote his energies to returning the lame-duck S-boats to active duty and also concentrate on training and the formation of new flotillas.

Since the threat to the German lines of supply was greater in the North Sea, on 24 April SKL transferred the torpedo boats and 2.SFltl. there to Group West.[12] Operating from Kristiansand, Stavanger and Wilhelmshaven, S-boats protected the transport route German Bight–Stavanger–Bergen, either as a direct anti-submarine force or standing off from a convoy for defence against surface warships. Bütow, who was also the competent authority for S-boat personnel and administration, criticised their use in the anti-submarine role, since this activity wore out the central engine. Using two engines, the boats were too fast, and with one outer engine the steering was irregular and the boats could not be kept on course, something the commanders had already learned in the opening months of the war in the Baltic. And he warned, 'If the use of S-boats continues at the same rate as previously, at the latest by mid-July the time will come when a major proportion of the boats of both flotillas will have reached the limits of engine endurance.'[13] SKL was aware of this but was forced to continue because of the lack of suitable anti-submarine forces: in the meantime another torpedo boat had been lost in the North Sea.[14]

The boats were now also being required to protect minelayers again, and in these circumstances on the night of 8 May 1940, 2.SFltl. sailing in loose line abreast met a British squadron composed of a cruiser and seven destroyers that had arrived to interfere with minelaying in the Skagerrak. Oberleutnant zur See

S-boat leaving depot ship.

2.SFltl. boats leaving harbour.

Opdenhoff in S 31 succeeded in torpedoing and seriously damaging the destroyer *Kelly*, which had to be towed home. A pursuit of the S-boats ensued, during which S 33 (Oberleutnant zur See Hans Schultze-Jena) twice rammed a British destroyer, sustaining serious damage, but returned safely to Wilhelmshaven.

Initially it had been assumed that HMS *Kelly* had been sunk, and SKL noted with pleasure, 'the first glorious success of our S-boat Arm'.[15] Ober-leutnant zur See Opdenhoff became the first S-boat man to receive the Knight's Cross.

> At the second ramming, the boat stopped when the technical NCO at the controls [*Fahrmaat*] fell across the drive lever. Sixty metres astern of the destroyer, the crew prepared the boat for scuttling while the technical crew (Obermaschinist Eigenbrod), still under fire, went over the machinery. Once the cause was found, the boat resumed progress and after twenty miles outdistanced its pursuers.
> (War Diary, 2.SFltl. 9 May 1940)

In the English Channel

On 10 May 1940, the offensive in the west began. Group West made an urgent request for S-boats in the English Channel. SKL hesitated in-itially, but on 12 May withdrew 2.SFltl. from escort duties. Two days later, 1.SFltl. was detached from Admiral West Coast Norway. This terminated the S-boats' participation in Operation *Weserübung*. It had been a naval campaign in which they had again been used in an unorthodox role for motor torpedo boats but had nevertheless proved their mettle. Admiral West Coast reported that S-boats had been 'indispensable for continual security duties, transport work and also in the sea pilotage service'.16 SKL and Group Commands East and West took a similar view, having relied increasingly on the S-boats, an arm for which only shortly before they had not seen a role. The torpedoing of the destroyer *Kelly* had highlighted the capabilities of these small craft if they were employed correctly.

3
Blitzkrieg in the Channel
May 1940–May 1941

Despite the state of war existing between France and Germany, there had been no major clashes on the Western Front during the winter of 1939. The period was termed 'the phoney war' by the British. The Allied side had no great offensive planned and the Germans considered that a direct attack through the Maginot Line on the common border involved too high a risk. Hitler was anxious to finish off the French. Despite the early successes, the political situation was becoming less favourable and there was a danger that the United States might enter the war if quick action were not taken.

OKH was dubious, seeing the only chance for a successful campaign as being a repeat of the World War One Schlieffen Plan, thrusting through the Netherlands and Belgium. The first three invasion strategies were therefore variations on this old theme. The Allied side massed troops on the Belgian border in anticipation. Hitler was hesitant and in the end postponed the attack date in the west on no less than twenty-nine occasions. The proposal by General von Manstein to scythe through the Ardennes with massed panzer formations and keep going to the Channel, cutting off the enemy from his rearward lines,[1] was decisive and adopted by Hitler.

The Kriegsmarine was neither involved in the tussle for the right plan nor consulted as to possible details. C-in-C Admiral Raeder had declined to become involved;[2] for him, the occupation of Norway, and its strategic geographic situation for the Atlantic battle against the British trade routes, was the paramount factor.[3]

The offensive began on 10 May 1940. Surprised by the speed of the thrust and its obvious success, SKL withdrew its former reservations and deduced:

The further expansion of the land situation will allow a swift mopping-up of the regions of northern France and western Belgium. There will be a very comprehensive evacuation involving enemy troop transports out of the ports on those coasts. At this time the S-boat Arm must be at readiness to strike with an adequate force in this area. No effort must be spared to obtain the base at Den Helder, and as soon as possible also the Hook of Holland, for use as S-boat bases. In the light of these urgent operational considerations, the equally important deployment of S-boats from the southern Norwegian coast must take a back seat.[4]

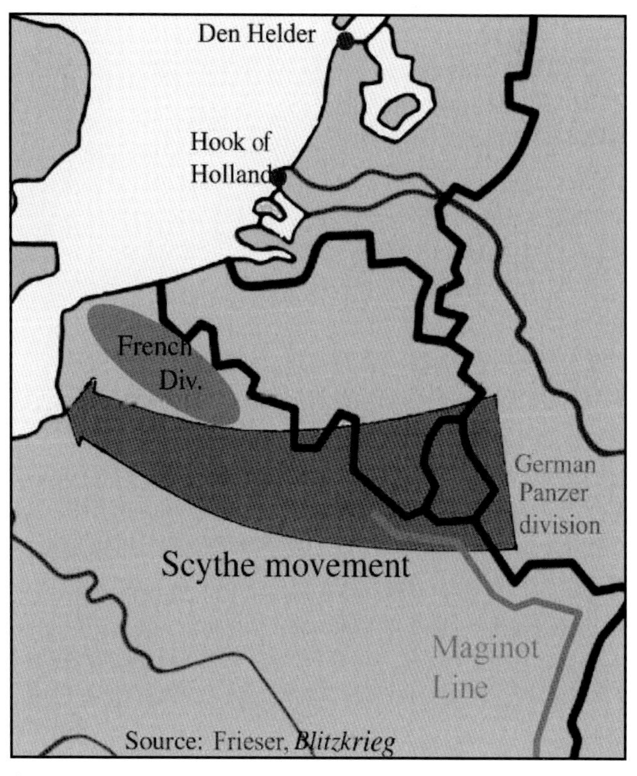

German Blitzkrieg, 1940.

First Operations

The following night, 15 May 1940, the first mission was sailed from the island of Borkum against Allied shipping off the Dutch–Belgian coast. A steamer was sunk. On the night of 21 May, the French destroyer *Jaguar* also fell victim, after which the boats moved into Den Helder, which had been hastily prepared. The base was ninety sea miles nearer the Channel, reducing the demands on engine-hours and allowing more time at sea during the short nights of spring. The FdT, Kapitän zur See Bütow, set up his headquarters at Den Helder. Since *Weserübung* he had been at Kiel without an operational role. In recognition that S-boats required quite different mechanics of command from those of naval squadrons, his application for readmission to the chain of command citing those grounds was accepted by SKL.[5]

His first task was to search for locations for new bases, to set up logistical and technical support, the supply of weapons and ammunition and the establishment of torpedo workshops. He contacted Army units responsible for coastal defence, sought Luftwaffe collaboration, a close relationship with German minesweeping units and adequate protection for his boats. These were all jobs that the flotillas could not have undertaken alone and which no higher levels considered to be their responsibility. Moreover Admiral Lütjens, Naval Commander West and also commander of the fleet, who acted under Group West, was too preoccupied with other operations to concern himself with the daily business of S-boats. This now came under the jurisdiction of the FdT. In order to maintain constant contact with the boats at sea and also Group West, through which all operationally relevant information passed, he set up a mobile radio centre.[6]

When German troops reached the Channel, they isolated the Belgian forces, which capitulated on 28 May 1940. Although the British and French armies fell back on Dunkirk as a last resort, the Germans held back outside the town,[7] allowing the Allies time to evacuate.

Dunkirk

On 16 May at 1857 hrs, Operation 'Dynamo' began. Over the next nine days, the sea was leaden and calm, unusual for the Channel. The Royal Navy seized its opportunity and sent an armada ranging from small, open motor launches to destroyers across the Channel to ferry back the Allied troops. The calm sea allowed them to be brought away across the sands, and a heavy overcast prevented effective Luftwaffe air attacks. RAF fighters, whose use Churchill had forbidden in support of the land fighting, protected the withdrawal from the air while French destroyers guarded the flanks.

The evacuation ran out along three routes. The S-boats were the only offensive naval craft at the disposal of the Kriegsmarine. In the dark nights it was difficult for their lookouts to spot the enemy, and their engines could be heard far and wide, which alerted the destroyer defences. Only at creeping speed and accepting lesser penetration could they approach the irregular armada, and never did they find a rewarding target for a torpedo. On the first night, when the steamer *Abukir* was sunk, the crewmen remaining aboard her saw what they thought was a U-boat conning tower and opened fire. It was a life raft from their own ship, and nearly all aboard it were killed.[8]

In order to penetrate deeper into the Channel, on 31 May the FdT transferred both flotillas to the Hook of Holland as a jumping-off point, with a base at Rotterdam. To his bemusement, on 1 June the commanding officer, 3rd S-boat Flotilla (Kapitänleutnant Kemnade), whom he had sent to Kiel to train urgently needed new crews, arrived with two boats. 'He is to take part in operations . . . on the orders of SKL without informing the FdT,'[9] he wrote in the War Diary, and pointed to the negative consequences for crew training. Group West objected, 'The criticism of the measures undertaken by higher authority which one finds in the War Diary are out of place.'[10] Support for Kapitän zur See Bütow came from Admiral Lütjens, who distanced himself from the reprimand. On the contrary, he considered

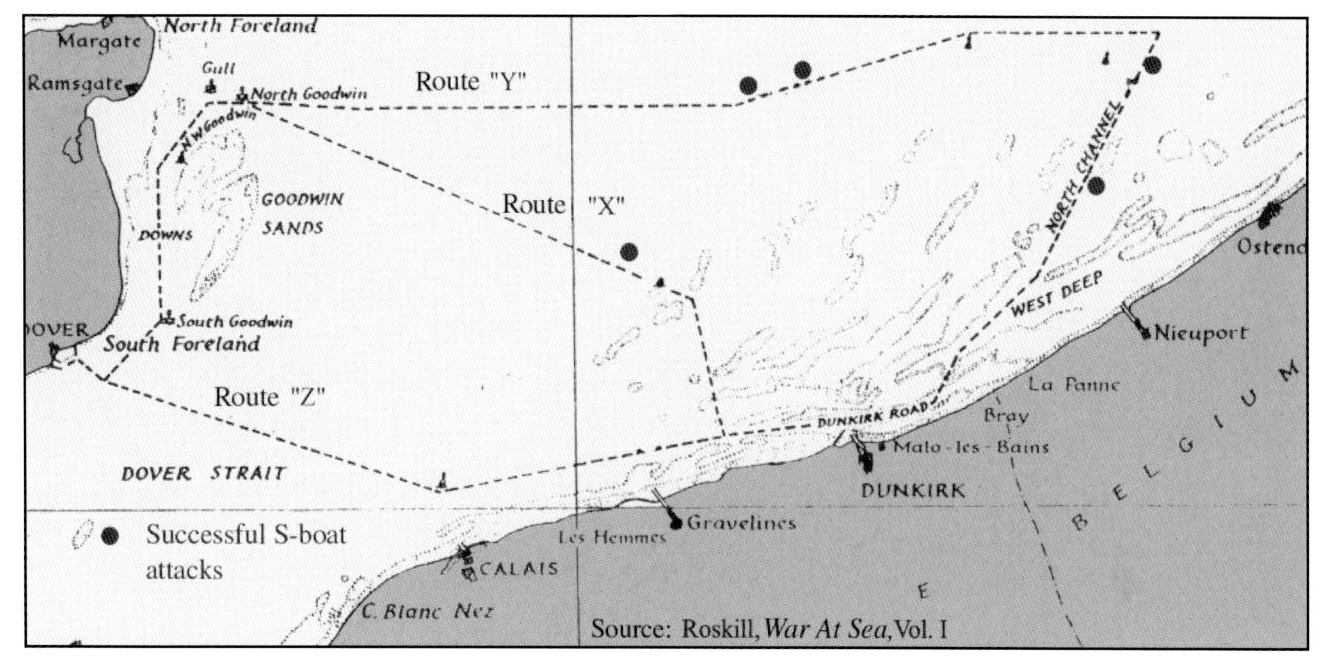

Evacuation routes from Dunkirk.

it to be 'the duty of every commander to point out those disadvantages which in his opinion are likely to arise from orders given. I consider it dangerous to impose restrictions on commanders as to the statement of their views in this respect.'[11]

Operation Dynamo ended on 4 June. Using 800 craft, including only fifty-six destroyers, within nine days the British succeeded in bringing back to England almost 340,000 men, although without their equipment. The Allied side lost seventy-two vessels during the operation, most of them sunk by the Luftwaffe.[12] Nevertheless the sinking of two destroyers, severe damage to a third, together with three steamers sunk, showed the capabilities of the S-boats despite there only ever being two or three out of a total of nine operational at a time because of engine troubles. SKL held a positive view of the future for the S-boat Arm: its performance provided 'a glowing testimony for the usefulness of the Arm and the outstanding training of its commanders which opens great prospects for success at those hotspots for continual naval operations'.[13]

While German heavy units left Norway under the command of Admiral Lütjens on the anti-commerce operation 'Juno', on the day following the conclusion at Dunkirk there began the second phase of the Western Offensive aimed at the French heartland. The French defences were quickly overrun: on 9 June Dieppe fell, on 18 June Cherbourg, and German troops reached the Swiss–French frontier. Four days later, France signed the armistice at Compiègne.

The War Goes On

Following the evacuation at Dunkirk, the FdT had sent out 1. or 2.SFltl. every night alternately against the British convoys on their east coast. Initially boats of 3.SFltl. were also used, but were returned to Kiel after ten days to train new crews. The convoy routes along the east coast had been plotted by German air reconnaissance and it was known that convoys had been sailing regularly between the Thames and Firth of Forth since September 1939.[14] The exact sailing times of the FN (Firth North, Thames to Firth) and FS (Firth South, Firth to Thames) convoys depended on the arrival or departure of Atlantic convoys, the tides in the Thames and the state of minesweeping along the route. The convoys consisted of twenty to thirty small merchant ships, following minesweepers and

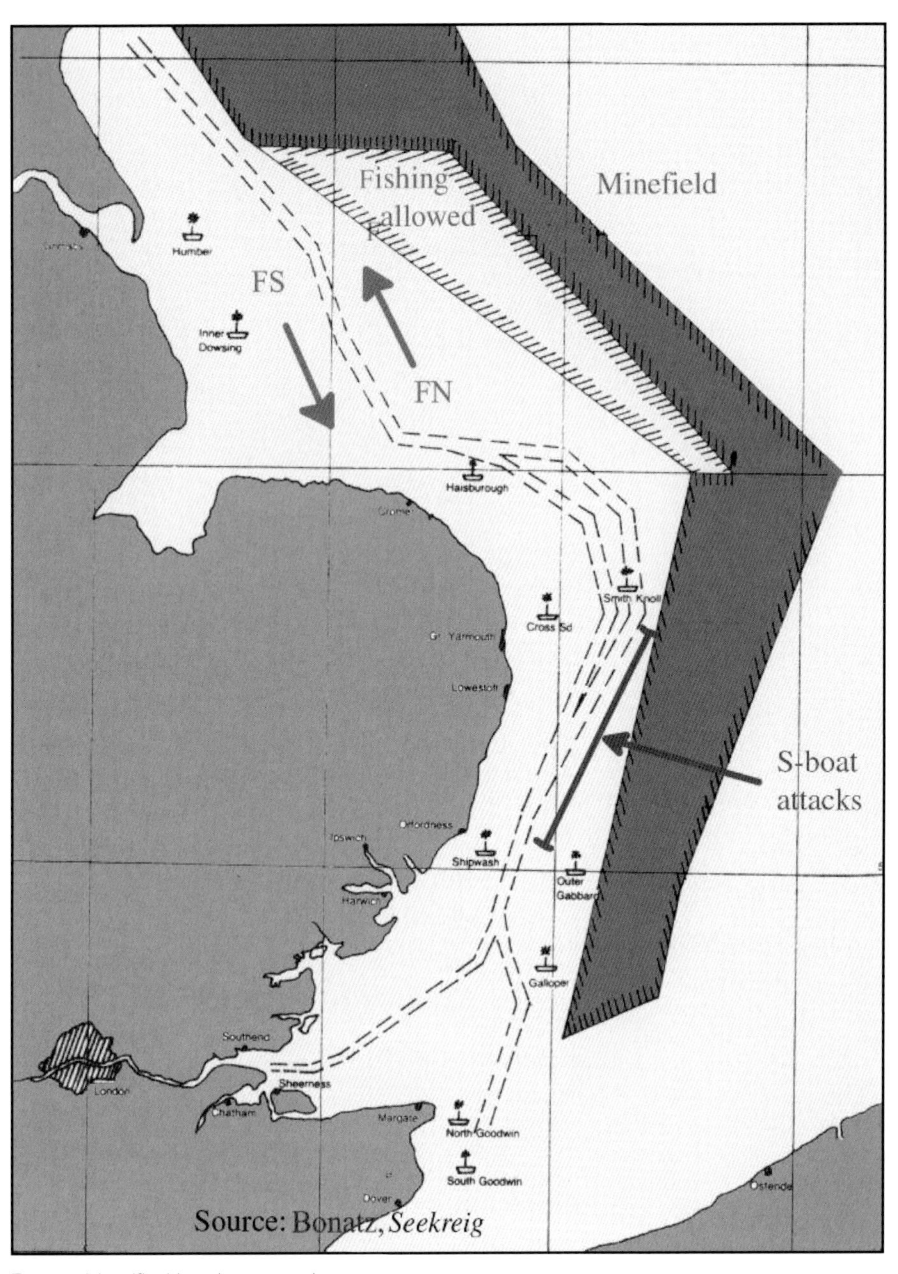

Routes identified by air reconnaissance.

escorted by destroyers or anti-submarine vessels.[15] Radio monitoring gave the Germans indications of the probable arrival or sailing time, but was not sufficiently precise to allow a concentrated attack to be launched. Here, only air reconnaissance could help with an exact position; a search by three or four boats over such a large sea area was not a viable proposition.

Because of the small operational strength, reduced by the eternal engine problems, ever more boats fell by the wayside. In the absence of an exact report, the force had to arrive at the sea lane and wait there for the enemy merchantmen to show up, or creep up to the position with slow revs. For this reason, by night the few boats could only ever cover a search sweep of less than one sea mile in breadth, keeping the shadow of the companion boat of the *Rotte* (paired boats) in sight at between 500 and 800 metres, often less, so as not to lose contact. Lying in wait was often unrewarding. Over eight consecutive nights, steamers were spotted, and attacked on three occasions, but without success; the boats were either forced to bear away early by the destroyer escorts, or the torpedoes missed. The main causes of the latter were overestimating the size of the target ship and unreliable torpedoes, mostly surface runners.[16] In July the first G7a torpedoes were delivered, with better depth-keeping and new detonating pistols.[17]

> During conversations about the Channel engagements, whenever I mention the importance of the sense of smell, people tap their heads. But it was so. In the early years when we lay in wait in *Rotten*, we might neither see nor hear a convoy for days on end, but if one was coming and the wind was right, the first warning would be, long before-hand, a whiff of the typical coal-steamer smell.
>
> (Dr Heinz Gillner, letter to the author, 15 June 1988)

Advance to Boulogne

Meanwhile the British were shipping their remaining troops, together with Canadian and Polish units, out of Le Havre, Cherbourg, Saint-Malo, Brest and the Biscay ports for England. SKL wanted to attack these troopships and pressed for the S-boats, the only available offensive force in the region, to be brought west. The FdT had identified Boulogne early on as a suitable base, but was wary of its vulnerability to air attack. On 11 June he wrote, 'There must be flak protection. I anticipate nightly air raids on the harbour and radio station.'[18] He gave in when SKL and Group West promised that a fighter group was stationed at Boulogne aerodrome. When 2.SFltl. entered Boulogne next morning, it was fired on by the German coastal defences, which had not received notice of its arrival. During the day, British aircraft attacked the boats three times; despite frequent changes of moorings they were found and hit before the German fighters could get airborne. The death toll was seven, including Oberleutnant zur See Kecke, commander of S 35; twenty-two were wounded, including Oberleutnant zur See Zimmermann, commander of S 30. That night, the flotilla returned to Rotterdam and only returned five days later, after a flak battery was installed. By now the troopships had moved further west and could no longer be reached from Boulogne.

From Boulogne, the convoys under the English south coast were very close at hand. There was a lack of reconnaissance reports, but since the enemy coast could be seen, it was a simple matter to plot the regular sailings CE (Coastal East, Falmouth to Thames) and CW (Coastal West, Thames to Falmouth). Only 2.SFltl. (Korvettenkapitän Petersen) operated initially; he had four boats. The 1st S-boat Flotilla (Kapitänleutnant Birnbacher) had returned to Wilhelmshaven for engine overhauls. In four missions, Petersen's flotilla found the enemy three times and sank three steamers of 7,000 gross tons but suffered its first loss when S 32, proceeding at slow speed in mid-Channel while listening out for a convoy, hit a drifting mine. The explosion tore away the forecastle as far as the wheelhouse. Oberleutnant zur See Koscky and six crew were killed. After a tow failed, the boat was destroyed with explosives.

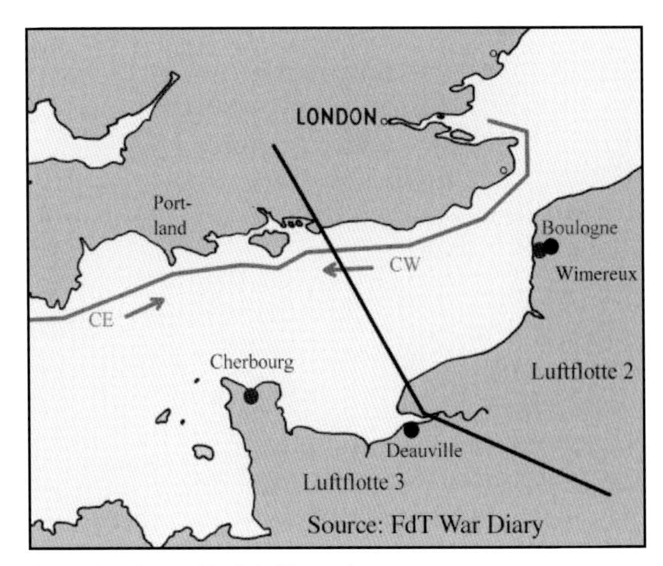

Operational area, English Channel.

Onwards to Cherbourg

During these operations, the FdT and his small staff worked to improve the flotilla's situation materially. At Boulogne, there was a radio station and the crews lodged in small summer hotels at Wimereux. Von Bütow had inspected Cherbourg and found suitable crew quarters in nearby Urville. Transport, fuel deposits, ammunition dumps, stores for spare parts and torpedo workshops had been set up. Although the flak protection for the harbours did not always meet his approval, it was at least in place and afforded the boats a certain security on their moorings. A request to Admiral Raeder for protective bunkers was turned down.[19] Close contacts had been established with the patrol flotillas guarding the French coast as far as Biscay. Their task was to keep open the routes for German coastal traffic, keep a constant watch on harbour entrances for newly laid mines and to sweep them when found.[20] After they had reported Cherbourg clear on the night of 27 June 1940, three boats of 1.SFltl., which had come from Rotterdam after engine overhauls at Wilhelmshaven, entered harbour.

'The end of June sees the U-boat Arm in a strategically favourable position. The operations from the two bases at Boulogne and Cherbourg cover the Portland–Thames Estuary area,' the FdT noted with relative satisfaction in his War Diary.[21] Despite this favourable position, however, the convoys were seldom found. The fault lay in having so few boats available – three operational boats per flotilla. The other reason was the running of convoys by day and close inshore. In the first half of July 1940, the boats found a convoy only twice, sinking two ships and damaging two.

S-boats and the Luftwaffe

The lack of naval reconnaissance, and of liaison between the Luftwaffe and Group West, forced the FdT to attempt to resolve the situation and so improve the chances of finding enemy convoys. In July, the Luftwaffe had begun to mount heavier attacks against shipping along the English south coast. Luftflotten 2 and 3 divided it between them and carried out operations independently, with little mutual exchange of information. By personal visits to the various Luftwaffe command staffs and their commanders, and obtaining direct decisions, von Bütow succeeded as far as he could in convincing the Luftwaffe to share with him their information about enemy convoys.[22] Operating with his flag lieutenant from Cherbourg, he had direct contact with Fliegerkorps VIII at Deauville and Luftflotte 3 in Paris. His staff officer, Oberleutnant zur See Rebensburg at Boulogne, liaised with the Luftwaffe command position at Ushant, where the Luftwaffe had set up a signals station to receive reports from Fliegerkorps I and II. Bütow and Rebensburg communicated by radio, telex or telephone.23 Direct contact between Luftwaffe aircraft and S-boats was not possible because of differing procedures, charts and radio equipment.

> At the beginning of June 1940 I was sent to Paris. I was already five years in the service, an oberleutnant without any staff training. I had to report our situation to the Chief of Staff, Luftflotte 2. As later with Luftflotte 3, my reception in the Luxemburg Palace was held in the most luxurious surroundings. The conversational partners of General Kesselring, later Sperrle, were usually colonels and generals. By reason of the situation, they understood the needs of the Kriegsmarine but their words and promises were purely theoretical in nature. It evinced their surprise that the Kriegsmarine should send only an oberleutnant for such very complicated problems, and from that they inferred that we did not want the naval war, or in any case not for the time being, since the bomber war would collapse England. (Rebensburg, *Erinnerungen*, p 17)

In the second half of July, the exchanges paid off. At first the information supplied was negative, reports that no convoys had been sighted. As a result, the FdT kept his boats in port to save on costly engine-hours and spare the crews. Generaladmiral Saalwächter, C-in-C Group West, was not in agreement: 'I do not share the opinion of the FdT that he can make torpedo missions dependent on air reconnaissance, since the area surveyed is relatively narrow and the departure of merchant ships from harbours on the English south coast is also possible by night.'[24]

Therefore the boats sailed but, with one exception, found nothing. The exception was the passenger steamer *Meknès*, returning 1,300 French officers and men to France, which had not – contrary to requirements – been advised to the Germans through diplomatic channels. Over 300 of those aboard were drowned.[25] Then, on the afternoon of 25 July, Fliegerkorps II reported successful attacks against a convoy proceeding south from the Thames estuary. Further attacks followed off Dover. When reconnaissance detected the enemy convoy again and reported the latest course change, the FdT sent out

1.SFltl. His three boats found the westbound convoy CW8 at the estimated position and three freighters were sunk. This brought the total to eight merchant ships and two destroyers sunk, plus two other steamers damaged.

The British could not sustain such high losses indefinitely. To halt the convoys was out of the question, not least because the south coast required 40,000 tons of coal weekly. Therefore the British suspended them temporarily in order to introduce new measures. For the air attacks, stronger fighter defences were prepared. Since there were insufficient aircraft for a total defence, 'strongpoints' were established. Special ships flew barrage balloons as a protection against low-flying aircraft, and well-trained gun crews went aboard for the more dangerous voyages, and returned on another convoy. The average number of ships in a typical convoy – twenty-five – was reduced by half. Minesweeping the route was carried out at night, the last search in the convoy's path. For defence against S-boats the new Hunt class escort destroyers with improved armament were brought in. The escorts were augmented by naval trawlers and motor launches (MLs), while orders were placed for heavily armed, fast motor gun boats (MGBs). The co-operation between the convoy escorts and shore radar stations was intensified.[26] All in all, this broad band of measures was based primarily on RN/RAF co-operation, contrary to the experience of the Germans, whose Luftwaffe and Kriegsmarine, throughout the war, remained independent and frowned on the very idea of a co-ordinated policy.

After all these new developments had been introduced within two weeks, the convoys resumed. The first passed eastbound without loss; the first westbound convoy CW9 was spotted by the Luftwaffe on 7 August. The 1st S-boat Flotilla sailed on this report and found CW9. Despite stiff resistance from the destroyers and naval trawlers, three ships were sunk. The report was passed back to the Luftwaffe, which attacked the scattered survivors afresh next morning – without success, as a result of the heavy fighter presence. Because of these air defences over convoys, and the increasing importance of the bomber war against Britain, the Luftwaffe began to concentrate more on land targets, leaving the convoys to the S-boats.

Loading mines at Ostend.

Mining Operations

For some time, SKL and Group West had been very much in favour of mining the convoy lanes. While it was realised that the few mines laid per boat per mission would not result in a breakthrough, mines unsettled Merchant Navy crews and tied down minesweepers that would otherwise be clearing the great belt of mines protecting German coastal traffic. The FdT was not pleased with this new task. It seemed to be alien to the purpose for which S-boats had been built. The mines were too heavy, each being over a tonne in weight, and had to be carried on the stern deck. 'The use of S-boats as minelayers has been forbidden in a fundamental OKM order,'[27] he wrote. Orders were orders, however, and he issued the instruction, organised technical personnel to prepare the boats, installed cranes for loading and assembled the newly arrived boats in 2.SFltl. at Boulogne for the job.

The first operation followed on 10 July 1940. Of the seven boats, three were each loaded with four EMC anchored mines.[28] The flotilla sailed in line ahead to the Thames estuary. Boats 4 and 5 each laid twelve explosive buoys as the anti-sweeping measure port and starboard of the twelve-mine field; boats 6 and 7 stood guard fore and aft during the laying.

Explosive buoys at the stern.

Next evening, while on a torpedo operation, 2.SFltl. lost S 23 (Oberleutnant zur See Christiansen) to a mine before reaching the convoy route. An attempt was made to tow the boat home. When this failed, the wreck was blown up. There were no losses to personnel. The FdT sharply criticised the flotilla commander (Korvettenkapitän Petersen) for involving all units in the tow and abandoning the torpedo operation.[29] This concern for the safety and protection of boats and men was a controversial characteristic of Petersen's leadership throughout the war.

While 1.SFltl. carried out further torpedo operations and were equipped with the larger, faster Type S 38 boats for the greater area they could cover, 2.SFltl., with its smaller, slower Type S 30s concentrated on minelaying.[30] To use shorter approach routes, at the end of July they transferred to Ostend, where an S-boat base had been made. Whenever the weather was favourable, they would sortie for minelaying to the English coast. It was important to lay the mines precisely in the narrow convoy lanes, generally about three cables (about 550 metres) wide,[31] no easy task in a strong current and with navigation aids limited to stopwatch, chart and magnetic compass. It was also essential to remain unobserved and the enemy had to be avoided or an alternative area sought. Psychologically, mining was unrewarding. Successes were rarely reported and were difficult to substantiate, and the missions demanded great navigational skill and ran a constant risk of contact with heavy enemy defences and with mines, which had already cost two boats. The 1st S-boat Flotilla, on the other hand, had torpedo successes with confirmed sinkings.[32]

Operation *Seelöwe*

Preparations were in hand for landings on the English coast ordered by Hitler in his Directive No. 16 of 16 July 1940. The measures were to be completed by mid-August. There was disagreement as to whether the landings should be on a broad front, as OKH wanted, or against a narrow sector of the coast, which OKM considered the best possibility. After long wrangling between the two, Hitler decided for landings principally across the Channel Narrows. Four sectors were planned, X-Day to be 15 September 1940, later postponed to 24 September because the naval side was not ready. The decisive factor in the view of both OKH and OKM was air supremacy.33 On 13 August 1940, '*Adlertag*', the Luftwaffe offensive began. It soon became apparent that the RAF fighter arm could not be weakened decisively, and therefore Admiral Raeder was dissuaded. The risk of a devastating defeat seemed far greater than the chance of forcing Britain to sue for peace through determined warfare on her maritime commerce. OKH also considered the operation questionable without adequate air support. Hitler hesitated initially and then on 17 September 1940 postponed *Seelöwe* 'indefinitely',[34] although he let the preparations continue because the tides and moon were favourable in October.

The preparations for the invasion of England had involved the S-boat Arm closely. Beginning with *Adlertag*, their numbers had been strengthened for the air-sea rescue role. This operation, '*Rosengarten*',[35] tied down the units and, since these would be daylight missions, they left no time for night operations. In the first week of the Luftwaffe offensive, S-boats rescued five Luftwaffe crews and consolidated the relationship between the two services. The role as lifeboatmen came to an abrupt end for 2.SFltl. in mid-August when the Ostend torpedo arsenal and nearby naval workshops were sabotaged. Exploding warheads destroyed forty-four torpedoes and damaged all four boats present (S 24, S 31, S 35 and S 37), forcing them to return to Germany for repair, from where they returned to Ostend in early September.

Immediately before the beginning of *Seelöwe*, the S-boats had had the task of laying flanking minefields either side of the intended troop-transport route right under the coast.[36] During the invasion proper, particularly following the second and third waves, the S-boat flotillas were to have protected the supply route. In order to provide adequate technical support for the operations as they unfolded, the depot ships *Carl Peters* (1.SFltl.), *Tanga* (2.SFltl.) and *Adolf Lüderitz* (3.SFltl.) were to move up to Cherbourg/Le Havre, Zeebrugge and Flushing respectively.

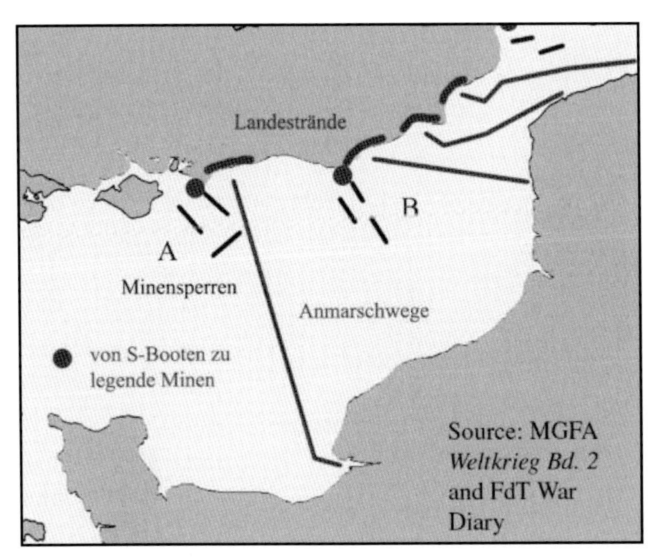

Operation *Seelöwe*.

The British were aware of the invasion preparations. They held back their heavy ships in reserve and pushed forward most of their destroyer force between Dover and the Humber. They left the Western Approaches undefended, even though this lightened the task of German U-boats operating there; fending off invasion was the first priority. As the build-up of German troop carriers continued in Channel ports – in the end 3,000 ships and boats – they were attacked with aircraft and destroyers. The continual air raids caused losses to transports and escort craft. Four torpedo boats were hit, of which one sank. A number of S-boats received damage and were rendered unserviceable for the coming operation. None sank, and the British destroyers found them a handful. This forced the latter to keep their distance offshore and bombardments of the Channel ports from the sea were few and far between.

Enter the Destroyers and Torpedo Boats

In order to cover for 2.SFltl. during its absence at Ostend for repairs, the FdT transferred 1.SFltl. from Cherbourg to Rotterdam and operated it from there against the Thames estuary. The boats sailed on only three occasions, because of bad weather, and found the convoys elusive. When 2.SFltl. returned to Ostend at the beginning of September, the flotilla worked with 1.SFltl. against the English east coast whenever the weather was favourable. On the night of 4 September 1940, 1.SFltl. sank five steamers and seriously damaged another; on the 6th, 2.SFltl. sank a freighter. On 7 September, 1.SFltl. returned to Cherbourg for engine overhauls, since its technical equipment and spare parts were there. Three days later, 3.SFltl. (Kapitänleutnant Kemnade), with four boats and the depot ship *Adolf Lüderitz*, arrived in Rotterdam to replace 1.SFltl.

In the wake of the *Seelöwe* preparations, other

surface warships had been brought to the Channel by Group West for use against the south coast convoys. The 2nd and 5th Torpedo Boat Flotillas laid mines in the Straits of Dover and sank two anti-submarine vessels and two coasters with gun or torpedo. Seven German destroyers operating at the western end of the Channel mined the convoy lane off Falmouth and searched for merchant shipping in the southern Bristol Channel but were forced away by the defences.

Missions sailed at this time were carried out by one class of warship – all destroyers, all torpedo boats or all S-boats. Differing sizes of vessel with their own sea-keeping properties and speeds, familiarity with other vessels within flotillas, knowledge and mastery of special tactics and in particular the appropriate cruising and attack formations, all militated against mixed-bag squadrons. There was also no mutual support in the sense of a unified battle command structure; the various staffs were not trained for, nor accustomed to, amalgamating various weapons systems into an integral whole. Instead, the idea was to employ diversionary tactics in an area adjacent to one in which action was taking place, in order to divide the enemy's attention and so protect German forces, but this was soon discontinued after smaller craft could not sail or were forced to make for port on account of bad weather.[37] Pure S-boat operations between mid-September and mid-October showed no rewards, except for the sinking of a coaster by 2.SFltl., and this was for the loss of its third boat, S 37, to a mine. Oberleutnant zur See Hans Schultze-Jena and twelve crew died; eleven were saved.

In order to increase the number of available boats, with the approval of Group West in mid-October the FdT transferred 1.SFltl. to Rotterdam so that he could operate three flotillas against the Thames estuary. This paid off, for after two unsuccessful missions a northbound convoy was found on the night of 17 October 1940; two ships were sunk and a third damaged. But this combined operational force would not last for long.

Concentration or Dispersal

After the final postponement of *Seelöwe*, SKL assessed the situation as follows in October 1940: 'Germany's strategic naval situation, controlling the entire coastal area from the North Cape to the French/Spanish border, provides us with exceptional possibilities for the fulfilment of the two basic principles of our naval policy: the battle against enemy sea communications and the preservation of our own.'[38] As clear as this assessment might be, its application in instructions to the Group North and Group West commanders on 14 October 1940 was contradictory. The task of Group North had the character primarily of coast protection, according to SKL, but included maintaining German freedom of movement in the North Sea, protection of Norwegian traffic, expansion of the warning areas and prevention of enemy minelaying. Together with these purely defensive arrangements there was an offensive element: war against commerce on the English east coast. For this task, Group North placed 2.SFltl. amongst two modern torpedo boat flotillas.

For Group West, according to SKL, coastal defence and security work was linked to the need for wide-ranging operational activities by surface forces, and for this purpose the Group received battleships, cruisers and more destroyers. SKL envisaged a lively minelaying programme in the Channel and along the south coast for torpedo boats and S-boats, while destroyers, when not mining the Bristol Channel, would maintain an offensive against merchant shipping in convoys proceeding to and from the Atlantic.[39]

Group West and Group North both saw immediately the problem that the allotted sectors caused for their offensives against convoys to and from the Thames estuary. The common boundary was the Cromer–Den Helder line. Group North wanted to operate in all the joint sea area and proposed that the boundary to be shifted westwards, the FdT to be leader of operations. Von Bütow opposed the splitting of the S-boat Arm and a transfer of the point of concentration northwards: 'There is no case to be made for weakening the concentrated

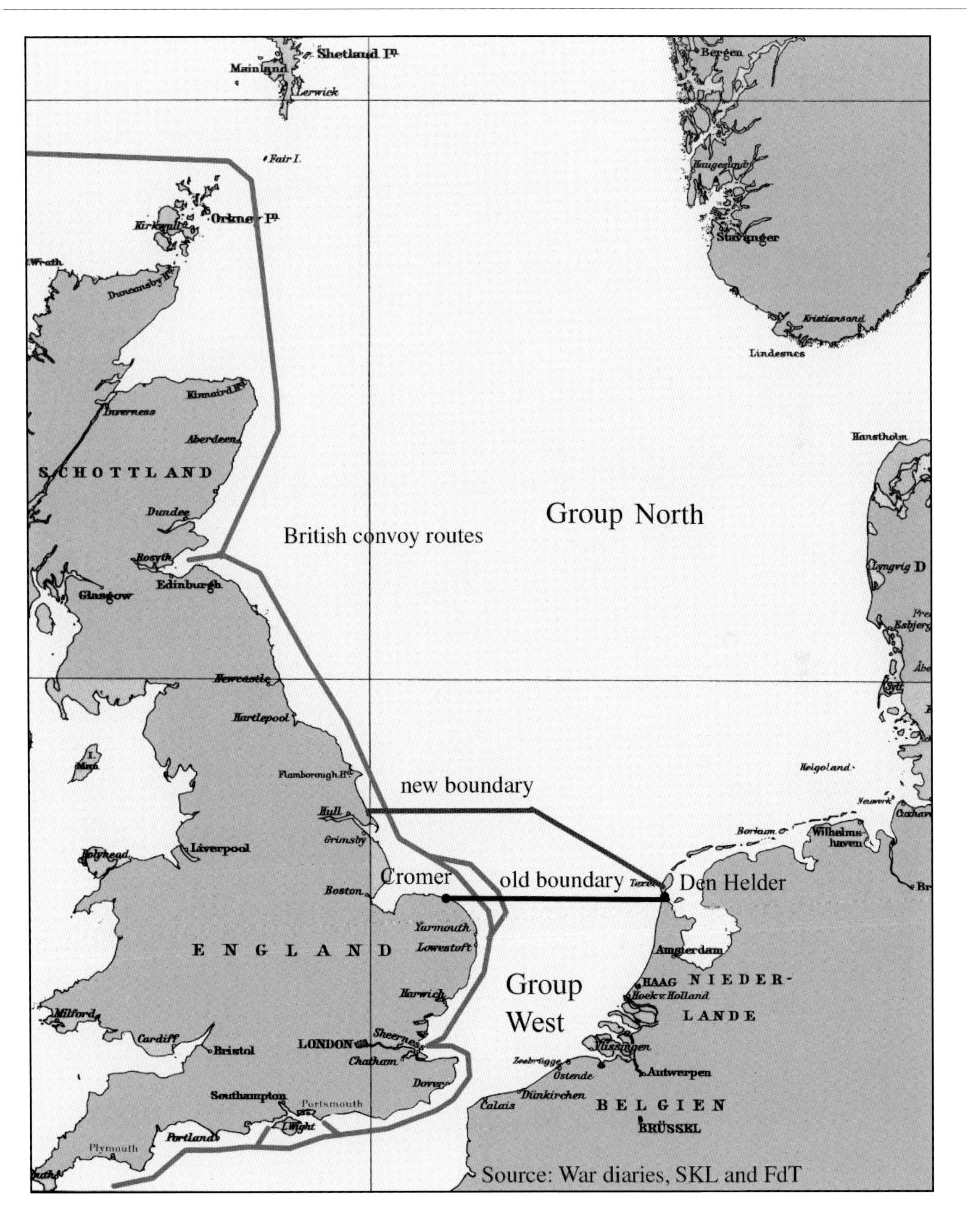

Shetland I^n
Mainland
Lerwick
Fair I.
Orkney I^n
Kirkwall
Duncansby H^d
Wrath
Bergen
Haugesund
Stavanger
Kristiansand
Lindesnes
Kinnaird H^d
Inverness
Aberdeen
SCHOTTLAND
Dundee
Group North
British convoy routes
Rosyth
Edinburgh
Glasgow
Hanstholm
Lyngvig
Esbjerg
Sylt
Newcastle
Hartlepool
I. Man
Flamborough H^d
new boundary
Helgoland
Hull
Grimsby
Liverpool
Holyhead
Wilhelmshaven
Cromer
old boundary
Texel
Den Helder
Boston
Yarmouth
Lowestoft
ENGLAND
Amsterdam
Group West
HAAG
NIEDER-LANDE
Hoek v. Holland
Harwich
Milford
Cardiff
Bristol
LONDON
Sheerness
Chatham
Vlissingen
Zeebrügge
Ostende
Antwerpen
Dover
Southampton
Portsmouth
Dünkirchen
Calais
BELGIEN
BRÜSSEL
Wight
Portland
Plymouth
Source: War diaries, SKL and FdT

S-boat offensive against the heavy traffic between Cromer and Thames in favour of occasional sorties against the more northern part of the east coast . . . Each night an average of two convoys transits the mentioned area. There is no compelling reason to shift the point of main thrust northward.'[40] He went on to argue that T-boats were no substitute. Their draught did not allow them to pass through enemy minefields off the English east coast. It was preferable to send them to the English south coast with the destroyers and compensate for the transfer of 1.SFltl. from Cherbourg to the Thames.

Group West agreed, being keen on destroyer and torpedo boat operations in what they saw as the rewarding area between the Scillies and the Isle of Wight, and asked for new torpedo boats while leaving 2.SFltl. with the FdT. SKL declined to make any changes to their instruction and remained doggedly by their fundamental operational concept of combining the Atlantic anti-commerce war with the U-boat war. Destroyers would be used as well as battleships and cruisers in the Atlantic. SKL criticised Group West for its apparent failure to see the strategic possibilities.[41] In the hope of resolving the impasse, Kapitän zur See Bütow requested to present a statement in person to SKL, and on 25 October 1940 delivered a comprehensive report regarding the situation on the English east coast and the parameters of the S-boats. SKL 'could not deny the clear proof from the FdT'.[42] Therefore, he remained operations leader in the area of responsibility of Group West and was made directly accountable to it after the departure of Admiral Lütjens on 26 October.[43] Shortly afterwards, the common boundary was shifted northwards, but only in order to preserve the unity of the operational area for S-boats.[44]

SKL also recognised the virtue of having all three S-flotillas in the western zone and rescinded the order to transfer out 2.SFltl. Probably to avoid denying Group North everything, SKL decided, against the newly accepted knowledge and strategic principle of concentrating forces, to move 1.SFltl. with its larger boats to Group North. Together with torpedo boats, they would escort the heavy cruiser *Admiral Scheer* during the initial stage of her cruise to the South Atlantic and Indian Ocean. The fragility of the arrangement was visible in the formulation of the order whereby *Scheer* was not to be dependent on the S-boats by reason of 'the possibility of their transfer away at the appropriate time'.[45]

As instructed, 1.SFltl. sailed from Rotterdam with *Carl Peters* on 27 October 1940 and escorted *Admiral Scheer* from Brunsbüttel across the North Sea and into Bergen. After that, the flotilla was used by Group North for escort duties between Norway and Denmark, which drew the energetic protests of the FdT, in view of the strategic objectives. To use S-boats for such extraneous purposes 'deteriorates and weakens this Arm best deployed in the urgent tasks along the English south and east coasts'.[46]

Group North (Generaladmiral Carls) rejected the sensitivity of the FdT: 'One would expect the front commanders to understand that only quite extraordinary circumstances would force Command to use that kind of emergency measure,'[47] although he reacted by proposing a foray by torpedo boats against the coast of Scotland and having the S-boat flotilla sail from Bergen to attack the traffic around the Shetlands. SKL did not approve: 200 sea miles' wear on the engines was not justified by the poor prospects for success. Apparently the FdT's speech on the special requirements of S-boat operations had had the desired effect, for in turning down Group North's proposal, Admiral Raeder ordered 1.SFltl. to be returned to the control of the FdT within fourteen days.[48]

Engine overhauls delayed their return, however. The six boats were strewn around various ports after their escort endeavours and it was not until mid-December 1940, after seven wasted weeks, that they arrived in Rotterdam ready for fresh operations against the Thames estuary traffic. Meanwhile, 1. and 3.SFltl. had had few successes to report. Severe storms had prevented sorties, while the British had drawn up a reserve convoy lane closer inshore and worked the merchant ships along one or other irregularly.[49] Although regular air reconnaissance flown by Fliegerkorps II reported convoys in the Thames estuary, it was not known which of the two lanes they would use. Since a flotilla could rarely send out more than three operational boats, it was not possible to search along both routes nor to penetrate the improved defences, which now embraced the recently arrived new Hunt class destroyers. The chances of successfully attacking a convoy were therefore poor, and the long absence of 1.SFltl. had made itself felt. In the period preceding the return of this flotilla, seven missions had been sailed, resulting in two skirmishes with convoy destroyers. On the night of 19 November 1940, S 38 (Oberleutnant zur See Detlefsen) was rammed in poor visibility by the destroyer *Campbell* and finished off by her guns. The destroyer picked up eighteen survivors, the first S-boat men to be captured.[50]

In connection with the loss of the vessel and crew, the FdT and SKL were concerned that the boat might have sailed with a full inventory of code books, contrary to orders that only material for the day should be taken to sea. As a precaution the codes were changed, but no information came to light later that secret material had been salvaged. In order to obtain details about losses, Fleet Command proposed 'that the FdT, as is already the case with the BdU, should compose a code giving captured officers the opportunity to report from captivity on important events'.[51]

Withdrawal

On 15 December 1940, all three flotillas sailed and found a convoy. Most boats were beaten off by destroyers but the remainder claimed two ships, each of about 2,000 gross tons, from the convoy behind the destroyers. Severe storms prevented further operations until 22 December, when a number of boats got through to a convoy to torpedo and sink a freighter and a naval trawler. More fierce winds made operations impossible until the beginning of January 1941. The Meuse was iced over and so 1.SFltl. went to the incomplete new base at Ijmuiden, 3.SFltl. to Boulogne. 2.SFltl. stayed at Ostend. Using a radar installation on the Channel coast, experiments were made at directing and attacking convoys passing Dover. The results were unsatisfactory and after a fortnight the trials were given up.

January and February 1941 were bad-weather months. On six forays, contact was made with the enemy, resulting in the sinking of the destroyer *Exmoor* and four freighters. During this time, it was noticed frequently that while drifting in wait or when near the convoy lanes, boats were approached directly by destroyers, this leading to the incorrect assumption that the enemy had shipboard radar. The destroyers were actually being directed by land stations or received their information from shipboard German-speaking radio operators who listened in on the lively oral traffic.

A Royal Navy Hunt class escort destroyer.

We were joined on board by a young German graduate Jew whose parents had gone the way of Auschwitz and whose first and only aim was to help bring about the Nazis' downfall... We called him Wolfgang... Twiddling the knobs in his stuffy little office night after night in the very remote chance of hearing a crackle in his native tongue must have been testing beyond belief, yet his hate sustained him and he had his reward.

'It is German speaking.'

Every nerve on the bridge twitched and the Captain ordered, 'Stand to!'...

' It is about torpedoes; I think he say, "Prepare to fire."

'They're probably attacking the convoy,' reasoned the captain. 'We'll go and augment the escort. Hard to starboard, full ahead both engines.'

The ship shuddered as the propellers bit, and listed with the turn.

'Ach!'

'Y-e-s?' I encouraged gently.

'He is swearing; he says, "Der Kerk hat Kurs geändert," the – in English I do not know how you say? – his course is changing.'

The full impact of a profound observation is often not felt for a moment or two – then,

'Whoops!' whistled one.

'Ow!' cringed another.

'Midships!' snapped the captain. 'Hard-a-port! Fire starshell all round!'

This was one of the patent drills and was well rehearsed. As the captain threw the ship from side to side to avoid the torpedoes which were presumably even then running towards us, we surrounded ourselves with a halo of light which revealed – absolutely nothing.

My ear went back to the voice-pipe. 'The swear is very bad; he say, "The enemy is awake now, stop the attack." '

'Wolfgang,' I cried, 'you've saved the ship.'

The E-boats had evidently spread for their attack and were scattered by our starshell, because they could not find each other again and the Senior officer became more and more exasperated. Finally he could bear his unit's truancy no longer and ordered, 'Join me instantly; I am about to fire a green flare stand by – green flare – now.'

And there it was; all we ever had to show that the battle we had almost fought was not a vivid dream.

(From Peter Dickens, *Night Action: MTB Flotilla at War*, p47)

Through constantly changing strongpoints, the FdT was attempting to unsettle the enemy defences and at the same time lighten the task of finding the convoys. He had agreed a procedure with Fliegerkorps II in which the evening reconnaissance would remain over the convoy and pass the contact-keeper's reports to the operations centre. This would then repeat the report, converted to naval co-ordinates, on the S-boat frequency. As the boats approached, the reconnaissance Ju 88, which had no equipment apart from flare bombs, would fire a three-colour recognition signal.

At the end of the bad weather period, this procedure was tried out for the first time on the night of 7 March 1941. The midday Luftwaffe reconnaissance had reported a southbound convoy and had shadowed it for some time so that despite the worsening weather, with winds freshening from north to north-east at force 7 to 8, the FdT sent out all three flotillas. The evening reconnaissance then reported an additional northbound convoy, which would be off Cromer at around midnight. The British MGBs had all run for shelter and the thick cloud cover prevented the RAF spotting the approaching S-boats.

While 2.SFltl. was forced into the warning area by enemy patrol vessels, 1. and 3.SFltl. arrived on the inner convoy lane and lay in wait. They attacked, first the northbound convoy in the inner lane, then the southbound convoy in the outer lane, sinking seven ships of 13,000 tons gross. This was the greatest success the S-boat Arm had achieved to date in one night. Despite the rough seas, S 28 (Oberleutnant zur See Klug) rescued the master of the *Corduff*, while S 101 (Oberleutnant zur See Christiansen) picked up two men from the *Norman Queen*. Forty-one British mariners and AA gunners lost their lives.[52] Nights of bright moon prevented a repeat, the S-boats being discovered early on and forced to turn away. The destroyers avoided their torpedoes, the electric propulsion G7e in use for the first time. As a result, the FdT admonished the flotillas that 'torpedoes fired at 3,000 to 4,000 metres' range at individual targets, particularly destroyers, are completely pointless, waste torpedoes unnecessarily and offer no prospect of success'.[53]

A Royal Navy British Power Boat type MGBA.

After a total of nine operations in which the boats were warded off, claiming only two steamers sunk, the FdT decided on an intensive minelaying programme. The inner lane was the target. This was to force the traffic to use the outer lane, where it ran the greater risk of torpedo attack. The principal mine used was the new TMB (Torpedo Tube Mine B) with magnetic detonator.[54] On 16 April 1941 the three flotillas laid 100 TMBs and sank a freighter, two others being damaged. Bad weather then interfered with the mining missions, and they did not resume until the end of April, when a freighter was torpedoed and sunk during the operation.

The bow flak MG C38 20mm, maximum range 4,900 metres, rate of fire 120 rounds/minute, weight of projectile 134g.

Initially, the Royal Navy had used the so-called motor anti-submarine boats (MA/SB) for defence against S-boats. These were equipped with hydro-phones. From the spring of 1940, they were converted into motor gun boats (MGBs) with one 3.7cm and two twin machine guns either side of the bridge. At the beginning of March 1941, the 6th MGB Flotilla, formed from these conversions, was sent from Fowey, near Plymouth, to the Coastal Forces strongpoint at Felixstowe.[55] The S-boats now came

S 19 of 4.SFltl.

up against this new opponent. In a long battle on 28 April 1940, the weakness of the S-boats, the lack of a forward gun, became obvious. At the beginning of December, the FdT had anticipated the development and ordered a 2cm gun for the foredeck.[56] Now, in April 1941, the weapon had already entered the test stage and the FdT demanded completion and installation on the boats at the front.

With that, the era of the first operations in the Channel came to its end, for now there came into force measures for 'a scheduled training period in the Reich for front flotillas',[57] this being camouflage for the attack on the Soviet Union in the Baltic.

To cover the absence of 1., 2. and 3.SFltl., it was the FdT's operational plan to employ 4.SFltl., newly formed in the Reich, against British coastal convoys in such a manner that 'the British are forced to maintain their strong defence forces at the same level as hitherto'.[58] Accordingly, missions would be sailed primarily from Rotterdam and directed towards constantly changing locations on the convoy route between the Humber and Orfordness. The flotilla would also occasionally engage in minelaying and machine-gun attacks on escorts, and operate now and again from Cherbourg.

Kapitän zur See von Bütow himself retired to Swinemünde in the Baltic, leaving behind only the operations officer of his staff, Oberleutnant zur See Rebensburg, to support the 4.SFltl. commander, Kapitänleutnant Bätge, with his knowledge.

The 4th S-boat Flotilla had only three operational boats, the old S 19, S 24 and S 25, all still without the enclosed forecastle. It sailed its first, unsuccessful sortie on 21 May 1941 while the other three flotillas headed for Wilhelmshaven or Kiel for a short refit. The British defences remained in what was for them a critical phase. They had not yet overcome the S-boat threat, but now they had a respite.

4
Intermezzo
May–October 1941

Following the transfer of the FdT and the 1st, 2nd and 3rd S-boat Flotillas to the Baltic for the attack on the Soviet Union,[1] from 20 May 1941 the 4th S-boat Flotilla (Kapitänleutnant Bätge) operated alone against the convoy routes along the English east coast, the principal purpose being to tie down the strong British defences there.[2] Operating from Rotterdam, the flotilla varied the locations for attack and alternated between mine and torpedo. Hoping to deceive the Royal Navy as to their numbers using the three old boats S 19, S 24 and S 25 was asking a lot, even at the end of May when S 20 and S 22 of the same old class joined them. These five boats were prone to engine breakdowns and only two or three were ever operational at a time. Only after July 1941 did the situation look up, with more and newer boats.

The command centre at this time was Scheveningen near The Hague, where a small staff headed by Oberleutnant zur See Rebensburg, FdT operations officer, received its orders directly from Group West.[3] Shortly after the first unsuccessful foray on the night of 21 May 1941, Group West threw all available forces to the Atlantic ports to provide assistance for the battleship *Bismarck* should it be required. The 4th S-boat Flotilla was ordered to Lorient, but departure was delayed by bad weather and then cancelled after the loss of *Bismarck* on 27 May. From then and throughout June, the flotilla concentrated on the area between Lowestoft and the Humber estuary with alternate mine and torpedo operations. The weather permitted only six sorties and the small number of boats found only one convoy and sank a large ship. This was not, as originally thought, the aircraft carrier *Hermes*, but a freighter disguised to resemble her.[4]

The Enemy Forms Up

Despite the poor success rate of 4.SFltl. against their coastal convoys, the British continued to expand the defensive measures they had introduced in the autumn of 1940.[5] While the Luftwaffe and Kriegsmarine made heavy work of co-operating, and achieved it mainly at the personal level, the co-ordination of the British armed forces was far more efficient. The naval forces were under a uniform structure on a regional basis of naval commands. The RAF was organised along similar lines. The merging of the two headquarters for a particular region ensured close co-operation and a continuous exchange of reports and measures. For the operational region of S-boat activity, the RAF's 16 Group, Coastal Command shadowed the naval commands of Nore and Portsmouth. Nore and 16 Group shared a common headquarters, Chatham, to which naval sub-commands Humber, Harwich, Nore and Dover, Portsmouth and Portland were subordinated. To the west, Western Approaches command and 15 Group shared a headquarters at Plymouth.

In the interim, Coastal Forces had organised, developed and begun to exhibit considerable strength. In 1939, the Royal Navy had only twenty-seven MTBs in four flotillas. The 1st Flotilla (six boats) was at Malta, the 2nd Flotilla (six boats) at Hong Kong. The 3rd Flotilla (six boats), en route for Singapore, was at Malta at the outbreak of war, and the 4th Flotilla (four boats) was in home waters. Five other MA/SB boats were used on anti-submarine duty. The twelve boats at Malta returned to England in November/December 1939 through the French canals and waterways (Marseilles, Lyon, Dijon, Paris, Le Havre), losing one boat on the way. The older types were assigned to

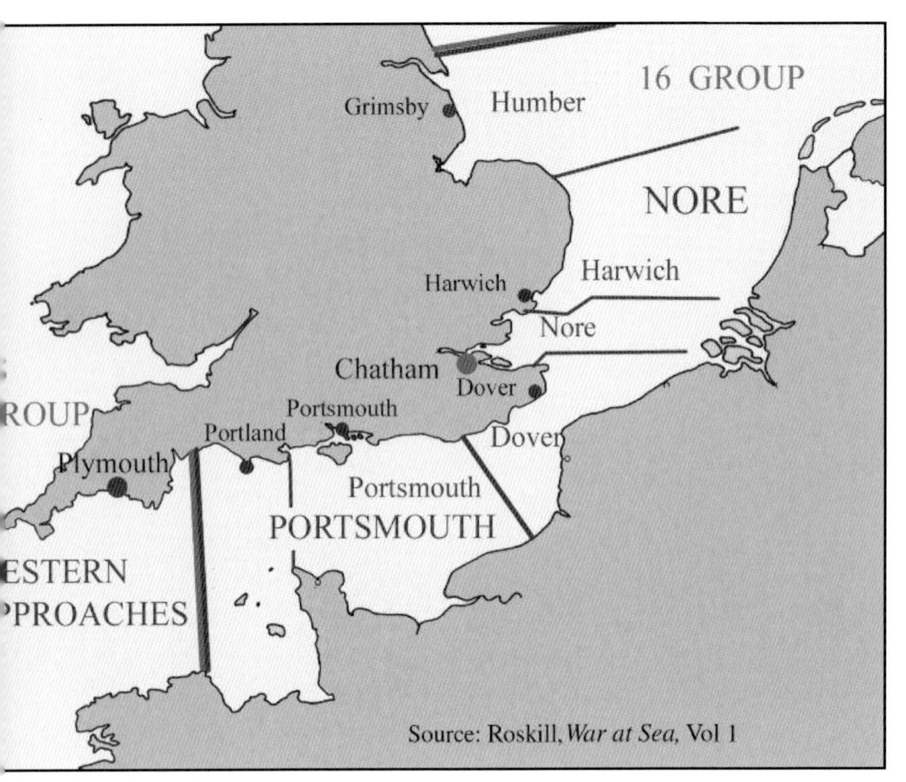

British RN/RAF sectors of responsibility.

harbour defence and air-sea rescue, the newer boats amalgamated as the 1st Flotilla at Felixstowe.[6] When it became apparent that U-boats were concentrating the battle in the Atlantic and not in English coastal waters, the MA/SB boats were converted into motor gunboats (MGBs) from the spring of 1940. In November 1940, the 6th MGB Flotilla was formed at Fowey, then transferred to Felixstowe for anti-E-boat duty in March 1941, where other Power Boat-type MGBs joined them that year.[7]

In common with their German counterparts, the British Admiralty did not appreciate the importance of small units for convoy protection in inshore waters until the war was under way, but with their typical pragmatism they reacted immediately, setting in train a comprehensive building programme that differentiated between MTBs as the weapon of attack against German coastal shipping, MGBs to ward off the S-boats from their own shipping, and motor launches (MLs)[8] for convoy protection. In November 1940, they created the post of Rear Admiral Coastal Forces (Admiral Kekewich) and made him responsible for personnel, training, supply, repairs, prosecution of the building pro-gramme and further developments of the arm. The regional commanders retained only operational control.

Shore training began in October 1940 at the newly established HMS *St Christopher* centre at Fort William in Scotland. In July 1942 a naval training centre, HMS *Bee*, similar to the German S-boat Training Flotilla, was set up at Weymouth. All crews and new boats went through a four-to-eight-week intensive and demanding sea training programme. Only after passing out were they drafted to regional commands and flotillas.

At the end of 1940 there were five Coastal Forces bases: at Harwich and Felixstowe for the east coast; Dover, Portsmouth and Fowey for the south coast. During 1941, Immingham, Great Yarmouth, Lowestoft, Sheerness and Ramsgate were added for the east coast; Newhaven, Cowes, Portland, Dartmouth and Falmouth for the south. These new installations were clear proof of the increasing strength and better distribution of Coastal Forces over the entire operational area.

The spectrum of operations for the Royal Navy boats appeared similar to that of the S-boats initially: air-sea rescue for ditched pilots during the Battle of Britain, torpedo attacks on German coastal convoys, minelaying off enemy ports, and patrols to deter attacking warships and boats. Additionally, they supported convoy escorts in driving off German aircraft. As was the German experience, British boats were lost to mines in operations near the enemy-held coast. In September/October 1940 alone, three boats were mined and sunk; the month before, two destroyers had foundered in a new minefield off Texel.[9]

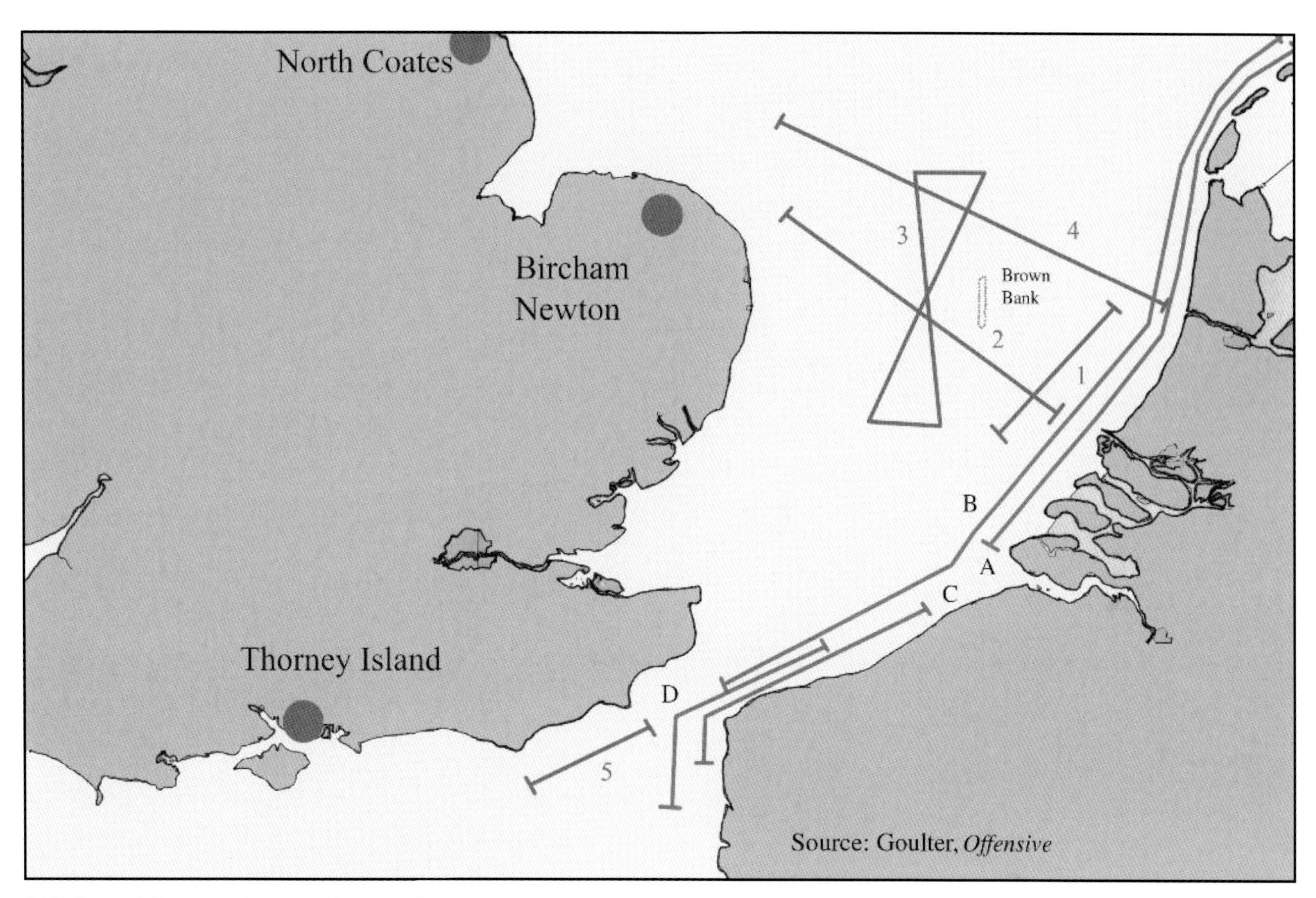

RAF Coastal Command reconnaissance flights.

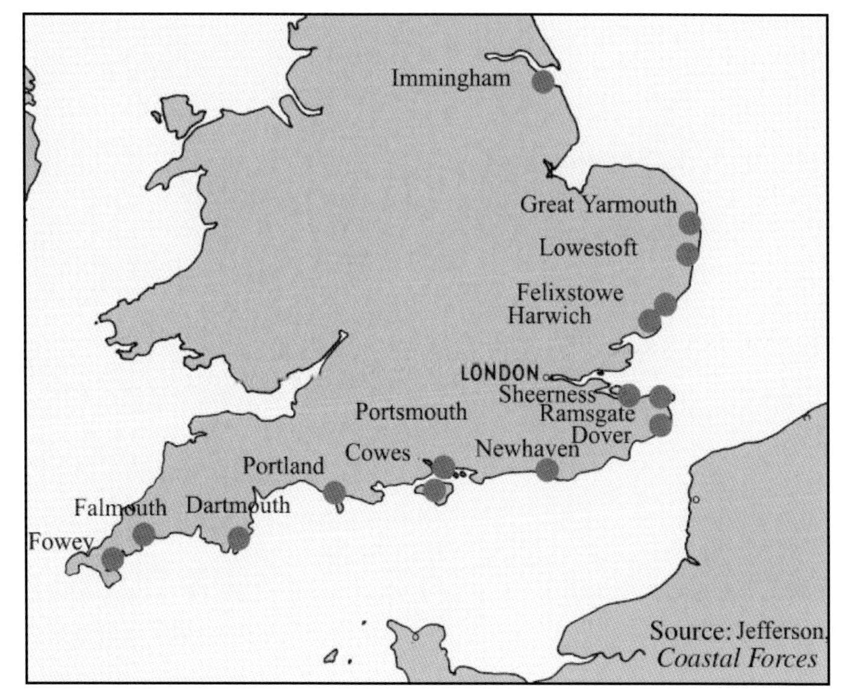

Coastal Forces bases.

Key to flights map (above)

1	One hour before sunset
2	15 minutes before sunset
3	30 minutes before sunset
4	With last of daylight
5	In combination with MGBs
A & B	During the night
C	At dawn and dusk
D	At dawn

The various minelaying operations of German forces by aircraft, ships and S-boats were rarely co-ordinated[10] but nevertheless inflicted serious losses. In 1940, 201 ships of over 500,000 gross tons were lost to mines, 116 of these (350,000 gross tons) in the Nore sector alone.[11] This forced a permanent minesweeping presence on the convoy routes. Following the German air attacks in the autumn of 1940, a nightly search, if possible immediately ahead of the convoy, had been instituted. The number of minesweepers rose from 400 in February 1940 to 698 in September 1940, to 971 in September 1941. The mine threat could be controlled to some extent with such a large force, but even so the losses in the autumn of 1941 from mines still ran at five to six ships per month.[12]

With the strengthening of Coastal Forces and the introduction of MGBs and MLs, the defence against S-boats was systematised. The MLs ran with the convoy while the MGBs patrolled the approach and return tracks, listening out for motor or screw noise or searching on the basis of RAF reconnaissance reports.

Naval War from the Air

In the summer of 1941, 16 Group, RAF Coastal Command began to fly regular and systematic reconnaissance of the most likely S-boat approach routes, and watched the sea lanes used by German merchant shipping for the opportunity to attack. For reconnaiss-ance and attack against vessels recognised as German, the Northern group had Nos 22 and 86 Squadrons (Beauforts[13]) at North Coates and 248 Squadron (Blenheims[14]) at Bircham Newton. Nos 404 and 407 Squadrons operated their Blenheims from Thorney Island, near Portsmouth.15

The co-operation between RAF and RN built up slowly. The S-boats were now being picked out from the air on their approach and attacked long before they reached the convoy lanes, while Coastal Forces began an offensive targeting the E-boats, as the British called them. (It is not certain what 'E' stands for. 'Enemy' has been suggested, but what were they called before 3 September 1939?) The first incident occurred on the night of 20 June 1941, when three Power Boats (MGBs 58, 59 and 65) intercepted two 4.SFltl. boats on the Brown Bank and chased them for twenty nautical miles to the Dutch coast. The British forward-firing twin machine guns were not reliable at high speeds and the German boats escaped unscathed. During this encounter, the susceptibility to break-down of the MG C30 gun had manifested itself, resulting in a request by the FdT that 'the equipping of all S-boats with the greatly improved Flak 38, as has been done with 1–3.SFltl.,[16] should now proceed urgently with 4.SFltl.'.

Brown Bank is a long, narrow stretch of sandy shallows about halfway between the Dutch coast and the British convoy lanes. It was used by S-boats for navigation purposes by means of an echo sounder.

Junkers Ju 88 bomber/reconnaissance aircraft.

Along with the request for better flak, the FdT also asked for light-buoys to be moored north and south of the Brown Bank as aids to S-boat navigation.

Bristol Blenheim reconnaissance aircraft/bomber.

Further West

Meanwhile, the first S-boat bunkers had been completed at Boulogne and Ostend.[17] These had been originally refused by Raeder, but the FdT had been dogged, and eventually convinced the C-in-C. Therefore, on 24 June, 4.SFltl. moved to Boulogne to operate in the Dover Strait from protection, and thus gave the impression of several operational centres. They did not remain there long. Since March 1941, there had been no minelaying by destroyers or torpedo boats along the English south coast, and even the Luftwaffe had dropped only a limited number of mines at the approaches to the southern ports. Group West was anxious to keep the enemy occupied in this sector and after a single sortie from Boulogne, 4.SFltl. moved west to Cherbourg to carry out torpedo and mine missions against the English south coast.[18]

Because of engine repairs and essential overhauls, it was a pitifully small flotilla that put into Cherbourg. On the night of 27 June 1941, the two boats sailed for the convoy routes; one turned back with engine trouble. The remaining boats of the flotilla arrived in July.

In the period between mid-October 1940 and the end of June 1941, when S-boats had been absent from Cherbourg, no systematic evaluation had been undertaken of the available reconnaissance reports, so that no up-to-date knowledge existed as to the convoy routes nor frequency of sailings. Strong British air defences in existence since the Battle of Britain had put paid to organised reconnaissance flown by bomber aircraft, and as a rule Ju 88s were used. Fighters could fly these missions, too, but the results would not be available until they landed, often too late for a useful S-boat sortie. The chances of locating a convoy with the few boats on hand were poor, and it was decided to concentrate instead on intensive minelaying.

When the flotilla strength returned to four boats on 7 July, operations picked up. Over a total of eight nights, the assumed convoy lanes between Portland and Portsmouth were sown with 155 TMAs (Torpedo Tube Mine A) and twenty drag-buoys, mostly close inshore, from where the boats came under fire on numerous occasions from coastal batteries, or were chased by destroyers, on one occasion across the Channel to within sight of Cherbourg. No losses or breakdown occurred, nor any direct successes.

At the end of July, the flotilla returned to Boulogne to keep the British defences on their toes. The Freya[19] radars erected at Cap Griz Nez, opposite Dover, were tried out for convoy detection. The equipment relayed data to the S-boat headquarters at Wimereux, near Boulogne. From there, the FdT passed the information in short-signal form to his S-boats at sea.

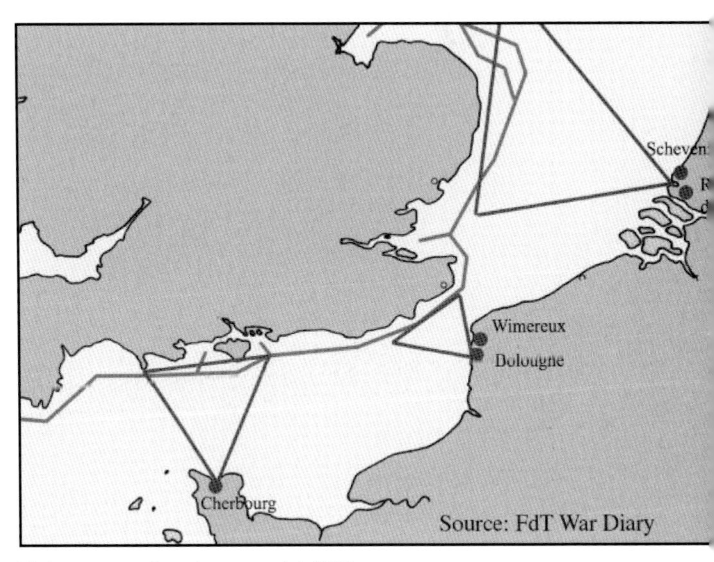

Various operational zones of 4.SFltl.

Taking torpedoes aboard using shipboard equipment.

Both sorties at the beginning of August 1941 were successful; convoys were found and ships torpedoed.[20] The Boulogne bunker offered good protection against the regular RAF air attacks, most of which were directed either towards the heavy units at Brest or the German coastal convoys and ports. Being required on the Russian Front, the Luftwaffe was no longer able to guarantee adequate protection, 'with a total of only a little more than six fighter groups, as against six full squadrons between the Hook of Holland and the Spanish border earlier on'.[21]

The lack of forces limited not only the Luftwaffe but also the Kriegsmarine. On 29 July 1941, Group North requested the long-term transfer of the Channel boats to the Baltic to supplement flotillas there short on engine-hours. The request was repeated on 5 August 1941, when the breakout of the Russian fleet from Kronstadt to Sweden was feared. In turning down Group North, SKL accepted the opinion it had obtained from the FdT, 'that the S-boat Arm, by withdrawing all boats from the West, will lose contact completely with the arch-enemy and his fighting methods, and will at the same time relinquish the provisions for co-operation with the Luftwaffe for our own operations'.[22] The 4th S-boat Flotilla remained in the Channel.

Back Again

As the British defences were now alerted, 4.SFltl. changed its target area to the English east coast, and on 18 August moved back to Rotterdam with headquarters at Scheveningen. The first sortie was successful, one steamer being sunk, a second torpedoed, but in following missions there was no contact. Co-operation with the Luftwaffe was especially good in the area because of the short distance between the airfields and Scheveningen but, even so, the reports were too long delayed and the convoy speed was difficult to gauge from the air. The few boats needed precise information to find a dark convoy on a dark night and, in addition, at the time of the reconnaissance it was not known which of the convoy lanes off the English coast the target formation would take.

The B-Dienst had very efficient DF and hydrophone networks along the Belgian–Dutch coasts, but these were not much help, since the minesweepers and the convoy following them would usually maintain strict radio silence. If attacked, they would report it by radio, however. On the night of 6 September 1941, when the Luftwaffe bombed a northbound convoy at dusk, the operations leader at Scheveningen was able to triangulate the transmissions and determine the convoy's exact position. S-boats, already at sea on the basis of earlier reports, found the convoy and sank two freighters. It was 'a good example of the importance of long-term efforts made by the FdT to establish close co-operation between Luftwaffe reconnaissance and bomber units, the MNO South West as the competent radio observation post and the operational leader of the S-boats',[23] the FdT noted with satisfaction.

It was an isolated event, however, for the Luftwaffe had few aircraft available in the west. The 4th S-boat Flotilla, now up to six boats, played the dual strategy of mine or torpedo, but deteriorating weather conditions with storms limited the number of sorties to nine, during which four ships were torpedoed and sunk. On 3 October, during heavy air raids on the port of Rotterdam, three boats were damaged, one seriously, and were unserviceable for up to a fortnight.

On 9 October 1941, 2.SFltl. (Kapitänleutnant Feldt) arrived at Rotterdam from the eastern Baltic. The FdT Staff also returned and directed the first joint operation of the two flotillas on the night of 12 October.[24] On this occasion, B-Dienst fixed the position of minesweepers and a convoy escort. The 2nd S-boat Flotilla sank two freighters in the outer convoy lane; 4.SFltl. was driven off the inner route by destroyers. Immediately after the attack, British destroyers, escort vessels and aircraft retaliated in such a manner that 'the commanders and crews were stunned and impressed'.[25]

Thus ended the intermezzo. Despite its few boats, 4.SFltl. had carried out its mission without loss to boats or crews in an outstanding and circumspect way. Nevertheless, a weakening of the German offensive capability by S-boats in the western theatre had been unavoidable. This had allowed the British to consolidate and expand their defences, a fact that they had now demonstrated to effect.

5

To the Baltic for Barbarossa

May – November 1941

Hitler's decision to attack the Soviet Union came to maturity in the summer of 1940. How he proposed to combine it with his war effort against Britain after the French capitulation (25 June 1940) was explained to the heads of the German Wehrmacht at Obersalzberg on 31 July 1940, within the framework of a conference on the overall war situation. The envisaged date lay in the spring of 1941.[1] In contrast to the infighting over the operational plan for the Western Offensive, there were no great differences in the Wehrmacht with regard to the Soviet Union. The attack 'had not been recommended by the Army, and the military leadership considered it unnecessary, but it was an achievable undertaking without serious difficulties'.[2] As the planning gathered momentum, the Kriegsmarine remained committed to its priority, the war against Britain, a war that it was their objective to intensify with U-boats and heavy surface units.[3] The Navy was therefore only prepared to commit light naval forces to oppose the Soviet Fleet in the Baltic, and even then the numbers would be few, having regard to the need to protect the European coastline from the North Cape to the Spanish frontier. Accordingly, neither the idea of a bold flanking operation with naval support from the Gulf of Finland towards Leningrad nor the preparation of the Baltic as a supply route for troops, weapons and equipment found favour.[4] The Kriegsmarine object-ions were accepted and reflected in Directive No. 21 'Fall Barbarossa' of 18 December 1940, in which Hitler set out his general concept for the attack on the Soviet Union. For the Navy, 'the priority remains, even during the campaign in the East, directed against Britain'.[5] The Directive stated that it would be the responsibility of the Kriegs-marine, beyond guarding the German-held coasts, to prevent the breakout of enemy naval forces. Once the German Army captured Leningrad, the Russian Baltic Fleet would be deprived of its last base and find itself in a hopeless position. Therefore major naval operations beforehand were to be avoided.

To comply with this instruction, SKL foresaw the deployment of minelayers, U-boats, S-boats, mine-sweepers and UJ-boats (submarine-chasers). The Soviet Fleet was to be prevented from sailing offensive sorties by a series of minefield barriers and then, bottled up in the Gulf of Finland, attacked by the Luftwaffe. S-boats were to protect the minelayers while U-boats kept watch over the central Baltic. Minesweeping flotillas would meanwhile keep the seaways clear and then advance with the land front while UJ-boats searched for Soviet submarines in the central Baltic.[6]

Soviet Baltic Fleet (per Potter and Nimitz, *Seemacht*, p 605): 2 battleships, 2 heavy cruisers, 2 flotilla leaders, 19 destroyers, 7 torpedo boats, 6 minelayers, 33 minesweepers, 48 MTBs, 65 submarines, 656 aircraft.

At the end of May 1941, the 1st, 2nd and 3rd S-boat Flotillas left the Channel for a short overhaul and exercises in the Baltic. Immediately before the beginning of the attack on the morning of 22 June 1941, S-boats were drawn up in the following waiting positions:

1.SFltl. (Kapitänleutnant Birnbacher): depot ship *Carl Peters* and six boats off the Prokhala skerries near Helsinki, together with the Kobra group of minelayers (*Kobra*, *Kaiser* and *Königin Luise*), plus half of the 5th R-boat Flotilla.

2.SFltl. (Korvettenkapitän Petersen): depot ship *Tsingtau* and eight boats off the Abo skerries near Turku, together with Nord group minelayers (*Tannenberg, Brummer, Hansestadt Danzig*) and the other half of the 5th R-boat Flotilla.

3.SFltl. (Kapitänleutnant Kemnade): at Pillau with ten boats, together with minelayers *Grille, Versailles, Skagerrak* and the 15th Minesweeping Flotilla. The depot ship *Adolf Lüderitz* had remained at Swinemünde because of the danger of air attack.

5.SFltl. (Kapitänleutnant Klug, S 28): newly formed from three boats of 1.SFltl. and two boats from 2.SFltl. and lay at Gotenhafen[7] with the 5th Minesweeping Flotilla.

6.SFltl. (Kapitänleutnant Obermaier): with four boats still in training and depot ship *Tanga*, sailed for Helsingör for escort duties, supporting the old battleships *Schlesien* and *Schleswig Holstein* in the Great Belt and Sound.

In charge of the Baltic operations was Vizeadmiral Schmundt, BdK (C-in-C Cruisers), at Swinemünde, with direct responsibility to Group North (Generaladmiral Carls). Subordinate to Schmundt were the FdT (Kapitän zur See von Bütow) at Helsinki, commanding operations in the Gulf of Finland and co-ordinating with the Finns, and Kapitän zur See Böhmer, FdM Nord (C-in-C Minesweepers, North). The latter had the task of securing the central and eastern Baltic, while the Baltic approaches remained the jurisdiction of Vizeadmiral Stohwasser,[8] BSO (C-in-C Coastal Security, Baltic).

Minefields were laid in the central Baltic between 18 and 21 June 1941. Some 1,500 mines and 1,800 explosive buoys formed the three ranks of the Wartburg barrier between Memel and Gotland. At the German request, the Swedes put down a mine barrier between the limits of their territorial waters and the foreshore.[9] Further fields were put down a few hours before the attack at 0300 hrs on 22 June 1941. Group Kobra, protected by 1.SFltl., laid the 'Corbetha' barrier at the entrance to the Gulf of Finland, while minelayer group Nord laid the 'Apolda' fields north of Dagö island extending to Finnish territorial waters. Four boats of 2.SFltl. protected the Apolda operation, while two *Rotten* of S-boats mined the Sounds of Moon and Solesund respectively. Further south, down the coast, five S-boats laid mines off the harbour approaches to Libau and Windau, while 5.SFltl. mined the Strait of Irben.

Camouflaged S-boat depot ship in the Finnish skerries.

Before hostilities began, SKL drew the attention of Group North and the Baltic commanders to the importance attached to the aim 'that our own activities in the war against Soviet Russia must avoid a preparedness to accept heavy losses, since these cannot be decisive for the war, and the military forces which we would lose are needed most pressingly for the further prosecution of the war against Britain'.[10] Because of telecommunications problems, this instruction to avoid unnecessary risks, which would later have an adverse effect on operations by the heavy units,[11] did not reach the FdT until after his S-boats were at sea. Despite misgivings, for 'this report will certainly give rise to doubts and possible disquiet amongst the responsible senior officers who are in

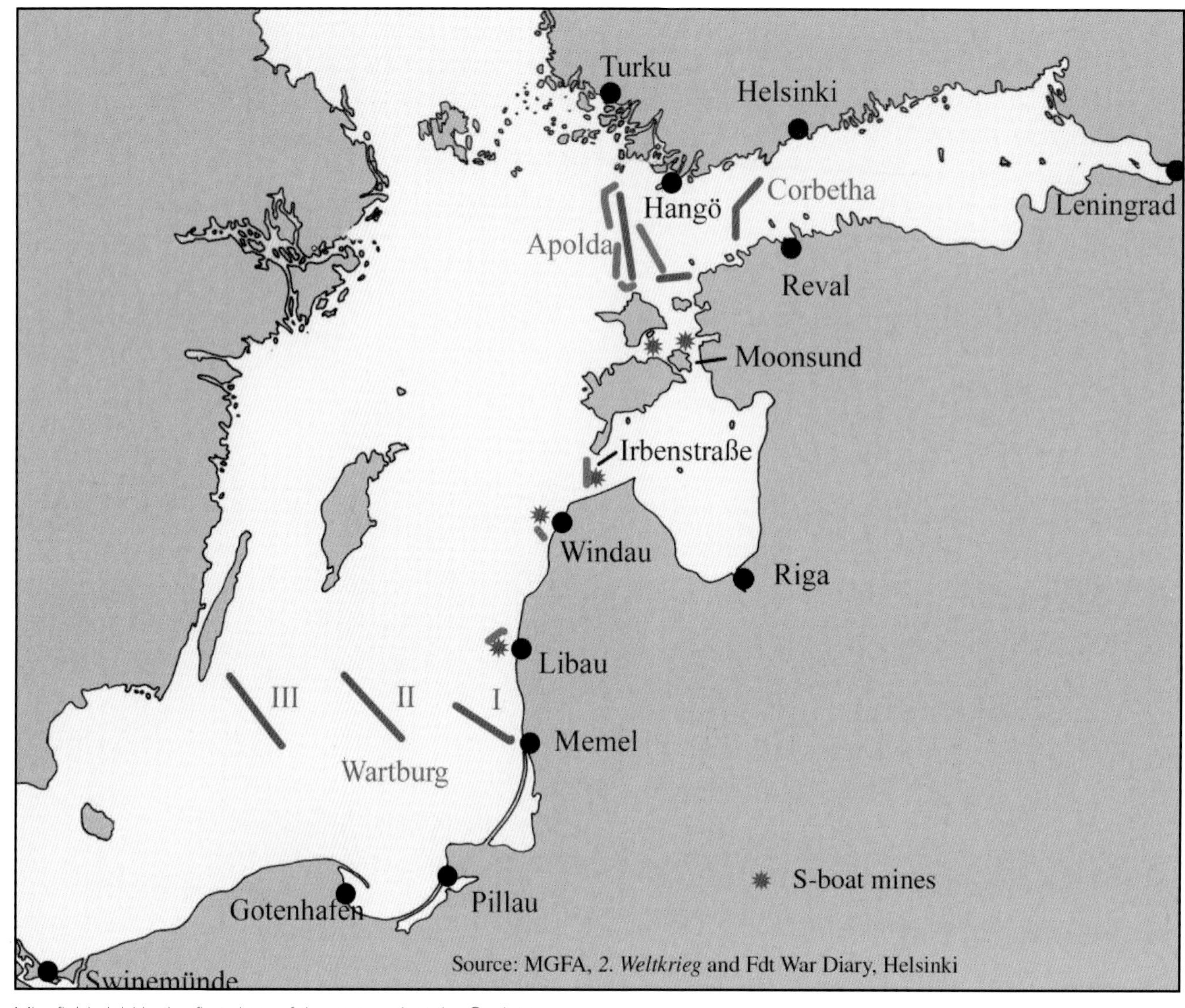

Minefields laid in the first days of the war against the Soviets.

large part committed to the operation',[12] he passed the instruction forward, since in his opinion it contrasted with previous orders and should not be withheld from the units involved. He phrased the instruction, which he had received in garbled form: 'Break off today's operation if the situation makes it seem pointless from the outset. No later operation as in the Norwegian campaign.'[13]

The Soviets were surprised by the attack, however, and there was no immediate resistance. Instead, 3.SFltl. sank two freighters after the minelaying, while 5.SFltl. brought in the Estonian steamer *Estonia*, later used as an S-boat accommodation ship. The same day, 2.SFltl. put to sea again and on the evening of 22 June 1941, south of the Soviet base at Hangö,[14] sank an Estonian steamer and a Soviet patrol boat.[15]

The Soviet countermeasures now set in train were not offensive naval actions but, as in other theatres of war, part of a general overall response. Thus, on the first night of the war in the east, the Baltic Red Banner Fleet began to close off the Gulf of Finland with a mine barrier to prevent the Germans doing what they had no intention of doing, namely to launch a massive thrust deep into the Gulf of Finland in order to threaten Leningrad, and to support the Finnish offensive coming from the north and into the rear of the Soviet units on the northern front. While the Soviet barrier was being laid east of the Apolda field, some of the escort units crossed into the German field. A cruiser and destroyer were mined and sunk, a second destroyer seriously damaged.

Next evening, the Soviet Navy laid minefields off Libau and Windau, which were intended to protect the ports, and in the Irben Strait in the Gulf of Riga. The Germans had the same intention. The 2nd S-boat Flotilla completed the mine barrier north of Dagö and 3.SFltl. came up from the south to mine the Irben Strait, all without meeting Soviet units. On the way back, however, S 35 and S 60 of 3.SFltl. surprised the submarine S-3 and sank it after a long battle. Subsequently the flotilla moved up from Pillau to Memel.

> Ten degrees ahead a shadow comes in sight, and is recognised as a submarine. Both S-boats fire their last torpedo. Both are duds. The one fired by S-60 sinks, the S-35 torpedo is a surface runner. Then both boats open fire with their deck guns. Numerous hits are observed. The enemy replies with a 4cm gun and numerous small-calibre machine guns and rifles. Both boats turn away as both MG C38s jam. Enemy attempts to escape to the north. Boats line up as close as possible despite heavy enemy fire and lob hand grenades and depth charges. Soviet crewmen are already abandoning the submarine despite its still being defended from the conning tower and running at high speed. S 35 picks up the first of them as a hand grenade from S 60 hits the conning tower, which begins to burn. The Soviet commander falls dead. S 60 drops a depth charge in the path of the submarine. This damages her astern so that she begins to sink slowly. Twenty survivors are rescued. (Battle report, *Rotte* S 60, S 35)

Germans and Soviets continued their mining operations. On the night of 26 June 1941, the minelayer *Brummer* laid a field near the island of Odensholm, escorted by 2.SFltl. On the return, S 43 and S 106 ran into the Soviet minefield laid three days previously and sank with nineteen crew. In the south, 3.SFltl., scouting off Windau, came across a Soviet group mining the Irben Strait and torpedoed a destroyer. A Soviet MTB damaged in the exchange of fire was found abandoned and drifting later by German minesweepers and towed in.

On the night of 27 June, S-boats sailed as escorts to the minelayers, or made reconnaissance voyages without sighting the enemy. There were few enough boats; an unusually high number of engine breakdowns cut the available number dramatically.[16] At the end of June 1941, only twelve of twenty-nine were serviceable. Nevertheless, the FdT wanted more minelaying, not at the approaches to the Gulf of Finland but on the routes directly under the Estonian coast. He was opposed to torpedo operations against the traffic there on the grounds of the lack of air reconnaissance. Moreover, on the orders of the BdK, Russian merchant ships were not to be sunk but taken in prize, a policy hardly feasible right under the enemy coast.[17]

In order to engage enemy warships, however, he sought approval to transfer 1.SFltl. to Kotka, where he had set up a base to strike at the units in the Bay of Kronstadt. Group North and the BdK turned down both the Estonian minelaying and the move to Kotka on the grounds that the priority was to prevent the breakout of the Soviet Fleet, and therefore the S-boats had to keep mining the Gulf of Finland: 'Having regard to the task in the west, no further operations are planned in the Gulf of Finland other than to support army operations and attack rewarding targets, and to engage the enemy fleet should it attempt to break out.'[18] The minelaying came to an abrupt halt when the transport *Phönicia* brought TMB mines with a carriage gauge that did not fit S-boat rails, and no suitable rails were aboard the S-boats for the larger EMC mines available in large numbers.[19]

Meanwhile German troops, having occupied Libau on 24 June, Windau on 1 July and Riga on 29 June 1941, forced vessels of the Soviet Fleet to fall back on

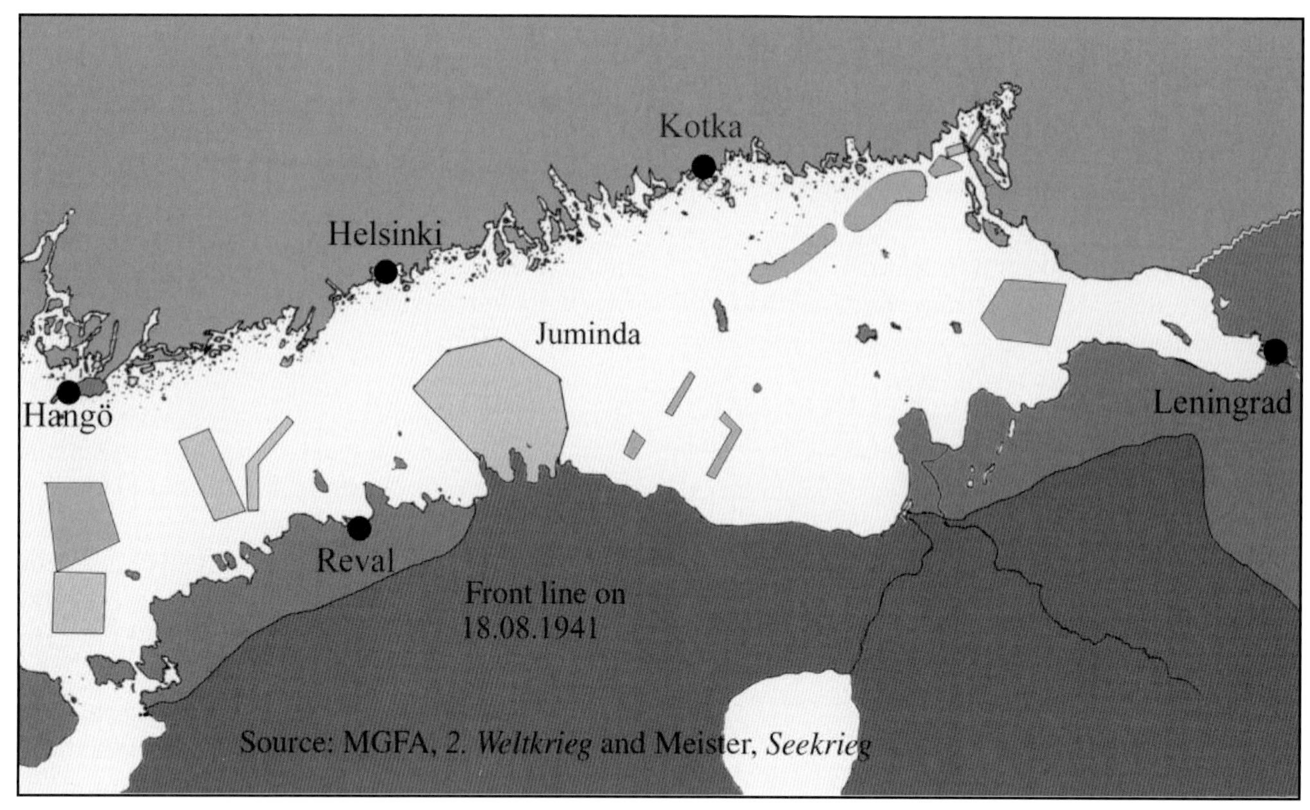

Minefields, Gulf Of Finland, August 1941.

Reval (now Tallinn). After sweeping clear the German and Russian minefields, on 4 July 1941 3.SFltl. entered Libau with the depot ship *Adolf Lüderitz*. Two days later, the entire coast was under German control and convoys of smaller craft began carrying aviation fuel and munitions to Riga. Soviet warships from the Sound of Moon attempting to interrupt this traffic were warded off by 3.SFltl. A Soviet destroyer was sunk in the process. To support the escorts, 2.SFltl. moved up to Windau in mid-July. In this period, the continual engine problems led to a reformation of flotilla compositions and strengths. Boats returning from refits or engine change in Reich shipyards were sent to the flotilla having the fewest operational units, while 5.SFltl. was disbanded and its boats shared around.

July ended without any major operations. 2. and 3.SFltl. patrolled in the south while 1.SFltl. protected occasional mining expeditions from Finland. The low operational levels of the boats worried Group North, which, in view of the expected breakout of the Soviet Fleet, requested that 4.SFltl. be sent from the Channel for support. As explained in the previous chapter, this was declined by SKL on the advice of the FdT because the war on English coastal traffic would have come to a complete stop.[20]

When German troops reached the Gulf of Finland on 6 August 1941, Estonia and the Reval base were finally cut off. At last, the FdT had the authority, which he had been demanding persistently, to lay the 'Juminda' minefield and so isolate Reval from the sea and blockade the naval units congregated there. From 8 August to the end of the month, a system of thirty-two fields covering a sea area of twenty-four by thirty-two miles was sown with 1,400 mines and almost 1,000 buoys. Security for the operation was run by 1.SFltl., based in Finland with seven operational boats. On the night of 12 August 1941, they sank a minesweeper and a tug and took aboard twenty-three survivors.

On 28 August 1941, German troops took Reval. The previous night, the Soviet X Rifle Corps had embarked aboard the ships of the Red Banner Fleet, which then sailed in four columns for Kronstadt through the Juminda minefields. Despite the advance guard of minesweepers, the great squadron suffered heavy losses from mines and air attacks. It anchored in the minefield overnight to allow the minesweepers time to do their job, and sailed again next morning. The 1st S-boat Flotilla attacked, but the cruisers' big guns kept the German boats out of torpedo range. Eventually over 100 vessels, the major part of the Soviet Fleet, and 20,000 fighting troops got through to Kronstadt to support the defence of Leningrad.

One week after the capture of Reval, Estonia was occupied and only the Baltic islands now remained in Soviet hands. In order to dislodge these forces, it was planned that the Kriegsmarine would carry out landings on Ösel and Dagö to divert attention away from the movement of German troops across the Sound of Moon. On 13 September 1941, the three operations began: '*Westwind*', on the west coast of Ösel, '*Südwind*', on the south east coast of Ösel, and '*Nordwind*' on the north coast of Dagö. The 3rd S-boat Flotilla formed part of *Südwind* together with torpedo boats, minesweepers, R-boats, minelayers and smaller craft, as well as two Finnish armoured coastal ships in the north, of which one was mined and sunk while returning. The feints passed off successfully; the German Army forces crossed over almost unopposed, taking Ösel on 5 October, and Dagö between the 12th and the 21st.[21]

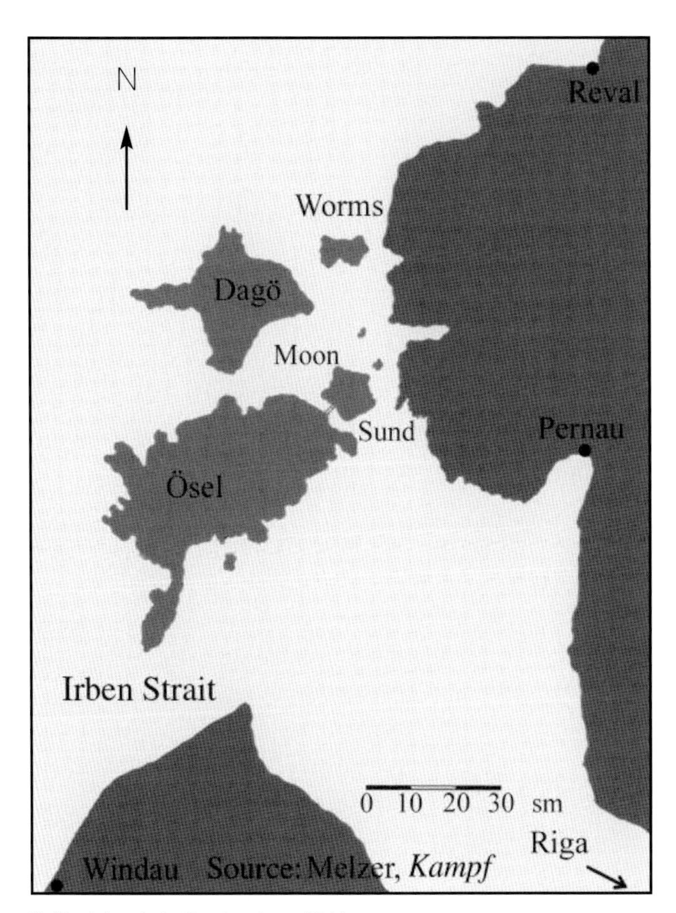

Baltic Islands In September 1941.

After the Germans completed the Juminda minefield and the Finns had laid other barriers in the Gulf, SKL considered a breakout by the Baltic Fleet in Kronstadt Bay as very unlikely. Hitler took the opposite view and argued that heavy ships should be put on station to frustrate any such breakout attempt. According to his directive, the battleship *Tirpitz*, the heavy cruiser *Admiral Scheer*, the light cruisers *Köln* and *Nürnberg*, three destroyers and five torpedo boats were formed into the 'Baltic Fleet' and sailed for the Aaland islands on 23 September 1941.[22]

The 3rd S-boat Flotilla with four boats was ordered to Finland in support, arriving at Turku on 21 September 1941. The light cruisers *Emden* and *Leipzig*, sent to Libau as the southern group, were supported by the two available boats of 3.SFltl. and two boats of 2.SFltl. that had meanwhile re-entered service. After Luftflotte 1 attacked the Russian warships on 24 and 25 September 1941, seriously damaging both battleships and a heavy cruiser, the German 'Baltic Fleet' was withdrawn next day.

The 3rd S-boat Flotilla now received orders to prepare for Mediterranean operations. The four northern boats returned with the *Tirpitz* group, while the other two escorted depot ship *Adolf Lüderitz* to Swinemünde, where all units met up on 26 September 1941. The 2nd S-boat Flotilla was also released by BdK shortly after (1 October 1941) for a return to the English Channel after a refit. Only 1.SFltl. remained in the Gulf of Finland for convoy escort duty; missions were sailed against Russian traffic entering and leaving the base at Hangö but these, lacking sea reconnaissance, involved the unnecessary expenditure of engine-hours and reported no successes. Even after the evacuation of Hangö on 26 October 1941, the flotilla remained in Finland to protect the last of the minelaying. When it was finally released, on 13 November 1941, ice had begun to form in the Gulf, threatening to trap the boats there for the winter. They were held back for ten days by bad weather and reached Germany on 24 November 1941, where the flotilla received orders to prepare for work in the Black Sea.

Thus ended the five-month odyssey of the S-boats in the central and eastern Baltic, an operation in waters difficult for navigation such as the Finnish skerries, and in which few opportunities presented themselves to use the S-boat's principal weapon of offence, the torpedo. Despite serious engine problems, especially demanding of the technical personnel, they performed all tasks required of them and proved once more their ability to perform many different roles.

Hits on the Soviet battleship *Marat*.

6

Back to the Channel

November 1941 – June 1944

As the Baltic campaign ended, the focus of S-boat operations reverted to the English Channel. Initially only the 2nd S-boat Flotilla arrived to support the 4th, which had held the fort since the summer of 1941. The 3rd S-boat Flotilla was preparing for the Mediterranean, the 1st for the Black Sea; the 8th went to the polar north, while the 6th was working up in the Baltic. Further flotillas were in the act of formation and would later reinforce 'the Channel workers', as S-boat men observed ironically. Their unspectacular, grim and often deadly missions would maintain a certain similarity over the coming few years. 'A fixed stipend on the British convoy routes' was how Oberleutnant zur See Klose, commander of S 70, described it later. Similar and regulated, because until the Normandy invasion in June 1944, neither the strategy nor the tactics really changed.

Week by week, the convoys ran to and from the Thames estuary along the English east and south coasts, protected by an ever more comprehensive system of aircraft, flying boats, gunboats, destroyers and land stations. The S-boats attempted to find gaps in these defences and so get through to the merchant ships of the convoys. That was how it had been and would remain until the invasion.

In November 1941, 2. and 4.SFltl. operated from Rotterdam. After several fruitless sorties in which no convoys could be found, on the evening of 19 November the Luftwaffe delivered the last known position of a southbound convoy it had spotted. The 2nd S-boat Flotilla, north of Smith's Knoll, found the ships immediately and sank three of 8,000 gross tons on its first approach. The flotilla then disengaged from the convoy escorts but, while regrouping for a second attack, two boats collided as the result of an ambiguous order transmitted by radio. S 105

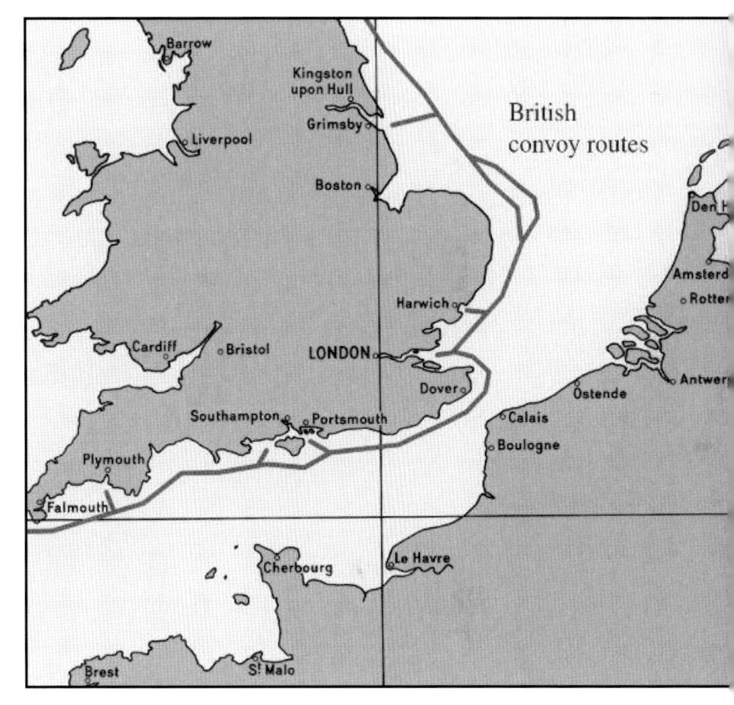

Convoy routes 1941– 4.

misinterpreted what the word '*stopp*' applied to and stopped dead in the water. S 41 and S 47, astern of S 105, collided while attempting to avoid the stopped boat and sustained serious damage. After each was taken under tow by a separate group, the two groups lost contact, but one group then ran into a force of two British gunboats. The MGBs had sailed from Felixstowe upon receipt of the enemy report and were heading for Brown Bank to cut off the S-boats' retreat. The Germans were surprised and, in the course of the skirmish, S 41, under tow by the stern, received further damage and had to be abandoned. An attempt to destroy the wreck by explosive charges was botched, the boat sinking slowly enough to allow an MGB to put a party aboard to salvage radio and ultra-short-wave equipment and navigation charts before S 41 went under.[1] 4.SFltl., further south, failed to rediscover the convoy and did not hear 2.SFltl. radio calls appealing for help. At dawn, 2.SFltl. came under heavy attack from British fighter aircraft and suffered further losses and damage. There was no German fighter presence because the flotilla's request to Jagdführer Holland command centre was not received. As a result, all surviving boats of 2.SFltl. arrived back in a shot-up condition and only 4.SFltl. remained operational.

In the two subsequent operations, 4.SFltl. found the reported convoys and sank a total of five freighters. From then until the end of December 1941, 4.SFltl. and three 2.SFltl. boats returning from the repair yard carried out four minelaying missions between Orfordness and the Humber. Before these operations, there had been differences of opinion between Group West and the FdT. The Group wanted to mine as large an area as possible, with at least a kilometre between mines. The FdT considered the need to remain unobserved paramount, which meant completing the operation as quickly as possible. Minelaying kept the entire crew busy, and since the number of lookouts had to be reduced, the job ought not to last more than forty-five minutes. A compromise was reached with group mining. Group West accepted the argument and a total of twelve ships of 50,000 gross tons were lost to this minefield.[2] On these operations, a short-signal code, the so-called '*Schnepfentafel*' ('tart' code), was tried out so that reports and information between the FdT and flotilla chiefs at sea could be encrypted into the normal radio traffic.[3]

During a mining operation, the two boats of a *Rotte* lost contact. The FdT showed understanding for this. That one of the two commanders should then return home with his mines led to his being relieved of command.

> The dark night made the highest demands of the commanders' seamanship. That the two commanders experienced difficulties in holding station is therefore understandable (the crew of S 24 was making its first enemy patrol). That S 109 failed to lay her mines in the operational area despite being there several hours is inexcusable. A commander who displays a lack of initiative of that nature must be removed. (War Diary, FdT, 22 December 1941)

As the result of experiences gained in recent months, at the end of 1941 the FdT requested the installation of a foredeck flak gun on all boats, since these had proved their worth in action with British naval vessels. He also asked for the introduction of the GA apparatus, which enabled the torpedo course to be pre-set prior to launching and did away with the need to aim the boat at the target, an awkward procedure that wasted time and gave the enemy opportunities to detect the flotilla.

Severe weather kept S-boats in harbour until well into February 1942, save for two outings to lay mines. Icing in the Meuse forced 2.SFltl. to remove to the still-incomplete base at Ijmuiden, while 4.SFltl. went to Boulogne. On 17 January, 6.SFltl.(Oberleutnant zur See Obermaier) came to Ostend. The British advantage in radar became clear at this time when, on the night of 18 January 1942, with visibility between fifty and ninety metres, S 39 received shellfire from escorting destroyers without being able to make out the muzzle flashes. The fire came from one of the first radar-equipped destroyers on the east coast.

At Boulogne, 4.SFltl. prepared to assist in the protection of the heavy units *Scharnhorst, Gneisenau* and *Prinz Eugen* in Operation 'Cerberus', the Channel Dash from Brest to Germany. Additional boats were drawn from 2. and 6.SFltl. to bring the force up to ten. For Luftwaffe identification purposes, the S-boats' upper deck was painted a luminous yellow from the stern to the rear of the raised forecastle, and from the bow to the front of the wheelhouse. Additional flak ammunition, smoke canisters and torpedoes were taken aboard. The 4th S-boat Flotilla formed part of the flank protection against aircraft, MTBs and destroyers. During the passage, S 64 was hit and sent into port. The 2nd S-boat Flotilla, at immediate readiness, remained in harbour because of the deteriorating sea state. Before the squadron of heavy ships had entered the Channel early on 12 February 1942, 6.SFltl. carried out an operation off the English south coast as a feint to draw off enemy naval forces.

After Cerberus, the alternating torpedo/mine missions resumed. When 2.SFltl. was pursued by British destroyers on the night of 19 February, S 39 and S 53 collided. S 39 limped home with a long gash in the hull, but S 53 (Oberleutnant zur See Block) was found by MGBs and had to be scuttled. Some of the crew were rescued by the British, but the commander was lost.[4]

Through February and March, 2.SFltl. operated with mine or torpedo against the east coast convoys, supported initially by 6.SFltl. until the latter transferred to Norway.[5] On minelaying operations at this time between Dover and Dungeness, 4.SFltl. confirmed that the boats were being tracked by enemy land radar and, since the locations of German minefields was known, enemy convoys were steering clear of them. The FdT now considered minelaying valueless in such a closely watched zone. Group West took another view and believed that 'a mining mission carried out with perseverance can cause the enemy many problems and his enforced evasive manoeuvres can provide favourable opportunities for torpedo attack'.[6] The FdT was not convinced that this was so and decided to suspend minelaying for the time being.

While 4.SFltl., based at Boulogne, close to the operational area, could generally give the slip to enemy pursuers, 2.SFltl. repeatedly came across defences on the alert. On the night of 14 Match 1942, after sinking the destroyer *Vortigern* in an action against a southbound convoy, the boats lost contact in poor visibility and returned to base either singly or in *Rotten*. Once they were safe in the bunker, a telephone message was received from the FdT that, according to the B-Dienst, an S-boat was involved in a battle with MGBs. The flotilla sailed at once in search of S 111. It appeared that after a delayed return, the reasons for which were not clear, S 111 had been intercepted by three MGBs lurking near the Dutch coast. Presumably S 111 had mistaken them for German air-sea rescue vessels on account of their white livery and proximity to Holland. S 111 had been taken by surprise and an attempt at flight had been ended by a depth charge dropped immediately before her bow; the boat had been captured and towed off in triumph. The 2nd S-boat Flotilla now came across the towing party, whereupon the British MGBs cut S 111 adrift and made into a fog bank. S 111 was now taken in tow by friendly vessels. A fighter escort requested by the FdT was unable to take off for low

4.SFltl. boats in the Boulogne bunker.

cloud, but eventually three *Rotten* of fighters got aloft. The first pair could not find the MGBs, the second pair were never heard from again, having presumably crashed into the sea in fog, while the third circled the towing team for a while before returning home for lack of fuel.

Shortly afterwards, eleven RAF Spitfires arrived and, in a thirty-minute skirmish, inflicted damage and injuries aboard all S-boats. In the confusion, S 111 was cast adrift once more and sank.

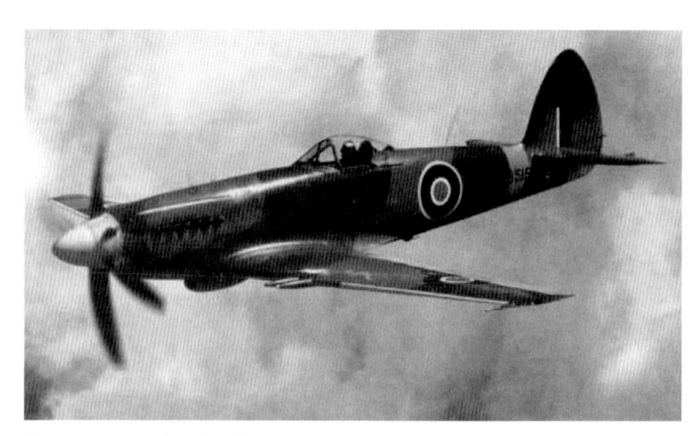
Supermarine Spitfire fighter.

> The white ensign flew at the mast. Bridge and superstructure riddled by machine-gun fire, in the command centre and wheelhouse lay seven dead: Oberleutnant zur See Popp, the commander, Oberleutnant zur See Jopping, commander-in-training, the coxswain, bridge-midshipman, helmsman, navigation AB and a stoker. Eighteen other men of the crew were missing.
> (2.SFltl. War Diary, 15 March 1942)

The S-boat Arm Becomes Autonomous

On 20 April 1942, there occurred a significant organisational change, whereby the post of FdT was discontinued, the torpedo boats passing beneath the umbrella of the FdZ (Führer der Zerstörer), while the S-boats received their own commander, the FdS (Führer der Schnellboote).[7] It made sense, for in the past the FdT had spent the greater portion of his time administering the S-boats, because the torpedo boats in certain operational areas had been taken from his control. Thus, the S-boat Arm found its place in the Kriegsmarine, after having been dismissed only a few years previously as a mere 'weapon of opportunity', lacking operational importance and of only limited usefulness. In this development, Kapitän zur See Bütow, FdT, had played a leading role. He was distinguished by his clear operational ideas, the ability to see them through, and his fearlessness before the thrones of the German Admiralty kings. He weighed the chances of success against the operational risk soberly and without emotion, always mindful of the crews' welfare. His soldierly qualities are highlighted by an entry in the War Diary after a torpedo boat sank an RN vessel: 'The term chivalry is not to be found in the behaviour of the commander of *Jaguar*. There was no reason to sink a boat unable to flee.'[8]

Bütow's successor as leader of the S-boat Arm was Korvettenkapitän Petersen, formerly chief of 2.SFltl., who would remain *Kommodore* until the end of the war. For the S-boats, the organisational reshuffle changed nothing. As before, they were directed from command headquarters at Scheveningen, but by the FdS instead of the FdT. Both posts were directly answerable to Fleet Command as regarded the men, and to Group West for operations.

Until the beginning of June 1942, 2. and 4.SFltl. at Rotterdam carried out mainly mining activities along the convoy routes skirting the English east coast. In May, 4.SFltl. was transferred temporarily to Boulogne to escort the merchant raider *Stier* through the Straits of Dover on her way to the Atlantic. On the night of 12 May 1942, British MTBs sank two of the four torpedo boat escorts, *Seeadler* and *Iltis*. Without ever having been in contact with the enemy force, 4.SFltl. picked up eighty-three survivors, plus three British mariners from the sunken MTB 220.

At the beginning of June, both flotillas moved via Ostend to Boulogne, from where the seven serviceable boats subordinated to 4.SFltl. commander would mine the British convoy lanes directly under

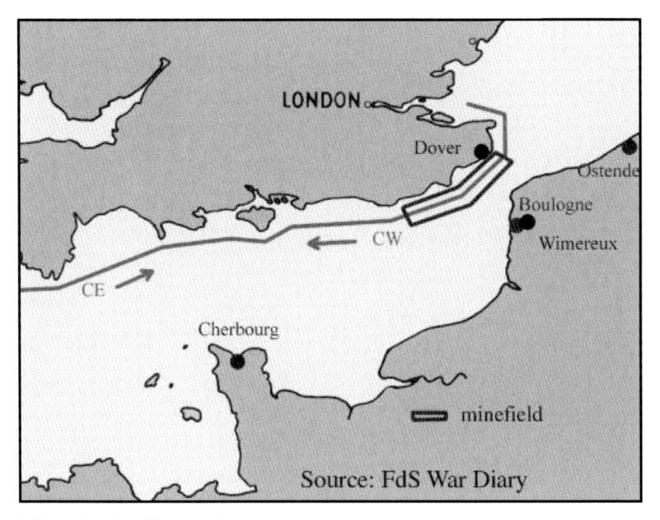

Mines in the Channel narrows.

the English coast.[9] Although it had been proved earlier in the year that the enemy was able to trace the boats and knew exactly where the minefields were laid, Group West considered the activity valuable, since it tended to divert attention from German convoys on the French side of the Channel and reduced British minelaying. The FdS moved his headquarters from Scheveningen to Wimereux to be in closer contact with the areas of operations and the Luftwaffe command centres.

The *Stichansatz*

At the end of June 1942, the boats moved to Cherbourg to operate against the east–west convoys. The flotilla commander 2.SFltl. was given charge, although the flotilla was directed by the FdS, which was new. The new tactic introduced was '*Stichansatz*' – the stab. The preconditions were B-Dienst or Luftwaffe reconnaissance reports. The stab would then proceed towards a dead-reckoned position for the convoy. The flotilla would disperse at about ten to fifteen nautical miles from the planned attack point, each Rotte putting about two nautical miles' distance between itself and the next, and creep up to the convoy lane to lie in wait adrift. If nothing was sighted within a given time, a search for the convoy would begin either side of the lane, because the dead-reckoned position could be up to eight or ten nautical miles out. The best possible situation was for a reconnaissance aircraft to be circling the convoy, illuminating it with flares, reporting its position constantly by radio and attempting to draw off enemy forces. To simplify the passing of orders, the convoy route on the chart would be given a reference point every two nautical miles.

The first attempt of this nature, on 6 July 1942, failed because the spacing between the *Rotten* was too small. The attack on an eastbound convoy on 8 July 1942, however, was fully successful, six ships of a total of 12,000 gross tons being sunk. The operational orders read: 'Convoy review 1715 in position . . . 2.SFltl. *Stichansatz* with one *Rotte* each at 0130 positions Max, Nanni and Otto. The 4th S-boat Flotilla at Quatsch. First to third *Rotten* lurk until 0145. Afterwards *Rotte* 1 westwards along convoy lane, *Rotten* 2 and 3 scout northwards. *Rotte* 4 lurk until 0200 hrs, then scout north-east. In contact with convoy, maintain contact until other *Rotten* arrive. Convoy consists of two large, six medium and five small steamers, two small escorts. Return 0315 hrs, tart-code 1A, ultra-short-wave channel 13.'[10]

In subsequent weeks, there was an absence of

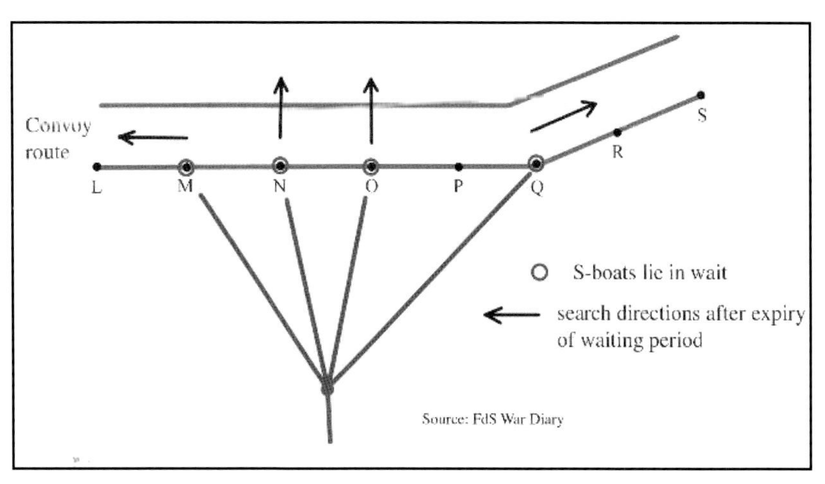

Stichansatz.

precise reconnaissance reports, as a result of which the FdS ordered more minelaying, which brought little success. Meanwhile, both flotillas had returned to full strength and, at the end of July 1942, 5.SFltl. (Kapitänleutnant Klug) arrived at Cherbourg. On 3 August 1942, the nineteen boats of the three flotillas headed for a westbound convoy, but the British defences were on the alert and their destroyers and MGBs drove off the S-boats. Three boats loosed off torpedoes, but no sinkings were reported.

The lengthening nights enabled the resumption of operations against the much heavier convoy traffic along the east coast, resulting in the return of 2.SFltl. to Ijmuiden and 4.SFltl. to Rotterdam. The 5th S-boat Flotilla remained at Cherbourg. The FdS returned his headquarters from Wimereux to Scheveningen. At the beginning of September, 6.SFltl. (Korvettenkapitän Obermaier) returned from Norway, joining 2.SFltl. at Ijmuiden, so that three flotillas were poised on the Dutch coast to strike at the convoy lanes.

Fairmile C class MGB, similar to MGB 335.

On 10 September 1942, flotillas returning from the English coast were intercepted on Brown Bank by four RN MGBs. During the ensuing skirmish, one of the MGBs was seriously damaged and abandoned. While some of the S-boats pursued the three British vessels, parties from S 80 and S 105 boarded the abandoned MGB and began a salvage attempt after removing two telegraphists. Despite many difficulties (lines parting, flooding, towing by the stern, waggling), the prize was brought in. British charts with plotted minefields, a signal book, radio apparatus and a radar set were found aboard, the latter proving how great were the strides the British had made in this respect. The capture of MGB 335 was kept secret, and the boat was claimed as sunk for the information of the British.[11] In this firefight, the 4cm gun had proved itself particularly valuable. S 117 was the only boat to have it installed, and two rounds from the weapon had pierced the bridge armour.[12]

After the battle, whose significance for crew morale was reported upon by the flotilla chiefs, the FdS laid down the following requirements for future operations:

S-boats are to leave and return to port together, to sail in large groups and to avoid the favourite waiting areas of enemy defences by sailing north-about routes;
S-boats are to be fitted with bridge armour as a priority;
S-boats are to have more guns;
more S-boats are to be fitted with radar, particularly radar detection devices.[13]

In the absence of air reconnaissance reports, minelaying missions followed. In addition, Group West ordered a number of boats to remain at thirty minutes' readiness to sail in the event of a repetition of Allied landing operations such as that at Dieppe on 19 August 1942. This made extra demands on men and materials.

During September and October, 5.SFltl., operating from Cherbourg, carried out alternate minelaying and torpedo forays but could claim only one naval trawler sunk. The principal reason for this lack of success was a shuffle in the convoy arrangements on the south coast in mid-October.

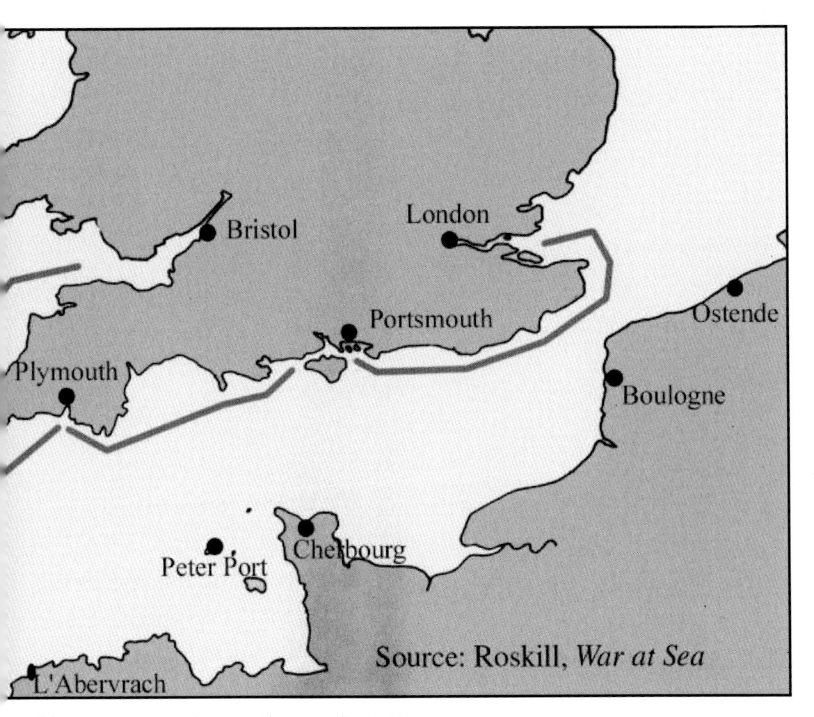

New convoy routes on the south coast.

The British were now sailing twenty ships between the Bristol Channel and Plymouth, in each direction, every second day. These were the WP (West–Plymouth) or PW (Plymouth–West) convoys. Smaller convoys of seven ships or so made the run every other day between Portsmouth and Plymouth, in each direction. CW and CE convoys, which sailed previously from the Bristol Channel to the Thames estuary direct, were now eighteen strong and ran six times a week between Portsmouth and the Thames. East-coast convoy timetables had been staggered in October, the frequency of sailings being raised from every other day to six per week, and up to thirty-six ships now formed the convoy.[14]

On the night of 6 October 1942 on the east coast, the B-Dienst report of a northbound convoy was confirmed by air reconnaissance, and seventeen boats from three flotillas attacked, sinking three steamers of 7,000 gross tons, a tug and ML 339. In this operation, the new GA torpedo director installed aboard S 80 enabled the torpedo to be fired on a bearing relative to the boat's fore-and-aft axis and was successful. One week later, in another attack on a northbound convoy, when only 6.SFltl. found the convoy and torpedoed two freighters, the FdS identified a clear failure in tactics and repeated the ground rules of *Stichansatz*:

> On the approach, navigation is the important factor. Before the flotillas are ordered to disperse by the flotilla commander, the leader boats are to close up to synchronise their navigational co-ordinates. This agreed position then serves for everybody, and the boats are then to spread out at the dispersal point. The distance between each *Rotte*, previously two miles, can be shortened to one mile if air reconnaissance gives sufficiently reliable reports.
>
> The attack point for the central leader *Rotte* stated in the orders relates to a particular time of day. In the event of delays during the approach, in order to calculate the new attack position, the speed of the convoy is to be estimated to be 7 knots. Corresponding to the tactical necessity to remain unseen until the attack begins, ultra-short-wave radio silence must be maintained until contact is established with the enemy. Ships of the convoy and destroyers must be reported by radio without delay. Any delay is a mistake. Only in this manner can the main body of boats get to the enemy. *Stichansatz* in *Rotten* is dictated by our own reconnaissance. Based on enemy reports, a massed attack is justified by coming up on the convoy from astern. It is incorrect if the flotilla, at the moment when the convoy is detected and the enemy defences take action, remains together. A destroyer cannot chase five boats heading in different directions. The correct course is to scatter in *Rotten* so that the enemy latches on to one *Rotte* and gives the others the opportunity to escape.[15]

Wintry storms and the lack of air reconnaissance permitted few sorties. In various engagements, one steamer was sunk and another torpedoed.

S 101 had become detached for a brief period and closed in on a number of MGBs which had been mistaken for friendly by their green light signals. In the exchange of fire, all the bridge personnel, including the commander, Oberleutnant zur See Miljes, were killed. Wounded signaller Obergefreiter Berghammer gave the order 'Full ahead all engines, course 90°' and so saved the boat, which then regained contact with the flotilla under the temporary command of coxswain's mate Hauser.
(2.SFltl. War Diary, 15 November 1942)

On the night of 12 December 1942, in a permutation of the FdS's basic principles, boats of 2. and 6.SFltl. on the flanks lured away the escorts, leaving 4.SFltl. with a clear field to sink five steamers of 7,000 gross tons from northbound convoy FN 889.

Measure and Countermeasure

At the beginning of the New Year, 1943, the four flotillas in the west had forty boats at their disposal. The 2nd S-boat Flotilla (Kapitänleutnant Feldt) and 6.SFltl. (Korvettenkapitän Obermaier) were at Ijmuiden; 4.SFltl. (Kapitänleutnant Bätge) and 5.SFltl. (Kapitänleutnant Klug) were based at Rotterdam and Cherbourg respectively. 2., 4. and 6.SFltl. (usually fourteen to sixteen operational boats) operated jointly against the British convoys on the English east coast, but the proven *Stichansatz* tactic was unsuccessful here. The enemy defences had become so strong that the boats tangled interminably with the escorts, unable to penetrate to the freighters. Air reconnaissance was a rarity because of a general lack of suitable aircraft, and even when the Luftwaffe actually did fly a mission, the fighter defences would force the aircraft away before the convoy could be sighted. Even reliable B-Dienst reports required confirmation by eye, according to the FdS, after fruitless forays on 24 and 26 January 1943, and he demanded the restoration of air reconnaissance to support the activities of the S-boat Arm. In general, there was none and instead the flotillas sustained losses.

On 9 January 1943, S 104 of 2.SFltl. was sunk; the same fate befell S 71 on 18 February under a destroyer's guns, but no report was made. The search set in motion the next day by the FdS, involving all three flotillas, led to an altercation with Group West. S 71 was missing, B-Dienst had not intercepted messages to clarify the situation and in the poor visibility it was possible that the boat was still afloat. Group West deplored the search because no operation with the entire fleet of boats could be justified except, under special circumstances, for an offensive when the opportunity presented itself. This amounted to a personal reprimand for the FdS, and he replied by an entry in the War Diary that attracted a sharply critical letter from the C-in-C, Group West. The personal differences were ironed out in a private conversation between Generaladmiral Marschall and Kapitän zur See Petersen on 21 March 1943, but thereafter there existed a rather tense relationship between Group West and the S-boat flotillas. This was fuelled by the attitude of the FdS and his staff towards operations, which was prejudicial to some degree to other branches of the service, but the main cause of discord was his vehement opposition to escort work and duties of a similar nature foreign to motor torpedo boat practice.

The next group of sorties brought no success. On bright moonlit nights, the flotillas laid mines in the convoy lanes, but British radar enabled the fields to be plotted accurately and then swept. From B-Dienst reports, the FdS was able to watch the British minesweeping vessels at work and to establish to some extent how accurate the laying had been. Nevertheless, successes were rare and the boats suffered fresh losses. In an attack on a convoy on the night of 4 March 1943, S 70 of 2.SFltl. sank fifteen minutes after colliding with a drifting mine. While returning from the same operation, *Rotte* S 74 and S 75 of 6.SFltl. was spotted at first light by two waves of Spitfires. S 74 received serious damage, while S 75 caught fire and

A boat being towed in after hitting a mine.

had to be blown up. All three boats sustained dead and injured.

Despite prior notification by the FdS, and although the machines were waiting at readiness, German fighters failed to appear. The request by the boats on the fighter frequency had not been received again by Jagdführer Holland. And once again it was clear how limited was S-boat operational freedom; they could sail only during the hours of darkness, whereas the enemy was so strong that he could assemble in daylight. All petitions and requests by the FdS for the deployment of German aircraft against British naval targets went unheeded. The Luftwaffe, permanently overburdened by work, was not available.

The real problem remained the finding of convoys. As a tactical variation, for the first time on 7 March 1943 the 'FuMB Lurk' was introduced. 2. and 6.SFltl. would form up for the scheduled *Stichansatz*, while 4.SFltl. would lie adrift away from the convoy route and only after the radar-carrier had obtained a fix would the attack point be set.

On this occasion, despite air reconnaissance over both convoys, there had been no successes because the British, contrary to practice, had run the southbound convoy down the inner lane and the northbound convoy, at a slightly later hour, up the offshore lane. Only 6.SFltl. made contact, but was beaten off by the destroyers without making contact. During the proceedings, S 119 and S 114 collided, the former being so badly damaged that it had to be scuttled after S 114 removed the crew.

The 'FuMB Lurk' by all three flotillas on 9 March 1943 was the logical next step. According to the operational orders:

> The boats will not enter the convoy lane until the ships of the convoy have been confirmed by radar. Experience shows that most radar-detection-equipped boats will obtain a fix on the convoy escorts using radar at about fifteen sea miles. The accuracy of the radar-detection observations has not been especially good hitherto. Only individual boats with long service and highly trained personnel have obtained precision results that justify the intended operational arrangement.[16]

This arrangement could not be tested in practice because of poor visibility in the operational area. Group West ordered instead that the boats should separate into three equal groups in preparation to repel an immediately imminent invasion. The FdS preferred an alternative division of his forces but accepted the decision for fear of provoking a new outbreak of wrath and also because the period of bright moonlight prevented offensive forays for the time being.

Accordingly, in mid-March 1943, 6.SFltl. sailed to Cherbourg to join 5.SFltl., while 4.SFltl. occupied the base at Boulogne and 2.SFltl. Ostend. After several false alarms, Kommodore Petersen requested the return of the flotillas, approved by Group West on 25 March 1943, the day when the new C-in-C

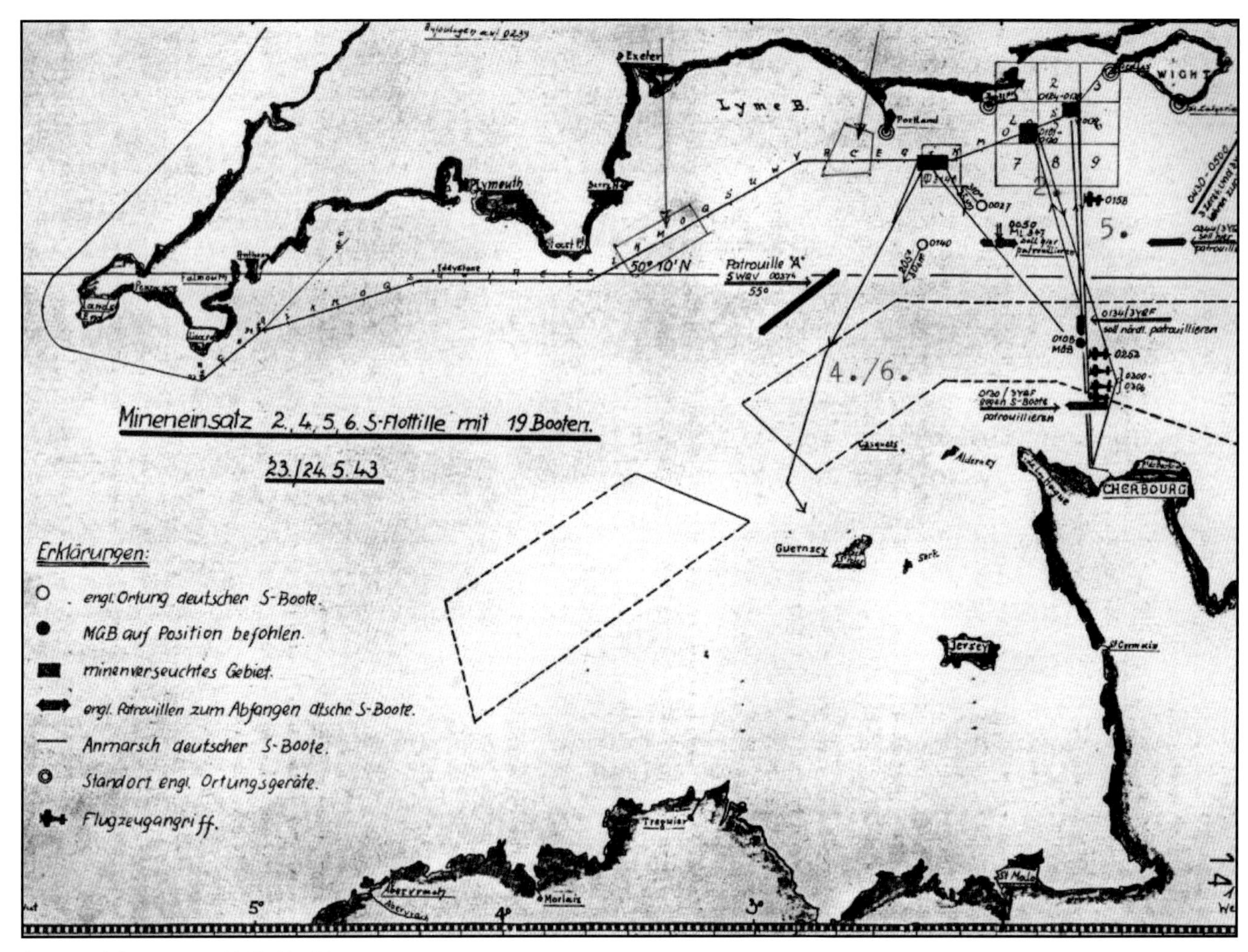

Sketch of Operations, FdS War Diary
'Minelaying operation, 2.,4., 5. and 6.SFltl. with 19 boats, 23 May 1943'
Key (to seven symbols, top to bottom):
1 German S-boats detected by radar
2 MGBs at positions ordered
3 German minefields
4 British patrols searching for S-boats
5 Route taken by S-boats
6 Location British radar
7 Attack by aircraft

Kriegsmarine, Dönitz, was inspecting 2.SFltl. at Ostend. The flotillas began their return to allotted bases on 27 March and 2. and 4.SFltl. launched a joint operation on the 28th. Before reaching the attack point, part of 2.SFltl. ran into two MGBs and in the ensuing mêlée at a range of 400 metres, the commander of S 29, Oberleutnant zur See Lemm, and bridge crewmen were killed. The boat limped away and found the rest of the flotilla at dawn. B-Dienst intercepted orders from the British naval area commander to his units at sea – also searching for the damaged German boat – to retire west at 0630, when air patrols would take over. Since no German fighter cover was available because of fog, the commander 2.SFltl. was ordered to scuttle S 29 and return to base. Shortly afterwards, B-Dienst heard the order to British units to continue searching, because British aircraft were now also grounded by fog. The FdS immediately rescinded the order to sink S 29, but this had already been carried out. The lack of bridge armour was responsible for the casualties – four dead and seven wounded.

On 14 April 1943, the three flotillas laid mines off the English east coast. The 4th S-boat Flotilla sank a patrol boat. The nights were now so short that it was no longer possible to make the entire round trip to and from the convoy lanes off Great Yarmouth in darkness. Therefore, as in 1942, the FdS switched his flotillas to the Channel for the summer: 2. and 5.SFltl. to Cherbourg, 4. and 6.SFltl. to St Peter Port, Guernsey, an emergency harbour without bunkers or arsenals for mines and torpedoes. The FdS changed his headquarters back to Wimereux, near Boulogne.

Because of enemy radar superiority over the whole region, which was not tied necessarily to fixed routes, Petersen did not rate his chances of success very highly and proposed using the summer months for a comprehensive programme of armour-fitting and refits. This would reduce the S-boat force in the Channel by half until August.

The 5th S-boat Flotilla had been operating alone until this point, laying mines in Lyme Bay and attacking convoys. In the majority of forays, the flotilla had been driven off by the defences before seeing the convoys, but on 26 February 1943, four ships of 6,000 gross tons had been sunk, together with a landing craft, from which eleven survivors were made prisoner. On 13 April, the success was repeated by the sinking of a steamer and the destroyer *Eskdale*. The flotilla was now to work jointly with the others against the south coast, although initially, on the orders of Group West, it operated against shipping off the Normandy coast that had either been tracked by radar or located by DF. After a number of wasted voyages, the FdS requested a halt to it on the grounds that the radar contacts were too vague for a directed attack and the DF had not been triangulated by a second DF unit. After long deliberation, the FdS staff carried the day since they had superior technical understanding of electronic detection devices and their tactical application. Not without ulterior motive, Petersen was rewriting the manual of technical warfare at sea.

At the end of May, the four flotillas began minelaying operations in the Channel. On the nights of 23, 28 and 30 May 1943, the south coast convoy routes were mined. The flotillas avoided enemy destroyers, MGBs and night fighters by the use of high speed, continually changing target areas, detours on the approach and return routes and circumnavigating enemy groups advised by the B-Dienst. The British divided their various areas between sea and air-sea forces and positioned MGBs and destroyers along the accustomed return routes, if possible close to the German bases.

The minelaying operation of 23 May 1943 is an example of a series of such operations. All flotillas avoided contact with the enemy, except 5.SFltl., which was attacked by night fighters because it used the homeward route for the outward voyage. All minelaying operations in the period were recognised by the British as such. On 29 May 1943, for example, B-Dienst intercepted a report at 0126 hrs: 'Germans are now laying suspected minefield at 220 degrees twelve nautical miles off Portland Bill.'[17] Had the Luftwaffe been available, they would now have pounced on the British minesweepers working to clear the field. Petersen requested such measures regularly, but in vain, for there was nothing available.

The last minelaying operations were conducted at the beginning of June. A total of 321 mines and eighty-four protective buoys were laid in the operations. The flotillas were now regrouped so that 4.SFltl. remained at St Peter Port and 5.SFltl. at Cherbourg, while 2. and 6.SFltl. went to Ostend. The FdS wished to keep open the opportunity of operating into the Thames estuary itself in order to force the dispersal of the British defences congregated in the Channel following the latest operations.

While 4. and 5.SFltl. carried out two mining

A boat with a new armoured bridge crosses astern of another, with increased armament.

court-martialled.

Operations were intensified as the nights grew longer. In a quick raid on a patrol group off Orfordness on the night of 3 August 1943, the seven boats from 2. and 6.SFltl. sank an escort. 4. and 5.SFltl. in the western Channel lost one boat and had six unserviceable for lengthy periods after an attack by aircraft in Baie de l'Aber Wrac'h, which they were using to get west of the convoys. Both flotillas remained in harbour for the coming weeks.

For 2. and 4.SFltl. the remainder of August was taken up with measures for anticipated landings. Frequent states of immediate readiness ordered by Group West alternated with escort duty for minelaying by R-boats and minesweepers together with S-boat mining activities to extend the existing barriers off the French coast. Despite frequent skirmishes with British light forces and night fighters, including the rocket-equipped Typhoons for the first time, the boats suffered no losses, but had no successes to report.

In September, the flotillas were almost back to full strength, each boat now having the new armoured bridge cupola and more 4cm guns. Boats of 5.SFltl. were now equipped with the new, more powerful diesels, MB511 (2,500hp), which provided a cruising speed of thirty-five knots.[18]

It was thought that the boats might be used to create a diversion for R-boats and torpedo boats engaged in minelaying. As to the benefits of these tactics, opinion was divided. The FdS considered that they would alarm the enemy unnecessarily, resulting in British defences building up swiftly in a short time. The superior tactical experience of the S-boat Arm considered that 'alerting the enemy as late as possible' was better: 'Dispensing with the S-boat operation in parallel, one could expect in a moderate seaway that T-boats, if they showed only the bow-on silhouette to Dungeness or Hastings, would perhaps not be

operations in the western Channel with the objective of forcing the British to move the convoy lanes further offshore and thus provide the S-boats with a better chance of torpedoing the traffic, 2. and 6.SFltl. did not venture out on account of bad weather. The FdS therefore decided to step up the programme of refits and repair. From 15 July, only five to six boats of either group were operational, until mid-August when others rejoined the flotillas from German shipyards. These latter voyages often resulted in skirmishes with radar-directed British MGBs and aircraft. On 25 July 1943 off Ostend, S 68 and S 77 were set upon by MGBs. Immediately, S 77 lost both machine guns and an engine, and the starboard torpedo exploded, causing a serious fire and flooding. After the boat was scuttled, the British picked up four crew, twelve men being rescued the next morning from a rubber dinghy, while the commander, Oberleutnant zur See Ludwig, and six men were lost. The leader boat, S 68, had disengaged and run for Ostend. She failed to transmit an enemy contact report and thus 2. and 6.SFltl. at Ostend at readiness were not ordered to sea. The commander of S 68 was relieved of command and identified until showing their broadside profile on changing course. The enemy would then have to give chase, which in our experience only rarely leads to contact between the two sides.'[19] After several interventions of this kind, these operations were ruled out for S-boats. Instead, they were ordered to keep watch on the possible approach routes for an enemy landing force. The FdS was not keen on this idea, for the boats would be detected early on by enemy radar and have no chance of torpedo successes. Moreover, the escorts would engage and chase off the S-boats before they had the opportunity to glimpse and confirm the invasion fleet.

The lengthening nights now allowed operations to be planned from the Dutch bases, and in mid-September 2. and 6.SFltl. moved up to Ijmuiden, 4.SFltl.(Korvettenkapitän Lützow) to Rotterdam, reinforced on 12 September by the newly added 8.SFltl. (Korvettenkapitän Zymalkowski). The 5th S-boat Flotilla remained at Cherbourg.

On 24 September 1943, the Dutch-based boats sailed on a mining offensive with Luftwaffe support. New detonators, which rendered the mines harmless at intervals, were intended to hinder minesweeping.

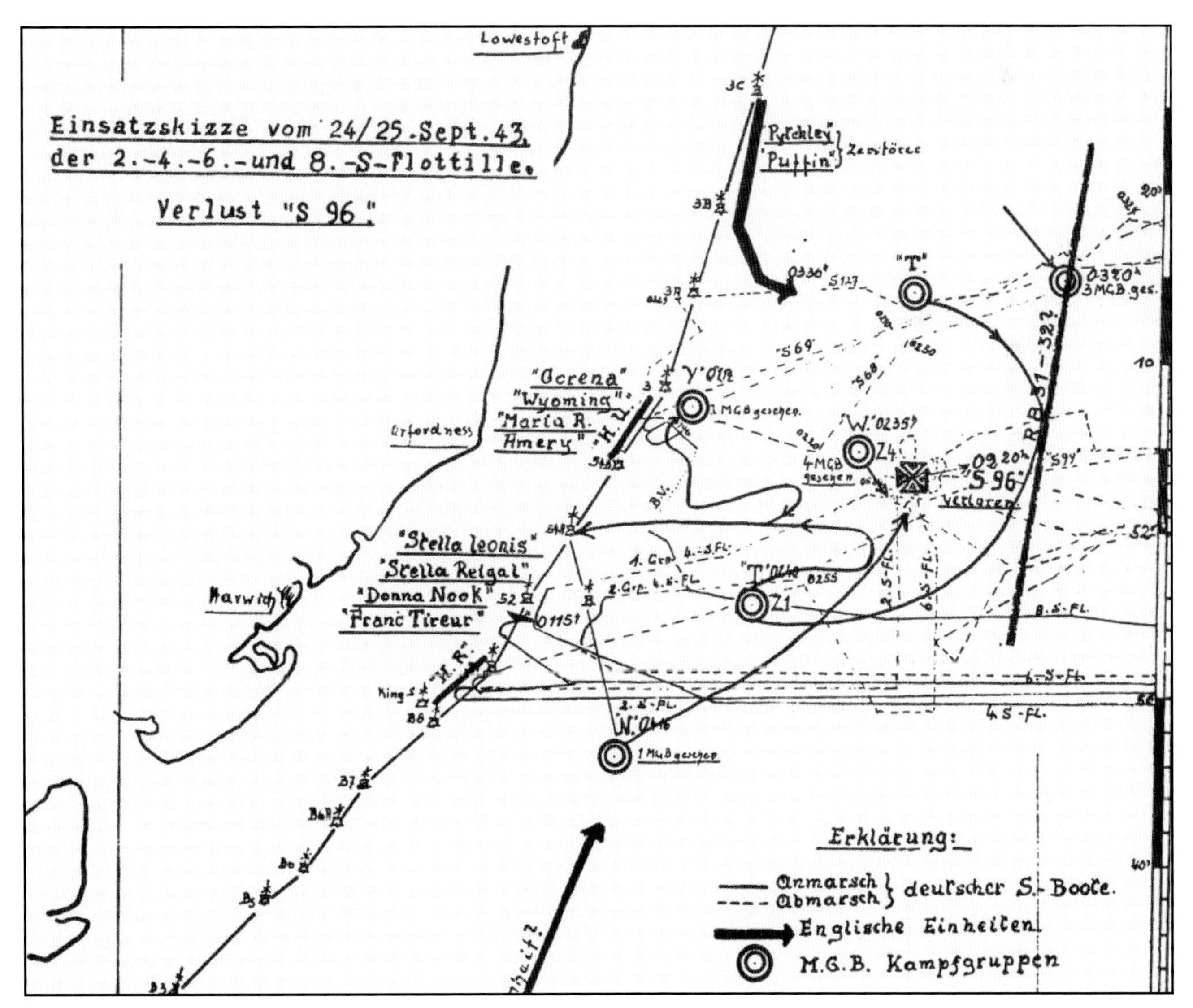

Operational sketch, FdS: the loss of S 96.

The British had introduced a new radio cipher that the B-Dienst had difficulty in decoding and the immediate reaction by the enemy to the mines could not be gauged. The minelaying itself, in the convoy lane off Orfordness, ran according to plan. After sinking a patrol boat, 4.SFltl. was surprised on the way home, S 96 being rammed and sunk by an MGB, which also sank. Two other S-boats were shelled and damaged the same night, while three more reported damage from unexplained explosions in the crank casings. The FdS's operational sketch demonstrates the confused situation in the battle area.

The minelaying missions were resumed on 7 October 1943. For the first time, the FdS placed one flotilla as a fighting group in a position poised to intercept pursuing destroyers and MGBs. The tactic could not be tried out on this occasion because bad weather forced the MGBs to hold back, while British destroyers kept to their patrol stations. 2., 4. and 6.SFltl. laid their mines according to plan.

The Luftwaffe, which during this period had carried out three minelaying sorties, terminated the common offensive on 10 October 1943 because 'by order of the Führer the focus of the air war in the near future is to be concentrated on bombing cities'.[20] Because of this, and information from the B-Dienst that enemy minesweepers had got the hang of the new detonators, Petersen abandoned the mining offensive ordered by SKL in favour of the normal variation between mine and torpedo, beginning sorties of this kind from mid-month. The extent of his autonomy – but also the minor degree of operational control exercised over him by superior command centres – is clear from the fact that Group West was not aware of his decision for two months, when finally they worked through his War Diary. SKL expressed their displeasure but did not reverse his decision. Therefore Petersen retained his freedom to make decisions in the operational sphere in the future.

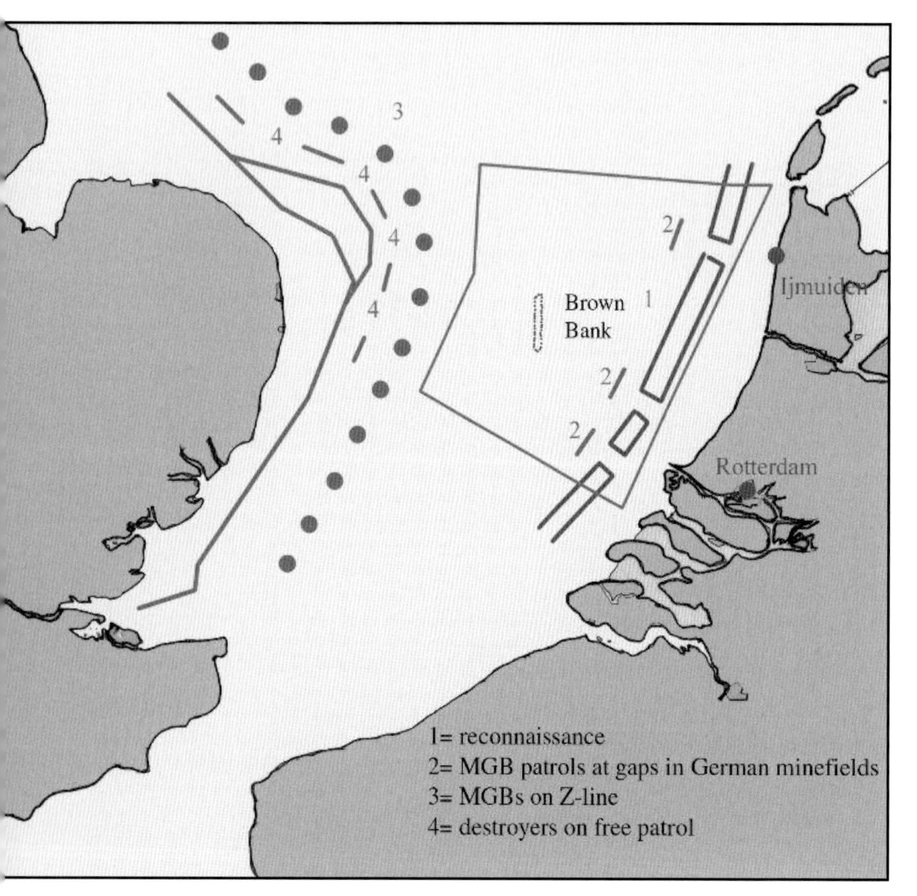

Increased naval defences in autumn 1943.

Increased Defences

The planned increase in US and British MGBs and MTBs and the release of escort destroyers from the Atlantic helped continually to upgrade the British convoy defences over the course of time. In autumn 1943 in the Nore, the main area of S-boat activity on the English east coast, there were 24 destroyers, 7 corvettes, 60 MGBS and 41 MLs on hand for convoy protection duty.[21]

The British defences would come to full strength as soon as a convoy assembled if, having regard to the weather, an S-boat attack had to be reckoned with. The most critical stretch of the route was between

Haisborough Sand and Smith's Knoll, where the north- and southbound convoys passed during the night. The entire S-boat approach area would be watched on such nights by aircraft of Coastal Command. Together with MGBs lurking near the gaps in the German defensive minefields on hydrophone watch, once S-boats were spotted they would alert the British area commander, who would respond by sending out his reserve groups. About ten nautical miles seaward of the convoy lanes, MGBs' waiting positions had been established, identified with code-names consisting of 'Z' plus a number. As a rule there were twelve such Z-positions, each occupied by two or three hydrophones-equipped MGBs. Between the line of Z-positions and the convoy lanes, destroyers patrolled freely. Their zones were identified by two-digit numbers for rapid transmission of orders. The destroyers and MGB groups co-operated to drive any S-boats discovered towards the MGBs. Shortly before the Z-line, they would stop and fire starshell so that the MGBs could see the S-boats clearly.

Close by the convoy itself would be the flag destroyer, two flank destroyers, two or three MLs in close escort either side and one or two MLs ahead and astern of the convoy, with several minesweepers well ahead of them all. After an attack, fighter-bombers would be alerted to search for the returning S-boats at first light, while MGBs supported by the reserve groups would be waiting for them at gaps in the minefields. In order to avoid problems of identification, the British area commander divided the whole area between aircraft and MGBs. His orders were regularly picked up by the B-Dienst and provided the flotillas with further reason to scuttle damaged boats in order to get back to base before dawn.

The first torpedo foray by 2., 4., 6. and 8.SFltl. against this enlarged defence occurred on 24 October 1943, when thirty-one boats under the personal command of Petersen aboard a 2.SFltl. boat operated a *Stichansatz* against a northbound convoy. There had been no previous air reconnaissance, and the boats were relying solely on B-Dienst reports. They detoured well north to skirt the defence and slipped past the occupied Z-positions at slow revolutions, but then four groups of S-boats encountered the destroyers on free patrol, were chased back to the Z-line MGBs and exchanged fire. Only the two groups of 2.SFltl. reached the convoy lane, where they found nothing; the convoy had been switched to the inner lane and already stood well to the north. A new *Stichansatz* by the most northerly flotilla, 8.SFltl., was ordered but not acted upon because the code tables on the leader boat had not been updated. The only success of the night was a straggler sunk by 6.SFltl. During the battle with destroyers and MGBs, two boats of 4.SFltl. (S 63 and S 88) were sunk. Korvettenkapitän Lützow, 4.SFltl. commander, Stabsobersteuermann Räbiger, commander of S 88, and eight crew were killed; sixteen survivors were pulled from the water by the British and twenty-four by German boats.

> The cause of the loss of the two boats was a misunderstanding between the senior engine-room hand and the commander of S 63 about readiness. After repair to shell damage to the port motor, the leading engine-room hand reported limited readiness for half ahead, meaning the port engine. The commander interpreted the report as referring to all three engines. On the basis of the commander's report, the flotilla commander detached S 88 and S 63 at twenty sea miles: subsequently an MGB group intercepted the two boats and destroyed them. This serves best as a lesson in blood about how important is a precise method of expressing oneself. (War Diary FdS, 25 October 1943)

On 4 November 1943, B-Dienst copied down a recall order on account of the sea state for British small craft off Great Yarmouth. In the opinion of the FdS, the weather did not preclude a minelaying operation. After four flotillas had laid their mines, 1st Group of 2.SFltl. ran into a patrol of destroyers, whose radars failed to spot the German boats until late because of the sea conditions, and the S-boats saw the northbound convoy. Two steamers were then sunk with FAT (surface–target-seeking) torpedoes used by S-boats for the first time. The 2nd Group of 2.SFltl. was engaged by the destroyers. 'Starshell by two destroyers with the full orchestra to follow. Ran off with all guns firing. One destroyer chased the Group for thirty-five minutes until twelve nautical miles from the convoy route,'[22] group leader Kapitänleutnant Klose noted in his War Diary. Because of the MGB recall, the British had sent out eight destroyers, three with the convoy, three on patrol and two to search the area. As the result of engine breakdown aboard one S-boat, 2nd Group of 6.SFltl. was still at sea at dawn and was promptly sighted and attacked by a flight of six Beaufighters. S 74 was hit and abandoned. The crew was rescued, less three dead. Two other boats received light damage. Although requested, German fighter cover was not available because of an expected heavy raid on the Reich and 'defence had priority according to the Führer-Order'.[23]

On 18 November 1943, the first four boats of the newly formed 9.SFltl. (Kapitänleutnant von Mirbach) arrived at Rotterdam, but all further operations until the year's end were prevented by severe storms.

Further west, 5.SFltl. had not been idle. On numerous occasions, the flotilla had escorted R-boats and torpedo boats on minelaying sorties, had mined convoy lanes itself and been driven off while attempting to attack convoys. On 2 November 1943, the flotilla was successful off Dungeness, sinking three steamers from a westbound convoy. Never-theless, the balance at year-end 1943 for the S-boat Arm was not satisfactory. During the year, only twenty-six ships of 44,585 gross tons had been sunk, compared to ninety-one ships of 214,885 tons gross in 1942.[24] As in the Atlantic, the enemy had blunted the formerly sharp sword of attacking German naval forces by means of a well thought out, technically and numerically superior combined defence. After a period of balance, the Allies had gone on to the offensive, and not in vain had Petersen spoken in November of a crisis amongst the S-boats.[25]

Nevertheless Onwards

On 20 January 1944, after a long spell of bad weather, the Holland-based flotillas made their first sortie, a combined mine/torpedo operation. While 4. and 9.SFltl. operating from Rotterdam laid their mines according to plan, the three Ijmuiden flotillas abandoned the mission on the grounds of fog. Not until mid-February could the next sortie be sailed. Despite the heavy defences, Petersen considered that

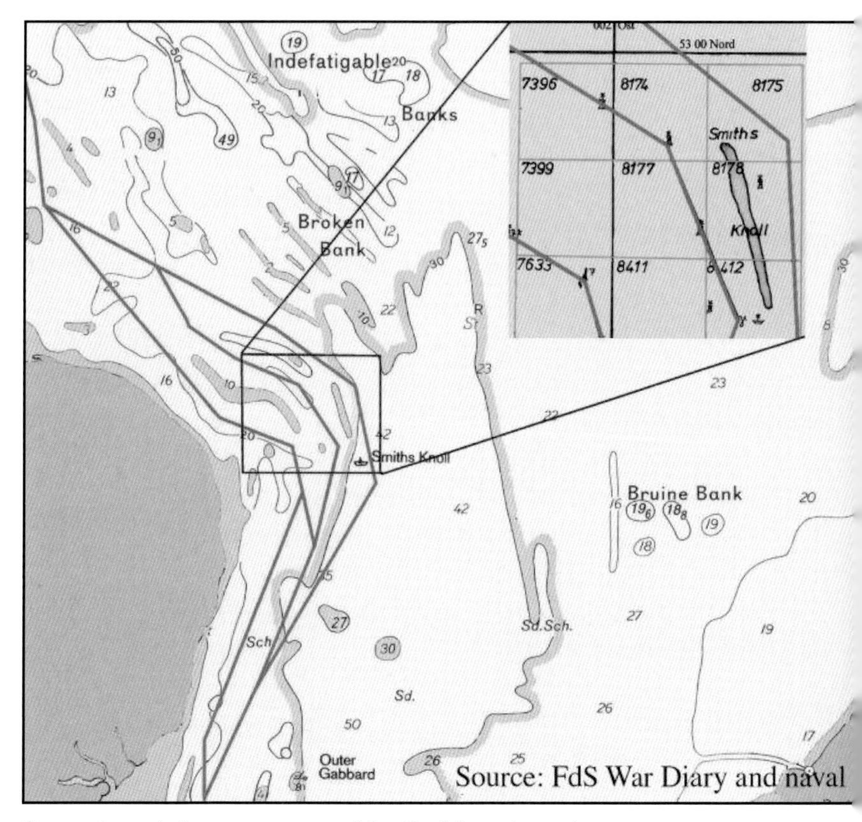

Convoy lanes in the narrow seas of the English east coast

the English east coast offered better prospects of success than the south coast. The enemy traffic was more prolific there and the convoys forced to keep to narrow set lanes dictated by the sea bottom and coastline. This made discovery by air reconnaissance more likely and evasive manoeuvres more difficult. Nevertheless, Petersen sent 9.SFltl. from the east coast to Cherbourg to improve 5.SFltl.'s chances of success.

Considering possible an Allied landing in the Pyrenees area, SKL had planned to transfer 5. and 9.SFltl. further south and prepared the ports of Bordeaux, Arcachon, Bayonne and St Jean de Luz to receive them. Nothing came of it all, and next SKL ordered instead that a flotilla be transferred to the Baltic. The FdS chose 6.SFltl., which departed Ijmuiden at the beginning of February. In the northern zones, 2. and 8.SFltl. remained at Ijmuiden and 4.SFltl. at Rotterdam, where the boats were to be re-engined, so that only twelve operational boats were actually available.

On 12 February 1944, the boats mined the British convoy lanes, this time well to the north, and 8.SFltl. sank a patrol boat. The British countermeasures were set in train after taking a bearing on the German ultra-short-wave traffic reporting the sinking of the patrol vessel, but their location was estimated too far south because the Cromer station had not managed to obtain a cross-bearing and estimated the boats much closer inshore than they were on the basis of signal strength. On the return voyage, the British patrols maintained a lively radio chatter and were easily avoided. On 14 February 1944, the minelaying operation was repeated by 2.SFltl., while 8.SFltl. sought battle with British MGBs in the hope of capturing one. The reason behind this plan was the need to clarify where the convoy lanes ran exactly, since such information could not be obtained by air reconnaissance. In the event, the opposing forces did not meet, although MGB groups that had taken station off Ijmuiden to ambush the returning S-boats were discovered and engaged by German VP-boats. Starshell was fired and beneath its light the returning 2.SFltl. spotted the second group of MGBs and launched a surprise attack. After smoke poured over the sea from damage to two German S-boats, the battle had to be discontinued. S 89 was towed in with shell damage. All the British MGBs were able to escape, despite numerous hits. The 8th S-boat Flotilla found the third MGB group and inflicted a lot of damage before the British retired. Requests by the FdS for Luftwaffe fighters to pursue the damaged British boats at first light went unheeded.

> Called command centre 3.Fighter.Div. Informed that day fighters not ready until 0700 hrs and then have to be requested. 0700 hrs rang 3.Fighter Div. again. Informed by orderly officer that flight by fighters will probably not be possible, as not available. Final decision not possible until 0800 hrs after call to One A, Major Grassmann. At 0715 report by FdS that at least seven enemy MTBs damaged and assembling in grid square AN 8438 for run in to Lowestoft. After another call to 3.Fighter Div. at 0730, final decision given that fighters cannot be deployed because aircraft are in rearward area and the weather is unfavourable. At 0800 hrs 3/F/122 I requested Schiphol to help against enemy MTBs. Orderly officer reports that operation possible, but approval to fly must first be obtained from aerodrome area commander, Major Drescher. At 0815 hrs reached him in Amsterdam, he said that operation had to be approved first by IX Fliegerkorps. Orderly officer of IX Fliegerkorps stated that permission to fly cannot be given as no suitable aircraft for this kind of mission are available and anyway the weather is unfavourable.
> (War Diary, FdS, 15 February 1944)

Poor visibility and storms put paid to further operations and not until 25 March did the boats sail on the next sortie. As in the four succeeding operations, they were either driven off prematurely by destroyers or failed to sight the convoy. The Allies, however, were stepping up their offensive against the S-boats. US Army Air Force Marauders – 385 aircraft in several waves – attacked the Ijmuiden base on 26

March 1944. While the bunkers for boats and mines were hit repeatedly but not breached, serious damage was caused to the new bunker under construction and to supply halls. Two 8.SFltl. boats moored outside the pens were sunk and a lighter foundered directly across the bunker entrance, so that access was possible only at high water.

In order to take measures to counteract the clearly impending invasion, SKL ordered Group West to mine the area around the Isle of Wight and so impede the sailings of enemy units from Portsmouth and Southampton. For this purpose, 4.SFltl. transferred to Le Havre, but even before their arrival the offensive had been called off because the Luftwaffe would not participate. After several objections had been lodged by the FdS, Group West agreed to leave the direction of operations in his hands and to allow more mine and torpedo operations independent of current developments, provided that active reconnaissance was maintained in the possible areas of enemy sailings towards Normandy.

Following the loss of a boat during a reconnaissance mission, Group West and Petersen were in agreement that, in future, a distinction should be made between a general reconnaissance, in which the flotilla commander had freedom with regard to carrying out operations and withdrawing from the area as necessary, and reconnaissance in force with the intention of observing a selected area over its entire length. Subsequently, the boats involved in the latter would only withdraw to spare men and boats if there were clear indications of an imminent invasion. With that as the background, at the end of May 1944 the flotillas were placed thus: Cherbourg – 5. and 9.SFltl.; Boulogne – 4.SFltl.; Ostend – 2.SFltl. The 8th S-boat Flotilla had been sent to Germany to be re-engined.

During this period, the Cherbourg flotillas reported successes. On 5 January 1944, 5.SFltl. sank three ships and a naval trawler, on 30 January two ships and a naval trawler. On 27 April 1944, the boats encountered a group of armoured landing ships practising for the invasion. By an oversight, the only protection was a frigate, and three landing ships were sunk. Soon it was June 1944 and everybody was braced for the long-expected invasion that had so far not materialised.

7
Norway
April 1941 – June 1944

After the occupation of Norway in 1940, it became the responsibility of the Kriegsmarine to defend the coast and protect the inshore traffic. For this purpose, three regional headquarters were set up: Admiral West Coast at Bergen, Admiral North Coast at Trondheim[1] and Admiral Polar Coast at Tromsø. Directly accountable to them at the most important ports were naval commandants who operated harbour protection flotillas and a coastal protection force consisting of minesweepers, patrol boats and anti-submarine vessels. Commanding Admiral Norway, with HQ at Oslo, had overall control. The fleet units that used Norway as a strategic departure base for oceanic warfare were directed by the C-in-C, Group North at Sengwarden, near Wilhelmshaven.

In mid-April 1941, the preparations for the German attack on the Soviet Union, Barbarossa, were begun in northern Norway. The Army placed at readiness on the Norwegian–Finnish border two divisions of mountain troops (Gebirgskorps Norwegen) to occupy the Finnish district of Petsamo and so secure the strategically important nickel mines there. Their other task was to capture Murmansk, the only ice-free port of the Soviet Union in the region. The Murman railway, which terminated at the port, was to be attacked at the same time, with the aim of either controlling the line or at least cutting it. Luftwaffe bombers with fighter cover were to support the Army, while the Kriegsmarine provided the necessary supplies from the sea. Actually covering or supporting the Army attack from the sea was not contemplated, for under the Barbarossa guidelines, the main task of the Navy remained the naval commerce war against Britain.[2]

On 22 June 1941, the Petsamo area was occupied according to plan. On 29 June, the German mountain corps began the attack on Murmansk with Finnish support. In the pebbly, treeless, uninhabited tundra, progress was difficult against a constantly growing enemy defence, for the Soviets appreciated the strategic importance of Murmansk and its railway for the desperately needed supplies from the West.

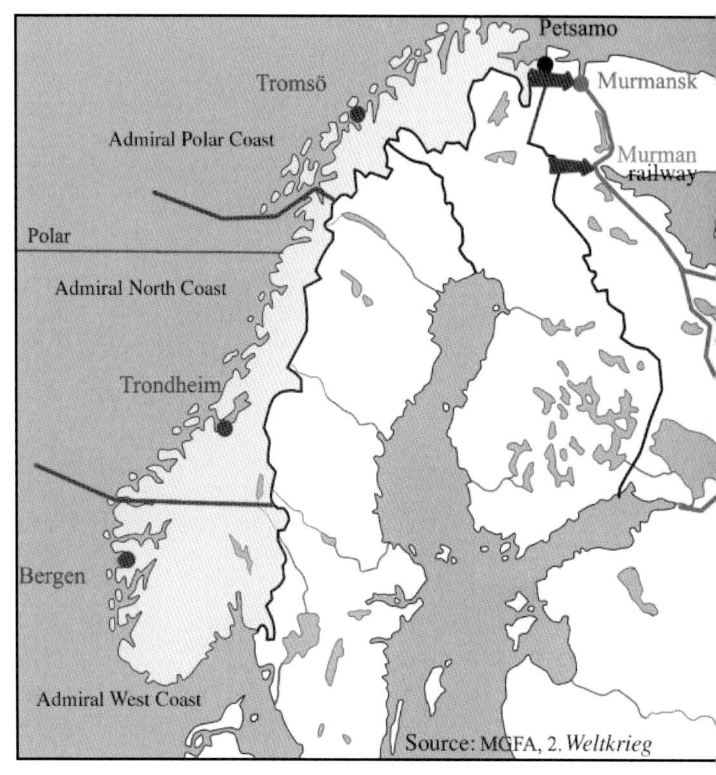

Norway and the operational planning against the Soviet Union.

Since the scanty German force had to concentrate on the operational objective of Murmansk, the Fisher Peninsula west of it was left untouched in the belief that later it would simply fall into German hands. Contrary to expectations, units of the Soviet Northern Fleet arrived to support their ground troops, presenting the Germans with a major difficulty. This was an interesting parallel to what happened later in the Black Sea, where the Soviet Navy did not pursue an independent war but always used its naval vessels as a branch of the overall armed forces and deployed them accordingly.

Here in the north, they landed troops on the flank of the advancing German corps, forcing the mountain divisions to break off their attack at the River Lisa. On 10 July 1941, destroyers of the German 6th Destroyer Flotilla arrived at Kirkenes but, instead of offering support to the troops ashore, they received purely naval work, looking for Soviet merchant traffic on the Kola coast.

They achieved minor successes, but were available neither to help the Army in its renewed offensive at the River Lisa nor to ward off landings of Soviet reinforcements in Lisa Bay at the German rear. Even the recently arrived U-boats refrained from patrolling the Soviet inshore sea lane and operated well out to sea off the Kola coast and the entrance to the White Sea.

Given a free hand by German naval forces, the Soviets reinforced the Fisher Peninsula with troops and heavy artillery and provided their front on the Lisa with such robust resistance that further attempts by the mountain divisions at the beginning of August, and again a month later, to break through to Murmansk were unsuccessful. To support their land front, Soviet submarines attacked German shipping along the Norwegian coast, cutting the sea route for a time and delaying the arrival of German reserves.

Lacking reinforcements, the German front stalled fifty kilometres from Murmansk and deteriorated into trench warfare, which remained unchanged until 1944. The attack on the railway line to the south also came to a halt short of the objective. Thus, the strategic supplies for the Soviet Union provided by Allied merchant convoys rolled unhindered southwards along the Murman railway.[3]

S-Boats Requested

Faced with these developments, at the end of September 1941 Hitler issued his instructions confirming that 'the ultimate objective of the operations in north and central Finland is to destroy the enemy forces around Murmansk and hold the Murman railway',[4] but the primary task was to protect the vital Petsamo nickel mines against possible Allied attack. As regards the Kriegsmarine, the instruction required 'the setting-up of an auxiliary base for light naval forces'5 and the strengthening of the coastal defences. Shortly afterwards, Hitler expanded the naval task to include 'attacking the enemy supply lines by sea to Murmansk and maintaining German maritime traffic in the Arctic according to available forces. To this end, light naval forces are to be reinforced as soon as possible and also S-boats transferred there. Kirkenes is to be developed and established as an auxiliary naval base.'[6]

Accordingly, on 19 October 1941 SKL ordered the formation of the 8th S-boat Flotilla (Kapitänleutnant Christiansen) with preliminary instructions to fit out four new boats (S 42, S 44, S 45 and S 46) and the depot ship *Adolf Lüderitz*. These units were to leave Kiel on 15 November 1941 so as to reach the polar north in the endless days of winter darkness. At the same time the freighter *Larsen* sailed to Trondheim for conversion to a workshop ship, while the steamer *Hernösand* would be converted to a torpedo arsenal and adjustment station. The depot ship *Tanga* was sent to Kirkenes as a command ship with a cargo of torpedoes, depth charges and other materials. Because of strong easterly winds, the S-boats did not sail on their 1,500-mile voyage northwards until 18 November 1941. They reached Bergen on 26 November 1941 and were then towed by patrol boats to spare the engines. From Bodø, the tow was continued by steam minesweepers to Tromsø, the flotilla arriving there on 14 December 1941. Heavy weather prevented departure, but the Christmas break was disturbed on Boxing Day when a British naval force entered West Fjord and caused damage to shore installations and merchant shipping.

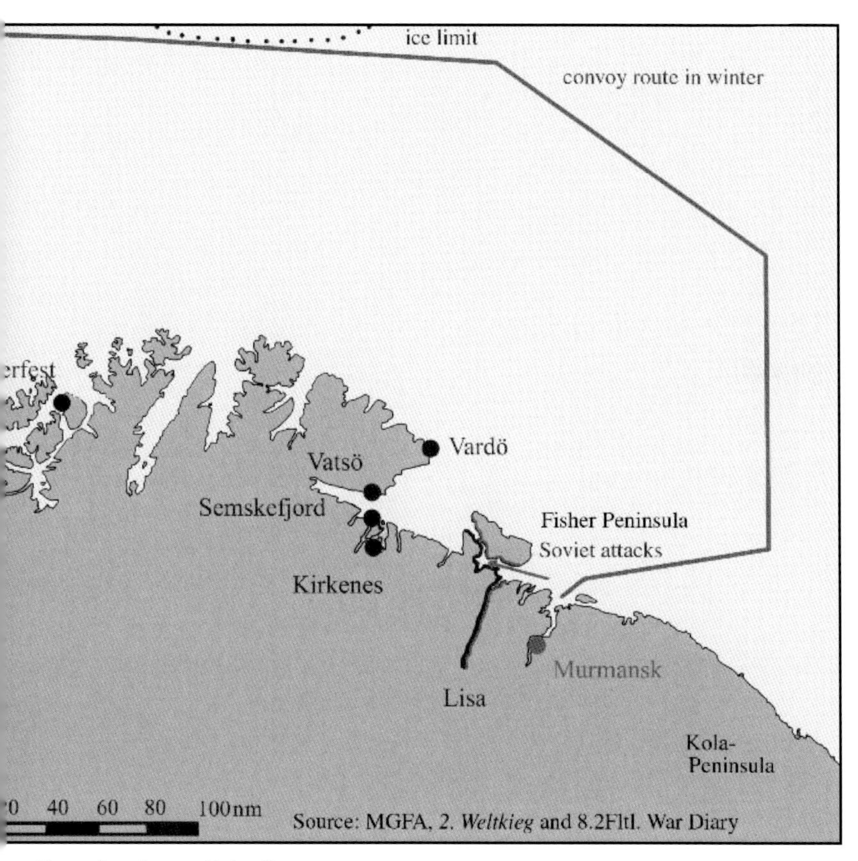

Operational area, Polar Sea.

A voyage of over 100 nautical miles through the coastal skerries was too far to go to reach the British ships, and when a second naval force penetrated the more northerly Vaags Fjord a day later, 27 December 1941, the S-boat flotilla was still at Tromsø. A search of the fjords as far as Narvik brought no results, because the enemy ships had set off for home immediately after their surprise raid.

Hitler was alarmed by the two British raids and on 29 December gave Raeder orders to transfer the heavy ships to Norway and bring the battleships *Scharnhorst* and *Gneisenau* and the heavy cruiser *Prinz Eugen* home from Brest – if possible through the English Channel.[7]

Meanwhile, on 15 October 1941, as an operational measure, 8.SFltl. had been placed under the control of Admiral Norway, who had been given responsibility for the operational direction of units on the coast and had chosen the S-boat depot ship *Tanga* at Kirkenes for his flagship.[8]

The long S-boat voyage resumed via Hammerfest to Vardø, where the flotilla arrived on 6 January 1942, seven weeks after leaving Kiel. It was quickly clear that the base would be unsuitable because of the almost perpetual high sea running directly into the harbour, and after searching for Russian naval forces to attack near the Fisher Peninsula, and finding none, the flotilla transferred to Vatsö.

From Vatsö, a second sortie looking for Soviet coastal and supply traffic drew a blank and a third patrol of Fisher had to be abandoned for a gathering storm. After these three operations, flotilla commander Kapitänleutnant Christiansen noted that the required conditions for operations, ie a sea state not exceeding force 3, had occurred only once despite a ridge of high pressure. As to the problems of an Arctic winter,

> At temperatures of minus 6 to 8 degrees (Centigrade), rear flak 38, depth charges, mine rails all unserviceable, totally iced over; in sea state 2–3 forward flak 38, torpedo aiming instruments cannot be protected despite measures taken against icing. Tube doors, guard arm giving only slight problem down to minus 13 degrees, solved with shipboard tools. Bridge personnel after six hours exposure to minus 8 degrees only limited effectiveness. Hull: outer skin, decking covered with tarpaulin, strong effects of frost and ice, eg upper deck.[9]

This bald description hardly portrays the strain imposed on S-boat crews by the polar winter: perpetual darkness, bitter cold, crammed together on a small boat, a deficiency of fresh food, illness, and never a success to report. Admiral Polar Sea, Admiral Schmundt, saw S-boats as being unsuitable for the sea area, but since there was nothing else to hand with

S-boats at sea in Arctic waters in sub-zero temperatures.

which to oppose enemy landing attempts, he had no choice: 'As long as the boats remain of value in the present tense situation around Kirkenes – if only in a defensive respect – I cannot agree to a withdrawal.'[10]

Admiral Norway (Generaladmiral Boehm) and Group Command North (Generaladmiral Carls) agreed and 8.SFltl. remained in the Arctic. In any case, no other decision was possible politically, for on 22 January 1942 when speaking to Raeder, Hitler described Norway as a 'zone of destiny' with a strategic significance for the outcome of the war, and he demanded that no effort be spared to strengthen the German presence in the region. He was worried about a possible invasion of Norway by the Allies aimed at depriving Germany of the Finnish nickel mines and extending into Sweden to disrupt supplies from the iron ore mines. As protection, he requested the urgent removal of the heavy units at Brest and the transfer to Norway of more U-boats, destroyers and S-boats. Regarding these last, he agreed to accept 6.SFltl. once the three heavy ships had returned to Germany.[11]

Meanwhile, in temperatures of -18 degrees, the sea at Vatsö had frozen with a five-centimetre-thick layer of ice, and 8.SFltl. had been forced to move to Kirkenes. From 28 January 1942, Semske Fjord near Kirkenes became anchorage and home base for the flotilla, far removed from any habitation. Engineers made the rocky mountainside sheer, so that *Adolf Lüderitz* could moor direct against the fjord wall for protection against air attack. Flak guns were sited either side of the fjord entrance and improvised remote-controlled mines blocked the approaches. Within, the boats were well protected but inactive, and until mid-March storms and ice allowed only one sortie, and even this had to be abandoned after four hours because of a developing storm front.

When spring came, the long polar night would give way to long days without darkness. The flotilla commander no longer saw the sense in having the boats remain and urged that other vessels should take over the role of harbour protection. Admiral Polar Seas agreed, while Group Command North pleaded the contrary on the grounds that, 'If the S-boat Arm in the Arctic is also a weapon of opportunity, there are periods of fog and very poor visibility very favourable for minelaying.'[12] This was wishful thinking, for even in April only two opportunities presented themselves to sortie, both being called off because of the weather conditions. On 15 April 1942, the flotilla commander was of the opinion that, 'It is proven that the Arctic is not suitable for the operational use of S-boats.'[13]

S-boats alongside the depotship *Adolf Lüderitz* in Semske Fjord.

Admiral Polar Seas supported this opinion and added, 'The offensive use of S-boats as torpedo-carriers can be seen as terminated as at 15 April, the first day of the year without darkness, since offensive torpedo operations during the period of endless daylight have no prospect of success. Offensive minelaying is also excluded for the time being for lack of suitable mines.' He concluded, 'The sea area is questionable for operations because even at moderate wind strengths a heavy sea builds up, which prevents high speeds by its steepness and the short periods between each swell . . . For these reasons the only conclusion to be drawn is that S-boats as torpedo-carriers are not suitable for offensive operations on the polar coast.'[14]

Admiral Norway agreed, but Group North held fast to its unshakeable resolve that 'even in summer there will certainly be periods of mist and fog that will allow minelaying off Kola Bay. The mines will be available by then. Until such time as an enemy landing in the Petsamo territory is ruled out, the flotilla must remain in the north for defensive tasks. In the event of landings, acting regardless of risks can result in very good, perhaps decisive, success in the fjords.'[15]

For certain, behind this stance there were worries about political repercussions arising from not abiding by the letter of the directive in the event of an invasion. Accordingly, the boats accepted the role of fjord defenders against enemy landings and even practised this once (28 April 1942) with Z Group Polar Sea destroyers. The mundane activities of the time were minor security jobs such as escorting the depot ship *Tanga* to Narvik and support of U-Jäger in anti-submarine work.

Change of flotillas at Semske Fjord; *Adolf Lüderitz* (far left) alongside *Tsingtau*.

A renewed attempt by the FdS to recall 8.SFltl. now found SKL approval, since Admiral Polar Seas saw no possibility of operations during the summer months, but the political requirement to defend the coast against invasion meant that the flotilla had to be relieved on station. On 23 June 1942, 6.SFltl., consisting of five boats and the depot ship *Tsingtau*, arrived at Semske Fjord; S 69, S 76 and S 13[16] remained as Group Narvik at West Fjord in nominal compliance with the Führer Directive.

The next day, 8.SFltl., which had spent six wasted months in this location, prepared to return south. The depot ship *Adolf Lüderitz* remained because its radio transmitter was needed as a repeat station for U-boat short-wave traffic. *Tsingtau* did not have the equivalent installation. *Adolf Lüderitz* therefore became depot ship to 6.SFltl. while 8.SFltl. set off for Kiel with *Tsingtau*, arriving safely two weeks later on 6 July 1942. There the flotilla was disbanded on 10 July, the boats being distributed to either 2. or 4.SFltl. *Tsingtau* was placed at the direct disposal of the FdS.

More S-Boats Arrive

Meanwhile 6.SFltl. (Kapitänleutnant Obermaier), complying with the Führer Directive, had arrived with eight boats (S 69, S 71, S 73, S 74, S 75, S 76, S 113 and S 114) and the depot ship *Tsingtau*, occupying the Svolvaer base in West Fjord near Narvik. Together with 8.SFltl., they awaited the landings that would never come. The two flotillas could not participate with the heavy units, U-boats and aircraft in the battles against Allied convoys for Murmansk and Archangelsk because the sea routes were beyond their range and the weather and sea conditions made a major operation impossible. Whilst the struggle against the English Channel convoys became ever more grim, and S-boats were needed desperately in the Mediterranean and Black Sea, on orders from above, two operational and well-equipped flotillas languished in the polar north. Although UMB mines did arrive at Kirkenes at the beginning of June 1942, plans to lay them in the sea lanes east of the Fisher Peninsula were all called off because of bad weather.

We had been squeezed together there close against the steep wall of the mountain for months, hidden beneath nets and camouflage tarpaulins, rarely venturing out, never attacking a convoy, and now a season unfriendly to S-boats had arrived, daylight twenty-four hours per day. So highly motivated men and outstanding boats spent their time in senseless inactivity while in the Channel and at other places the S-boat Arm was experiencing successes and losses. Additionally supplies from Germany were gradually drying up, partly as the result of freighters being sunk en route, others, as we learned later, being diverted to Narvik and surrounding fjords to supply primarily

> *Tirpitz* and other ships. Neither did it raise the morale of our flotilla, from the commander down to the most junior ordinary seaman, to have to accept a restricted diet in addition to our inactivity. There was no more fruit or fresh vegetables, and despite the best efforts of the cook, the dried potatoes were dreadful, and the dried vegetables awful. We got round it by buying fresh fish from the trawlermen for schnapps, and we found whalemeat steaks extremely tasty thanks to various alternative methods of preparation. The attempt to lay a minefield off Murmansk failed, as so often, because of the weather conditions, as did the modest probes to the Fisher Peninsula. There was a plus in all this though – no venereal disease amongst the men for lack of opportunity for contagion! (Letter from Dr Heinz Gillner to the author)

The 6th S-boat Flotilla remained in inactivity in the north until August 1942, when SKL put an end to it by sending both groups quietly back to Kiel on the pretext of engine overhauls. On 16 August 1942, after five months in Norway, the flotilla arrived in Germany, had a refit, and then proceeded to the English Channel.

Back North Again

On 19 November 1942, at the Berghof, Hitler ordered Admiral Raeder to send light naval forces to Norway, 'fearing landings in the long nights, based on reports before him. An S-boat flotilla should be sent to Trondheim.'[17] The 8th S-boat Flotilla was reinstated with effect from 1 December with Kapitänleutnant Zymalkowski as commander. The flotilla equipped briskly with a view to sailing on 15 December. The force was *Carl Peters* (depot ship), six boats (S 44, S 64, S 66, S 69, S 108 and S 118) and the torpedo-adjustment ship *Hernösand*, coming from Finland. Delayed by bad weather, the flotilla eventually sailed the week before Christmas 1942, spent the holiday period bottled up at Stavanger and reached Bodø on 19 January 1943. In order to accommodate the wishes of the Führer, at the beginning of December SKL had sent to Trondheim four old S-boats now serving with the so-called fast *U-Jagdgruppe* (submarine-chasers) to hold the fort until 8.SFltl. arrived, after which they returned to Bergen.[18]

The 8th S-boat Flotilla now lay in readiness at Bodø, some boats equipped with radar detection equipment (FuMB). Torpedo firing practice was arranged and exercises held with the Luftwaffe *Jagdstaffel* at Bodø, but no operations were lined up.

After British MTBs with Norwegian crews had penetrated the skerries repeatedly in January and February and disrupted the coastal traffic, Group North had the idea of responding with an attack on the Shetland Islands. This had been suggested before, in the autumn of 1940, when SKL had demurred.[19] It required a move down the coast to southern Norway to avoid a long sea run and SKL refused again, pointing to a lack of targets and the Führer Directive that tied the flotilla to harbour protection duty. Group North then proposed that the flotilla move to Hammerfest, from where it could operate against the northern convoys until the end of April, and then return to the Channel once the polar night ended. SKL declined:

> The Führer has provisionally refused the suggestion of the ObdM [Dönitz] to withdraw 8.SFltl. from Norway. Decisive for this is his view that S-boats present a significant strengthening of the Bodø–Narvik defence forces, which the Führer does not presently believe he can reduce. S-boats at Hammerfest cannot serve this purpose because it is too far distant for them to intervene in a timely manner against landings at Bodø–Narvik or Kirkenes–Petsamo. Prospects for operations against convoys on the basis of previous experience are too poor.[20]

At the end of May 1943, SKL saw a lessened likelihood of landings in Norway and was looking for the opportunity to return the boats to where they could be useful and were urgently needed. This time,

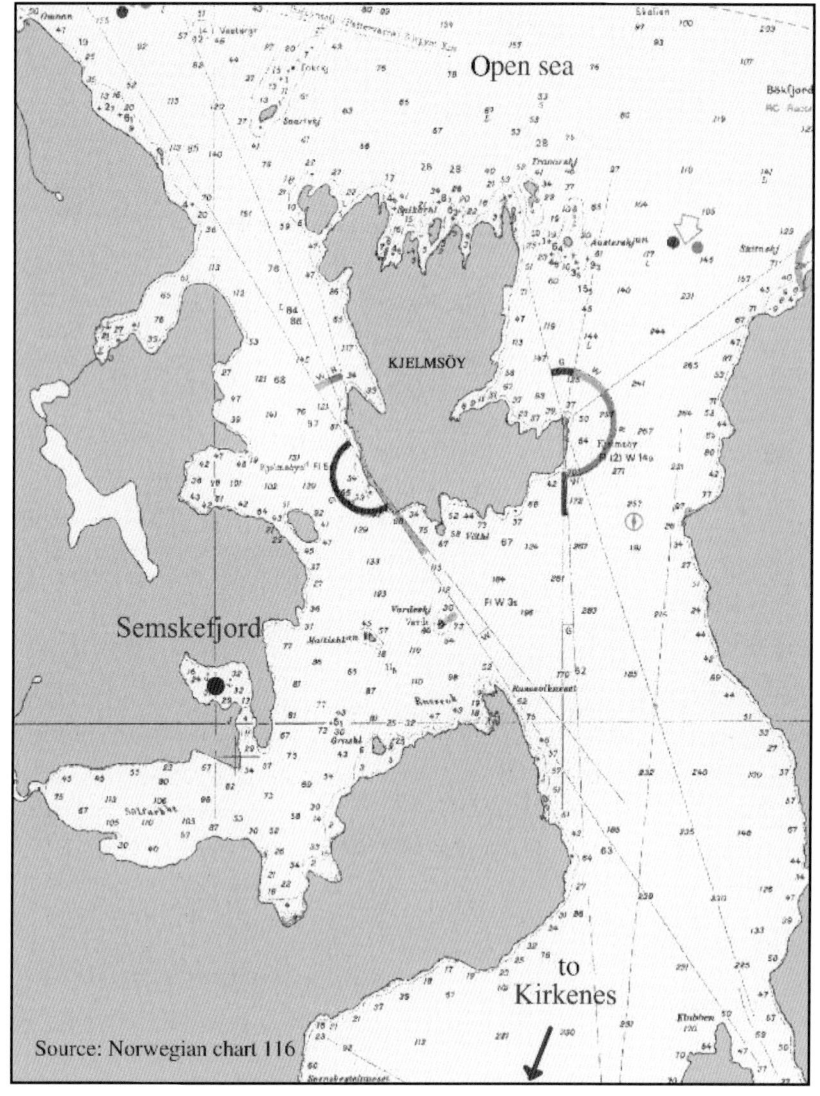

Semske Fjord, miles from anywhere.

SKL told their liaison officer at Führer HQ 'to mention in a situation report at FHQ'[21] that it was intended to return the flotilla to Germany for engine overhaul. When no objection was raised, 8.SFltl. and depot ship *Carl Peters* received orders at the beginning of June 1943 to head for Germany, and arrived at Kiel on 18 June for a refit and reinforcements before joining the Channel flotillas. Once again, a flotilla had wasted more than six months on a useless assignment and had been lost to operations against the main enemy.

The requests persisted, however, and in August 1943 Naval High Command Norway[22] indented for an S-boat flotilla, since this 'could be really effective in warding off the cruiser and destroyer raids expected in winter'. SKL spurned the approach, pointing out that to strengthen Norway 'was only possible by weakening other theatres. The enemy is increasingly active in all theatres, however, so that transfers of forces are not possible.'[23]

Unwilling to take no for an answer, Naval High Command Norway kept up the pressure for an S-boat flotilla with a medley of applications: in October 1943 (protection for damaged battleship *Tirpitz* in Alta Fjord), in March 1944 (fighting off possible enemy landings in Petsamo area) and again in September 1944 (protection of *Tirpitz*). SKL rejected them all with the explanation that the main strength of the boats lay in offensive torpedo operations, for which, on the basis of all experience to date, there was no requirement in northern Norway.

The game of applying and denying revealed the shortage of naval units, which left many areas of risk exposed, and highlighted the importance attached to the S-boats after they had proved their worth in the Channel and elsewhere. It was an importance that often led to an overestimation of their capabilities and to demands the boats could not fulfil, simply on account of widespread ignorance as to their possibilities and limitations.

To Norway Again

Scarcely had SKL turned down the latest request of Naval High Command Norway when Hitler looked afresh at northern Norway. After the evening situation conference at Führer HQ on 17 October 1944, SKL recorded, 'Führer fears that an agreement may ensue between the Russians and Anglo-Americans whereby German forces may be trapped in a pincer movement in the far north. This would involve Anglo-American landings on the northern coast of Norway and a simultaneous Russian attack from the east. Fears further major disruption of troop transports returning by sea.'[24]

Seizing upon the Führer's worries, without waiting for his orders, Dönitz ordered the immediate transfer of an S-boat flotilla of at least eight boats to Admiral Polar Seas. On 19 October 1944, 4.SFltl. (Korvettenkapitän Fimmen), selected by the FdS for the task, was recalled from Holland to Kiel, where the boats were fitted with increased armament before the flotilla (S 201, S 202, S 203, S 204, S 205, S 219, S 220 and S 703 and the depot ship *Hermann von Wissmann*) headed north. The boats called in at Frederikshavn and Kristiansand and put into Lindesnes to shelter. Here, S 203 collided with an R-boat and had to be scuttled.

Meanwhile, Allied submarine attacks on coastal convoys had caused a serious setback to Hitler's plans to return two divisions to the Reich from Norway. Naval High Command Norway had therefore requested a second S-boat flotilla. Since the general situation precluded it, SKL ordered 4.SFltl. to remain with Admiral West Coast acting as convoy escorts, and not to continue to the Arctic until relieved by the 1st S-boat Training Flotilla.

The Ardennes offensive required a concentration of S-boat forces in the Channel,[25] and without waiting for the 1st Training Flotilla (Kapitänleutnant Wilcke), 4.SFltl. returned to Holland on 28 December 1944 after nine weeks of useless wanderings around the Norwegian coast. Eventually, the training flotilla arrived at Egersund, from where it ran convoy escort until the cessation of hostilities.

In the last days of the war, 8.SFltl. (Korvettenkapitän Zymalkowski) transferred from Holland to Kristiansand to support the 1st Training Flotilla, and at the capitulation lay at Egersund. Thus the circle had closed for a section of the S-boat Arm. Given convoy protection duty in the opening months of the war, for a lack of suitable vessels they had the same role at the end, a task for which they were neither intended nor equipped.

S-boats spent over eighteen months in Norwegian waters. The crews endured hardships and showed great commitment. In the inhospitable north of the country they fired no torpedoes nor laid a single mine. The enemy did not perceive them as a threat there, being unaware of their presence.[26] Most importantly, they were absent from the decisive area, the Channel, and all efforts of S-boat Command to remedy that situation were in vain.

8

North Africa and Southern Mediterranean

November 1941 – June 1943

When Italy entered the war on Germany's side in June 1940, precipitately and without adequate preparations, and expanded the conflict by attacking Greece on 28 October 1940, new possibilities, but also great dangers, presented themselves to the German leadership in the war against Great Britain. Incorporating the Mediterranean into the Axis area of operations threatened Britain's sea route to India and might have resulted in the loss of all British bases and possessions in the region. On the other hand, it ran the danger of tying down substantial forces for no major return. When the Italians had no victories to show, and suffered defeats in Greece, North Africa and in naval battles with the British fleet, Hitler felt obliged to support Mussolini. For this reason, in February 1941 Army and Luftwaffe units arrived in North Africa, and in April 1941 in the Balkans.[1]

The German leadership first discussed the possibility of sending S-boats to the Mediterranean in the spring of 1941. Nothing came of this idea because the preparations for Barbarossa were in hand and SKL was obliged to commit flotillas to the impending Baltic operations. After initial successes, Rommel's offensive in North Africa ground to a halt because of the catastrophic supply situation. To protect the transports and drive off the British forces attacking them, in May 1941 Rommel requested German naval units for the Mediterranean. SKL refused; U-boats could not be released from the Atlantic and S-boats and R-boats were tied down in the Baltic.

When Hitler, in his Instruction No. 32 of 11 June 1941, 'Preparations for the Time after Barbarossa', ordered that the transfer of S-boats to the Mediterranean should be considered,[2] SKL decided to send a flotilla there as soon as the Baltic operations were concluded. Raeder informed Hitler of this on 25 July 1941 in the hope of avoiding a demand for U-boats in the Mediterranean,[3] but he was to be disappointed, for the increasing losses on the transport route to North Africa were causing concern and Rommel was becoming ever more insistent about naval support. In August, Hitler said that he wanted U-boats and, when SKL did not conform immediately, in September he ordered that six U-boats should be transferred to the Mediterranean theatre.[4]

Whereas the U-boats would pass through the Straits of Gibraltar, S-boats would transit the Rhine–Rhône Canal. This suggestion had been made by Kapitän zur See von Conrady who, as chief of the 1st S-boat Flotilla in 1937, had sailed the Rhine as far as Worms. Because the French locks were only thirty-five metres long, the smaller S-boats that preponderated in 3.SFltl. were chosen. At the end of August 1941, SKL released Kapitänleutnant Kemnade, commander of 3.SFltl., to reconnoitre the Rhine–Rhône route and the French Mediterranean coast to Sicily.[5]

After 3.SFltl. was released from Barbarossa at the end of September 1941, the boats completed a short refit at Wilhelmshaven and then moved off in two small groups. For reasons of secrecy, and in order to provoke as little interest as possible while passing through France, the boats were disguised at Rotterdam as harmless black tugs. A dummy funnel was fitted, the crews wore civilian dress and the deck weapons in plain view were dismounted.

On 9 October 1941, the first five boats left. After a long wait on account of low water at Ecuelles on the Rhône, they arrived at La Spezia in Italy on 18 November. Here, the armament was remounted and

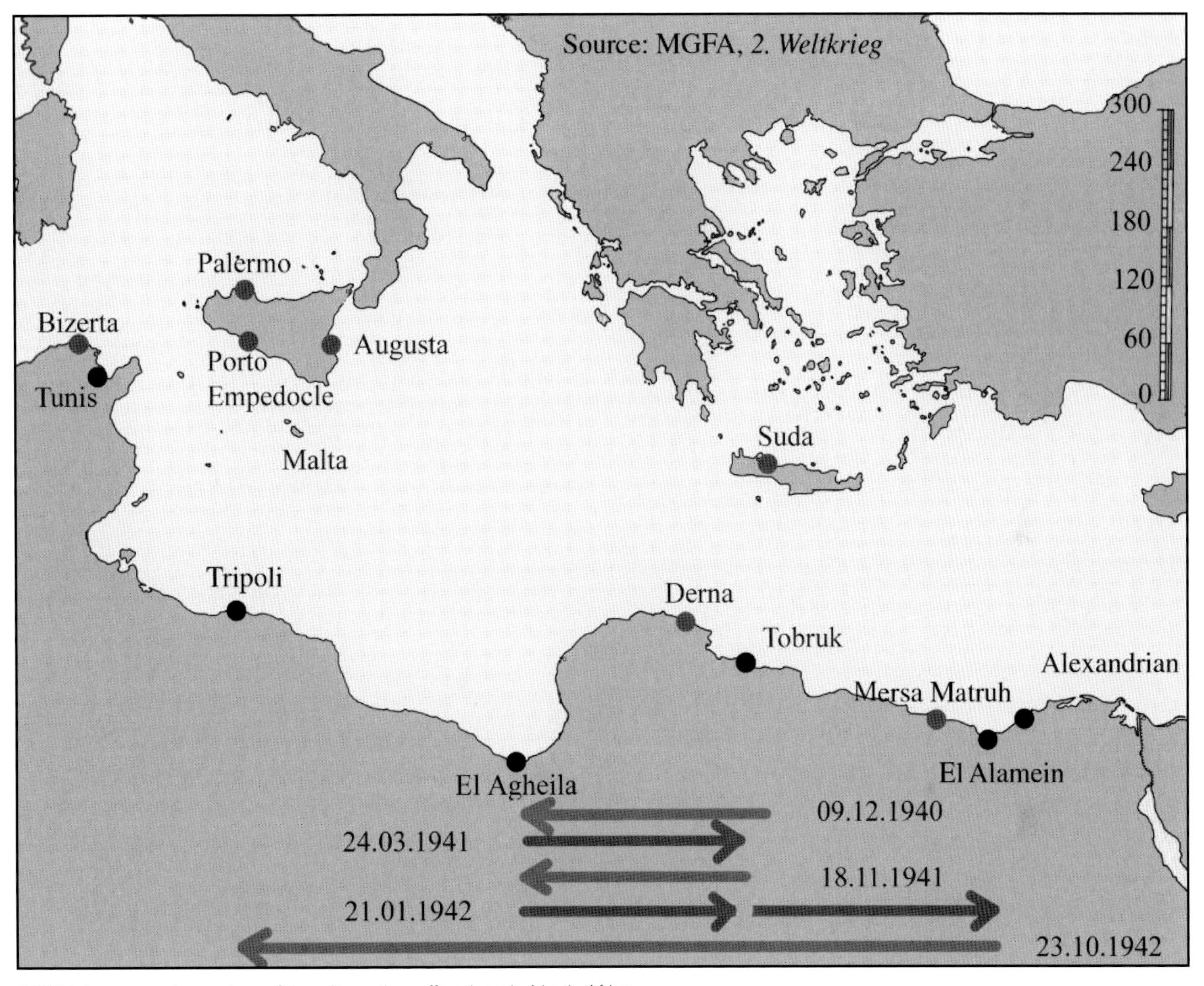

3.SFltl. bases and overview of the alternating offensives in North Africa.

the boats fitted out for operations. After ten days at La Spezia, they sailed via Gaeta for Augusta, Sicily, their new base. After loading torpedoes and an engine overhaul, on 11 December – two months after leaving Germany – the flotilla was reported operational to Vizeadmiral Weichold, C-in-C German Naval Command (DMK) in Italy, with headquarters in Rome.

The second group, also of five boats, left Wilhelmshaven on 10 November 1941 and arrived at Augusta on 5 February 1942. The third group, with four boats, followed the same route in May 1942 and put into Augusta on 24 May. The flotilla thus stood at fourteen boats.

Augusta had been agreed as a base by DMK with the Italian navy for its proximity to Malta. It was from Malta that aircraft, submarines and surface vessels attacked Rommel's supply lines. British successes had risen steadily from June to September 1941, with the result that the Afrika Korps had become bogged down and was unable to take Tobruk, in British hands and encircled, but still capable of being supplied from the sea. Finally, the British offensive in Cyrenaica, begun on 18 November 1941, had forced the Germans back to El Agheila, which had been their original starting point in March 1941. Therefore it was essential to overcome Malta, and in December 1941 II Fliegerkorps began nightly bombing raids on the island, the S-boats supporting them from the sea.

Minelaying off Malta

On 12 and 13 December 1941, the boats spent six hours lurking off Valetta harbour but sighted nothing. On the orders of DMK, minelaying began on the 16th of the month, once mines became available. DMK was the competent authority for operating the flotilla and co-ordinated work with the Italian navy at the same time. Operational orders would then be telexed to the flotilla directly from Rome. The mining of Malta lasted from December 1941 to May 1942. The need was for a sea state of not more than force 3, because of the heavily laden boats, and no full moon so as to avoid too great a possibility of being sighted.

The mosaic arrangement of the minefields, some of which were laid so close to the shore that searchlight operators could be seen on the beach, required extremely precise navigation and an undetected approach. For exactitude in establishing the co-ordinates, the boats formed in a line and took soundings on the Hurd Bank, north-east of Malta. This enabled them to plot a course allowing for the three-to-four mile deviation caused by the strong

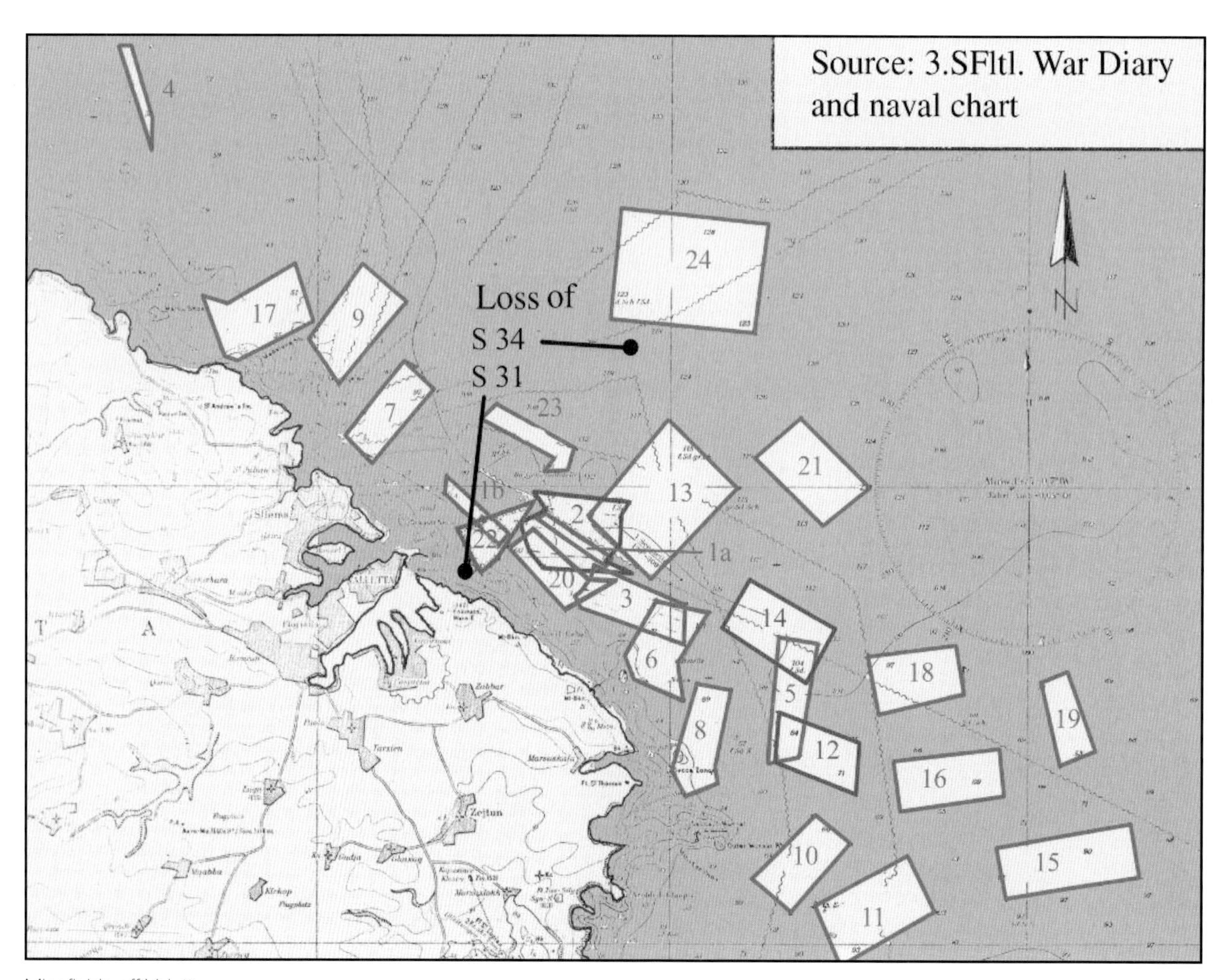

Minefields off Valetta.

S-boats at Augusta, Sicily.

current usually running. It was planned that minelaying should coincide with Luftwaffe bombing raids to distract the enemy and drown out the noise of the boats' engines, thus permitting a close approach to shore.

Generally the aircraft arrived and on time, but the boats were often delayed, either by having to avoid patrol craft or lie stopped off the coast to avoid intense searchlight activity. A total of 557 mines, of various types, and 416 protective buoys were laid in twenty-four minefields. The modern TMA (Torpedo-tube Mine A) was unreliable and would often explode shortly after being dropped, which would tend to alert the defences on the coast. In skirmishes, the British ML 130 and a naval trawler were gunned and sunk. The first German losses occurred at the end of the minelaying period on 10 May 1942, when S 31 was mined 700 metres off the Valetta mole-head. The boat broke up at once and sank, taking ten crew with her. The survivors were rescued by the leader boat. While withdrawing, the boats came across the forty-knot minelayer *Welshman* sailing alone. The torpedoes all missed as a result of underestimation of the target's speed. The cruiser got into Valetta behind a smoke screen, bringing urgently needed anti-aircraft ammunition, and left for Gibraltar six hours later.[6] On 17 May 1942, on the last mining sortie, S 34 was hit by salvoes from shore artillery and had to be abandoned.[7] Three men were lost, the remainder saved by the leader boat.

While S-boats tightened the noose around Malta from the sea, the constant bombing by II Fliegerkorps reduced the harbour and dock installations to rubble. This offensive reduced the danger from Malta to the extent that shipping losses were cut back, allowing Rommel to advance at the end of January 1942. In April/May, the Royal Navy evacuated its ships from Malta on the grounds that the harbour approaches were unsafe and there was no protected anchorage inside.[8]

Once Malta had been practically neutralised as a base for British submarines, surface forces and aircraft, the Germans planned to occupy it and so finally remove this threat to the Axis supply lines to North Africa, but Hitler and Mussolini reached agreement that Operation 'Hercules' should be held back until after the fall of Tobruk.[9] This prompted the Luftwaffe to call off its offensive against Malta and disperse most of its units there to Russia or North Africa in support of Rommel's siege of Tobruk. The 3rd S-boat Flotilla followed, arriving at Derna on 21 May 1942.

> The hope of an early torpedo engagement heartens commanders and men tremendously. Especially at the time when we sustained our losses it was clear to the crews what they had achieved. It was very fortunate and psychologically favourable that the survivors and wounded could be saved from both boats we lost.
> (War Diary, 3.SFltl., 19 May 1942)

North Africa

There was no proper harbour at Derna and the boats lay off at anchor. Water and fuel was shipped out to them in barrels aboard infantry lighters. Torpedoes were stored and adjusted under canvas, shipped out aboard the same lighters and hoisted inboard using a small crane, all in the roasting heat of a desert summer. Small repairs and overhauls had to be carried out with shipboard tools, although the Luftwaffe repair hangar at Derna airfield often lent a hand. Engine overhauls continued to be handled at Augusta, but the 500-mile transit was costly in engine-hours.

The British were supplying Tobruk from a fleet of small coasters, which sailed close inshore and were therefore difficult to find.[10] S-boats stationed at Derna had the task of disrupting this supply line. From then until the fall of Tobruk a month later, the flotilla sailed eleven sorties along the coast between Mersa Matruh and Tobruk. Escort craft were spotted on four occasions, and a naval trawler sunk, but the coasters could not be pinpointed for lack of air reconnaissance and detection equipment between Tobruk and Alexandria.

S-boat at Mersa Matruh.

While 3.SFltl. was on the North African coast, the British used the respite at Malta to replenish the island with its most urgently needed supplies by means of heavily guarded convoys arriving in mid-June 1942. The ex-Gibraltar convoy Operation 'Harpoon' was discovered late and engaged by Italian naval units in the Strait of Sicily. Dive-bombers sank three ships. Off Malta, the remainder ran into the minefields laid by 3.SFltl. and suffered further losses. Two of the six freighters reached Malta and brought a certain relief. The escort vessels left unobserved.

Convoy Operation 'Vigorous' coming up from the east was spotted early on by Luftwaffe air reconnaissance and attacked from North Africa and Crete throughout 14 June, two ships being sunk and two more damaged. The same evening, 3.SFltl. sailed and sighted the enemy ships at dusk. The vessels were then identified as British and attacked by Italian aircraft and Ju 88s; all escaped unscathed. Once darkness fell, it was found to be impossible to approach the convoy because the contact aircraft insisted on firing parachute flares into the night sky so as to keep the British ships in sight. Despite agreement with the Luftwaffe command centre at Derna, orders not to illuminate the sky were ignored and S-boats were unable to get through the escort destroyers to attack the merchant vessels. On a return approach at very high speed, a Luftwaffe aircraft homed in on the long wakes and attacked – again without success – with a bomb run. The flotilla commander now decided to attack the escorts. This resulted in S 55's sinking the destroyer *Hasty*, while S 56 hit the cruiser *Newcastle* with two torpedoes, damaging her severely. After these setbacks and news that the Italian fleet had sailed, the Royal Navy called a halt and turned the convoy back to the east. The 3rd S-boat Flotilla found it the following night, quickly establishing contact with a destroyer group, but could not manoeuvre into position to attack.

A few nights later, the flotilla lay off Tobruk waiting to intercept the enemy fleeing the citadel. As most vessels had already sailed on 20 June 1942, only the slow ships could be found.[11] Seven of these were gunned and sunk, and six captured, and a total of 175 prisoners taken. Several S-boat crew were wounded and two boats damaged and forced to return to Sicily after attack by enemy forces and Me 109s mistaking the boats as British. Oberleutnant zur See Geiger and the flotilla surgeon Dr Mehnen both fell during the attacks.

The high number of engine-hours run allowed no long-distance reconnaissance voyages, and the flotilla remained at Tobruk until the end of June 1942, leaving occasionally to escort supply convoys. At Tobruk, as at Derna, there were no proper harbour installations and the boats lay at anchor, being supplied by infantry lighters. The same procedure was followed at Mersa Matruh, to where the flotilla relocated on 29 June 1942 after Rommel captured the port. The torpedo adjustment personnel followed by road in several captured British lorries. Four days later, the boats sailed in search of merchant shipping off Alexandria, but on this, and in the next two sorties, nothing was sighted. On several nights, the British retaliated with air attacks against the flotilla at anchor while destroyers shelled Mersa Matruh. The destroyers were radar-equipped and were surprised only once, but the torpedo was avoided. The enemy also flew night reconnaissance using radar, bathing the boats in the light of flares shortly after they sailed, then gunning and bombing them, but only one hit was ever reported.

The constant threat of air attack and the limited opportunities for operations resulted in boats being sent to Suda Bay, Crete for undisturbed exercises instead of Mersa Matruh, after refitting in Sicily. While at Suda Bay, Kapitänleutnant Kemnade received orders to intercept a Malta convoy arriving from Gibraltar. He took his flotilla of four boats to the Channel between Sicily and Tunisia where, on the night of 12 August 1942, he attacked convoy Operation 'Pedestal'. Its ships had already been mauled by U-boats and air attack and the two *Rotten* of S-boats had no difficulty in finding their targets. Despite stiff resistance they sank four.[12] During the fighting, Oberleutnant zur See Wuppermann, acting commander of S 58, was wounded seriously. The S-boat attacks – during the night, Italian MAS boats had also arrived – scattered the convoy, so that first light provided easy pickings for German aircraft. Only five from a total of fifteen ships reached Malta, but the island received desperately needed supplies, particularly aviation spirit.[13]

> Defences opened fire on our boats with everything they had. 10.2cm hit in compartment III, two seriously, one lightly wounded. Rudder jammed hard to starboard. Boat was heading south-east towards enemy squadron, fire broke out in compartments II and III. Chief engineer got both fires under control, canisters pouring out a thick curtain of smoke. Boat still turning to starboard. Using starboard and later also central propeller at top speed I attempted to slew boat round to port. Enemy still firing with all weapons, our boat trapped in beams of five searchlights. This lasted about fifteen minutes. I could see no way to escape. Then the rudder came free. I headed north and later north-east at top speed. The searchlights still penetrated our smoke, but enemy fire died away.
> (War Diary, *Rotte* S 58, S 59)

After this action, the boats sailed 700 nautical miles to Mersa Matruh to operate off Alexandria in support of Rommel's attack on El Alamein on 30 August 1942. The seas were empty of traffic and a week later the boats returned to Augusta, since agents had reported another Malta convoy coming up from the west. Nevertheless, September and October remained quiet, and 3.SFltl. transferred to Porto Empedocle to leave Augusta free for 7.SFltl., which arrived in mid-December as reinforcements.[14]

At the beginning of November, 3.SFltl. laid three minefields off Malta. The island now had radar installations; the boats were tracked each time and the mines swept. Another Malta convoy was announced and the ten serviceable boats moved to Trapani: 'The existence of the Afrika Armee depends on the destruction of the British convoy. I expect a victorious action, regardless of the risks. The Führer.'[15]

He expected in vain, however, for the reported convoy was not heading for Malta but North Africa, where it landed troops in the early morning hours of 8 November 1942 at Algiers and Oran, well beyond the operational reach of S-boats.

Tunisia

After Rommel began his retreat westwards following the British offensive at El Alamein on 23 October 1942, the Allied advance from Algeria threatened his rear and, to protect him, German and Italian troops occupied Tunisia three days after the landings. 3.SFltl. entered Tunis harbour, seizing its installations. This allowed unhindered passage out for troops and equipment, while the port continued to act as a distribution centre for incoming supplies. Two days later, the flotilla captured Bizerta undamaged for use as an S-boat base. Patrols off Tunis and Bizerta were aimed at preventing anticipated commando landings and the possible breakout of French ships that had sought refuge in an inland bay near Bizerta after the occupation of Tunis.

As a direct result of the Allied landings in North Africa, Germany and Italy had occupied Vichy France, at which units of the French fleet at Toulon had been scuttled.[16] The Allied advances from west and east in North Africa raised doubts as to how the remaining French forces in Tunisia might react, and

Type S 151 boats of 7.SFltl. in a lock of the Rhine–Rhône canal.

on 8 October 1942 the French units at Bizerta were disarmed. At the same time, 3.SFltl. entered the inland bay to capture a total of sixteen French warships, amongst them six submarines and three torpedo boats plus four steamers, in order to prevent their being scuttled as at Toulon.[17] The crews were put ashore and placed under German Army control, the ships being given to the Italian navy four days later.

Tunis was slowly beginning to assume the same kind of importance as Stalingrad; if lost, it meant the loss of North Africa and exposing the 'soft underbelly' of the Axis. It was therefore considered essential to throw in everything available to shore up Tunis. It became evident from early on that Italy was mindful of the postwar period and not disposed to operate its available units unconditionally.[18]

It was the role of 3.SFltl. to attack the Allied forces that were causing heavy losses on the German–Italian supply route to North Africa, but the Allied naval units based at Malta and also on Bone could not be found without air reconnaissance.[19] Having no success, the boats worked with Italian warships as distant escorts to the supply transports; during these operations only one transport was lost, and this to air attack.

Meanwhile, Rommel had been forced back ever more westwards while the Allies in the west had gained ground, giving the Germans cause for concern that coastal landings at Rommel's back could collapse the very stretched Wehrmacht defences.

In order to forestall this possibility and at the same time disrupt Allied supply lines, in the second half of 1942 S-boats laid twenty-two minefields off the North African coast. From 7 January 1943, 7.SFltl. (Kapitänleutnant Trummer) joined the force, enabling minelaying by one flotilla while the other protected the flank. On one such escort mission on the night of 27 February 1943, the broadly dispersed 3.SFltl. suffered its third casualty when S 35 was lost with all hands, probably after colliding with a mine.[20] On the night of 12 March 1943, when the two flotillas ran across a British destroyer group, they sank the destroyer *Lightning*.[21]

On the Defensive

Whereas in their previous bases the S-boats had lain relatively quietly to anchor, at Bizerta they were kept constantly at immediate readiness by heavy air attacks on the harbour and town. Bombing raids also followed on the Sicilian ports, and at Augusta on 30 January 1943 three S-boats were seriously damaged and put out of action for a month. On 1 March 1943, S 56 was bombed and sunk at Palermo.[22]

The minelaying continued into May; the last mines were sown directly off the Bizerta harbour entrance on the afternoon of 6 May 1943, when the city was under enemy artillery fire. Then, after embarking the remaining base personnel and as many troops as the boats could carry, they sailed, the last German naval units to leave North Africa. On the voyage to Sicily in heavy weather, they fought through a blockading ring of sixteen destroyers to reach Porto Empedocle/Trapani, where the smaller 7.SFltl. boats had assembled, having not been able to hold their course against the heavy seas coming from the east.

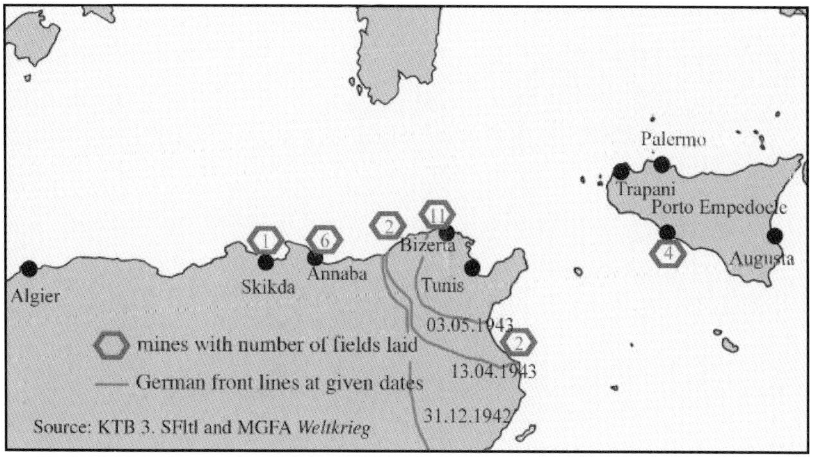

German minefields on the North Africa coast and Sicily.

9

The Northern Mediterranean, Adriatic and Aegean

June 1942 – August 1944

After the endless mining operations and the frequent lying at immediate readiness in the face of air attack, the boats found themselves in urgent need of a refit and engine overhaul. The fouling of propellers and shafts was causing a drastic reduction in speed, but the operational boats of the 3rd S-boat Flotilla were sent out to lay mines off Porto Empedocle as a defence against enemy landings, and then followed sorties against Allied convoys around the North African ports or Malta, and also against Allied warships bom-barding the island of Pantelleria. None of this could be successful without air re-connaissance, while the Allies protected sensitive areas below an air umbrella by day and with strong destroyer/MGB groups at night.

The omens for a major Allied landing were building. Would it be Sicily or Greece? At the beginning of June 1943, SKL issued instructions to set up supply and operational bases for S-boats and R-boats in the Aegean.[1] As a precaution, 7.SFltl. moved to Porto Vesme on Sardinia at immediate readiness in the event of landings there.

So that a major invasion could be resisted jointly with the Italians, at the beginning of June 1943, 3. and 7.SFltl. were placed under Messina Command of the Italian navy. The different approach to operations and the fact that Messina Command issued its pages-long orders in Italian, which lost valuable time in translation, resulted in an interview on 20 June 1943 between the commander of 3.SFltl. and German Naval Command Italy in Rome, after which the latter took back jurisdiction over the S-boats.

Fouling of shafts and propellers.

> The instruction in the operations order to attack enemy destroyers only if they opened fire on the island of Pantelleria must be an Italian idea. I would have brought to account any commander who complied with this order and let a chance to shoot go begging. (3.SFltl. War Diary, 8 June 1943)

Four days before the Allied landings in Sicily at the beginning of September 1943, heavy air attacks were commenced on Porto Empedocle. American fighter-bombers flew raids against the town and docks by day.

Boats under camouflage at Porto Empedocle.

Higgins-type boat of 15th US MTB Squadron at Bastia, Corsica.

After two boats were damaged and required long-term repair, S 59 was hit and sunk. This was the flotilla's fifth loss. The constant harassment from the air prompted a request by 3.SFltl. to transfer to Trapani, but the Italians refused. Instead, the same evening, the flotilla received orders to move to Augusta. On the way, they encountered seventeen boats of the 15th US MTB Squadron led by the destroyer *Ordronaux*, which had set out for Porto Empedocle to neutralise the S-boats there.[2] The flotilla turned away, unaware that the US operation formed part of the Allied landings, and out into Palermo at 0830 hrs on 10 July 1943. At 1920 hrs they received not-ification of the landings occurring that morning when German Naval Command Italy ordered: 'Go at once to the Strait of Messina, launch attack at Syracuse.'[3]

Although the boats put to sea at once, it was light before they could get to Syracuse, and the threat of air attack forced them to turn back to Messina and put into Salerno. Thus was lost the last chance to attack the invasion fleet in the disembarkation phase at sea. The next evening, 7.SFltl., coming from Sardinia, joined 3.SFltl., and the two flotillas sailed in company from Messina for the landing beaches. These beaches were covered by a force comprising six battleships, two aircraft carriers, fifteen cruisers and 128 supporting destroyers, and were thus too well defended to approach.[4]

The two flotillas had been weakened by engine breakdowns

and cases of jaundice amongst the commanders, who could not be replaced from Germany at short notice. Until the final evacuation of Sicily by German and Italian forces on 17 August 1943, the few serviceable boats sailed a handful of torpedo missions, all frustrated by strong defences. To Dönitz's enquiry into the reasons for the lack of success, Vizeadmiral Ruge, C-in-C German Naval Command Italy, attributed it to strong MGB groups on both flanks of the landing zones and long-term engine problems encountered by 7.SFltl.[5] In addition, at this time the flotillas had no clear information as to the overall situation and were shunted from pillar to post in the absence of a recognisable operational plan, dispersed haphazardly amongst ports such as Salerno, Viareggio, Crotone, Trapani, Cagliari, Civitavecchia or Vibo Valentia, which had no facilities for S-boats and not much fuel. Weapons and ammunition, and above all torpedoes, never arrived.

> After the Allied landings, everything in Rome seemed completely confused and we were obliged to fall back on ourselves and our own devices in every respect. (Albert Müller, *Erinnerungen*)

In order to unify the dispersed and mixed operational boats of 3. and 7.SFltl., at the FdS's suggestion SKL had ordered the formation of the 1st S-boat Division on 17 July 1943. This unit was commanded by Korvettenkapitän Herbert-Max Schultz, who took over 3.SFltl. at the same time as successor to Korvettenkapitän Kemnade.[6]

German uncertainties grew as to the future intentions of Italy after Sicily was lost and the Allies crossed the Straits of Messina to the Italian mainland. If Italy gave in, German forces had instructions to disarm Italian troops, prevent their vessels sailing and take them prize if possible. When this order,

7.SFltl. boats in dry dock.

codenamed 'Achse' (Axis) reached the flotillas, SKL warned OKW in Berlin that it would not be possible without the support of the Army on the spot.[7] In the confusion at the various ports, the talks ordered by German Naval Command with local Army offices were hardly possible and, as occurred at Taranto for example, the Army commander confessed himself perplexed as to how he should go about seizing an intact Italian fleet. On 8 September 1943, the Allies landed at Salerno and the Italian government ordered a ceasefire. The seventeen S-boats of the two flotillas were dispersed that day as follows:

Civitavecchia – 3 boats
returning there from Salerno – 2 boats
Pola – 2 boats
Taranto – 2 boats
in dock at Toulon – 6 boats
in dock at Salamis – 2 boats

The Italian naval strength at Pola and Taranto made it impossible to execute Achse locally. At Civitavecchia the S-boats were alone; other ports were closed and so they headed for the Gulf of Salerno, sinking the US destroyer *Rowan* on 11 September 1943, but were otherwise driven off by the destroyer and MGB/MTB defences.[8]

At Pola in the Adriatic, the U-boats, R-boats and S-boats gathered there thought better of trying to leave, in view of the threatening attitude of Italian units present. When the latter sailed to surrender to the Allies, and the German Army occupied the town, the S-boats regained their freedom to operate, subsequently escorting transports conveying Italian prisoners and supporting the Army in its struggle against partisans in the Dalmatian islands.

At Taranto, S-boats and a naval ferry were assisted to sail by the Italians. Although supposedly under Italian supervision, the three German units were allowed to mine the port entrances but, after leaving, the slow naval ferry had to be scuttled when warning was given of the approach of Italian warships from seawards. S 54 (Oberleutnant zur See Klaus-Degenhardt Schmidt) and S 61 (Bootsmaat Blömker, deputising for the jaundiced Oberleutnant zur See von Gernet) headed north and sank a destroyer and a gunboat and captured three steamers.

> Shortly after we stopped the steamer, a destroyer hove in sight from the north-west. Boat sheltered alongside the freighter out of the destroyer's view, and the prize crew boarded. They made a constant lee for S-boat by use of rudder and engine telegraph. Destroyer stopped immediately off steamer's bow. As we crossed the steamer's keel-line we fired both tubes in succession. Destroyer shooting at eighty metres' range fired high after torpedoes hit forward of bridge and amidships port side causing heavy list. One minute later sank without trace. Steamer under command of prize crew was left to pick up survivors. (War Diary, *Rotte* S 54/S 61)

The two S-boats entered harbour at Venice with the three steamers that evening. The next morning, the Italian garrison capitulated when threatened with attack by dive-bombers and panzers; the 10,000 Italian navy men surrendered later to the German Army.

Concentration in the Adriatic

The operational situation in the Mediterranean after the Italian capitulation, the military advance of the Allies in Italy, the increasing partisan activity in the Balkans and the ever open question of if and where the Allies would effect another invasion caused a rethink in German tactics at sea, in particular how the seventeen S-boats were to be divided. There were henceforth to be eleven in the western Mediterranean and six in the Adriatic/Aegean. From 1 November 1943, OKW demanded 100,000 tonnes of supplies monthly by ship to meet the running demand and the winter requirements of the Army units along the Dalmatian and Albanian coasts, since rail and land transport alone was inadequate.[9]

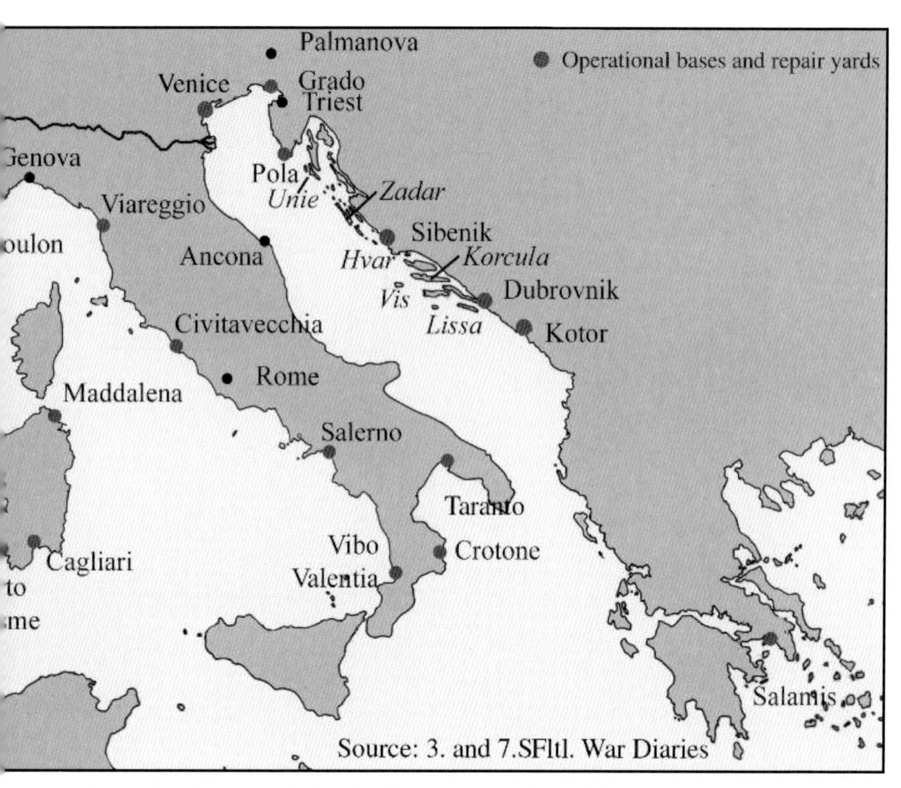

Operational bases of S-boats after the evacuation of Sicily.

Auxiliary Services to the End

Initially, the primary task of the S-boats was the protection of German maritime supply routes against British destroyers and MTBs in the Adriatic, but other needs soon arose. One of these was to disrupt the increasing support for Albanian and Yugoslav partisans from small fishing vessels and motor-sailers, another to mine coastal sectors of the Italian east coast open to possible commando raids behind the German mainland defences. As Tito's partisan army advanced, S-boats covered German Army operations to reoccupy islands that the Germans had lost, to shell partisan-held harbours and land installations and land German commandos in the enemy rear.

Against this background, on 27 October 1943 SKL decided to concentrate all S-boats in the Adriatic to help safeguard the supply route. A later transfer to the Aegean was not excluded.[10] C-in-C South, Generalfeldmarschall Kesselring, protested and called for at least some S-boats to remain, since even the few serviceable boats had tied down light enemy forces to a remarkable extent in the region, contributing substantially to a reduction in losses to German coastal traffic. SKL considered the task in the Adriatic/Aegean more important, however, and ordered all S-boats into the Adriatic.

At the same time, the naval command structure in the Mediterranean was subdivided into three regions, the jurisdiction of German Naval Command (DMK) now being limited to naval forces west of Italy.[11] Accordingly, the 1st S-Boat Division was transferred from the competence of DMK to Group South, Admiral Adriatic or Admiral Aegean, depending on the operation involved. The 1st S-boat Division headquarters was originally Venice, then Palmanova and, in December 1944, Pola.

Between these activities, operations took place in the Aegean to shield the removal of German units from the Greek islands or to escort captured Italian and Yugoslav warships into the Aegean. From the multitude of missions sailed, the following are a few examples:

On the night of 8 January 1944, S 36 and S 55 sank two motor-sailing vessels carrying ammunition and fuel, and shelled the harbour at Vis.

On the night of 20 May 1944, after an unsuccessful patrol in the Strait of Otranto, S 36 and S 61 sank a fishing boat and brought in four captives.

On the evening of 31 May 1944, four boats of 7.SFltl. sank six fully laden coasters mad a small tanker off Lissa island, and took prisoner 159 men in uniform, including British and Americans, thirty-seven women and five children.

On the night of 6 September 1944, three boats of 7.SFltl. covered from offshore Operation 'Seydlitz' (cleansing western part of Hvar island).

On the nights of 20 to 23 September 1944, S-boats escorted the captured torpedo boats TA37, TA38 and TA39 (TA = *Torpedoboote Ausland*, or 'torpedo boat, foreign') from Trieste to Athens.

On 18 November 1944, three S-boats sailed from Pola to search for survivors of the hospital ship *Tübingen*; of 120 aboard, 115 were saved.

On 19 November 1944, off Ancona, S-boats sank two auxiliary sailing vessels.

On the night of 19 December 1944, S-boats covering a minelaying operation off Sibenik attacked enemy MGBs without success, but a rummage party found nine partisans aboard a fishing boat outside the harbour.

On the night of 9 January 1945, the first operations of naval sabotage unit MEK 71 went ahead on the Dalmatian west coast and Italian east coast; the commandos were transported by S-boats; in Zadar harbour, two steamers were sunk; on the Italian east coast, three bridges were demolished.

Spectacular successes were not to be expected with the initial six available boats, of which as a rule never more than four were operational at a time because of engine overhauls and repairs to hull damage. The transfer of other units by road from Genoa to the Po river and then downstream to Venice lasted into the summer of 1944.[12] The last four boats of 7.SFltl. arrived at Pola on 20 June 1944, where, after an eight-month pause, working-up exercises were necessary to return the boats to operational readiness.

In the spring of 1944, another fifteen small LS-boats were brought by rail from Eckernförde and incorporated into the 1st S-boat Division as 21. and 22.SFltl., but their fighting value was not highly rated.[13] Thus, in October 1944 the nine boats of 22.SFltl. were passed to the Croat navy. They sailed no missions at any time for the Germans or Croats.

The six boats of 21.SFltl. were used as convoy escorts in the Aegean for lack of other suitable units, and were soon sunk or decommissioned. The flotilla was therefore disbanded in October 1944.[14]

Four obsolescent ex-Yugoslav boats and seven ex-Italian-navy MTBs made up 24.SFltl. and were used in the Aegean, but their fighting value did not compare with German S-boats. All operations proceeded under enemy air supremacy day and night. As a result, in a single week of March 1944 over 50 per cent of the available coastal capacity in the Adriatic was lost to air attack: 'The situation has peaked into catastrophe. The continuation of absolute enemy air supremacy leads us to expect the loss of all warships soon.'[15]

In addition, the zones of operation were being whittled down continually. Whereas the boats were based initially in Kotor Bay and the ports of Sibenik and Dubrovnik, during the course of 1944 they were forced back while British forces moved up to Vis and

LS-boat of 21.SFltl. in the Aegean.

then used Kotor[16] as a base for their destroyers and MGBs/MTBs. In the final months of the war, the German boats controlled only the inner Adriatic from bases at Pola, Venice and Grado, and their losses began to mount:

11 January 1944 – S 55 was sunk by air attack while running into Korcula;

12 January 1944 – S 153 sank after a fight with two destroyers north of Hvar island;

19 August 1944 – S 57 was scuttled after receiving serious damage in a battle with British MGBs;

25 October 1944 – S 158 sank at Sibenik after a direct hit by a bomb;

10 January 1945 – S 33, S 58 and S 60 ran aground on Unie island and had to be destroyed after all attempts to refloat them failed;

21 January 1945 – S 154 was condemned as irreparable at Pola after receiving damage in an air raid;

1 May 1945 – west of Trieste, S 157 was sunk by land artillery.

After the Balkans were as good as lost, Naval Group Command South was dissolved in December 1944 and the S-boats returned to German Naval Command control, known from 1 January 1945 as Naval High Command South (MOK Süd). By October 1944, the thirteen available boats were concentrated as the 2nd Group of 3.SFltl. after 7.SFltl. was disbanded. Following the evacuation of the Aegean, the seven boats of 24.SFltl. were redesignated the 3rd Group of 3.SFltl. They were almost never sailed in the Adriatic and were at Grado when the war ended. The surviving boats of the 1st and 2nd Groups of 3.SFltl. were condemned to inactivity in the last days of the war for lack of fuel and spare parts; they sailed only a few missions and stayed mainly at Pola. Under Kapitänleutnant Wuppermann, last commander of the 1st S-boat Division, the Pola boats sailed for Ancona to surrender to the Western Allies on 2 May 1945, once Tito's partisans began to occupy the town.

So ended the operations of the German S-boat Arm in the Mediterranean region. It was a theatre that had strategic importance at the outset because the survival or otherwise of Malta had a direct bearing on the supply situation for the Afrika Korps. As in no other theatre of war, in the Mediterranean the questions of advance or retreat, and the outcome of the war on land, at sea and in the air, depended immediately on the transport situation.

> We could not remain at Pola. None of us fancied being a prisoner of Tito. So we decided to ship as many naval personnel as we could from Pola and leave at midnight. We left for Italy in eight boats absolutely crammed full with sailors. Our goal was Ancona, a large port. We arrived at dawn. Nobody saw us put in. The harbour was full of British warships. The British commander received me. He could not agree to my request to return to Pola after disembarking the passengers. Thus we had to leave our boats, haul down the war flag and go miserably into British captivity. (Wuppermann, *Erinnerungen*)

The Allied landings in North Africa began for the Germans a defensive phase in which S-boats played an active and successful role. The oppressive enemy naval and air superiority swallowed Sicily and began to roll northwards up the map of Italy. This left the boats with no chance and scattered them in all directions. Concentrating them in the Adriatic provided no better prospects. Here, it was no longer naval warfare but simply a freight service for the Army fighting a hopeless struggle on both sides of the Adriatic Sea. The small, valiant S-boat force achieved what it could in a side-show far from the central theatre and its history-making events. In the closing months, when the Italian ports abandoned the blackout, German crews glimpsed a life after the war. Their boats were forced ever further back until deprived of all freedom to manoeuvre, and were finally bottled up in the northernmost ports of the Adriatic. Here they chose to surrender to the Western Allies rather than chance it in the hands of Tito's partisans.

10
The Black Sea
June 1942 – August 1944

At the commencement of hostilities with the Soviet Union on 22 June 1941, Army Group South, supported by Romanian divisions, headed for the Black Sea, where they encircled Odessa and pressed on for Rostov at the estuary of the Don. Odessa held out for two months with the help of the Soviet Black Sea Fleet, which initially opposed the besieging armies and later evacuated over 80,000 men and their equipment from Odessa and Sevastopol.

On 16 October 1941 Odessa fell, and two days later German forces crossed the Perikop Narrows to capture the Crimea, although Sevastopol held out. On 16 November, the last Soviet troops outside the stronghold left Kerch by road.[1]

The siege of Sevastopol began a month later, but was broken off soon afterwards when the Soviet fleet landed troops on the Kerch Peninsula, at Feodosiya and in the western Crimea. Generaloberst von Manstein, C-in-C 17 Armee, was now faced with a critical situation in the Crimea, but could not act until the muds hardened in the spring of 1942. Meanwhile the Soviet fleet, as in other theatres, played an integral role in overall military policy by supporting their troops ashore and attacking the encirclement at Sevastopol. This involved the transport of troops, materials and provisions, while ships' companies joined the defenders in the citadel.[2]

In response, OKH requested naval help to prevent further landings and to secure its own supplies. Naval Group South, responsible for the Black Sea/Aegean region from July 1941, had received a request for a Black Sea S-boat flotilla, to be sent after operations in the eastern Baltic ended, to supplement the poor-quality Romanian naval forces in the area.

Upon receipt of a repeat request in December 1941, SKL reviewed the matter and, after obtaining a positive answer, ordered six boats with experienced crews to be transferred to the Black Sea under the commander of the 1st S-boat Flotilla. At the same time, the transport of eight R-boats was also ordered; six small U-boats were to follow later.[3]

> Soviet fleet in the Black Sea: 1 battleship, 5 cruisers, 3 flotilla leaders, 13 destroyers, 84 MTBs, 44 submarines, 626 aircraft.

In November 1941, 1.SFltl. was the last flotilla to be released from Baltic operations.[4]

After a scheduled refit, preparations began for the transfer to the Black Sea. In order to obtain uniformity of equipment and armament, a number of boats were exchanged for those from other flotillas. Once the Elbe was ice-free at the beginning of April 1942, the boats were towed to Dresden without propellers. On the slip at Dresden, the motors were removed, the foredeck, command deck, torpedo tubes, rails, flak and navigational instruments

S-boat hull on the slip at Dresden.

On the autobahn to Ingolstadt.

dismantled and the hulls hung inside a scaffolding drawn along the autobahn by a Kuhlemeyer low-loader with locomotives front and rear. At Ingolstadt, the hulls were returned to the water and towed to Linz for full reassembly. After arriving at Constanta under tow from Linz, the boats ran speed trials, radio equipment was charged, transmission and sounding equipment calibrated and the hulls degaussed. The first two boats left Hamburg Vegesack on 4 April 1942 and were operational on 1 June. The next four boats followed in two pairs (S 72 and S 102, then S 27 and S 40) a week apart.

At Germany's request, since May 1942 the Italian naval presence in the Black Sea had been four MAS 500 type MTBs and three small submarines. During 1942, this force was supplemented by another six MAS boats and three more submarines. Between 8 and 15 May, von Manstein regained full control of the Crimea, and resumed the siege of Sevastopol on 7 June. He needed the city to be sealed off from the sea.

Off Sevastopol

The operations of the German and Italian forces in the Black Sea were directed by Group South, Admiral Black Sea (ASM), Vizeadmiral Wurmbach, with headquarters at Eforia, near Constanta. He placed the four operational boats of 1.SFltl. (Kapitänleutnant Birnbacher) west and south of Cape Kherson, the Italian boats south of Cape Sarych. From 3 June 1942, the boats lurked for several nights off Sevastopol in the channels between the Russian minefields, the positions of which were relatively well known. Enemy ships eluded them, although the Luftwaffe found and sank one destroyer, a torpedo boat and two transports.

In order to shorten the long sea voyage from Constanta, from 10 June the boats used Ak Mekshet, north of Sevastopol, as their new base for sorties. It had only a small wooden jetty, used for loading fuel and ammunition, but it saved a voyage of 150 miles and allowed substantially more time in the operational area. In 1914, the German warships *Goeben* and *Breslau*[5] had reported the Black Sea as having an innate phosphorescence that made torpedo tracks easy to spot. This same phosphorescence gave

Under tow to Constanta.

Soviet destroyers and torpedo boats time to take avoiding action. Thus, while enemy forces were sighted, no successes ensued although a transport was torpedoed and sunk by S 102. While a reserve torpedo was being loaded aboard S 26, the warhead exploded, causing a fire and putting S 26 out of commission for three months, leaving only three boats operational.

As no torpedoes were available at Ak Mekshet, the boats were forced to return to Constanta to reload. Here they shipped mines to close down the existing swept channels at Sevastopol, but Soviet literature does not mention any losses. After the first mission

Shipping mines at Ak Mekshet.

was completed, the Germans received the surrender of Sevastopol. Immediately beforehand, 1.SFltl., now with five boats, waited off the approaches to the port on the night of 1 July 1942 after the B-Dienst reported that transports would sail with Communist commissars aboard.

Two submarine-chasers emerged and were sunk after a gun battle lasting almost four hours. S 40 was so seriously damaged that the boat was obliged to return with S 26 to Linz for repair. Thirty-seven Russian survivors were picked up, including the last deputy commander of the citadel, the captain of a cruiser sunk in harbour, one political commissar and a female harbour pilot.

The fall of Sevastopol was a favourable juncture for the boats to have their 300-hour engine overhaul at Constanta,[6] while flotilla staff commissioned a new base at Ivan Baba at the eastern end of the Crimean Peninsula, which was surveyed in June and deemed suitable for operations against the Caucasian coast still in Soviet hands. Ivan Baba was named after its 170-metre hill with a precipitate cliff face. In the past the base had served as a torpedo testing station and it had two small moles, offering relatively good shelter. Adequate buildings were on hand for use as quarters, workshops, torpedo adjustment stations and bunkers for fuel storage.

For protection against air attack, an 8.8cm flak battery and a whole series of smaller-calibre guns were installed.[7] Two days after Ivan Baba was occupied, about twenty Soviet bombers attacked the harbour but were driven off by the very accurate fire of the flak defences.

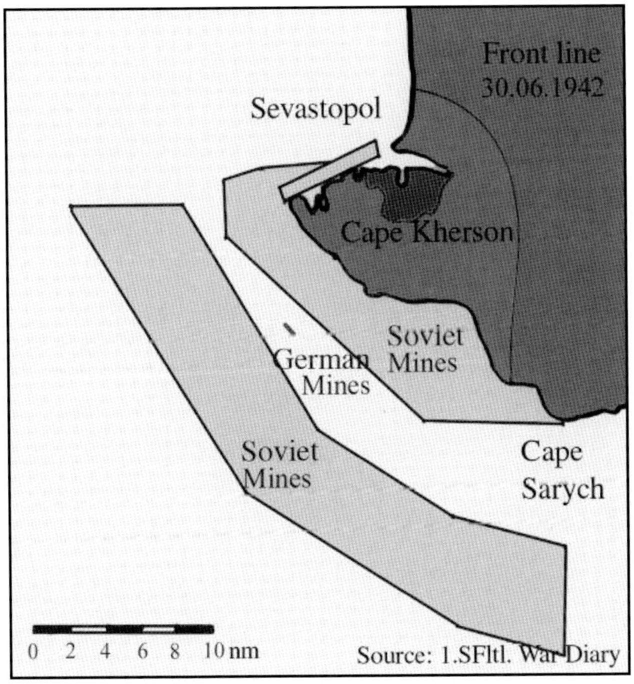

Mining operation of 29/30 June 1942.

Off the Caucasian Coast

When the four boats of 1.SFltl. entered Ivan Baba on 30 July 1942, the summer offensive of Army Group South had brought it to the shores of the Sea of Azov with the Romanian Army, while 17 Armee had reached the Kuban river and begun to overrun the region. Whereas the Soviet fleet had held back in the final weeks, they had now ventured forth to evacuate their troops from the Sea of Azov area, retreating before the German–Romanian advance. The S-boats were ordered to interrupt these activities.

From then until the end of August 1942, weather permitting, missions were sailed against the supply routes along the Caucasus coast between Tuapse and Sochi. This involved a round voyage of 140 miles, ten hours at 27 knots' cruising speed. Because of the danger of air attack, the boats sailed under cover of darkness, leaving them only a few hours in the

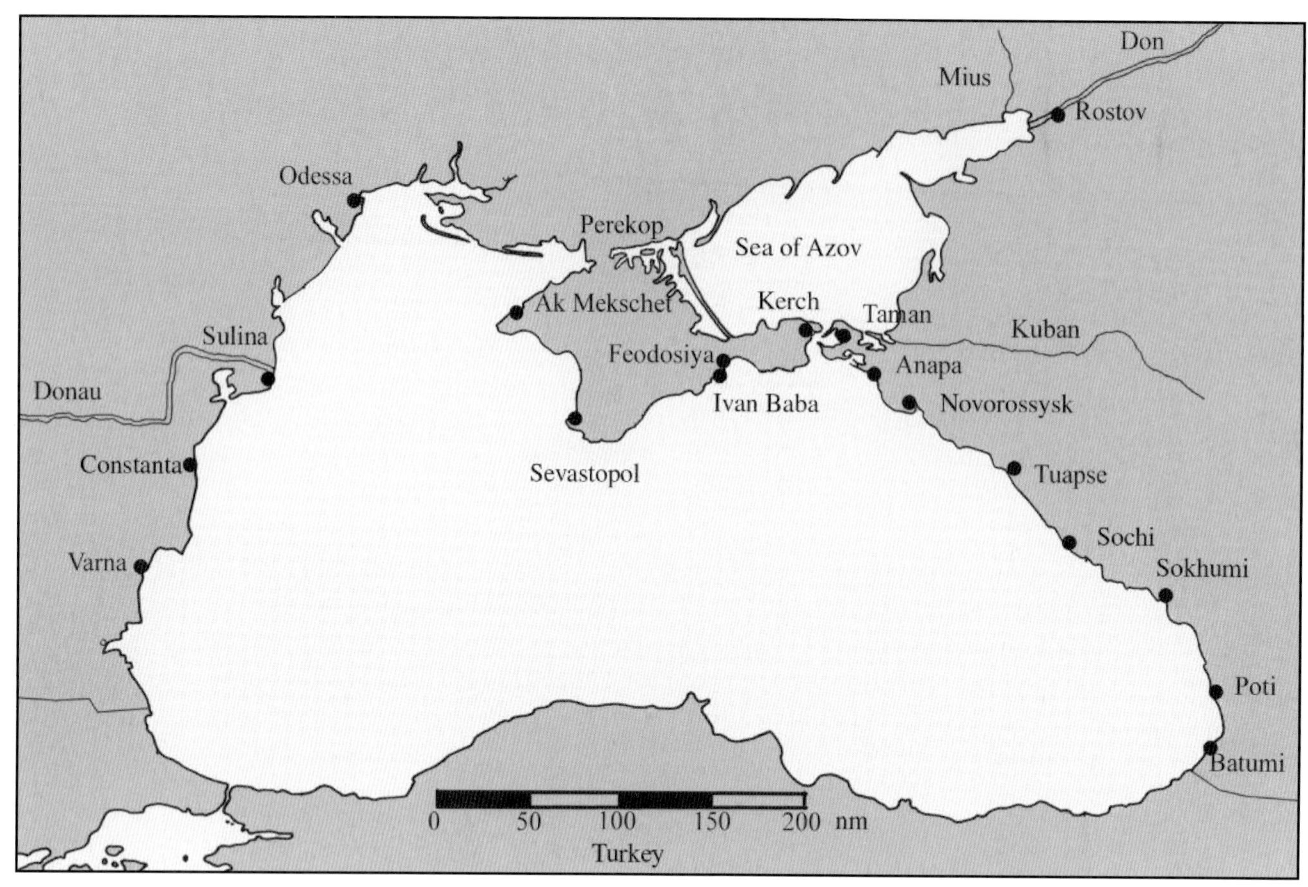

The operational region.

operational area to find ships that sailed alone and kept to no fixed sea lanes. Three were found and sunk in the course of six sorties, a number of torpedoes being avoided when betrayed by phosphorescence.

The Romanian 3rd Army had by now reached the Taman Peninsula, while 17 Armee, surrounding Anapa and Novorossiysk, could now cross the Strait of Kerch to join up with the Romanians. To cover this operation – codenamed 'Blücher' – and disrupt the anticipated withdrawal of Soviet forces, the four boats of 1.SFltl., under Kapitänleutnant Christiansen,[8] and the Italian MAS flotilla were positioned off the south coast of Taman Peninsula on 1 September 1942. German S-boats made several attacks on gatherings of vessels attempting to carry out the evacuation and on their own estimates had sunk twenty by 5 September. Then the operation terminated as Army Group South encircled the Sea of Azov.[9]

On the night of 5 September 1942, 1.SFltl. suffered its first loss when S 27 intercepted a torpedo fired by S 72 and sank with twelve crew. A number of seriously wounded were brought back to Ivan Baba, where the flotilla surgeon Dr Haenesch died of his injuries. The next day Anapa fell, but though German troops beset the town of Novorossiysk they could not take it. The two operational boats – the other three had reached their 300 engine-hours and were recalled to Constanta for engine change – thus returned to the Caucasus coast to attack the Soviet supply route. The sea area was vast for just two boats to comb, but by the end of September they had found and sunk three freighters. In this month, Ivan Baba was frequently the target of Soviet air attacks, these always being unsuccessful because of the effective flak. The transfer of the Luftwaffe 8.8cm battery to the Strait of Kerch to protect supplies flowing eastwards across the narrows

Ivan Baba naval base.

An S-boat off the Caucasus coast.

to the German Army units on the Caucasus front, and its replacement by a naval artillery unit, highlighted the lack of adequate forces on the Eastern Front. The Luftwaffe was flying ever fewer missions over the Black Sea because the aircraft were needed increasingly for the Battle of Stalingrad. On 23 September 1942, 17 Armee began a major offensive to capture Tuapse but became bogged down twenty kilometres short of the town in difficult terrain against a reinforced and determined defence.

Although 1.SFltl. had all five boats again from 12 October 1942, they seldom met enemy vessels and faced additionally the onset of autumn and winter storms that made operations impossible or resulted

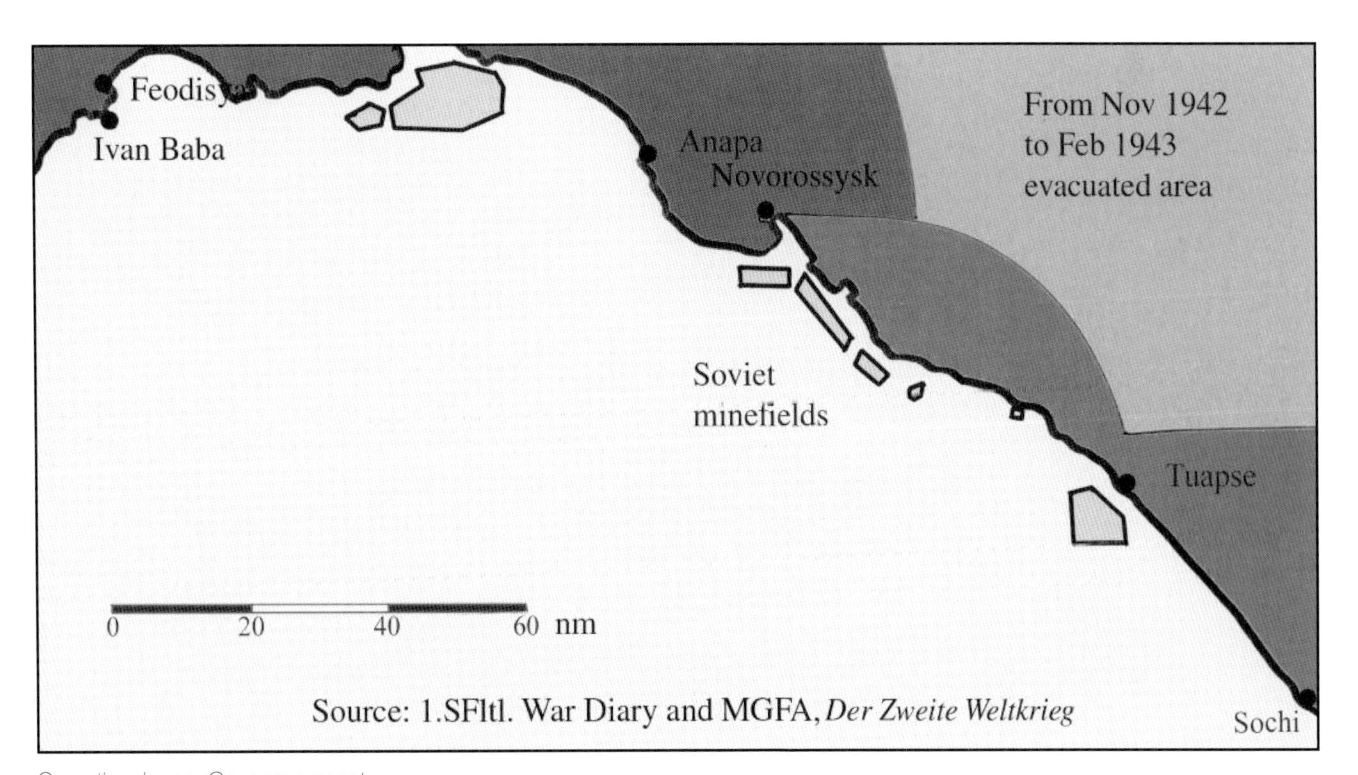

Operational area, Caucasus coast.

Even in the Black Sea, S-boats were armed with 4cm cannon and later received a cupola bridge.

in boats' being recalled while proceeding at sea. In contrast to Soviet shipping, which ran in the shelter of the coast, S-boats had to cross great expanses of open water in which the seas were short and high. The south-eastern region lacked weather stations, Black Sea U-boats provided no regular weather information and the weather forecast was therefore often wrong. Shifting base to Anapa, much closer to the area of operations, was rejected because of the greater danger of air attack there. Accordingly, Ivan Baba was prepared for winter and heating units were laid on for boats, torpedoes and accommodation. As a rule, only three or four boats would be operational at one time. Reasons included commanders falling sick with jaundice, engine breakdown, damage to shafts or hull damage as a result of skirmishes with Russian MTBs.

In autumn 1942, four more boats (S 47, S 49, S 51 and S 52) were sent to the Black Sea as reserves without crews.[10] Even before September, the flotilla had begun to transfer crews from boats under long-term repair to commission the reserve boats. Thus, when S 40 was decommissioned at Linz on 17 August 1942, the crew transferred to S 49 at the same time. The request by Group South for two new crews was not met because it meant recruiting from operational flotillas in the west. Only after the 1st S-boat Training Flotilla at Swinemünde was up and running was it possible to transfer three more boats (S 42, S 45 and S 46) to the Black Sea with their crews.[11]

Soviets on the Attack

The Soviet offensive that began at the end of November 1942 quickly expelled German forces from the Caucasus and reached the Sea of Azov. This cut off 17 Armee from the units at Rostov. On 17 December 1942, Hitler approved a retreat on the Kuban river to the Gothic Line. Troop concentrations in the Soviet-held Black Sea ports caused concern

In dock after receiving shell damage.

that landings were to be made in the German rear, and 1.SFltl. patrolled off the Taman Peninsula in January 1943 to repel such a move, as far as sea and ice conditions allowed. No enemy units were sighted. Landings occurred north and south of Novorossiysk on 4 February 1943. While the northern bridgehead was quickly overthrown by the Germans, the Soviets landed troops and equipment in the south near Cape Myshaka. Throughout February 1943, the flotilla's three operational boats worked to interfere with the flow of supplies to this point.

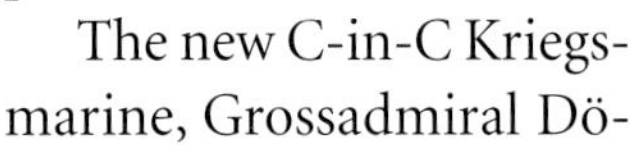

The new C-in-C Kriegsmarine, Grossadmiral Dönitz,[12] exhorted the men: 'The Eastern Front is locked in bitter fighting. Therefore even the most minor success by our naval forces is important. The most determined commitment is essential to help our comrades on the land front. Use every chance to get at the enemy.'[13]

In these operations, enemy vessels were sighted and torpedoes fired, but no hits were observed. Thus on the night of 17 February 1943, four torpedoes fired at a steamer all missed, as did six more aimed at a surfaced Soviet submarine on 23 February. The FdS, to whom the boats were subordinated in matters of personnel and administration, and who had jurisdiction over battle procedures and tactics, lamented the firing of torpedoes singly and ordered that the flotilla should attack in force and fire off salvoes of torpedoes or attack simultaneously from different bearings. The commanders, however, preferred to remain lone wolves in an extensive area of operations rather than operate in groups, as was usual in the Channel, particularly since boats were constantly in and out of the repair yards. Nevertheless, at the end of February 1943 they achieved successes and off the Caucasus coast they sank a minesweeper, a gunboat, a coaster and a tug.

Although the Luftwaffe had no machines available for anti-shipping raids close inshore, from March 1943 reconnaissance aircraft equipped with Lichtenstein radar flew over the sea area by night. In order to pass intelligence regarding enemy shipping to S-boats as quickly as possible, it was agreed between 1.SFltl. and the naval liaison officer (MVO) of VIII Fliegerkorps that aircraft would mark the convoy at once with parachute flares and report on the Luftwaffe contact-keeper frequency. The MVO would then pass the information to the Fliegerkorps command point for relay over the S-boat frequency. Aircraft would fire the second flare ahead of the convoy's course. As the Luftwaffe and S-boats had no access to each other's radio channels, it was proposed to install another receiver aboard the leader boat and *Rotte* boats so that the commanders could tune in to the tactical contact-keeper frequency.[14] By mid-April 1943 this system was in operation, but had limited success. A 6,000-ton tanker was tracked and sunk by a *Rotte*. On two occasions, the contact-keeper aircraft had to leave before the S-boats arrived and the boats could not find the convoy, while on two reconnaissance missions the aircraft failed to find any ships.

On 17 April 1943, the five operational boats of the strengthened flotilla moved to Anapa, together with R-boats and Italian MAS boats, from where it was hoped to maintain rolling support for the Army in its efforts to break down the defence south of Novorossiysk and finally capture the town. Admiral Black Sea had forwarded ammunition, fuel and additional medical support to Anapa, but no torpedoes were available there. For better firepower,

Hits on S 26.

in addition to the new 4cm gun aft, the S-boat armament had been increased by a 2cm and a Russian 1.3cm machine gun located above compartment I.[15]

Until the end of April 1943, the boats operated almost every night off Cape Myshaka, destroyed the landing moles with torpedoes, shelled the bridgehead and fought patrol boats and transports. Two Russian patrol boats were sunk, along with numerous freighters. Despite this naval support, the German Army was unable to improve on its initial successes and abandoned the attack at the end of the month.

As a result, the boats returned to Ivan Baba to resume the normal routine. The Soviet advance was now gaining momentum. Although Group South under Generalfeldmarschall von Manstein, by a castling of armies, gained the initiative and recaptured Kharkov in the northern sector, the front to the south shrank back to the river Mius and contact with the Kuban bridgehead was lost.[16]

Danger now threatened at many locations and Vizeadmiral Kieseritzky, Admiral Black Sea,[17] had to react vigorously. S-boats were now sailing reconnaissance into the Sea of Azov from Kerch, alternating with patrol work off Anapa, and operations off Novorossiysk and Tuapse. Only seldom did they sight traffic, always small coasters. Seven of these vessels were sunk in May 1943. All eight torpedoes fired at a Soviet cruiser and destroyer missed on account of the high sea running. As a rule, the boats were now being attacked by Soviet aircraft during the voyages out and back:

6 May 1943 – group consisting of S 51, S 52 and S 102 attacked by five Douglas Boston bombers; no hits, one aircraft shot down, two aircrew saved;

11 May 1943 – *Rotte* S 51 and S 26 attacked by ten SU-2s; no hits, one aircraft probably shot down;

12 May 1943 – seven SB2s and six PE2s attacked *Rotte* S 72 and S 49; about sixty bombs dropped, no hits;

20 May 1943 – eight to ten aircraft attacked *Rotte* S 72 and S 49 again; S 72 sustained fifteen hits and five wounded; S 49, 136 hits, one dead, three wounded; later, Me 110s provided protection;

29 May 1943 – air attack on *Rotte* S 52 and S 26; S 26 one dead, two wounded; German fighters flew from Anapa to give cover.

Even Ivan Baba itself was now attacked, an indication of the importance the Soviets attached to destroying the S-boat threat. On 21 April 1943, a Soviet submarine attempted to fire torpedoes into the harbour; these became entangled in the anti-torpedo

Ivan Baba harbour with torpedo netting.

wounded, the damage reducing 1.SFltl. to four serviceable boats. The Soviets were becoming more offensive in outlook and their MTBs had begun to tackle Axis convoys under the coast, so that 1.SFltl. occasionally supported 11.SFltl. in escort work to protect these im-portant supplies for the German Army.

For swift reaction to anticipated shelling of the coast by Soviet destroyers, Admiral Black Sea formulated a plan originating from the strategy of Rittmeister Zieten (1699–1786), in which, upon the arrival of enemy forces, S-boats would lay smoke under the coast and emerge at high speed with artillery support to surprise and overwhelm the attackers. The boats lay at immediate readiness for several days before standing down and resuming normal duties.[19] In the Sea of Azov and along the Caucasus coast in the summer months, no spectacular successes were expected against the ant-like traffic, although eight coasters, two gunboats and an MTB were sunk.

netting across the entrance. On 1 May 1943, Russian destroyers shelled the harbour, killing one man and inflicting light damage.

Throughout the summer of 1943, S-boats continued their activities across a broad spectrum. On 20 May 1943, the seven remaining Italian MAS boats were taken over by the Kriegsmarine, renumbered S 501 to S 507 inclusive and formed into 11.SFltl. From Feodosiya, they sailed mainly coastal reconnaissance, provided an escort for Axis convoys along the Crimean coast to the Taman Peninsula or performed anti-submarine duty. Because of their worn-out machinery, they were rarely used on torpedo operations and their fighting value was low.[18]

From June 1943, 1.SFltl. had seven boats available after three new arrivals with fresh crews, but instead of concentrated work against Soviet shipping the boats were divided to operate either in the Sea of Azov against Soviet landings in Temriuk Bay or the supply routes off Novorossiysk and Tuapse. Returning from a mission south of the Kerch Strait on 8 July 1943, S 102 was mined and had to be scuttled. Eight men were lost.

Air attacks continued, claiming dead and

On the Defensive

In the late summer, the Soviet Army began to surround the Sea of Azov. On 28 August 1943, Führer HQ ordered: 'Situation requires urgently immediate naval support for southern sector, Mius Front. Führer has therefore ordered that all available artillery lighters, R-boats and S-boats are to proceed for operations into the Sea of Azov.'[20]

S-boats returning from a mission near Tuapse on the night of 28 August were attacked and damaged by aircraft, leaving only four able to comply with the Führer's order. They spent several nights patrolling the Sea of Azov and sank a gunboat; nothing else was about.

After a call at Ivan Baba, the flotilla proceeded to

Ilyushin Il 2 armoured fighter-bomber.

the Caucasian coast, where the Soviets had opened an offensive against the Gothic Line. On 1 September 1943, 1.SFltl. lost S 46, its third casualty, when eight to ten Il 2 fighter-bombers made a surprise swoop on the column of four S-boats, concentrating on S 46 at the rear. Her engines stopped, the starboard torpedo exploded and tore off the forecastle. After one dead and two wounded had been shipped aboard S 49, the wreck was scuttled. German fighters took off immediately upon receiving the alarm but did not arrive over the flotilla until the attack had finished. The Luftwaffe was not able to offer permanent air cover for lack of aircraft, but co-operation was good: S-boat commanders flew on air operations while flight-leaders shipped aboard S-boats to gain an impression of operations and better estimate what was necessary. As a result a common signal code was devised and agreed for shorter and more precise exchange of information.

The situation ashore had continued to deteriorate. The Soviet North Caucasian Front was beginning slowly to bring intolerable pressure on the Kuban bridgehead. 17 Armee received permission to retreat and ship out men, weapons and equipment. These transports had to be protected. After Anapa fell, on 21 September, the Soviets used the harbour as a base against the German convoys. Weather permitting, they were opposed by 1.SFltl. (Kapitänleutnant Büchting).[21] On the night of 27 September, 1.SFltl. sank an ammunition ship and two minesweepers, and damaged another two vessels. Co-operation with the Luftwaffe paid off when aircraft parachute flares lit up Anapa so brightly that the boats could easily pick out their targets. A short while later, further such co-operation resulted in a major naval victory when two groups of S-boats, one on escort duty, the other coming out from Constanta, fought a delaying action with three Soviet destroyers, luring them towards the Crimea. Stukas of I Fliegerkorps intended for other missions were quickly bombed up and sent out at dawn to attack the destroyers, sinking all three. After this debacle, the Soviet leadership ruled that all future operations by larger units required their approval beforehand.[22]

At the beginning of October 1943, 11.SFltl. of former MAS boats was disbanded, the boats decommissioned and towed to Linz for major refits.[23] This left 1.SFltl. alone in the Black Sea, supported only by R-boats and artillery lighters to protect the withdrawal of 17 Armee, provide distant escort to convoys, attack Anapa and patrol off the southern entrance to the Strait of Kerch. On 9 October 1943, the retreat to the Crimea, Operation 'Brunhild', was completed. On 21 October, the Soviets were repulsed when attempting landings at Kerch. Romanian troops reported other landings at 36°E, but when 1.SFltl.

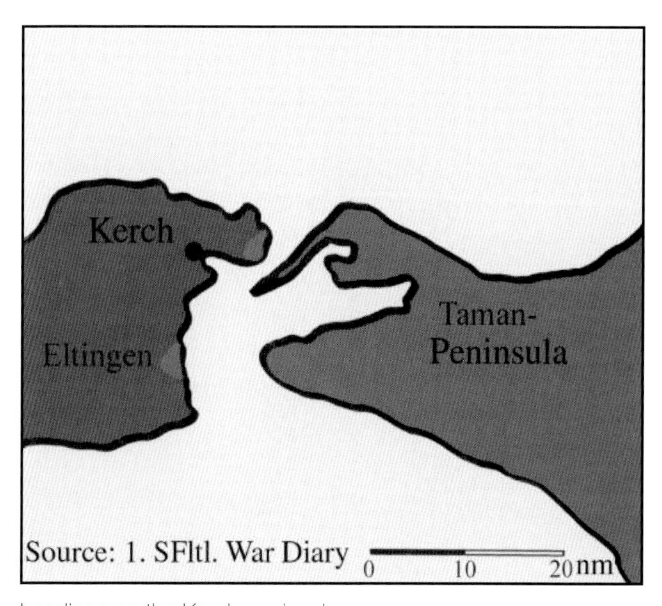

Landings on the Kerch peninsula.

attended, it found nothing, this being later confirmed as a false alarm.

The next evening, the boats patrolled again off the supposed landing beaches, acting under orders from Admiral Black Sea in which, 'All vessels, including more powerful groups of commando boats and other enemies found in the areas threatened with landings along the Crimean coast, are to be attacked without regard to conditions of visibility or armament.'[24] This 'final' operation had been ordered in terms that showed clearly how the situation in the Crimea was being viewed, and also the Führer's nervousness. Nothing was seen, however, and the flotilla resumed its activities against enemy shipping around Anapa. When unnecessary personnel and materials were despatched to Constanta, the column was recalled the next day, 31 October 1943, by Admiral Black Sea. In response to the flotilla commander's suggestion of relocating the main base at Sevastopol, using Ivan Baba only as a jumping-off point, the admiral retorted, 'The Crimea is to be held with everything available. No allurements or transfers are envisaged.'[25] A request four days later for a number of boats to return for scheduled engine overhaul was refused. The Führer and C-in-C Kriegsmarine had ordered the Crimea to be held, and nobody in the intermediate command levels would stray very far from that.[26]

The Soviets made further landings at the beginning of October. At the narrowest place in the Strait of Kerch, they could not be dislodged but, in close co-operation with R-boats, the S-boat flotilla attacked the second bridgehead at Eltingen, sinking several ships and landing craft. This denied Soviet troops ashore necessary supplies, enabling 17 Armee to destroy the bridgehead.[27]

On 8 November 1943, the extremely stretched situation in the Crimea prompted SKL to schedule another three S-boats for the Black Sea. While the FdS recommended used boats, SKL chose the new models S 131, S 148 and S 149. This proved unwise later, when important parts were found to be missing during reassembly work at Constanta. Standard spare parts would not fit and special mountings had to be sent for. This was the sort of problem that would normally have been ironed out by the New-Warship Testing Command (EKK).[28]

The German and Soviet navies were now hindered by the onset of winter storms. From the end of November 1943 to the beginning of February 1944, twelve sorties were sailed against the Caucasus coast, including a minelaying operation off Tuapse. No enemy ships were seen. Since the Soviets were now running their coastal shipping by day in the absence of the Luftwaffe, S-boat sorties by night were a waste of time. As it was essential to cut engine-hours for the anticipated final battle for the Crimea, in February and March 1944 only three operations were sailed. Two gunboats were sighted, but otherwise the seas were empty.

Meanwhile, Ivan Baba was receiving frequent air raids. Almost regularly every day between 0830 and 1000 hrs, a formation of bombers and fighter-bombers would fly in from seaward, cross the narrow spit of land and bomb the base and boats. Often a second attack would follow between 1300 and 1400 hrs. Although many aircraft fell victim to the well-positioned flak, the Russians persisted stoically. Initially they improvised 17.2cm shells as bombs, inflicting minor injuries and light damage to buildings. In March their aim improved and two boats required repair at Constanta. Splinter damage was handled at Ivan Baba. Losses in personnel also rose. German fighters were no longer available for defence.

Evacuating the Crimea

On 8 April 1944, the North Ukraine Front began its long expected push over the Perikop Narrows. Two days later, they had regained such vast tracts of territory that at 1125 hrs on 10 April, 17 Armee issued codeword '*Adler*' to commence the planned evacuation of the Crimea.[29] Under this plan, Ivan Baba was to be abandoned on X-Day+2, ie 12 April. At midday on 10 April, Hitler rescinded Adler and ordered the front held; only the Kerch Peninsula was to be evacuated.[30]

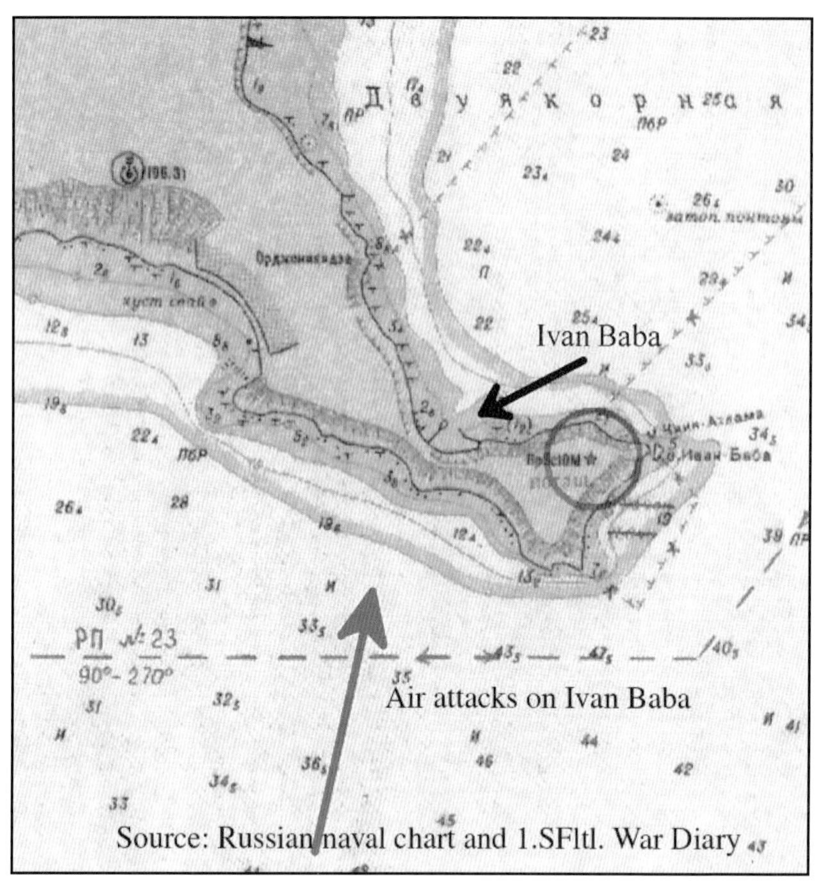

Air attacks on Ivan Baba.

Despite the Soviet advance, Hitler insisted that Sevastopol be held:

> According to the personal instruction of the Führer to the ObdM [Dönitz] that the bridgehead Crimea–Sevastopol is to be held, the Navy has to commit itself fully to this task. Work together closely and energetically with the Army so that adequate stocks of anti-tank weapons, ammunition and provisions can be brought in.[32]

For the S-boats this was nothing new. Every night – bar the three occasions when it was impossible because of heavy weather – they protected convoys against Russian MTBs and were always successful in driving them off. The flotilla was operational with ten boats, having received three recent additions. Minor damage and engine breakdowns were repaired at Constanta so that operational readiness was never less than ten. By the end of April 1944, more than 80,000 persons had been brought out and 1,100 fighting troops supplied to Sevastopol.[33] Meanwhile Balaclava had been abandoned and the S-boats stationed there joined the Sevastopol group.

The Soviets rolled forward and Adler was reactivated on 12 April by Army Group South Ukraine. After countermanding it again, on 13 April Hitler decided that there should be no general evacuation of the Crimea as proposed by Adler, but that the Gneisenau Line was to be held at Sevastopol, although personnel and material not essential to the defence could leave.[31] Ivan Baba could now be evacuated. The order had been anticipated and the most important special equipment and tools were already on boats heading for Constanta. What remained to be done was to destroy the important harbour installations before the personnel set out along the road to Sevastopol. The boats had moved back to Sevastopol or Balaclava two days earlier. From there, they were at sea each night, the Balaclava boats securing the Axis convoy route from Yalta, while the Sevastopol group covered the sea lanes to Constanta.

From 4 May, the enemy had the port within artillery range and the encirclement was tightened to bring the guns closer. Air attacks on the city and port followed, and three days later the boats moved to Kamshevaya Bay, south of Sevastopol. Although subjected to artillery and air attack here, necessitating constant changes of anchorage, they maintained their escort roles by night, keeping enemy MTBs at a distance.

Finally, on 9 May, permission was received to evacuate Sevastopol. The German Navy mobilised everything that floated and could transport cargo. A co-ordinated evacuation was no longer possible because the docks at Sevastopol were under permanent bombardment. Transports sank, others sailed only half-full, others again fell victim to Soviet aircraft, while bad weather made sea voyages difficult for smaller vessels.

> Situation slipping towards catastrophe. Unauthorised departure 'Patria' and delay in arrivals of convoys for bad weather is forcing Army to delay 24 hours. Because of lack of ammunition, condition of men and also enemy air supremacy, this means almost certain destruction of major part of force if substantial shipping space does not arrive at the last minute. (Radiogram, Naval Commandant Crimea, 1412 hrs, 10 May 1944)

In view of the situation, 1.SFltl. set aside escort work to concentrate on the evacuation. The flotilla organisation was dissolved. As soon as boats were full, they sailed for Constanta, disembarked passengers and equipment, refuelled and sailed back. Despite air attack and artillery bombardment, they took everybody they could, including the C-in-C 17 Armee and the Naval Commandant, Crimea, who then directed embarkations from S 149. Air attacks were a permanent feature; the Luftwaffe had only four Me 110s available over Sevastopol. This was not enough and losses continued to rise.

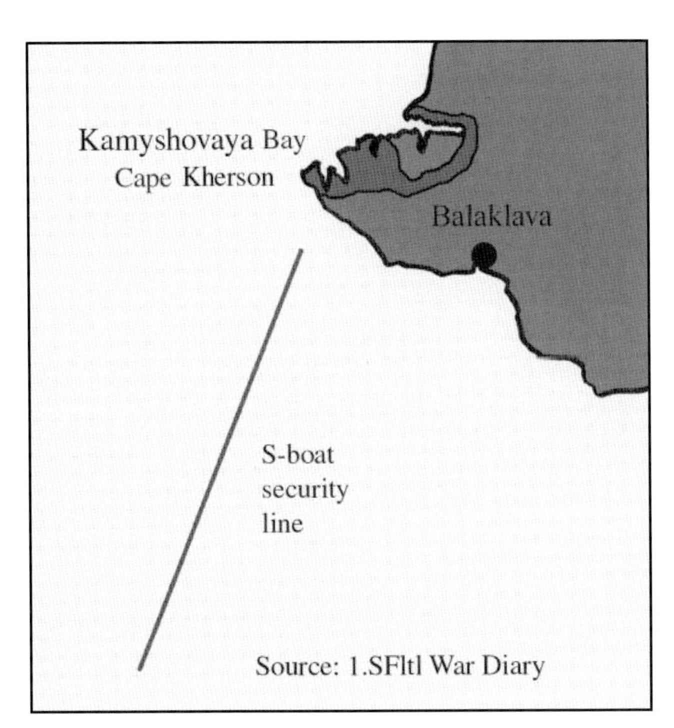

Evacuation of Sevastopol.

> Embarkation under the heaviest enemy attack by fighter-bombers, bombers and artillery, practically without reply on our side. 'Romania' burning, 'Tissa' sunk. Where are our long-range fighters? (Radiogram, Naval Commandant Crimea, 0934 hrs, 1 May 1944)

On 12 May, Sevastopol fell and the fate of 20,000 German soldiers remained uncertain. On the night of 13 May, a few dispersed groups were picked up by S-boats at Cape Kherson, and on subsequent nights they searched the bays near Sevastopol in the hope of finding more survivors. It was in vain: empty floats and numerous drifting corpses supported by life jackets bore mute testimony to the tragedy. On 16 May 1944, the last three S-boats made fast at Constanta after five weeks of unremitting operations. The following numbers of survivors were picked up by individual boats of 1.SFltl. in that period:

S 28 (Leutnant zur See Neumeier) – 128
S 40 (Oberleutnant zur See Weisheit) – 51
S 42 (Oberleutnant zur See Mohs) – 150
S 47 (Leutnant zur See Behrens) – 95
S 49 (Oberleutnant zur See Richter) – 135
S 52 (Kapitänleutnant Seevers) – 81
S 72 (Oberleutnant zur See Deckert) – 217
S 131 (Stabsobersteuermann Neumann) – 130
S 148 (Oberleutnant zur See von Dülong) – 165
S 149 (Oberleutnant zur See Wülfing) – 113
Total 1,265, of which one-third were wounded, and including two women and one child.[34]

In the Trap

Until the end of May 1944 the crews rested. The boats were repaired, engines overhauled. Subsequently, activities were scanty. In June, two sorties were sailed in the search for enemy shipping off Sevastopol and Yalta but nothing was found. Fuel shortages then restricted operations, which could only be allowed against targets identified by reconnaissance, and these were few, since the Soviet fleet rarely ventured anywhere. But their landfront advanced. To retire the S-boats through the Danube could not be entertained politically, for tremendous efforts were being made to sweeten the Romanians for their oil. Another two boats were thus sent down from Germany; these and two others were to be donated to Romania.

As events in the Black Sea came to a head, on 8 August 1944 S 86 and S 89 left Linz. On 19 August, while attacking Soviet units, three boats at Sulina, S 26, S 40 and S 72, were sunk, a fourth boat seriously damaged, during an air raid. Dead and wounded resulted. On 20 August, more air raids followed against Sulina and Constanta. Thirty to thirty-five bombers with fighter cover attacked the port in four waves without warning and sank numerous vessels, including S 42, S 52 and S 131. Two other boats were seriously damaged. On 21 August, S 148 was mined and sunk off Sulina. On 23 August 1944, Romania changed sides and on 25 August, after German aircraft bombed Bucharest, Romania declared war on Germany. At 1700 hrs that day, the serviceable German units left for Varna, the last open port in Bulgaria. S 28 and S 149, already damaged, were scuttled. On 26 August, Bulgaria left the Axis and declared neutrality. In order to avoid internment under the 72-hour rule, the last boats, S 45, S 47, S 49 and S 51, left Varna on 29 August 1944 to scuttle outside the harbour.[35] The crews became adventurers, heading for home through the now hostile Balkans. Most made it. The last two boats on the way to the Black Sea reversed course on 28 August and moored at Linz on 21 September 1944.[36]

Thus ended S-boat operations in the Black Sea. It was a theatre of war in which the boats had supported the land front for two years, a battle against a stubborn enemy, special weather conditions, involving long runs between shore bases and operational zones that demanded outstanding seamanship. S-boats caused no rethinking of strategy, and their sinkings were modest, but they tied down substantial enemy forces and often kept them at a safe distance from the fighting. Lacking adequate air cover, they succumbed gradually one by one to enemy air attacks until – linked to the fate of the German Army ashore, sitting in a trap with no way out – the crews were forced to scuttle their boats and head for home on foot.

11
The Invasion
June – August 1944

At conferences in Washington and Casablanca in 1943, Roosevelt and Churchill had set out the guidelines for the continuation of the war in Europe. This was not a simple matter. Churchill was primarily in favour of securing the perimeter and then moving in on the Reich slowly through Italy, the Balkans and possibly Norway. Roosevelt argued for an early leap from England to the occupied mainland with a view to an earlier end to the war.[1] Eventually Roosevelt's choice prevailed and in August 1943 the Allied Planning Staff that had been set up to plan the invasion began its first deliberations. The main bridgehead was to be Caen, fed through several Channel beaches simultaneously. Initially, supply was to be shipped through artificially created ports, fuel through a submarine pipeline. After this operation was successfully concluded, there would be a second invasion in the south of France, so that the country would be liberated by drives from north and south, after which the Allied forces would turn east to strike at the Ruhr and so rob Germany of her last sources of energy.[2]

From the autumn of 1943, the Germans had thought it likely that there would be a major invasion from England, although the target area remained unclear. SKL had long expected the attack to come in southern France,[3] and the Army did not at first believe that the Channel coast could be the objective. It was an open question as to whether the Allies would launch a single major invasion or several smaller landings. The Germans were certain, however, that the most effective defences possible were essential, for nobody doubted for a moment that the invasion would be of decisive significance for the outcome of the war, although the conviction was not reflected by the High Commands' organisation or conceptions about the defences.[4]

France, Belgium and the Netherlands were theatres of war controlled by OKW, but the competent C-in-C West, Generalfeldmarschall von Rundstedt, had only limited authority over the Luftwaffe (Luftflotte 3, General Sperrle) and the Kriegsmarine (Group West, Admiral Krancke). The latter leaders were directly responsible to their respective High Commands, both of which kept a jealous watch on their independence and resisted with vigour all attempts to introduce exterior influences. In addition there were the Wehrmacht C-in-C for France and the Netherlands, leaders of the Waffen-SS units and Generalfeldmarschall Rommel in his dual role as head of the invasion defences and also C-in-C Army Group B, subordinate to von Rundstedt.[5]

Rommel believed that German forces in the west could not repel an invasion attempt because of Allied naval and air superiority, and he therefore stationed reserves along the Channel front in order to strike at the enemy before the landings could properly deploy. The commander of the German armoured divisions, General Geyr von Schweppenburg, favoured keeping combined operational reserves to the rear but poised for a massive thrust against the strongpoint of the enemy offensive once it became known. Even in the face of Allied air superiority, he believed that free operational movement would be possible. Von Rundstedt inclined towards von Schweppenburg's view but could not fully rule out the logical argument of the battle-experienced Rommel, and thus a compromise was worked out in which three reserve panzer divisions would be placed at the Channel coast, plus three more in the south of France, and three panzer divisions plus a motorised panzer-grenadier division would remain as the operational reserve.[6]

Parallel to this panzer controversy, the Army and Navy fought amongst themselves over coastal artillery. The Kriegsmarine emerged victorious; firing at shipping was obviously a maritime task. Once the enemy was ashore, overall control of the coastal guns would pass to the Army. Thus there was a mixture of army and naval artillery units on the coast, directed independently.[7] This was sensible so long as the security of German coastal convoys was the principal consideration, but it was quite inadequate for defence against invasion.

The Luftwaffe, lacking any reserves, had a plan to move its forces to reserve airfields and bring up its flak units.[8] Because of the stretched situation everywhere, the Kriegsmarine had no further units available for duty in the Channel. Requests by Group West for the transfer of torpedo boats and an S-flotilla from the Baltic were turned down in May 1944.[9] The naval preparations were concentrated on expanding the coastal artillery ashore and preparing at short notice to sow *Blitzsperren*, minefields to be laid as the occasion demanded. Besides this work, known gaps in the Channel fields were to be closed and other mine barriers laid between the main belt of minefields and the German coastal lanes. The '*Landwirt*' ('farmer') U-boat pack remained in reserve at Brest, while S-boats had orders to augment their armament.[10]

In his capacity as Inspector of Defence Measures, Rommel worked energetically to upgrade those sectors of coast thought likely to be subject to landings. He had built gun emplacements and beach and coastal fortifications, prepared stakes fitted with explosive charges (the so-called 'Rommel asparagus') in areas suitable for paratroop landings, co-ordinated alarm measures between the Army units and persevered in his attempts to bring all reserves to the coast.[11]

Rommel was not convinced that the *Blitzsperren* could be laid in time, and opposed the conviction of Group West that both the time and place of the landings would be known sufficiently in advance to allow the mine barriers to be sown successfully. The source of Group West's confidence is difficult to establish, for the Luftwaffe had for some time not been in a position to fly regular reconnaissance over the English south coast, and the S-boats could not guarantee the provision of timely information. If they met a landing force, they would have been driven off by its escorts and pursued. They would merely have reported a meeting with enemy destroyers and being driven off by them, but such a report would be treated as mundane and would not give rise to suspicions that an invasion of the mainland was under way.[12]

SKL accepted Rommel's argument and, at the end of April 1944, ordered a section of *Blitzsperre* to be laid in the Scheldt estuary, south of Boulogne, and between Cherbourg and Brest. This was against the advice of Group West, which feared a rapid deterioration of the mines in the tidal waters of the landing zones. More mines were laid in Seine Bay, on both sides of the Marcouf beaches, the later Utah beach.[13]

Since the question of where and when one or more landings would occur preoccupied the German commanders in the west in 1944, synchronising countermeasures rather faded into the background. Rommel's concerns about Allied air and naval superiority in the event of invasion were not addressed by any of the three Wehrmacht services. Thus no overall plan was devised nor any agreement reached on co-operation in combining the available German forces so as to offer some kind of limited superior opposition to the invader when he came, if only somewhere and some time. The nebulous idea that air and naval reconnaissance would provide clear advance warning of an approaching enemy invasion armada and give time to put in place the first defensive measures, and bring up the reserves, dominated German thinking.

The Army therefore concentrated on how they would repulse the invader once he was ashore, while the Navy did not believe an invasion could be repelled. The extent to which they did not believe in combining forces was made clear in a Group West war game on 12 April 1944 respecting the operation of naval forces in the event of invasion, attended by the most senior commanders and chiefs. Adhering slavishly to previous thinking, the main preoccupation was not co-operation, nor joining forces, but rather to ensure that 'individual flotillas have freedom to manoeuvre so that in the event of invasion those flotillas at sea do not meet up with each other'.[14]

Moreover, they were counting on fourteen days' warning before the invasion fleet sailed, during which time, together with the Luftwaffe, they would be able to sow the British invasion ports with the new pressure mine and so make substantial inroads into the invasion force. When SKL refused permission for this minelaying activity at the beginning of May 1944 for fear of having the weapon compromised prematurely, Group West decided instead to mine the British convoy routes with old mines. In mid-May they learnt that the Luftwaffe would not be taking part in the common minelaying offensive, and all further efforts to convince the Luftwaffe otherwise failed because 'the task of mining English coastal routes does not lie with IX Korps'.[15] And that was final.

These multifarious organisations and concepts stood in stark contrast to the clear leadership and unequivocal operational plan of the Allies. Eisenhower was C-in-C of the Allied Expeditionary Force. His mission was set out in classic tactical terms: 'You are to land on the European continent and in common with other United Nations carry out operations towards the heartland of Germany and destroy its armed forces.'[16] To accomplish this, he had full power of command, and the commanders of the land, air and naval forces were all subordinated to him unconditionally. Because of their special importance, special staffs had been set up for the artificial harbours and the submarine oil pipeline, but the respective leaders obeyed Eisenhower.

The invasion forces had been in the process of building without interruption since the autumn of 1943. The original sailing date of 1 May 1944 had been postponed to allow for a further month's production of landing craft, and after the landings in Sicily and at Salerno the boats and ships no longer required there returned to England. The demand was so great that the loss of three landing ships by the 5th and 9th S-boat Flotilla attack of 27 April 1944 in Lyme Bay exhausted the reserves completely. Every additional loss would have led to a reduction in the transport space or a further postponement.[17]

For the landings themselves, the following conditions applied: bright moonlight, so that the airborne divisions could foregather and reach their objectives before sunrise; early morning, to provide visibility for air attacks and naval gunnery; rising tide, so that naval frogmen could find submerged obstacles, and to allow landing craft to unload and then withdraw. As high tide approached, the subsequent waves would have less beach to cover.[18] All these conditions were met approximately three days each month – in June 1944 on the 5th, 6th and 7th. Eisenhower thus selected 5 June for the landings between 0630 and 0735 hrs, depending on the individual beach. For the first attack, there would be three airborne landings plus two US and three British divisions invading five stretches of beach.

Despite their clear supremacy at sea and in the air, the Allies regarded with some misgivings the strongly fortified continent and the six German divisions stationed along the intended landing zones. They appreciated the fact that the winner would be the side that succeeded in bringing up its reinforcements faster, so turning the relationship of forces in its own favour. It was therefore essential to keep the Germans in the dark as long as possible as to where the landings would actually take place. For this purpose, a comprehensive and widespread deception was practised, while pinpoint air attacks destroyed the communications network to the rear of the planned landing zone in order to complicate the bringing up of German reinforcements. Luftflotte 3 drew the correct conclusion and indicated the area between Cherbourg and Le Havre as the probable invasion zone. The Kriegsmarine also noted the concentration but ignored the implications. Even the sinking of the three landing craft in Lyme Bay on 27 April had not led them to suppose a connection between the practice beach and the possible invasion zone. Because the Luftwaffe and Kriegsmarine conducted their own reconnaissance and evaluated it separately, and neither sought contact with the other, there was no consolidated opinion. The pointers were either overlooked or not pursued. Thus the question of where the landings would come remained open.[19]

Landings and the First Line of Defence

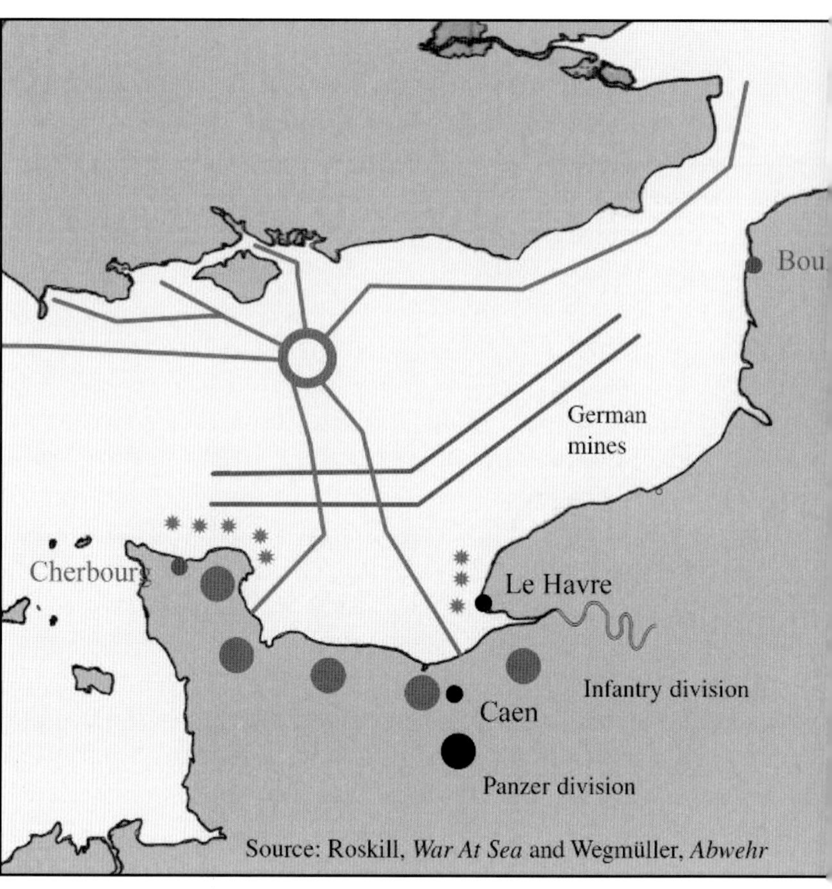

The Allied attack.

On 2 June 1944, the first ships of the invasion fleet left their far-flung ports for the northern Channel coast. The previous evening, Abwehr heard the BBC broadcast the first line of Paul Verlaine's 'Autumn Song' ('The endless sighing of autumn violins . . . '), which, according to their intelligence, was to advise the French Resistance movement of the imminent invasion. No alarm was raised and nothing happened, for a sudden low-pressure system forced an interruption. Eisenhower brought to a halt the complicated machinery, turning or ordering to heave-to the great operational units at sea – and all without dropping a hint to the ever-watchful German B-Dienst. When the meteorologists reported an intermittent period of high pressure with a temporary drop in wind strength, at 0415 hrs on 5 June 1944 Eisenhower gave the order, 'OK. We'll go.'[20]

Four thousand landing craft with the troops and equipment of five infantry divisions, escorted by over 900 warships, including 6 battleships, 23 cruisers and 100 destroyers, now headed for the French coast. More than 200 minesweepers cleared eight lanes through the German mined belt, for each landing beach one lane for slow and another for fast convoys. The Coastal Forces protected the flanks and laid mines off Cherbourg and Le Havre. The brief spell of calmer weather had escaped the attention of the Germans because their weather station '*Schatzgräber*' ('treasure seeker') on Greenland had been evacuated at the beginning of the month and no weather U-boat had arrived in the area.[21] Therefore on the afternoon of 5 June, Admiral Krancke considered an invasion 'on the night of 5 June in Holland and on the Channel coast unlikely'.[22] Dönitz went on leave, Rommel returned to Germany on service business, the patrol boats stayed in port. Even when the second line of 'Autumn Song' (' . . . wounds my heart with endless yearning . . . ') was broadcast by the BBC that evening, it was interpreted as a further preliminary indication of imminent invasion, not as the starting signal.[23]

The first reports of paratroop landings were received at 0015 on 6 June 1944. An hour later, 7 Armee and 15 Armee raised their state of alert to Alarm Stage II, followed by Group West at 0130 hrs and Luftflotte 3 at 0210 hrs. After radar reports of unidentified units near the coast at 0410, C-in-C West raised the general alarm in his area of jurisdiction two hours before the first landings and ordered the reserve panzers to immediate readiness.[24] The landings did not find the Army asleep but strategic surprise had been won, and thus the war now entered its decisive phase.

Although SKL decided the same day 'that the possibility of this actually being the great decisive undertaking against western Europe does not enter into question',[25] C-in-C West and Admiral Krancke hesitated. Was the enemy really attempting to invade at a place that had no major port in the vicinity or was the whole thing a massive diversion to tie down forces and mislead the Germans as to the true bridgehead? For this reason, von Rundstedt held back his reserve panzers while Krancke ordered the laying of *Blitzsperren* off selected beaches from Le Havre to the Scheldt and reinforced his coastal patrols. At the same time, the four destroyers on the Biscay coast left for the Channel, while SKL ordered the *Landwirt* U-boat pack out of Brest.

At this point the S-boat flotillas were dispersed as follows: 5. and 9.SFltl. – Cherbourg, 4.SFltl. – Boulogne, 2.SFltl. – Ostend, 8.SFltl. – Ijmuiden. On the morning of the invasion, at the raising of the alarm, the two flotillas at Cherbourg sailed north-west and north-east respectively but broke off the search at dawn, having found nothing but empty sea. The 5th Torpedo Boat Flotilla, which left Le Havre at the same time, ran into the flank of the Allied force and sank the Norwegian destroyer *Svenner* with torpedoes before withdrawing behind a smoke screen.

By the end of the first day, the Allies had taken all five beach sectors (US – Utah and Omaha, British – Gold, Juno and Sword). The well-directed fire of the battleships, cruisers and destroyers[26] paved the way for the troop landings, the air forces sealed off the battle region, constant fighter patrols dominated the air space. Only rarely did the Luftwaffe reach the landing zones to support the Army units; their chances of success were few. The Luftwaffe flew 319 sorties, the Allies 14,674 – an oppressive superiority.[27]

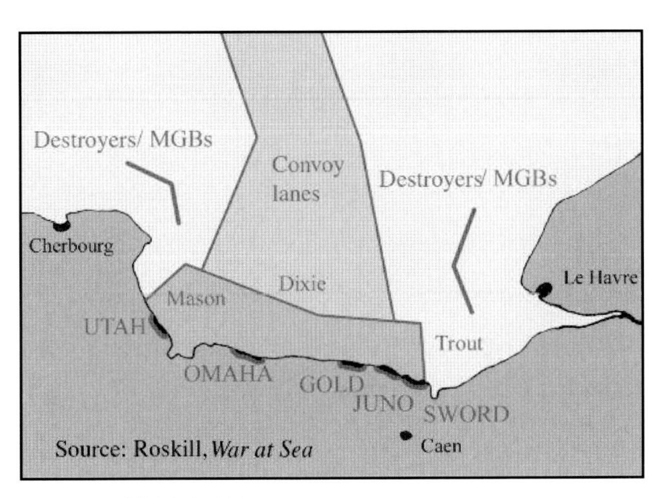

The area of the landings.

When night fell, the heavy ships withdrew to more secure positions offshore. Destroyers and smaller escort craft took over protection duties along the lines Mason, Dixie and Trout,[28] while the convoy routes, along which continuous supply convoys were now passing, were protected by destroyers and Coastal Forces (MGBs/MTBs). These vessels were not directed by the commanders of the landing areas, but by Naval Command Portsmouth, along with all other escort vessels.

On the German side, during 6 June the belief had set in that the Allied invasion was concentrated on the Seine Bay, but suspicion remained that it might be a feint. On the night of 6 June, therefore, Group West ordered 5. and 9.SFltl. from the western Channel and the 5th Torpedo Boat Flotilla from the eastern Channel to attack the landing force. The 2nd, 4th and 8th S-Boat Flotillas were to keep watch on the coasts fronting Boulogne, Ostend and Ijmuiden respectively. The other coastal security units were to lay *Blitzsperren* off Le Havre, either side of Dieppe and south of Boulogne.

This was by no means the concentration of forces in the opening phase of the landings that Rommel had demanded persistently and which might perhaps have provided the opportunity to break down the Allied superiority at a still-critical stage.

The thirty-six *Landwirt* U-boats were split up by SKL so that nineteen formed a security line to oppose possible landings on the French Atlantic coast, while the other seventeen now became the '*Holzbein*' ('wooden leg') group in the Channel (including eight snorkel boats). On the night after sailing, they came in for heavy air attack, since the Allies monitored the entire Channel by radar. Six U-boats were forced to retire to Brest in a damaged condition. On the morning of 7 June, they were joined there by the three destroyers of the 8th Destroyer Flotilla from Royan in the Gironde estuary, and the torpedo boat T 24, all of which had been attacked from the air but sustained no major damage. The 5th Torpedo Boat Flotilla returned to Le Havre with nothing to report, but 5. and 9.SFltl. from Cherbourg had run into convoy traffic. Both flotillas fired off torpedoes at the escort destroyers and landing ships without scoring a hit, and on the run home S 139 and S 140 were mined and sunk in the Greengage minefield laid by the Allies shortly before the landings. 'S-boat successes at the present time are not satisfactory,' Admiral Krancke noted, and instructed the FdS 'by telephone to engage the S-boats fully against the invasion fleet'.[29]

The German divisions had begun their counter-attack on land. The 21st Panzer Division, stationed near the coast, split the British bridgehead and pushed through to the sea. Here it received heavy fire from the battleships and heavy cruisers offshore and was forced to pull back under air attacks. The Luftwaffe, intimidated by the oppressive enemy air superiority, could offer no help. 'Enemy forces on the English coast make further major operations on other sections of the coast seem probable,'[30] Group West recorded, and ordered more *Blitzsperren* laid. While 8.SFltl. remained on coast watch at Ijmuiden, 4.SFltl. moved from Boulogne to Le Havre to help oppose the invasion fleet, and 2.SFltl. occupied Boulogne from Ostend.

As on the previous night, 5. and 9.SFltl. sortied from the west to attack landing craft in the Seine. The 4th S-boat Flotilla and 5th Torpedo Boat Flotilla were to join forces. While the torpedo boats kept watch, 4.SFltl. headed north and found a supply convoy. Torpedoes were fired, several hits were obtained and two armoured landing ships (LSTs) were sunk.

On the other side of Seine, 5. and 9.SFltl. made skilful use of the now charted Greengage minefield, which was restricting Allied shipping in its movements. The 9th S-boat Flotilla got through the ring of escorts, fired four torpedoes and sank two smaller landing craft. The 5th S-boat Flotilla engaged a squadron of warships and fired torpedoes at cruisers and destroyers. The US Fleet destroyer *Meredith* was hit and sank the next morning. In his appraisal, Petersen, while welcoming the results and raising the spirits of the flotilla chiefs and commanders, added a note of caution that 'the enemy defensive system is not yet fully in play . . . and in the framework of the landing fleet, numerous new British and, particularly, American units, have been deployed which lack experience of the Channel . . . so that the recent successes should not be overestimated when considering the prospects for future operations.'[31]

Further Actions

On the night of 8 June, S-boats changed to operations in which the daytime positions of the battleships were to be mined to cut back the naval bombardment of German land positions. It was unsuccessful, for during the night Ultra decoded the instructions so that the area was avoided and then swept.[32] This always happened when orders were passed by encoded radio signal instead of telex.

> MOST SECRET – IMMEDIATE – A.M. 081317B para. 5th and 9th E boat flotillas have been ordered to lay mines in area bounded by 49 deg. 30 min. N, 49 deg. 36 min. N 01 deg. 00 min W, 01 deg. 10 min. W which is used by battleships by day for shelling the coast. They are to concentrate on the south-westerly corner of this area but are not to lay where depth of water exceeds 25 metres. On outward passage they are only to attack worthwhile torpedo targets and are to enter Cherbourg at dawn with freedom to attack on return passage. (Ultra message, 8 June 1944)

The same night, two of the remaining *Holzbein* U-boats were sunk, two others damaged; others again fired off all their torpedoes at U-hunter groups. Of the seven survivors, the five snorkel boats were ordered back into the Channel on 9 June; the two non-snorkel boats were sent back because of heavy enemy air presence, but were lost on the way.

Steam gunboat (SGB) involved in security duty.

The same day, four other snorkel boats heading out into the Atlantic were recalled for the Channel. While at least some U-boats got through, the Allies were informed of all intentions, including those of the German destroyer group moving from Brest to Cherbourg, by decoding their radio transmissions. At 1230 hrs on 8 June, Ultra advised that the destroyers were to sail that night. At 1405 hrs, it reported that they would leave Brest at 1830 hrs, head for Cherbourg at twenty-four knots and make port at 0500 hrs. Further details followed at 1505, 2017 and 2028 hrs.[33] It was therefore a simple matter to keep the German destroyers under aerial observation until Force 26 with its eight destroyers ambushed them. Z32 and ZH1 were sunk early on 9 June; Z24 and T 24 got back to Brest.

Only S-boats and torpedo boats now remained in the vicinity of the invasion fleet. On 9 June, they repeated the operation of the previous night. 5. and 9.SFltl. were unable to penetrate the security ring and stood off Cape Barfleur, east of Cherbourg. The 4th S-boat Flotilla came up from Le Havre, mined the convoy route, found a supply convoy and sank a large submersible section of Mulberry harbour that the Allies were setting up off Omaha and Gold beaches. The 2nd S-boat Flotilla, ordered provisionally to Cherbourg, was unable to get through and put into Le Havre. The torpedo boats fired eighteen torpedoes but were also unable to breach the concentrated ring of destroyers, MGBs and fighter-bombers.

Supplies at Le Havre were now scarce. It was not an S-boat base and had neither a torpedo arsenal nor an adjustment workshop. The difficult transport situation ruled out any continuity of supply. Those torpedoes that did arrive needed major adjustment, which could only be done on an improvised basis. The 4th S-boat Flotilla had only thirteen torpedoes available for the coming operation. Only 2.SFltl. had a full stock. The 4th Flotilla boats therefore had to sail to Boulogne to load, the passage and the short nights making severe cuts in their time spent in the

Artillery lighter.

operational area. Petersen was visibly impressed by the claimed sinkings to date: 'S-boat successes against invasion fleet first class! Special recognition for sinking the cruiser. Keep at it! Now you have plenty of targets – at them!'[34] And the boats responded. On the night of 10 June, 5. and 9.SFltl. coming from Cherbourg broke through the security ring and fired torpedoes at the reinforcement traffic. Two tugs and an MTB were sunk, a destroyer and a landing ship damaged; S 136 was lost. A *Rotte* got through to Le Havre. From the eastward, 2. and 4.SFltl. laid mines before attacking the reinforcements, sinking an ammunition ship and two other vessels, after which they headed for Boulogne for more torpedoes.

The following night, the attack profile remained unchanged. It was becoming obvious that S-boats needed more support to break the ever-growing ring of security ships east of Cherbourg, and the 4th Artillery Flotilla was ordered out from the coast to attack and draw off the chain of destroyers off Barfleur.[35] It was the first time that this kind of co-operation had been tried, and it was effective. The boats got through and claimed torpedo hits, although these were never confirmed. In other encounters, hits were claimed by the Germans but no corresponding losses ever admitted by the Allied side. This may have happened because insufficiently precise observations were made during the heat of battle, while the Allies declared the losses of small craft without differentiating the cause of loss as torpedo, mine or bomber attack. Coming from Boulogne the same night, 2. and 4.SFltl. were unable to reach the invasion fleet for lack of time and attempted to attack the supply traffic to the north instead. They were driven off by destroyers on free patrol and put into Le Havre with a full load of torpedoes.

Bitter Losses

A commitment of all available naval forces was intended for the night of 12 June. The S-flotillas coming from west and east would attack the supply route north of the Bay of the Seine, while R-boats protected by torpedo boats from Le Havre would lay mines to the south. This was frustrated when the T-boats were driven off by British destroyers, MGBs and fighter-bombers 'with remarkably good co-operation',[36] but S-boats of 5. and 9.SFltl., supported by artillery lighters and coastal artillery, broke through the Allied ring off Barfleur. They found no traffic, however, for Naval Command Portsmouth had stopped the convoy run south of the assembly area off the Isle of Wight at night because of the losses.[37] A number of S-boats had sustained damage in skirmishes. Because of this, and the fear that, having got through the ring once, it would not be possible to repeat the trick the same night, both flotillas put into Le Havre.

The 2nd S-boat Flotilla searching to the north sighted nothing and headed for Boulogne, where 4.SFltl. joined it after a chase by MGBs and fighter-bombers, one boat being mined. The British knew the intentions of the German naval forces in the area more frequently now, for Group West resorted to Enigma-encoded messages, transmitting its outline instructions for the coming night on the coastal short-wave band at midday. Ultra could decode these messages in time for the Allied naval commanders to have them before the S-boat operation began. Apart from the early warning, there was little tactical advantage to be gained against S-boats, however, because they received most of their orders, advice and warnings from the FdS once the sortie was under way, and these took too long to decode to be of use.

It was different if sailing instructions were intercepted, as for example on the night of 12 June, when Group West ordered 2.SFltl. either to return to Le Havre or to make for Boulogne. The Allies had the decoded the order at 2141 hrs[38] and, from midnight onwards, British fighter-bombers patrolled over Boulogne. At 0430 they sighted the S-boats and attacked in waves. S 178, S 179 and S 189 were sunk, as was R-boat R-97, which came up to help. The C-in-C Luftflotte 3 refused fighter cover for the surviving damaged boats because 'all available aircraft were operating against the bridgehead, and to detach aircraft for the requested purpose did not justify weakening the air defence force'.[39]

Despite these sinkings, an operation against the invasion fleet was scheduled for the night of 13 June. It was considered important that the concentration of S-boats at Le Havre should be reduced by having 5. and 9.SFltl. return to Cherbourg. Freshening force 7 winds backing to the north-west forced 4., 5. and 9.SFltl. to abandon the operation and run for Le Havre. As soon as the Allies had decoded the message reporting the flotillas' return, they realised their unique opportunity finally to wipe out an always-elusive opponent, and C-in-C Allied Naval Forces, Admiral Ramsay, made a personal request for an air attack to the Chief of Bomber Command.

Air Vice-Marshal Harris responded immediately and before the S-boats' evening sortie on 14 June, 221 Lancaster bombers, escorted by fighters and led by Mosquito fighter-bombers, attacked Le Havre in two waves.[40] Because Luftwaffe air activity had been advised over the target for later, the flak commander had orders from Luftflotte 3 that all flak batteries in

Avro Lancaster bomber.

the city were to remain silent from 2200 hrs. Although the incoming bombers were clearly identified at a distance of twenty kilometres as enemy, and were impossible to confuse with German aircraft, the flak received no amending instructions. Of the fifteen boats making up the three flotillas at Le Havre, only S 167 escaped.[41] Additionally, three of the four available torpedo boats, eight minesweepers, eight VP-boats and numerous smaller craft were also sunk. Casualties were eighteen dead, including the commander 5.SFltl., Kapitänleutnant Johannsen, and twenty-five wounded, including the commander 9.SFltl., Götz von Mirbach, and four boat commanders.

I arrived at Le Havre aboard S 144. Her commander Beck was wounded. The boat tied up at a wharf. At 2232 hrs on 14 June 1944 Lancaster bombers attacked the naval harbour area. There were three torpedo boats and fifteen S-boats there. The air raid lasted about half an hour. Cdr of S 167, Sager, was wounded, also flotilla commander von Mirbach after a Knight's Cross celebration on the torpedo boats. These latter were all sunk. In the adjacent basin I could see four S-boats, two *Rotten* moored together by a loose halter, and which had drifted away from the pier and were undamaged. The harbour lay under a dark cloud of smoke, fire and explosions. A bomb hit on the deck had hurled a steel plate across the stem of S 144. We could not get the boat free and had to abandon her. We went aboard the next free boat, S 167. Most of the crew had vanished when the bombers came, although some were caught on the wharves. I went into her armoured bridge. As we were removing our gear from S 144, the second wave of bombers arrived at 0114 hrs. I had no desire to go through a repeat of the raid in harbour and ordered 'start up engines'. Some of the men (a mixture from the two boats) ran for cover, others reported to their stations aboard. We got two engines running and 'sailed' on a compass bearing – blindly – through the smoke-enveloped harbour to the anti-submarine nets, and then past Roeder's boat at anchor (S 146 was hit later, the crew got ashore in rubber dinghies), got through the barrier, headed for the open sea, not a scratch but the near misses kept us moving pretty fast. We looked back and thought the Allies were going to make more landings there. When nothing arrived, at daybreak we put back and reported to the bunker. We were the only boat to have survived both attacks. (Information from Hans Schirren to the author, 14 April 2003)

The following night, the Allied air forces attacked again. This time, Boulogne was their objective in an attempt to destroy the offensive capability of the Kriegsmarine in the Channel. They sank nine minesweepers, two patrol boats and three minesweeping tenders. The 2nd S-boat Flotilla sailed from the bunker before it was hit and suffered no serious damage. The overall effect of these air raids was to reduce the number of operational boats from thirty-one at the beginning of the invasion to thirteen.[42]

Countermeasures

In view of this dramatic reduction in the offensive capability, Petersen was faced with taking three immediate steps.

First, it was necessary to deny the enemy time to rest and to prevent S-boat crews obtaining the impression of having sustained a defeat. Accordingly, on the nights following, the few surviving boats resumed operations.

Second, the flotillas had to be reorganised and the basis for operations rethought. Therefore, the boats of 2. and 4.SFltl. were merged under the flotilla commander, 2.SFltl., and 5.SFltl. personnel sent to the Reich to re-form the flotilla. Regrouping at Le Havre was out of the question. Since Boulogne was under permanent radar watch from the English coast, was vulnerable to Allied air attack day and night and the run to the operational area was long, Dieppe was chosen as an additional base. It had no bunkers, but the risk had to be accepted. In any case, whether such bunkers offered protection now that Allied heavy bombs had penetrated bunker roofs at Rotterdam and Le Havre was open to doubt.[43]

Finally, reinforcements had to be brought up as soon as possible. On 13 June, SKL had approved the proposed transfer of 6.SFltl. from the Baltic, and 8.SFltl. was to be brought up to strength with new boats for operations from Boulogne.

For the time being, not much could be achieved by the handful of surviving boats, and Cherbourg was being gradually evacuated. After 9.SFltl. boats had

Mulberry artificial harbour.

tried unsuccessfully on successive nights to break through the Allied security ring, on the orders of the Führer they sailed to Saint-Malo to supply the beleaguered garrison with 21cm ammunition. Shortly before the loss of Cherbourg on 26 June, they reached Dieppe, leaving the damaged S 112 and S 145 behind. During this period, there were no successes to report, so oppressive was the security ring of destroyers, MTBs, MGBs and fighter-bombers. Great hope was being placed in the new pressure mines (DM1), of which SKL had authorised the release on 7 June. From 14 June, the Luftwaffe began mining the landing zones; mines for S-boats did not begin arriving at Le Havre and Dieppe until 19 June. When they had them, the would-be minelayers failed to get through to the landing zones, and S 190 of 2.SFltl. was sunk in a skirmish with two destroyers. Petersen therefore requested freedom of manoeuvre for the flotilla commanders, this even being approved by Group West, so desperate was the situation, and thus mines were laid in locations that could still be reached despite the enemy countermeasures. The mines served as a flanking barrier and provided more freedom to operate from Le Havre, at the approaches to which enemy naval forces had virtually set up camp.

Initially the Allies suffered a series of losses in the landing zones attributable to the new mine, but after examining the detonator of a mine dropped ashore in error by the Luftwaffe, they discovered that ships making five knots or less were immune. Allied naval units were advised accordingly on 3 July and thus the new weapon was robbed of its potency.[44]

Group West was alert to the lack of success and blamed the S-boats: 'The orders for attacks regardless of the dangers in the case of invasion have been forgotten, and are broken off prematurely too often in conditions of visibility short of ideal.'[45] After being notified of this criticism by Admiral Krancke, Petersen travelled immediately to Le Havre to address flotilla commanders and boat captains, but did not vary the nature of operations or the conditions. In his view, the relationship between chances and risk had to be measured, and in proportion.

Meanwhile, new weapons were being introduced. On the night of 25 June, the first Linsen explosive boats made their debut; the one-man torpedoes Neger and Marder followed shortly. They claimed to have sunk a fair number of ships, but this is not confirmed by Allied archives. It is possible that the ships had been sunk deliberately as breakwaters seaward of the two artificial harbours and not identified by the Germans as such at that stage. On 28 June, Group West requested long-range cameras 'in order to clarify the assembly of shipping off the Orne estuary', since for the first time the possibility was being considered that 'there could be ships of no value sunk as breakwaters for the landings.'[46]

Vain Striving

The successes obtained by S-boats, mines and the K-Verband (special operations by frogmen) had not been significant; the uninterrupted flow of supplies to the Allies in Normandy had been too overwhelming. During the first month, every day, 200 ships arrived in the landing zones, including 9 troop transports, 25 Liberty ships, 38 coasters and 135 landing craft.[47] The unimpeded growth of Allied forces on the ground was so great that the German reserves had no hope of keeping pace with it. The Germans were even still thinking that a second invasion was coming, and von Rundstedt and Rommel argued in vain with Hitler, at a conference north of Paris on 17 June 1944, to move up reserves still being held back.

Hitler's main concern was to protect the Channel coast for the imminent V-1 offensive, and he would not release 15 Armee stationed there. He also refused to fire the V-1s on the landing zones or allow operational freedom, because he wanted to retain the option of switching from 'holding firm' to 'flexible' leadership. The attempts by the two field marshals to combine Wehrmacht supplies also failed because of outright refusal by the Luftwaffe and the Kriegsmarine.[48] This left the command structures divided and immobile. On 29 and 30 June 1944 at Obersalzberg, Rundstedt and Rommel were unsuccessful in an attempt to make Hitler reconsider. The fanatical will to hold out and the belief in new rockets, jets and U-boats prevailed. The next day, in reply to Keitel's rhetorical question, what else could one do other than hold the front? Rundstedt told him, 'You should put an end to the war, you idiots.'[49]

By now, the Allies had twenty-eight divisions in the landing areas poised to spread out immediately through France. Rommel considered the situation and, in a three-page memorandum lacking niceties, he set out the position, pointing to the strength of the Allied land forces and to the German losses of nearly 100,000 men (including 2,360 officers, 28 generals and 354 troop commanders), for which 6,000 reserves had been called forward to replace them and concluded, 'They are fighting heroically everywhere, but the unequal struggle is approaching its end. I must request you to draw the necessary inference of the situation without delay. I feel compelled, as C-in-C of the Army Group, to state this clearly.'[50] Two days later, Allied fighter-bombers attacked the car in which he was travelling and Rommel was seriously wounded. The Army thus lost not only a senior commander, but above all a possible Resistance leader.

The details of the 20 July 1944 assassination plot have been widely covered.[51] Apart from short factual statements in War Diaries, the S-boat Arm remained silent. It is not to be expected that, in the situation prevailing at that time, commentaries would be made in official documents. From the coolness of the reports, however, one can see a certain distance being kept, a distance from the will to continue a struggle whose prospects were daily less hopeful, and a leadership increasingly a stranger to reality. Distance also, however, from the attempt to remove the head of state by murdering him. It could not be expected that the units at the front engaged in daily sorties against the enemy would have the necessary insight into the overall situation respecting the policymakers at the highest level and the criminality of the regime.

Even by mid-July, the Germans had not ruled out a second major invasion. This fear tied down forces that could have bolstered the front against the first invasion. It was not the fact of the landing, not the chosen place, nor the day and the means, but simply that the Allies were relying on a single landing without a nearby port and would receive their supplies through artificial harbours and an underwater pipeline; this was the real strategic surprise that baffled them. Slowly the truth began to dawn among the German staffs, and finally SKL gave in to the repeated urgings of the FdS for reinforcements, and pulled 10.SFltl. out of the Baltic on 30 July 1944. The newly re-formed 5.SFltl. could not be ordered westwards as well; it was needed urgently in the Baltic to help protect the seaward flank of the Army against the Red Army offensive.[52]

The Allies in the west had begun to prepare their breakout with massive air strikes. The German forces were at an end. Lacking reserves and operational freedom, they were in no condition to offer serious resistance. The defence against the invasion had finally collapsed.

New Weapons – More Losses

Despite the arrival of 6.SFltl. and the completion of 8.SFltl., the S-boat Arm had achieved no further success by mid-July. In view of the ever more difficult task of piercing the Allied security ring, at the beginning of the month Petersen had requested the issue of the new target-seeking T5 Zaunkönig torpedo, hoping to disperse the ring with it and penetrate to the landing zones. With Dönitz's agreement, the first Zaunkönigs were delivered on 14 July 1944, but even this torpedo, proven by the U-boat Arm, brought no turn in the tide. The surface war differed too substantially from the U-boat war against escort destroyers. Frequently the Zaunkönig, homing in on the destroyers, would be drawn off by MGBs and MTBs. Even at a running depth of three metres it scored no hits, and the reason was found in later tests. The torpedo ran at twenty-four knots, which was not fast enough to catch an alerted destroyer.

Petersen would not give in. If the supply line could not be attacked near the Bay of the Seine, he would have to try somewhere else, he decided, and consequently reverted his operations to the convoy operations along the English coast. On the first night, 26 July 1944, 6.SFltl. sank two freighters off Dungeness, while 2.SFltl. tied down the security ring near Le Havre. In a skirmish, two British MTBs and S 182 were sunk. This was the only loss in the thirty-eight sea fights and twenty fighter-bomber attacks during July.[53]

Three nights later, 30 July 1944, there were further successes when 2.SFltl. tied down the Allied security ring and, together with part of 6.SFltl., deceived the Allies as to the purpose of the operation. The 2nd Group of 6.SFltl. attacked an eastbound convoy off Dungeness, sinking one freighter and damaging three Liberty ships. The Allies were so concerned at these fresh losses that British bombers struck at Le Havre the next day, damaging three S-boats, and again on 2 August, when S 39 and S 114 were sunk and two others damaged.

Despite these losses, the boats sailed again on 2 August to draw off the Allied security vessels and allow Linsen explosive boats and Marder one-man torpedoes favourable opportunities. At the same time, the Luftwaffe attacked with the intention of tying down Allied forces and supplying navigation aids by flak gunnery and fires. Almost two months after the invasion, this was the first attempt to combine various machines of war by inter-service co-operation. The K-Verband sank three ships. It was modest but still a success, and also showed what could be achieved by combining command structures. But that was an end to it, for the Luftwaffe had no more aircraft to offer, and new K-Verband craft had to be brought in.

The S-boat Arm now received a new weapon, Dönitz ordering delivery of the T3D Dackel long-range torpedo. On 4 August 1944, as the tide made at Le Havre, the Dackel, composed of two ordinary G7e torpedoes, was fired towards the invasion beaches on a direct course. Timed to arrive at the period of still water between high tide and the beginning of the ebb, the Dackel would then search the area in long, pre-programmed zig-zags.[54]

Petersen was sceptical, fearing that the tide would be too strong for a torpedo running at only nine knots, and also worried that the boats, after firing the Dackel, would then run back as a flotilla to load mines or torpedoes and not be available the same night for operations. After the first six sorties in which seventy-six Dackel were discharged, he remained dubious, and refused to share in the euphoria engendered by Group West 'since we have no observations of ships sinking and the B-Dienst has not reported messages about torpedoings, damage and sinkings, etc.'[55]

A total of ninety-one Dackel were fired between 4 and 18 August 1944, on eight missions. It seems confirmed that four ships – an old cruiser, a minesweeper, a freighter and a workshop ship – were sunk.[56] Petersen employed his non-Dackel boats on mining or torpedo operations on the English coast.

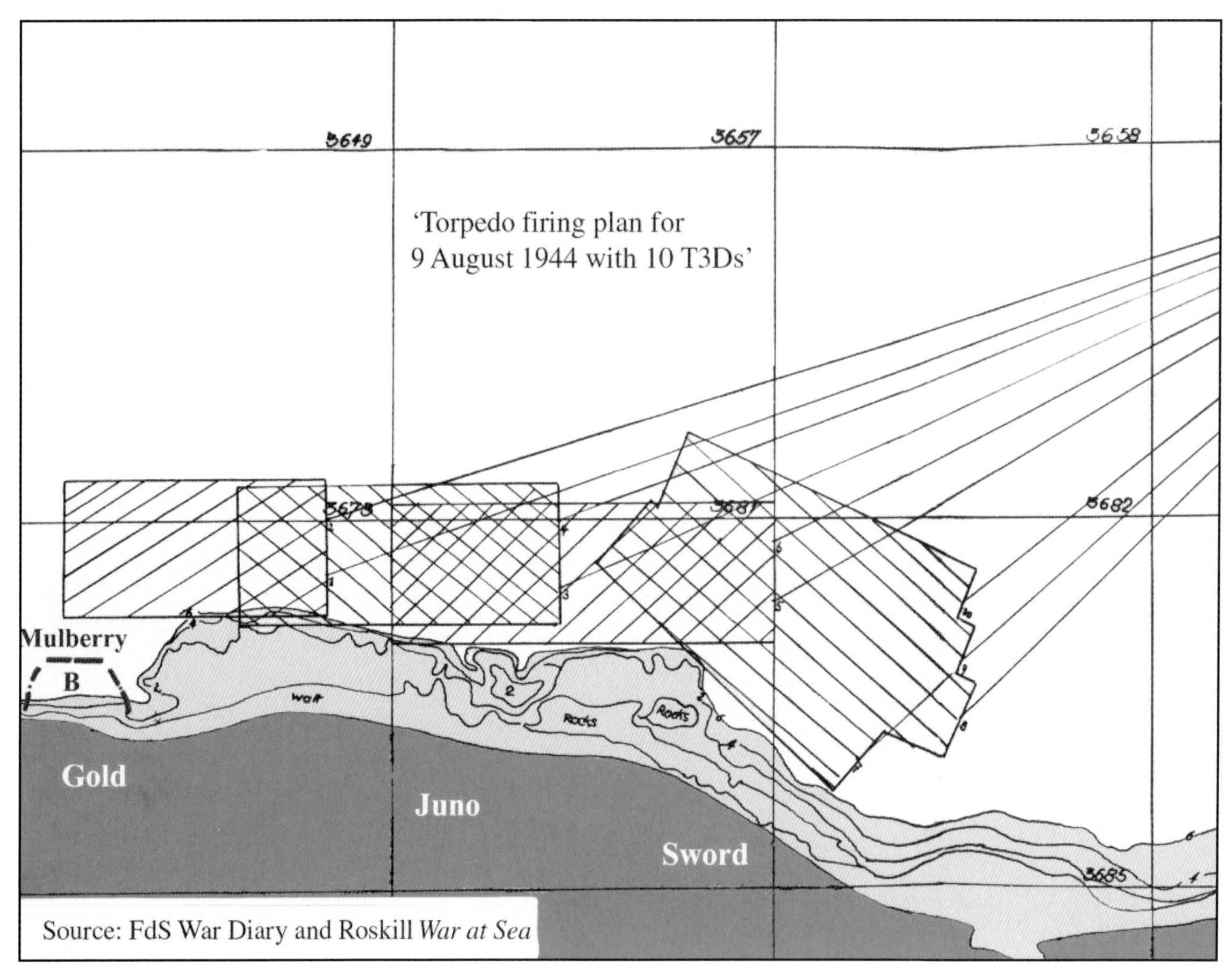

Operational sketch of Dackel torpedoes.

10.SFltl., which had meanwhile arrived at Ostend, carried out two mining operations in the Thames estuary. Apart from tying down enemy naval forces, nothing was achieved. British radio cryptanalysts delivered timely warning, and against an alerted enemy the boats had no prospects for success. In skirmishes, 6.SFltl. lost S 91.

Meanwhile, the Allies had landed in southern France (Operation 'Dragoon', 15 August 1944). As a result, Petersen made provisional arrangements to pull back all boats and personnel not necessary for immediate operations. This was a dangerous policy having regard to the uncompromising orders to hold out issued by the political and military leadership. On the night of 29 August, 2.SFltl. was the last unit to leave Le Havre. After mining the harbour entrance, the flotilla headed for Boulogne. Six nights later, this port too was abandoned, 10.SFltl. being the last unit to leave. Heading eastwards, S 184 was sunk by coastal artillery. 'Remarkable', Petersen commented, 'is the fact that after four years' warfare in the Channel, only in the last passage by German S-boats through the Channel Narrows did enemy shore-based guns score a hit for the first time – albeit a lucky one.'[57] Thus the operational theatre Northern France–Belgium had been abandoned for good, signalling the opening of the period of the 'Final Struggle'.

12

From the Ardennes to the End in the West

September 1944 – May 1945

At the beginning of September 1944, as the war entered its sixth year, the Wehrmacht, despite great efforts and as a result of shortages in men, materials and fuel, was being forced back to the original Reich borders by an enemy superior on all fronts.[1]

In June 1944, in the east, Army Group Centre had collapsed, in July Army Group North–Ukraine had been overcome, and shortly afterwards Army Group South–Ukraine had been almost wiped out, with the consequence that – following the capitulation of Italy in the autumn of 1943 – Germany's allies Romania, Bulgaria and Finland left the Axis.[2] On the Western Front, the Allied armies had broken out of the Normandy bridgehead and, after the landings of American and French troops in southern France (15 August 1944), were advancing on broad fronts. The German Army in the west fell back to a line stretching from the Scheldt estuary through southern Holland to the Westwall south of Trier. German forces still held some ports and islands in the Channel, which tied down Allied forces, but these were not significant for the Allies, who had now opted to build a major strongpoint at Antwerp. It was through this useful port that the great mass of their future supplies would pass for the thrust to the Ruhr.

Faced with this threatened collapse, Hitler's hopes were based on a dashing military success in the west aimed at upsetting the balance of the enemy coalition. On 16 September 1944, he announced to a small OKH circle that he proposed descending on Antwerp from the Ardennes with about thirty new *Volksgrenadier* and panzer divisions to strike a telling blow against the Allied forces there. Operating during bad weather, so that enemy aircraft would remain grounded, he would provide the British with a new Dunkirk and ring the changes in Germany's fortunes.

The preparations for *Wacht am Rhein*, especially the planned co-operation between OKH and Luftwaffe, were to be kept top secret.[3]

As in 1940, the Kriegsmarine was not involved and was not asked to keep its limited forces at readiness.

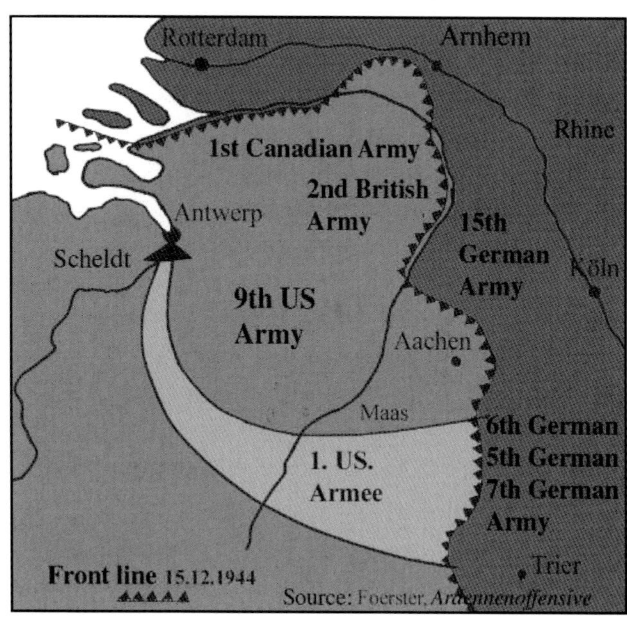

Operational plan for the Ardennes offensive.

For the direction of operations in the Channel following the dissolution of Group West, MOK Nord (Naval High Command North Sea)[4] had only patrol boats, minesweepers and S-boats at its disposal. All destroyers and torpedo boats had now disappeared permanently from the Channel following the loss of the last ships there in August 1944.[5] The U-boat Arm, which since 1943 had been sustaining high losses at the hands of overwhelming defences for no worthwhile returns, were needed urgently in other theatres and were unsuited for use in the shallow waters off the Scheldt and English coast. The Luftwaffe, needed on all fronts and desperately overstretched, had for long considered itself unable to provide operational support, while the idea of helping to prosecute the war at sea from the air could not now even be entertained.[6] The K-Verband had Biber 6-tonne midget submarines and 1.2-tonne Linsen remote-controlled explosive motor boats arriving at the front, but even SKL considered these 'primitive explosives-and-weapons carriers' to be 'mere weapons of opportunity', whose use was 'very dependent on the weather' and whose navigation 'was extremely unsound'.[7] Thus, it fell to the FdS alone, with his three available flotillas, which as a rule never had more than eight to twelve operational boats at Rotterdam (9th

Vickers Wellington bomber.

S-boat Flotilla) and Ijmuiden (8th and 10th Flotillas), to pursue the long-term offensive against the Allied supply routes. The former Channel flotillas were now either in Germany for rest and refits (2nd and 6th), in the Baltic (5th) or heading for northern waters (4th).[8]

Grouping up the flotillas and holding them in provisional readiness for a concentrated operation with the maximum number of boats possible, thereby supporting the Ardennes offensive from the sea, did not enter the reckoning at all, because the FdS had not been made aware of the Führer's intentions.

The naval surface war, which the FdS was leading practically by himself at this point, was straitjacketed by its limited operational basis and technological and numerical inferiority. Targets along the English coast were almost impossible to attack from the German-held Dutch ports. The continuous stream of troops and materials flowing through the artificial Normandy harbours now lay well beyond the range of the boats.[9] Sorties were still possible, but not surprise sorties.

Moreover, the enemy had expanded his defence forces. Air reconnaissance flown by 16 Group, RAF in the Nore region up to the Dutch coast could call upon nearly 100 aircraft. Not only did they report S-boats passing through the swept channels of the minefields, but now attacked with a new kind of bomb that exploded immediately above the surface. The Group had been reinforced with Wellington bombers equipped with radar and Leigh lights. These had been engaged previously in anti-U-boat patrols and had been reassigned. New radio apparatus enabled direct telephone connections between the aircraft and destroyers, which, as during the invasion, generally worked with two or three MGBs. The tactics were tried and tested. After receiving the aircraft report, the destroyer/MGB group waited at an intercept position. With its improved radar, the destroyer itself then tracked the S-boats and directed the MGBs to engage.[10] If the defence forces had been clearly superior numerically in the past, the imbalance now weighed far heavier against the S-boats. On 10 October 1944, the Dover area coastal forces transferred to Nore region, together with other patrol vessels at a loose end, so that the Nore naval defences now consisted of 35 destroyers, 15 frigates, 19 corvettes and more than 160 Coastal Forces vessels, including 60 MGBs, 40 MLs and 60 MTBs, the latter craft being intended mainly for attacks against German coastal convoys.[11]

As the German front contracted, the Coastal Forces advanced from Zeebrugge to Flushing, while RAF units (Spitfires and Typhoon fighter-bombers) started from Belgian and Dutch airfields.[12] The loss of

Royal Navy MTB.

the radio DF station on the west coast and the implementation of more secure codes for use by British coastal traffic had complicated the task of the FdS in locating convoys and directing his flotillas to intercept them. It had become less often possible to protect his operations by pinpointing destroyer groups and providing warning of approaching MGBs.

On the Allied side, Ultra could read operational orders and tactical instructions when Enigma-encoded and morsed, and German intentions were secret only when passed by telex. If the boats remained in their bases until the operation, telex was the rule, but if they moved along the coast first – for example from Rotterdam to the Hook of Holland – then the enemy would know the plan.[13]

Astonishingly, S-boats often managed to reach the convoy routes and score successes. This was achieved by switching between mine and torpedo missions in different areas, by taking advantage of marginal weather conditions that caused the smaller British boats sea-keeping problems, staggering the involvement of flotillas, and relying on leadership practice proven over the years.

In a total of ten operations in the autumn of 1944, the convoy routes were mined and merchant vessels sunk. The Germans sustained losses only on the night of 18 September, when four S-boats were bringing supplies into besieged Dunkirk.[14] Three boats of 10.SFltl. (Kapitänleutnant Karl Müller), S 183, S 200 and S 702, sailing a diversion, ran into a British patrol consisting of a frigate and MTBs. Two S-boats collided, after which all three were sunk. Fifty-seven crewmen, including the flotilla commander, were fished out of the water the next morning by British MTBs; the remainder had either been killed during the battle or, drifting in the cold water, died of exposure during the night.

After S 200 was sunk, two MTBs stopped at the spot where she had gone down, making no attempt to pick us up. About ninety minutes later another British vessel appeared, which looked to me like a steam gunboat, but this boat also made no attempt to rescue survivors. I find this attitude by the British incomprehensible. During the battle the inflatable boats were so badly shot up as to be unserviceable. Our only remaining life-saving equipment was a large French kapok float on which I first put the wounded. The conduct of the crew in the early stages after the boat sank was very confident and correct. Since the non-wounded were in the water alongside the raft in a 2–3 sea state, after four to five hours the first signs of exhaustion began to appear. The life jackets with the collar ring proved good and easy to wear. After about six hours in the water many of the men began to display a ruthless, impulsive urge for self-preservation and only by admonitions hinting at the direst punishment were excesses prevented. The exhausted men in the water were intending to occupy the float to the detriment of the wounded aboard it.

It was clearly proved once more that sailors thinly and scantily clad succumb far sooner to the effects of cold water than those wearing leather suits and woollens. I watched the wounded commander of the leader boat and three other men die of exposure after seven or eight hours in the water. Shortly after 0800 hrs, some British MTBs appeared sailing in a broad line abreast and began searching for survivors. These boats picked up eighteen survivors from S 200. Especially valuable were the nets let down on either side from all MTBs. They were about 5 to 6 metres long and hung from the upper deck to about a metre below the water surface. Nearly all survivors were now so weak that they could not climb to the upper deck of the MTBs without assistance. As the MTBs were making a few revs, it was not possible to hold on with the hands alone, and it was lucky that one could put both feet through the broad mesh of the net and in this way provide the arms with a decisive period of rest. (Report, 1 December 1944, Kapitänleutnant Karl Müller, repatriated on exchange basis)[15]

Since S-boats could not be totally wiped out at sea, the RAF was called upon again and, on 15 December 1944, seventeen Lancaster bombers attacked Ijmuiden. Giant Tallboy bombs penetrated the bunker. S 198 was destroyed and another boat seriously damaged, while the remainder all received medium to light blast damage. Casualties were thirteen dead, five wounded.[16] Since the bunker no longer offered safety, the FdS ordered the boats to be spread loosely around the port.

The next day, 16 December 1944, the Ardennes offensive began. At last, the Kriegsmarine was informed, and directly from Führer HQ: 'Development Offensive *Wacht am Rhein* provides Kriegsmarine with principal task of preventing sailings of British ships for Antwerp. Führer requests ObdM [Dönitz] to prepare everything possible in this respect.'[17]

Dönitz informed Admiral Förste, C-in-C Naval High Command North Sea personally and gave him 'the naval side of the support operation . . . as a special obligation'.[18] It was, of course, too late. Neither a large pack of S-boats nor a provisional holding-back for a concentrated operation by the maximum number of serviceable boats was possible, but at the suggestion of the FdS, the following flotillas were ordered at once to Holland by SKL: 2. and 6.SFltl. from Germany; 4.SFltl. from Norway, relieved there by the 1st S-boat Training Flotilla; and 5.SFltl. from the eastern Baltic.[19]

Although the units put to sea immediately, the planning neglect at the highest levels of command could no longer be made up for. The reinforcements arrived only when the Ardennes offensive had run its course and the war in the west was as good as lost. Although the FdS sailed his eight serviceable boats to attack the Scheldt traffic at once, they returned empty-handed for lack of air reconnaissance reports about the convoys. Accordingly, in subsequent operations, minelaying was given priority. This aroused the disapproval of Dönitz on 26 December 1944, since he feared it would compromise the Seehund midget U-boat operations then imminent. On the same day, he ordered that 'until further notice,

Seehund exhibited at the Wehrtechnisch Collection, Koblenz.

no more mines are to be laid in areas that may prejudice Seehund operations now or later'.[20]

This order robbed the S-boats of their most effective weapon and deprived operational command of the possibility of exploiting gaps in the enemy defences by mining strongpoints. Now the flotillas were not only forced to outmanoeuvre destroyer/MGB groups on free patrol, but also had to compete against the full convoy escorts. Dönitz also ordered that the S-boats should set aside their offensive missions to clear the way for Seehunds, should the need arise.[21] Naval High Command North Sea considered the possibility of 'providing protection for K-Verband craft setting out . . . to be slight'[22] and suggested, since the Scheldt traffic sailed mainly by day and was thus impossible to attack operationally, that the S-boats should concentrate against the English east coast, and he requested a free hand for minelaying in that area. On 5 January 1945, Dönitz agreed, but left the ban on minelaying in the Scheldt in place, for he had invested great hope in the new Seehund and, two days earlier, had reported to Hitler that if they fired 100 torpedoes per month at enemy shipping, 'it will mean 100,000 gross tons sunk if only 20 per cent of them hit'.[23] This was pure moonshine, as the U-boat and S-boat operations of the last few years had shown. Nevertheless, the FdS used the new operational freedom, reinforced by 2., 4., 5. and 6.SFltl., which gave him more than twenty-six boats,[24] distributed thus:

Den Helder: 2.SFltl. (Korvettenkapitän Opdenhoff), 5.SFltl. (Kapitänleutnant Holzapfel)
Ijmuiden: 8.SFltl. (Korvettenkapitän Zymalkowski)
Rotterdam: 4.SFltl. (Korvettenkapitän Fimmen), 6.SFltl. (Kapitänleutnant Matzen), 9.SFltl. (Kapitänleutnant von Mirbach).

After a period of bad weather that hindered operations, on the night of 14 January 1945 the boats mined the convoy route off Cromer and the Thames estuary. S 180 was mined and lost close to Den Helder. Oberleutnant zur See Pillet and eleven crew lost their lives. On 15 January there followed a torpedo operation stabbing at various points. The six flotillas were divided into three groups to attack convoys off Cromer, the Thames estuary and Zeebrugge. Near the Thames, a large landing ship was sunk.

When the FdS had reported personally to Dönitz on the S-boat war in the Channel two days earlier, he had been rebuffed with the question, 'why had boats not been concentrated for the most important task of attacking the Scheldt traffic?'[25] In his written response supplied at the request of SKL, Petersen set out the principles of his leadership developed over the years:

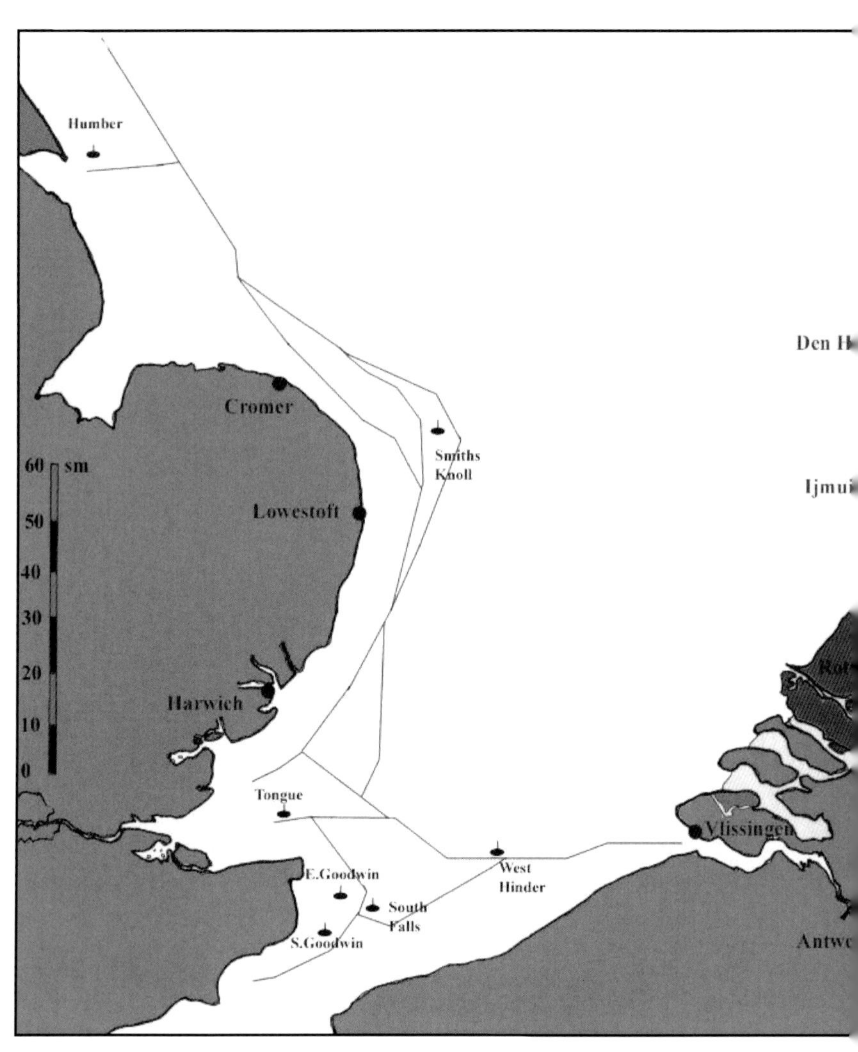

'Old' convoy routes and Scheldt traffic.

> As the S-boat is not in a position to overcome security vessels on close or distant escort, it has to pass between them. This requires freedom to manoeuvre.
>
> A number of S-boats operating against a single target determine amongst themselves the breadth of their attack front, the geographical considerations and the least distance between units.
>
> An attack unit is three to four boats, distance between the group at least five sea miles; where there are three groups experience shows that one group will get through.
>
> If the convoy cannot be attacked from all points, a maximum of four groups can operate at the same time against a convoy four sea miles in length.
>
> If enough time is available, a maximum of sixteen boats can attack in waves. The second wave attacks about two hours after the first wave.

In conclusion, the FdS requested 'freedom to operate, which will allow me to attack the enemy supply routes with torpedo and mine where the best prospects for success can be found, ie freedom to attack by all forces in the entire area . . . setting up regular air reconnaissance . . . and further development of radar and radar-detection equipment'.[26]

C-in-C Naval High Command North Sea confirmed the tactics and operational thinking of the FdS as sound and underlined the need for operational freedom with all available means. He reflected – as had Petersen – on the importance of regular air reconnaissance as a prerequisite for favourable deployment of the boats.[27]

> The morning after the operation, we had sent a short signal 'success assumed'. At about 0900 I received a telephone call – I was still in my bunk – Dönitz was on the line: 'Rebensburg, I have to see the Führer. The Führer is very down in the mouth, the Navy at least must give him something encouraging. Can you?' (From 27th Historical and Tactical Fleet Convention, 1987)

Dönitz had recognised the basis for the operations on 15 January, and Petersen had submitted his paper on 22 January, but now Dönitz had the impression 'that too-strict guidelines have been imposed for the operational leadership of the S-boat Arm so that no permanent test of its purposefulness is possible because of too little fighting activity on a sufficiently broad basis'.[28]

This reproach was repeated a few days later in a personal letter to Petersen. In particular Dönitz admonished him, 'that too much emphasis was placed upon sparing our forces and avoiding big risks when weighing up demands, exigencies and pressures needed to inflict extensive harm on the enemy'. He went on, 'Things were, and are, different in the U-boat Arm . . . sparing our forces and avoiding too high a risk does not play anything like the role it does in the S-boat Arm.'[29] And he insisted that the following questions should be subjected to an immediate practical investigation:

1. Is the maximum really reached with four groups of four boats each, must the second wave really not attack for another two hours?
2. Is there no chance of engaging a destroyer pursuing the boats?
3. If it is true of the S-boat as a weapon of attack that fighting is more important than protecting, is it therefore necessary to escort home a damaged boat?
4. Should two kilometres be the least operational distance for shadowing?

This criticism in question form concluded: 'Even with the relatively small number of boats, the idea of sparing the crews and avoiding risk has to take second place to the will to destroy the enemy. Great successes are only obtained when great chances are taken.'[28]

Although mortified by the indirect accusation of cowardice, Petersen set out in a cool and factual manner the rationale for his principles of engagement, tried and tested over the years. German air reconnaissance had ceased, the number of S-boats available was much reduced, the enemy defence forces and radar superiority had increased greatly and enemy supremacy in the air was total. Other than that, none of the basic principles had changed. In response to the four particular questions he replied:

1. The maximum of four groups is reached if, as on the Thames–Scheldt run, the attack can only be mounted from one flank and the convoy itself is compact. The attack by the second wave occurs after the first wave has retired and the enemy defences have spread out again, and darkness again covers a battlefield always illuminated by starshell during the action. When the second wave attacks, it embroils itself in a running gun battle, twisting and turning in and out of friendly S-boats and enemy MTBs, the laying of smoke making it impossible to distinguish between friend and foe. The first wave has to report its attack finished on the actual convoy or the second attack is doomed to fail.
2. The aim of the enemy destroyers on free patrol is to disperse the S-boat groups so that the MGBs can intercept and destroy them. The chances of hitting a destroyer with a torpedo are extremely poor because of the destroyer's rapid and irregular changes in course and speed. Of fifty-six torpedoes fired to date at destroyers, only one has hit. Moreover the aim of the torpedo operations is the merchant ships of the convoy.
3. The limit of distance to base over which a damaged boat must be escorted back is now extended. Nevertheless, depending on the situation, the flotilla commander must have the right to decide

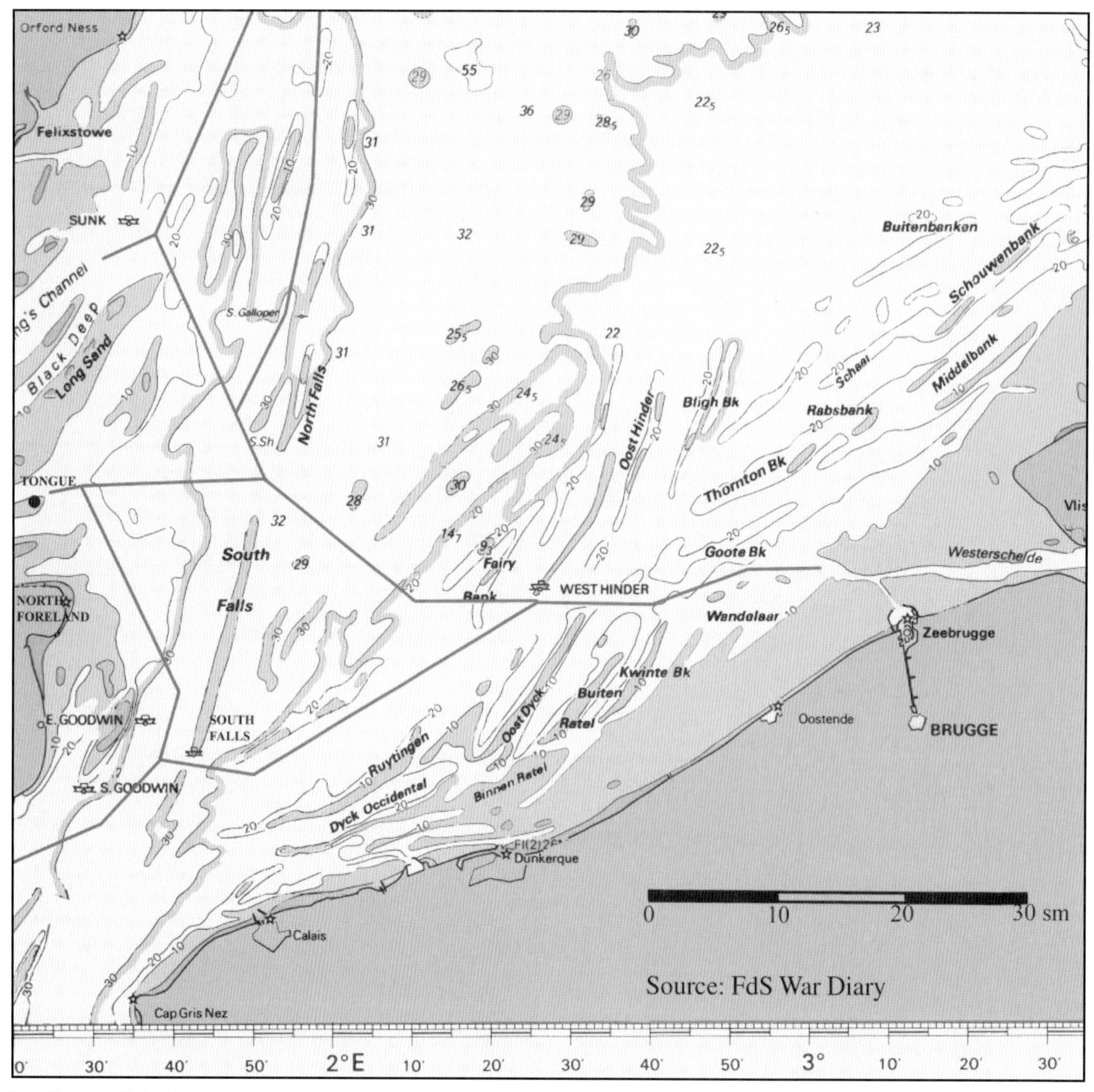

The Thames–Scheldt convoy route.

at what stage a boat is to be released for home either alone or with an escort.

4. Regarding least visibility on minelaying operations, this is the ability to make out the shadow outline of a vessel at 1,000 metres. On torpedo operations, less than 2,000 metres is not acceptable, for even coming across a stopped target, the barely two minutes available is insufficient to weigh up the situation and develop the attack. One has to bear in mind moreover that the enemy tracks our boats by radar from early on, and is already on the alert.[31]

This was a German naval commander speaking

who, as no other, knew surface warfare from almost daily operations and recognised the significance of enemy radar superiority, a reality in which the 'blind' had scarcely any chance against the 'sighted'. It was a reality not appreciated by Naval High Command, who maintained that if only one believed in success, success would follow. Petersen was also a military leader mindful of his responsibilities to his crews and who was prepared, as in the past, to demand full commitment, within which the risks could be controlled. He was never in favour of kamikaze tactics.

In conclusion, Naval High Command North Sea was of the opinion that, 'The ban on minelaying robs S-boats of their currently most effective weapon in the fight against enemy supply routes,'[32] and asked for a free hand to mine the Thames–Scheldt route between 2°15'E and 3°E, this being the critical convoy lane for Antwerp traffic running east and west of the West Hinder lightship. Even though Admiral K-Verband, Vizeadmiral Heye, agreed, Dönitz declined. The Seehunds, whose operations on the Thames–Scheldt route began on 14 February 1945, had priority for him.

On 20 February 1945, Dönitz was tempted to transfer all S-boats to the Baltic to combat the appearance of Soviet MTBs there, because 'in bad weather S-boats in the west cannot operate and have no prospect for success, while the K-Verband can replace them in good weather conditions'.[33]

The C-in-C Naval High Command North Sea, the fleet and Petersen were horrified, and it was explained to him in an unequivocal memorandum that the withdrawal of the whole S-boat Arm would release at a stroke a huge enemy naval force ranging from destroyers to gunboats. Even the massed deployment of K-Verband units could not tie down naval forces as did the S-boats. Since SKL concurred with this opinion, and an S-boat operation off Great Yarmouth on 22 February 1945 had proved successful,[34] Dönitz agreed to leave the S-boats in the west and transfer only one flotilla to the east. The 5th S-boat Flotilla was chosen because it had not yet been re-engined with supercharged motors and was thus slower than other S-boats in the western theatre. Once 5.SFltl. had its sailing orders, Petersen changed his mind and suggested that 1.SFltl. should go instead, since the flotilla was already in the Baltic and was manned by experienced crews who had previously fought the Soviets. Dönitz agreed and 5.SFltl. remained for the time being in the west.

At the end of March 1945, the flotilla left for Sassnitz after Naval High Command Baltic asked Dönitz for a second flotilla to support the deteriorating situation on the Pomeranian coast. After receiving orders on 25 March 1945, the first four operational 5.SFltl. boats left Den Helder two days later for Wilhelmshaven and Kiel, the remainder following a few days after that.[35]

Together with his agreement that the S-boat Arm should remain in Holland, Dönitz also gave the nod to mining the Thames–Scheldt convoy route.[36] Petersen wasted no time and two missions were sailed to the very limits of the permitted areas. It was suspected initially that the mines had been laid outside the specified areas, and SKL reacted angrily: 'Undoubtedly in the present situation we have here a lack of skill. The S-boats were only freed for minelaying operations after the gravest doubts and long deliberation.'[37] Dönitz saw it the same way and, without awaiting the results, on 24 February 1945 he reduced the authorised area for minelaying from 2°25'E to the Scheldt estuary. To restrict the force even more, he also ruled that 'S-boats may only lay mines if their position in the convoy lanes is known definitely from navigation buoys'.[38]

The new limits put stretches of convoy route west of the West Hinder lightship out of bounds, preventing a broader approach, greater freedom of action with the few available boats and a better chance of penetrating the security vessels. (On the week following the 'unskilful' minelaying, the field claimed six ships of 25,000 gross tons.) The new instruction reached Petersen during the operation of the night of 24 February 1945. Although the minefield due to be laid was outside the new limits, he held back the instruction 'in order not to unsettle the operation in progress'.[39] This was his understanding of independent and responsible command.

Despite the new restrictions, efforts had to continue to be made to deceive the enemy defences as to the night's intended objective, whether it were a convoy attack or to mine the sea lanes. This deception might be attempted by changing the approach route halfway, or unsettling the enemy by a very fast approach, causing him to resort to the radio telephone for information about the defences and the convoy itself. The Allied defences could be split by launching minor feints in many areas. The Allied approach to either minelaying or convoy attack was different in the two cases: minelaying called for wide-ranging cover, torpedo attacks required escorts to congregate around the convoy. Two examples show this clearly.

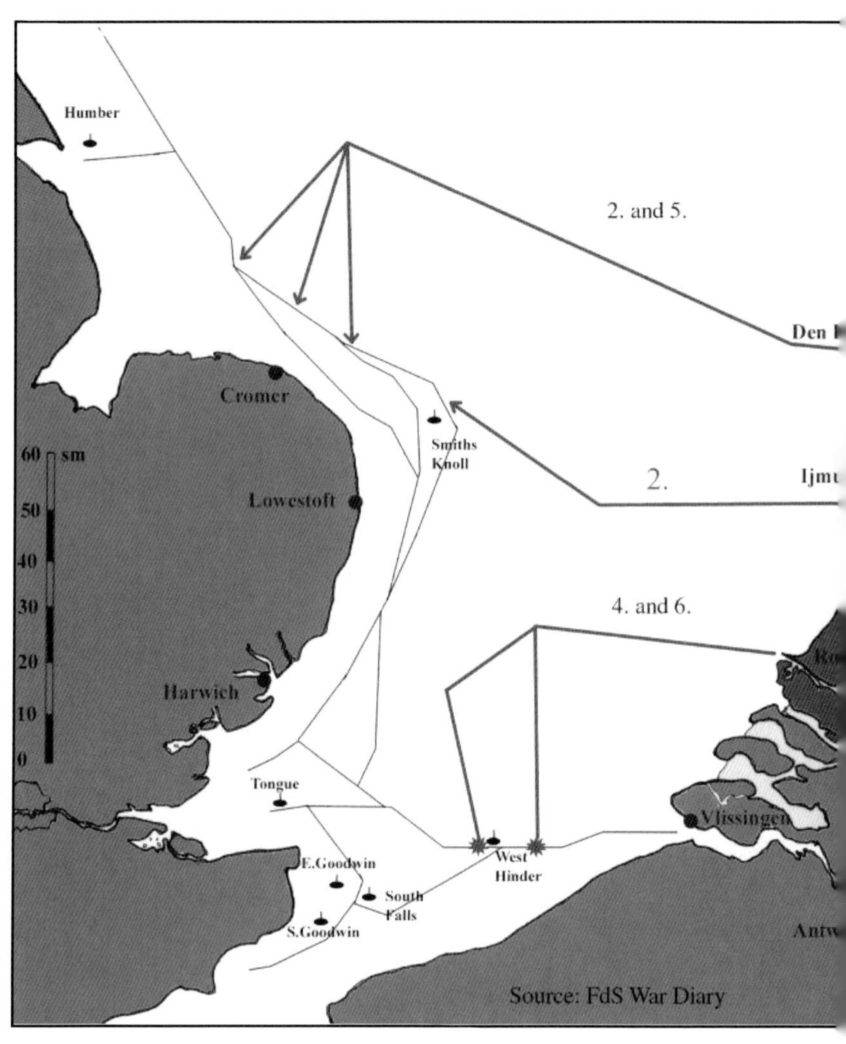

Mission on the night of 28 February 1945.

Night Mission of 28 February 1945

After two previous mining operations on the Scheldt route, Petersen decided to attempt to deceive the enemy into believing that mines were to be laid that night off the English east coast near the Humber, Lowestoft and Harwich. Accordingly, the 1st Group of 2.SFltl., and 5.SFltl., left Den Helder, the 2nd Group of 2.SFltl. sailed from Ijmuiden, and 4. and 6.SFltl. set out from Rotterdam. The actual intention was a torpedo attack on a southbound convoy expected north of Smith's Knoll lightship.

Uncertainty as to its exact whereabouts required that the approach be on a broad front. It was planned to lay mines to the south again, provided the boats could penetrate the Allied defences from the northern side. In the event, the flotillas to the north were driven off by destroyers on free patrol before reaching the convoy lanes, and for the first time enemy aircraft kept the boats in sight even after they reached the security zone of their own escort forces. The S-boats were hit repeatedly and suffered casualties of one dead and two wounded. To the south, the boats attempted in vain to fight through the naval defences. Some of the mines were dropped in the vicinity of the sea lane. S 220 was sunk.

'To force a way through while getting pushed around like that was not possible,' the FdS reported, and admitted with resignation that the unbelievable number of Allied vessels in the defence 'deprives us of any chance of surprise since there are no variations we can try in our approach run, nor can we increase our potential because of the narrowness of the operational area'.[40]

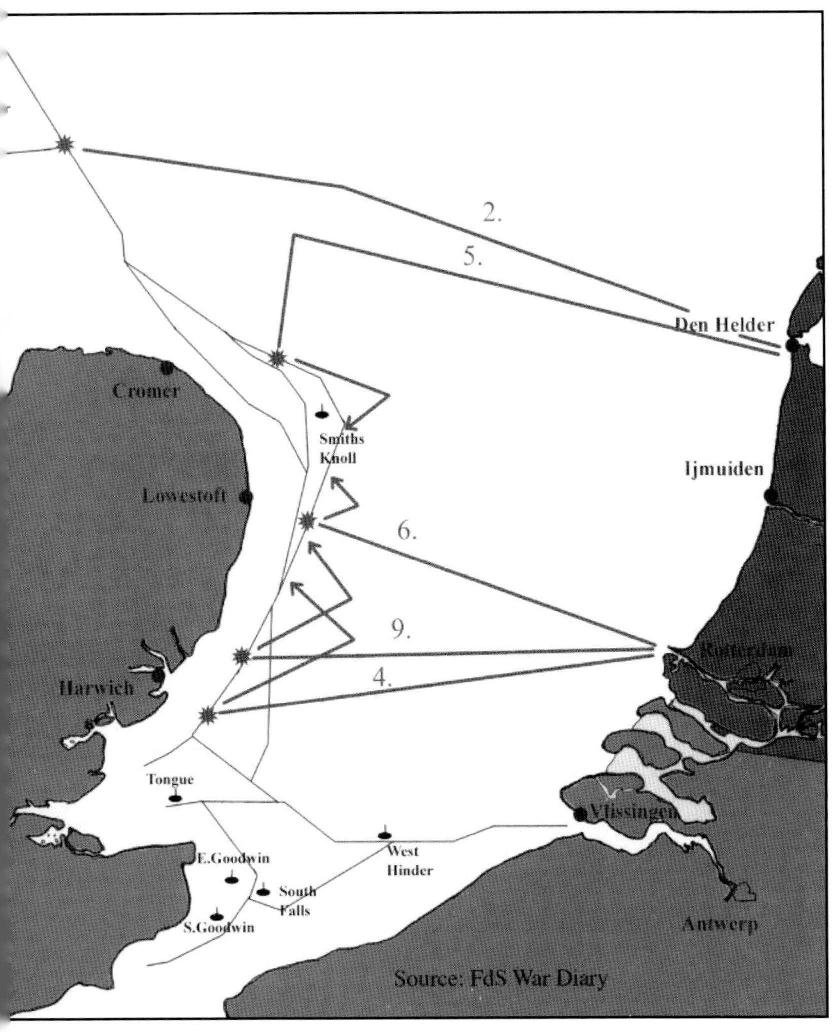

Attack on the night of 18 March 1945.

The Attack of 18 March 1945

On 17 March 1945, mines had been laid on the Scheldt route and off Cromer. It was proposed to mine other coastal stretches and attack a convoy expected from the north. On 18 March 1945, 2., 4., 6. and 9.SFltl. ran directly to the operational area while 5.SFltl. bore away south from the Humber track. Despite his continuous observation from the air, the enemy was taken by surprise and all five flotillas reached the convoy lanes, where 129 mines were sown. After the Allied naval defences arrived, only 6.SFltl. got through to the convoy. Despite a battering, the flotilla managed to sink two freighters. To the north, 2.SFltl. encountered two MGBs and tangled with fighter-bombers, with the result that all boats of the flotilla received further damage, two of them so seriously that they remained unserviceable for a long period.

> Leader boat 2.SFltl. had 5.7cm hit, entire electrical installation shut down, smoke canisters damaged, visibility nil due to smoke, situation complete confusion, S-boats and MGBs milling around, danger of ramming. Aircraft attacked with cannon, set S-boat on fire, took 45 minutes to extinguish. (Battle report, 2.SFltl., 10 March 1945)

Whereas the S-boat Arm lost nineteen boats at sea in 1944, the figure was already twelve by the end of April 1945, and many of the rest had been damaged in action and remained unserviceable over ever-longer periods for lack of repair capacity.

The Western Allies had encircled German land units defending the Ruhr and, once these were overcome, had moved forward to northern Germany and reached the North Sea coast. Holland was therefore cut off. 'Once the whole East Frisian area falls, the possibility of continuing naval operations from Holland will hang in the balance,'[41] Naval High Command (MOK) North Sea declared on 5 April 1945. As it was, Fortress Holland held out because the Canadian 1st Army, arriving at the southern shores of the Zuider Zee, feared that if they advanced further the Germans would destroy the dykes and so flood the land.

While the FdS, with SKL approval, moved his organisational and flotilla staffs from the west to

Roll-call in the bunker before sailing.

Sonderburg, Naval High Command North Sea gave instructions for 75 per cent of the 900 cubic metres of naval fuel stocks in Holland to be released to the FdS. They reckoned that 'conditional on many uncertain factors, the possibility of S-boat operations from Holland exists for about another four weeks, dependent on the weather and frequency of operations', adding that 'an end to the possibility of S-boat operations will be determined by consumption of the fuel stock or the crippling of the facility for repair'.[42]

A week later, on 16 April 1945, 500 cubic metres of fuel was available for S-boat operations, with no possibility of resupply. On 17 April, Dönitz ordered half of it diverted to the Army, leaving 150 cubic metres for operations and 100 cubic metres as the reserve for escape.[43] Thus, S-boat offensive activities in the west came to their end. During 1945, the S-boat Arm sank 6 ships of 12,972 gross tons by torpedo, 25 ships of 75,999 gross tons by mine, and seriously damaged 7 ships of 26,408 gross tons. The total losses of S-boats in 1945 was fifteen.[44] The remainder now awaited their last operations or the order to make for home ports. When the instructions came from Dönitz on 5 May 1945, only a few boats headed for the German Bight. At the end of the war, S-boats of 2., 4., 6. and 9.SFltl. still languished at Den Helder and Rotterdam.[45]

S-boat putting out to sea.

13
Last Station – the Baltic
February 1944 – May 1945

On 14 January 1944, three Soviet fronts began their attack on Army Group North. The latter quickly abandoned the siege of Leningrad and fell back on the Narva river. At the beginning of February, Army Group North asked Dönitz for naval support to prevent enemy landings west of the Narva.

Some days before, at the suggestion of Group North, SKL had instructed Petersen to transfer an S-boat flotilla from the North Sea to the Gulf of Finland.[1] Korvettenkapitän Obermaier, commanding the 6th S-boat Flotilla, sailed with eight boats from Ijmuiden on 6 February 1944 via Kiel for Reval (now Tallinn), where he met up with the depot ship *Carl Peters*, which had left Swinemünde on 16 February. Here they waited at readiness for the possible Russian attack, broken only by a spell of exercises at Libau. Meanwhile, the Russian fleet remained bottled up at Kronstadt. To maintain the blockade once the ice in the Gulf of Finland began to break up, the the Kriegsmarine set about supplementing the existing minefields at the eastern end of the Gulf. Their primary concern was to prevent the breakout of Soviet submarines, for which purpose they also set nets.

Between March and May 1944, over 2,000 mines and 1,100 protective buoys were laid between the Narva estuary and Suursaari island. To the north the Luftwaffe dropped mines, extending the defensive line stretching from the Finnish shore. Old Soviet mines were also present there. All of this activity was aimed at ensuring that the Soviet fleet remained embayed at Kronstadt. Monitoring these minefields against Soviet minesweepers were German steam minesweepers, R-boats and artillery lighters. From May, they became the target of attack by Soviet aircraft and small warships. To fend off the latter, 6.SFltl. arrived at Helsinki and then sheltered in the skerries west of Kotka, from where the flotilla sailed three operations into Kronstadt Bay, engaging the enemy on each occasion. Two Soviet boats were sunk, two damaged.

Following the Normandy landings on 6 June 1944, 6.SFltl. was ordered to return to the west, but the flotilla did not leave Finland until 16 June, because of bad weather, and arrived only on 26 June at Ijmuiden. While the invasion front was the centre of attention, the situation in the Baltic deteriorated rapidly. On 10 June 1944, the Soviet Union began its attack on Finland in Karelia. Although the forces there offered tough resistance, the task was beyond them and they were forced to retreat. Naval High Command Baltic (Admiral Schmundt) reported that after the Russian attack began, the Fins in Karelia showed a certain nervousness: 'This was also noticeable after 6.SFltl. was withdrawn. The Russians moved their minesweepers along the newly won coast and the Finns did not know how to respond to this.'[2] Schmundt did not request the flotilla's return, but SKL felt obliged to consider how the Finns could be propped up. On 21 June, when the major offensive was launched on Army Group Centre, it became known that peace feelers had been extended by the Finns to the Soviets, and it now became the primary task to keep Finland in the Axis.

Together with the promise of weapons supplies, including four S-boats, SKL ordered an eight-boat flotilla to be formed from the 1st S-boat Training Division for the Gulf of Finland.[3] The FdS chose 5.SFltl., which had lost all but one boat in the Channel and was now being reconstituted practically from scratch. As Dönitz was pressing for results, the three serviceable boats of 5.SFltl. (Kapitänleutnant Holzapfel) set out at once for Reval in company with the depot ship *Hermann von Wissmann*, arriving on

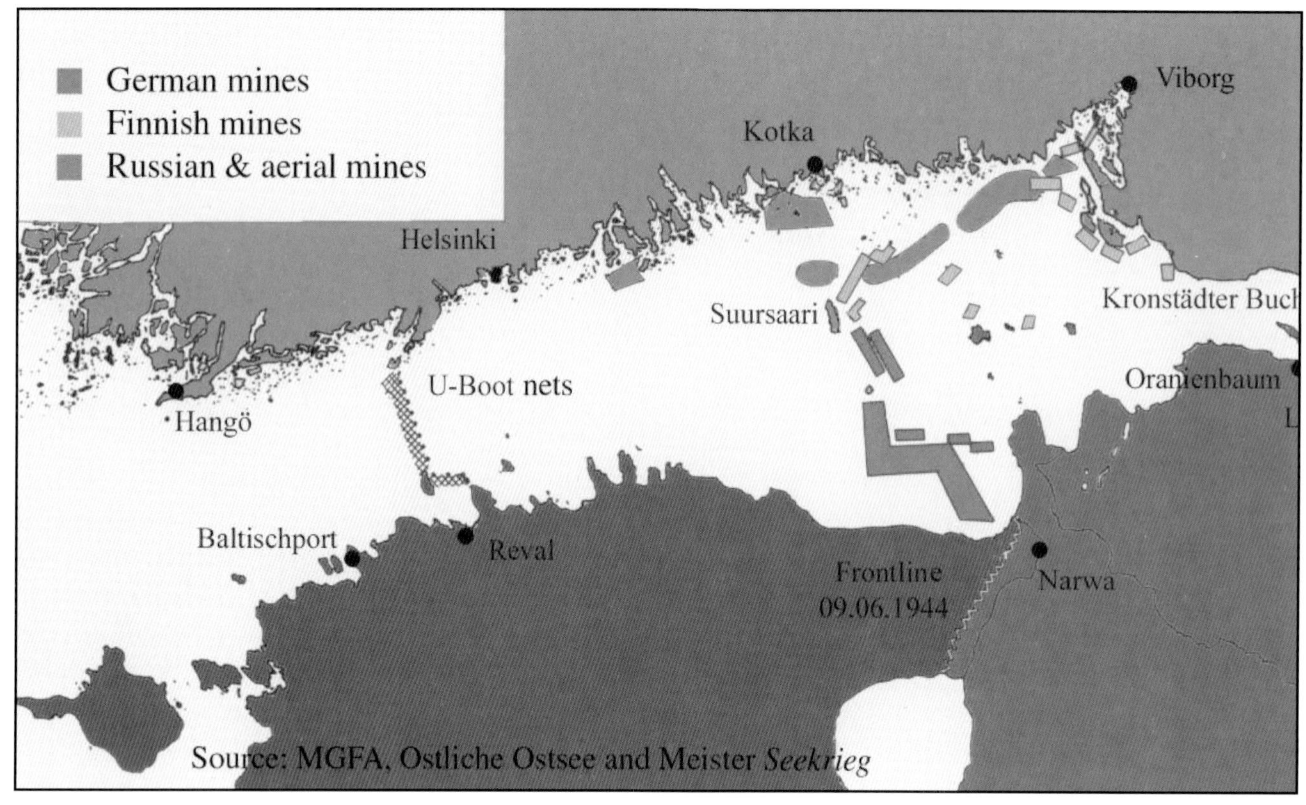

Situation in the Gulf of Finland, 1944.

15 July 1944, and from there proceeded to the Kotka skerries, where 6.SFltl. had lain in the spring. Other boats followed once serviceable, and so by August the flotilla strength stood at eight boats as ordered, although the depot ship was west of Helsinki for fear of air attack.

To compensate for this, a provisional land base was set up and from here the flotilla sailed a few minor operations, searched for survivors of the three German torpedo boats sunk in their own minefield while laying mines, and dropped mines around the watery grave of U-250 off Viborg to prevent the raising of the submarine.[4] Shortly after laying these mines, S 80 hit a mine and sank, with five crew.

On 4 September 1944, Finland abandoned the struggle and gave German forces notice to leave Finnish soil by 15 September. German naval units operating from the skerries pulled back, 5.SFltl. and the depot ship putting into Baltisch Port (now Baldieski).

Without the support of the Finns, the minefields that had kept the Soviet fleet trapped in Kronstadt Bay could no longer be maintained, and the presence of Soviet units, particularly submarines, was now to be feared in the central Baltic. This meant that the German convoy route for the Swedish ore traffic, for troop transports to the northern sectors of the Eastern Front and the vital U-boat training grounds off the Baltic coast were all now under threat, the possibility of which Dönitz had frequently drawn to Hitler's attention.[5]

In order to protect the minefields, from mid-September 1944 an attempt was made to occupy Hogland island, since Soviet minesweepers could be engaged from there by coastal artillery. To protect the landing, 5.SFltl. laid mines off Kotka to prevent Finnish MTBs leaving, but contrary to expectations the Finns on Hogland offered stout resistance and the landings failed. A number of German ships and boats attempting to land troops were sunk by Finnish MTBs, which had found another way to leave Kotka.

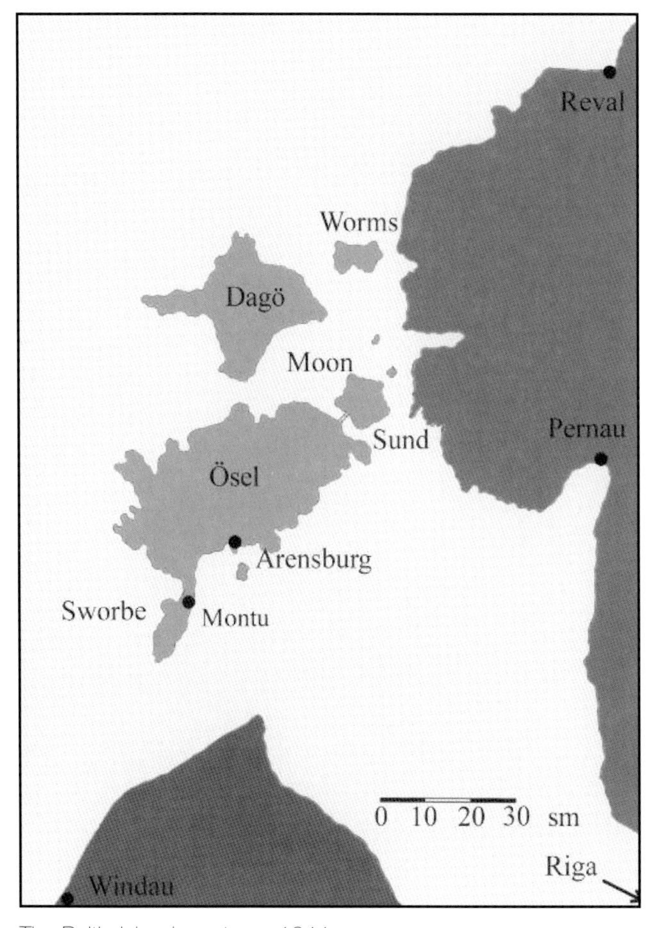

The Baltic islands, autumn 1944

The 5th S-boat Flotilla was unable to intervene, since it did not receive the full orders for Operation '*Tanne Ost*' until after its return from the minelaying at Kotka.[6] Even a successful occupation of the island would have served little purpose, however, for when 6.SFltl. brought off the remaining personnel in Finland on 15 September, the long-expected Soviet offensive against Army Group North began. By 21 September the Soviets had taken Reval, and a few days later Baltisch Port followed. These were the last two German naval bases in the Gulf of Finland and all naval vessels, including 6.SFltl., withdrew to Libau and Windau.

It now became the operational objective to prevent the occupation of the eastern Baltic islands. For this purpose, SKL requested another flotilla but, after discussions with Petersen, accepted the 2nd S-boat Training Flotilla under Kapitänleutnant Klose with an initial four boats. On 28 September 1944, the flotilla came alongside the depot ship *Tsingtau* at Windau. The 5th S-boat Flotilla was also there after having mined Reval.

The two S-boat flotillas now carried out a string of mining operations in the Sound of Moon, off Riga and also Pernau, but without causing the enemy any noticeable delay in his advance. On 29 September, Soviet troops crossed Moon and occupied the islands of Hiiumaa, on 2 October, and Saaremaa, on 5 October.

After the Führer had ordered Sworbe to be held to the last round on 8 October 1944,[7] the efforts of naval support forces and the two S-boat flotillas were concentrated on bolstering the land front. A battle group of cruisers and torpedo boats formed in the Baltic joined the defence. S-boats mined the coast of Sworbe and repelled several minor landing parties, but all efforts proved vain, for the defence was gradually overcome and, on the night of 23 November 1944, the 9th Security Division sailed with the last troops.[8]

> Commanding Admiral with C-in-C Army Group North and other generals taken by S-boat *Rotte* from Windau to Sworbe. Reached harbour Montu without being attacked. Both S-boats returned at midday. Boats of the 2nd S-boat Training Flotilla arrived at top speed. On leaving harbour, a wire hanging from a splintered beam tangled in propeller of first boat, central propeller of second boat hit underwater obstruction and was put out of service. This reduced top speed of *Rotte* to twenty knots. At sea, attacked by around eight foreign bombers with fighter protection. Our own fighter cover, four aircraft, unable to prevent. Leader boat hit by rockets, on fire forward. Torpedoes discharged because of fire risk. While Commanding Admiral and generals transferred to No. 2 boat, one of torpedoes returned on circular course and was only narrowly avoided. (War Diary, Admiral Eastern Baltic, 25 October 1944)

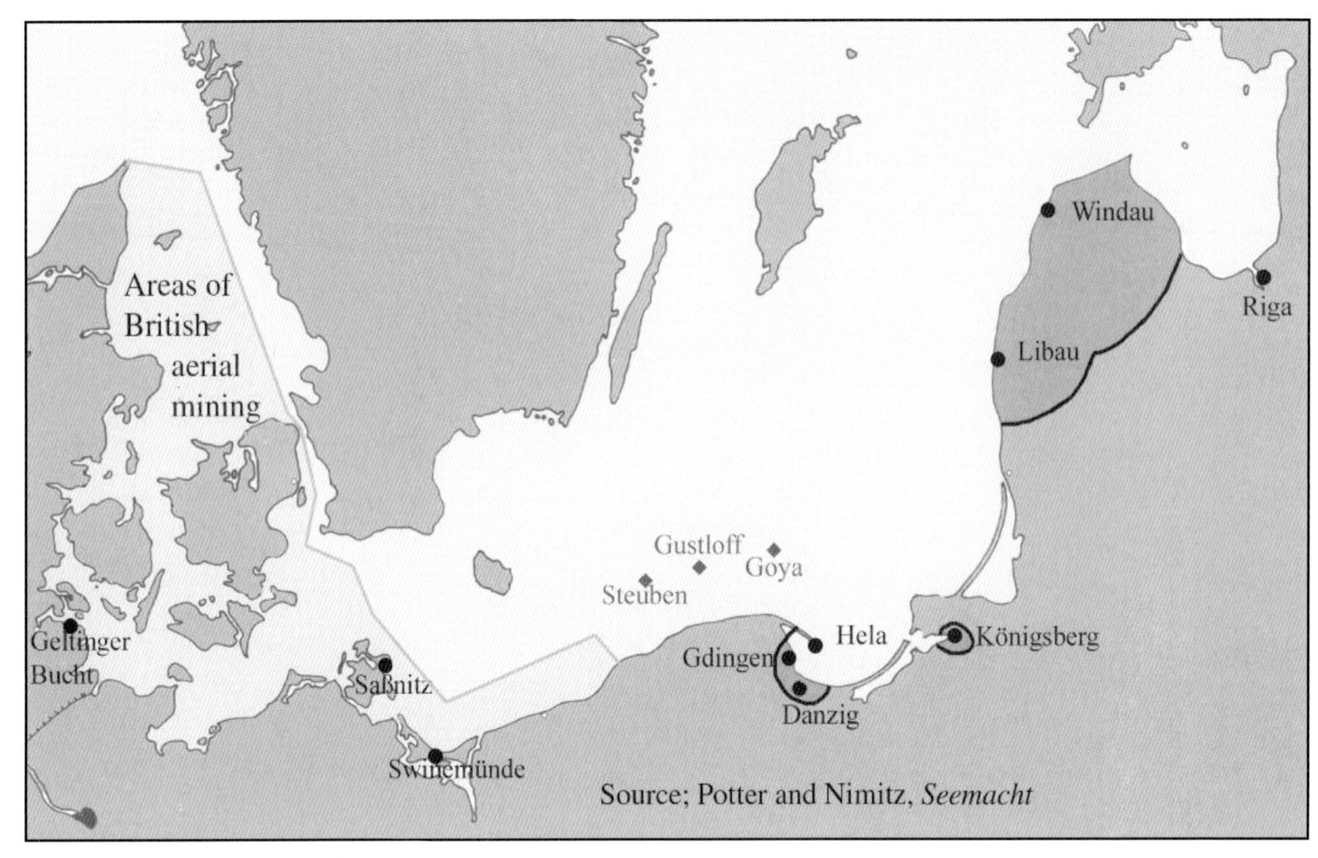

Situation in the central Baltic, spring 1945.

Following the evacuation of Sworbe, more minelaying ensued, from the south coast of the Sworbe peninsula and in the Irben Strait, to prevent passage of Soviet units, while, in a number of operations, agents and sabotage troops were landed in the Gulf of Riga. Meanwhile the operational strength of both flotillas had been much reduced by damage received in action, because of engine changes and collisions.[9] This was mainly 5.SFltl., while the 2nd Training Flotilla had been reinforced by four more boats from the 2nd Group.

When the Battle of the Ardennes began, a new offensive build-up in the west was ordered and, four days before Christmas 1944, 5.SFltl. left Windau. After an inter-flotilla exchange with the 1st S-boat Training Flotilla of the best boats at Swinemünde, 5.SFltl. (Kapitänleutnant Holzapfel) arrived at Den Helder at the beginning of January 1945 to strengthen the existing flotillas there.

Despite the ice season in the eastern Baltic between December 1944 and February 1945, the 2nd S-boat Training Flotilla sailed from Windau on mining operations, to land sabotage troops and occasionally fire on enemy positions in the Gulf of Riga. From 1 March 1945, they had the support of 1.SFltl. (Korvettenkapitän Büchting), operational despite some engine problems, and with new, well-armed boats to replace those lost in the Black Sea.

Meanwhile, Soviet troops had advanced as far as the coast of Pomerania. German troops were massed in encirclements at Kurland and in the Bay of Danzig, amongst them countless thousands of refugees hoping for evacuation by sea. On 22 January 1945, Dönitz decided, 'Whilst maintaining unconditional priority for military transports, the Kriegsmarine is to support the evacuation of the civilian population, above all women and children, from threatened regions, also by the use of warships.'[10]

The cruiser *Emden*, two target ships and various torpedo recovery vessels were made available for transport purposes. Naval High Command Baltic had a free hand to begin the greatest mass evacuation of all time. Eventually the fleet also comprised former passenger ships, freighters, small craft and vessels that happened to be passing through the area. The main impediment to the evacuation was British aerial mining of the western and central Baltic, which made heavy demands on the minesweeping flotillas. Soviet submarines operating in the Baltic avoided the minefields and attacked only shipping using the deep-water shipping lanes.

From March 1945, Soviet MTBs began to molest minesweepers and transports. To combat these activities, 1.SFltl. and the 2nd Training Flotilla took over convoy protection duty, but the task proved beyond the capabilities of many 1.SFltl. engines. In skirmishes with Soviet boats, the 2nd Training Flotilla sank three and damaged several more. On the night of 9 April 1945, a tragic accident occurred when two boats of 1.SFltl. sank a ship refusing to identify itself and not responding to recognition signals. On approaching the site of the sinking, it was found that the casualty was the German steamer *Neuwerk* with 1,034 people aboard, of whom seventy-eight were picked up by the S-boats.[11]

To strengthen the escorts, on 25 March a further S-boat flotilla was ordered to the Baltic. On 27 March, on the instructions of the FdS, the four serviceable boats of 5.SFltl. (Kapitänleutnant Holzapfel) left Den Helder, to arrive at Sassnitz at the beginning of April.

The other boats followed a little later. Throughout April, all three flotillas were used as escorts to transports. Despite major losses when *Gustloff*, *Steuben* and *Goya* were sunk, more than two million people were saved from the Soviets and brought to the West.[12] Although the partial capitulation came into force in the west on 5 May 1945, the sea transports continued in order to evacuate troops from the Hela and Kurland encirclements. On the night of 8 May 1945, the last transports sailed for the west. The S-boat depot ship *Tsingtau*, filled with wounded, and nineteen S-boats of 1. and 5.SFltl., and the 2nd Training Flotilla were the last naval units to leave Libau, bringing out 2,000 German soldiers.

Soldiers lifted off Kurland aboard an S-boat.

Last return from operations.

After disembarking passengers in Geltinger Bay, they joined boats of the 3rd S-boat Training Flotilla and 10.SFltl. with the depot ships *Hermann von Wissmann*, *Tsingtau*, *Tanga*, *Carl Peters* and *Buea*. On 1 May 1945 at 1100 hrs, the last ceremonial flag parade was held before the FdS. The lowering of the National Socialist war flag marked the end of operations involving the *Schnellboote* of the Kriegsmarine during the Second World War.

14
The Technological War

Scarcely in any other field of S-boat operations was competition so intense as that for technological equipment and its conversion for use in tactical situations.

At the outbreak of war, both sides had radar equipment in use. In Germany the Kriegsmarine had Freya sets, a land-supported system giving warning of aircraft, and Seetakt for shipboard use. The pocket battleships, battleships and heavy cruisers were equipped with the latter by the end of 1939. By April 1941, destroyers had radar, as did all major units by the end of 1942. The aerial was four square metres in size, however, which precluded its use aboard S-boats.

British radar was geared primarily to air defence. At the beginning of hostilities, Britain had set up a chain of early warning centres, with twenty units extending from the Isle of Wight to the River Tees. By 1940, a second chain had been set up for defence against low-flying aircraft and to direct RAF fighters. Early on, the British had decided to establish a centre to evaluate radar, the common command centre at Uxbridge. The effectiveness of their installations would be proven in the Battle of Britain.

In parallel, air intercept (AI) and air to surface vessel (ASV) sets were developed, and these were to be found in series production by September 1939.[1] A scientific team (Operations Research) worked on improvements to existing sets, converting them for shipboard use. Based on the air defence chain, which used the 12m frequency, they made rapid advances towards policing the coasts using shorter-wave equipment on the 1.5m band. S-boats were aware of these developments in 1940, after destroyers ran directly for their positions as they lay adrift in fog. The supposition by the Germans that the British were using 'decimetre telephony' (DT) or range-measuring devices (EM-2) was not correct at this stage. Destroyers were directed by the coastal radar stations, but in the final phase the enemy had to be found visually. Not until the winter of 1941 did British convoy escorts receive converted ASV sets. Atlantic escorts had priority over coastal destroyers and it was January 1942 before east coast destroyers received radar.[2]

In the autumn of 1942, Coastal Forces (MGBs, MTBs and MLs) were equipped with simple devices, one of which fell into German hands when MGB 335 was captured. According to a statement by a radar operator taken prisoner aboard this boat, the pinpointing of S-boats was still not possible at that time, whereas the coastal radar watch was almost absolute. In December 1942, the Nore radar net was completed, enabling observation from the foreshore to twenty miles out.

This signified two things for the S-boat Arm. First, a sneak approach to the convoy lanes under the coast after a long period lying in wait was no longer possible. The *Stichansatz*, involving almost immediate contact with the enemy *somewhere* was the logical consequence. Second, conditions of poor visibility, previously of great value for S-boats, now ruled out such sorties. Even at night, an S-boat required a minimum visibility of two nautical miles in order to avoid being surprised and fired upon by a radar-equipped destroyer. This limited further the freedom to operate. It was therefore logical that the FdT, and later his successor the FdS, should make repeated and ever more urgent requests for S-boat radar.[3]

Since the technical development could not be forced, however, pressure from U-boat Command, which suffered severely from the advantage of the British side in electronics, resulted in the production

Naxos radar with various aerial configurations.

of a radar warning device (Metox), tested aboard S-boats in the Mediterranean and Channel in May 1942. Positive reports led to series production, but U-boats had priority and not until August 1942 did two to three boats of each S-flotilla receive a Metox. In the spring of 1943, when U-boats reported being attacked without the 'Biscay Cross' having given warning, technical investigations discovered emissions from the Metox. This led to the assumption that the enemy could home in on the radiations and so the use of Metox aboard U-boats was abandoned.

British radar now operated on wavelengths in the centimetre band, a measure that the Germans had for long considered impossible. When, in August 1943, four boats of the 9th S-boat Flotilla sailed to Bordeaux in preparation to be handed over to Spain, the opportunity was taken by Signals Experimental Command (NVK) to survey the activity of British aircraft in the Channel. It was deduced that RAF fighter-bombers had devices in the 9cm band. Nevertheless, not until the autumn of 1943 did the S-boat Arm abandon Metox; by then, all British radars in the Channel had been converted to centimetre band and Metox no longer picked them up.

New radar detection devices (FuMB) followed: first Naxos with various aerial types (Fliege, Mücke, Cuba Ia); later Tunis and to some extent Korfu.[4] These were all receivers accurate to within three degrees and gave good warning, provided the enemy did not have too many radar carriers in the vicinity. 'I often had to switch the set off,' a commander wrote.[5] 'I simply couldn't stand the endless screeching and buzzing.' Obviously there could only be a warning if the enemy set was switched on. In the case of radar 'silence', or if British escort vessels were being directed by land stations, there was no warning, and for this reason the FdS had to emphasise the need for two nautical miles' visibility in order to guard against surprises.

In June 1942, an experimental radar (FuMG), Lichtenstein, which had been developed for night fighters, was tested on S 112. The results were still unsatisfactory. The maximum range was two kilometres and gave readings only thirty-five degrees either side of the boat's keel-line. For other angles, the aerial had to be unfixed and rotated. A rotatable aerial introduced later was found useful but increased the boat's radar-reflective surface so greatly that it would always be the first boat to receive enemy fire, and the installation received the nickname 'enemy-shell collecting box'.

The British also developed radar detection devices, mostly located ashore and aimed primarily at obtaining warning of the approach of German aircraft. When S 112 was equipped with the Lichtenstein set for the first time for an attack on a northbound convoy, British naval units deceived

Cuba 1a aerial (also called Fliege) for the Naxos anti-radar.

vicinity. By 1943, the British had already developed the rotating indication common to modern radar screens.

The panorama that such units provided was first discovered by the Germans in the spring of 1943 when they retrieved an intact set from a crashed bomber at Rotterdam. The extent of the British lead in the technology was so great that it could not be overhauled. The Arbeitsgemeinschaft Rotterdam laboratory therefore recommended that the captured equipment be reproduced as a copy.[7] Work on this was held back by problems with materials and long completion dates due to increased Allied bombing. The copy version for S-boats, the Berlin-S, was only ever available in small numbers, and was first tested on S 302 in the Baltic in March 1945.[8]

Parallel to the development of German detection devices, trials were held to see if the reflective surface of boats could be reduced, or eliminated, by the use of an absorbent coat. Codenamed 'Netzhemd', trials were run aboard S 147 off Pelzerhaken in Lübeck Bay in the first two weeks of January 1944. Two U-boats and an uncoated S-boat also took part as checks. Dönitz visited the trials and was visibly impressed, but the method was never used operationally.[9]

German land radar was erected early on at Cap

themselves into thinking that German aircraft were approaching because the device had only previously been used by the Luftwaffe.

At the beginning of 1944, an improved Hohentwiel was tested aboard S 87. Siting the aerial eight metres up in March 1944 gave better results but was not convincing for tactical purposes on operations, since it failed to provide the force commander with an overall view. Along with the poor extent of the field, the principal drawback was having the range shown on a Braunsch tube[6] and the bearing on the screen. The two had then to be combined, a very difficult proceeding on a darkened boat with no operations room, particularly when, as was usual on S-boat missions, there were many enemy vessels in the

First, fixed Lichtenstein radar.

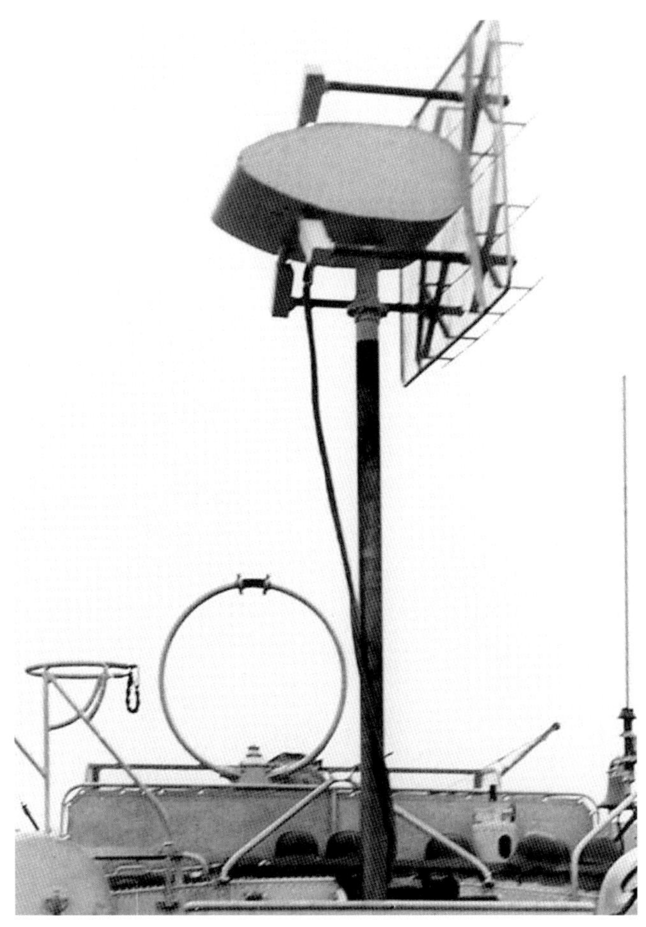

Rotatable Lichtenstein radar, also known as the 'enemy-shell collecting box'.

Trials of the Hohentwiel radar off Heligoland.

Griz Nez, near Calais. Frequent attempts were made to direct S-boats to detected targets, but the quality of the equipment was poor, and no successes ever resulted. The radar was also unsuitable for coastal watch because of poor range, indifferent bearings and general inaccuracy.[10] The FdS had no answer to the Allied concentration of radar carriers on land, at sea and in the air. The means by which he attempted to counterbalance the superiority of the other side was by the B-Dienst (Beobachtungsdienst = radio monitoring service).

Radio Monitoring

At the outbreak of war, the B-Dienst was already well trained and efficient.[11] After the fall of France, radio receiving and locating stations were set up on the occupied coast. Naval Direction-Finding (DF) Division Flanders especially was able quickly to assemble information relating to the rhythm of British coastal convoys and the procedures employed by British naval forces. This data was used at once by the FdT.[12] Loose co-operation initially became closer at the operational level as the need by staff planners for immediate access to results grew. This led to direct telephone links between the FdS and DF centres, and to the setting up of a DF centre at FdS headquarters. From 1 August 1942, there was even a B-Dienst unit at the FdS command centre.

As soon as the B-Dienst telegraphist wrote something down, the decrypt writer watching over his shoulder decoded the material with the help of a code table so that, almost as soon as the message terminated, he had the complete text. As this was done in the situation room behind a curtain, the FdS had the enemy report in his hand within seconds. Then, thanks to a precise and immediate knowledge of British reports and orders, he could pass his instructions forthwith to his S-boats at sea. (Bonatz, *Funkaufklärung*, p 156)

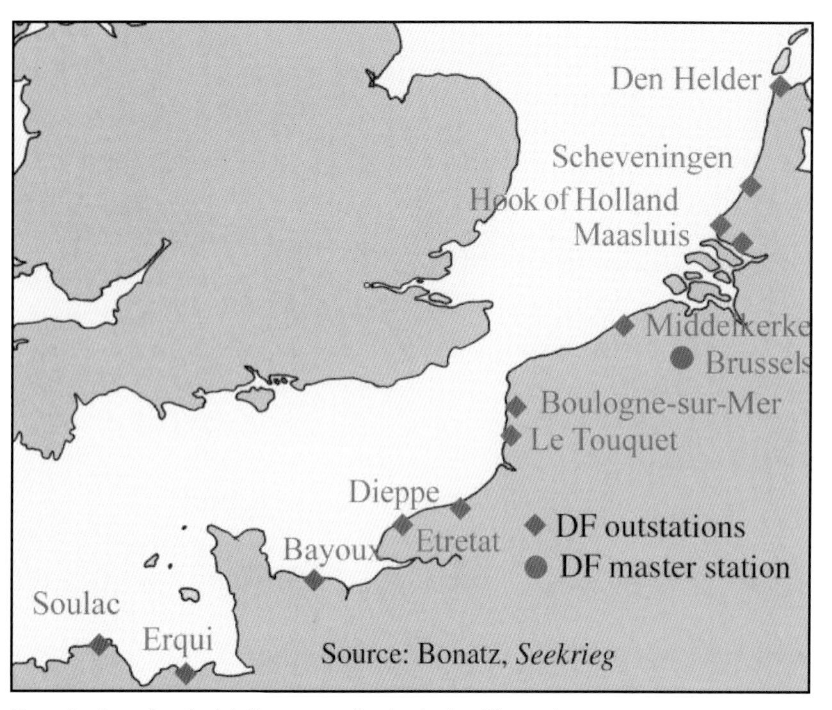

Organisation of radio intelligence-gathering in the Channel.

The Royal Navy codes were simple affairs and, providing enough material was transmitted, presented no great difficulties to the cryptanalysts. As a general rule, this enabled enemy radio traffic to be read at the beginning of night operations. Thus, once S-boats sailed, they would know if they had been detected by radar, if their minelaying had been spotted, if (importantly) the enemy had alerted his forces and how he was planning to intercept the S-boats on their return to port. The charts found aboard MGB 335 provided additional information regarding the predetermined interception spots and, from the spring of 1943, enabled the waiting MGB groups to be avoided. There was a black spot at around midnight when the British made their daily code change. Normally it required up to ninety minutes to break the code, but in this period the British would often signal *en clair* shortly before contacting S-boats in order for their units to react more rapidly. The immediate transmission of the decoded texts on the S-boat frequency meant that information was being passed to German and British naval vessels in the Channel at almost the same time. As an example, an operation of 2 September 1943 yielded the following signals:

0103 hrs. B-Dienst reports: '6.SFltl. detected by radar.'
0103 hrs. 'Information: 6.SFltl. your presence known.'
0119 hrs. B-Dienst: 'MGBs . . . steer south.'
0126 hrs. 'Information: 6.SFltl., MGBs coming from north.'

Ultra-short-wave voice radio in the wheelhouse.

Thus, by use of a system of short encoded notes, the so-called 'tart code', the FdS gained a time advantage. In the autumn of 1943, the British introduced a new code for operational radio-telephone traffic with its coastal forces, robbing the Germans of some of this advantage. 'This made itself very noticeable at Command,' the FdS recorded[13] after the operation of 24 September 1943.

The importance of radio monitoring for the Germans led them to introduce a strict radio-telephone discipline. The Radio-Telephone (Ultra-Short Wave) Regulations applied in the protective bunkers; boats left port under radio silence and, to synchronise position or for conversations at sea, had to find the partner boat and use loud-hailers. Only once contact had been made with the enemy was radio-telephone traffic permitted, although those *Rotten* out of immediate contact had to continue radio silence so as not to betray their presence prematurely.

The British had begun to decode Enigma traffic in the spring of 1940. The organisation involved in the work at Bletchley Park gave it the code name 'Ultra'.[14] Its priority was to read radio traffic to and from U-boats. The decoding required time, but an immediate supply of text, contrary to the requirement in the Channel, was not urgent in the Atlantic. It was sufficient to know the intentions, rendezvous with supply ships and the routes taken out and back. Initially, Ultra provided little on S-boat operations. In the Channel, operational orders from the FdS to the S-boat bunkers were passed by secure telex connections that could not be intercepted. At sea, the morse key was used, and because of the urgency, texts were passed by the 'tart code' instead of Enigma. This provided only a few hours' security but was ample for exchanges in battle situations. It was a different matter if the boats were operating at a fixed station and they received their orders as Enigma-encoded signals. Then Ultra could read them and the British commander would react. Thus, when 4. and 5.SFltl. transferred from St Peter Port on Guernsey to the Baie de l'Aber Wrac'h, north of Brest, on 11 August 1943, they had scarcely arrived when they were attacked by fighter-bombers. S 121 was sunk and six other boats seriously damaged.

Ultra came into its own after the invasion when some of the telex network was destroyed, forcing Group West to send its operational orders by radio telegraphy. The losses inflicted at Boulogne (13 June 1944) and Le Havre (14 June 1944) resulted from Ultra decryption.[15] In the Mediterranean, as a rule telex was used for messages between the flotilla staffs and Naval High Command in Rome. As there was no fixed command centre and the flotilla commander led from a boat, there was little important information usable by Ultra.[16] The British received indirect information regarding the first operations of 3.SFltl. operations when Ultra decoded messages sent to U-74 on 21, 22 and 23 December 1941, advising the submarine of S-boat operations off Malta.[17] In the Black Sea and Baltic, Ultra was not significant.

An Enigma code machine.

15
Training and Working Up

On 1 September 1939, the two S-boat flotillas, the 1st (Kapitänleutnant Sturm) and the 2nd (Kapitänleutnant Petersen), each had six to eight active boats with experienced crews, plus two boats in reserve in home ports, used for training purposes. A midshipman and a seaman branch NCO (whose next appointments would then be as the No. 1 and boatswain) and, from time to time, an engine room artificer also scheduled for a new boat, would be responsible for the training of a boat's complement aboard each reserve boat.

The flotillas had a mix of engines. The boats of 1.SFltl. had Daimler-Benz diesels, 2.SFltl. the older and less reliable MAN diesels. The training extended to both nautical and technical instruction and lasted three months. During this period, the crews under training lived aboard an accommodation ship in the Scheerhafen because the two depot ships, *Tsingtau* (1.SFltl.) and *Tanga* (2.SFltl.) had a limit of six crews from the operational flotillas.[1]

As further flotillas were created during the war, the crews were trained by flotilla senior personnel. The first new flotilla, 3.SFltl., was formed on 15 May 1940 from the reserve boats of the first two flotillas (S 10, S 11, S 12 and S 13). As flotilla commander Kapitänleutnant Kemnade had only three commanders at his disposal, he started the training with only three boats, but then received orders that within three months, by the end of September, he should have completed training all four crews plus two more for 1. and 2.SFltl. as well. *Tsingtau* was assigned as depot and target ship, replaced later by the newly commissioned depot ship *Adolf Lüderitz*.[2]

Before joining the flotillas, the crews completed basic training in ships' core companies (*Schiffs-Stammabteilungen*), and then the appropriate instruction in the technical schools of the various inspectorates:

- Navigation schools (*Inspektion des Bildungswesens*)
- Naval gunnery, coastal artillery and flak schools (*Inspektion der Marine-artillerie*)
- Naval engineering schools (*Inspektion des Schiffs-Maschinenwesens*)
- Torpedo schools (*Torpedo Inspektion*)
- Signals schools (*Marinenachrichten Inspektion*)[3]

These schools also provided extended technical instruction for NCOs qualifying as mates, of whom most would have served previously on S-boats. As a rule, engine-room personnel also received instruction at the various engine manufacturers' premises.

In working up a flotilla, the crew had to master the boat in all states of wind and weather, to repair damage occurring during operations or from enemy action and to use the boat's weapons effectively. First by day, then night, all roles on the boat had to be practised until they could be performed blindfold. Training aboard the assigned boat was followed by work in *Rotten* (pairs) and then as a flotilla, evolving correct methods of reconnaissance and attack. Torpedo firing was practised using the depot ship as target; for gunnery, a tug towed a target float. Sailing in formation also had to be worked at. For 3.SFltl. the programme was:

- five individual boat training exercises
- three *Rotte* training exercises
- six attack practices
- seven reconnaissance and attack practices
- two gunnery practice shoots
- three practice torpedo exercises, with thirty practice torpedo shoots for commanders and boatswains
- six flotilla formation exercises

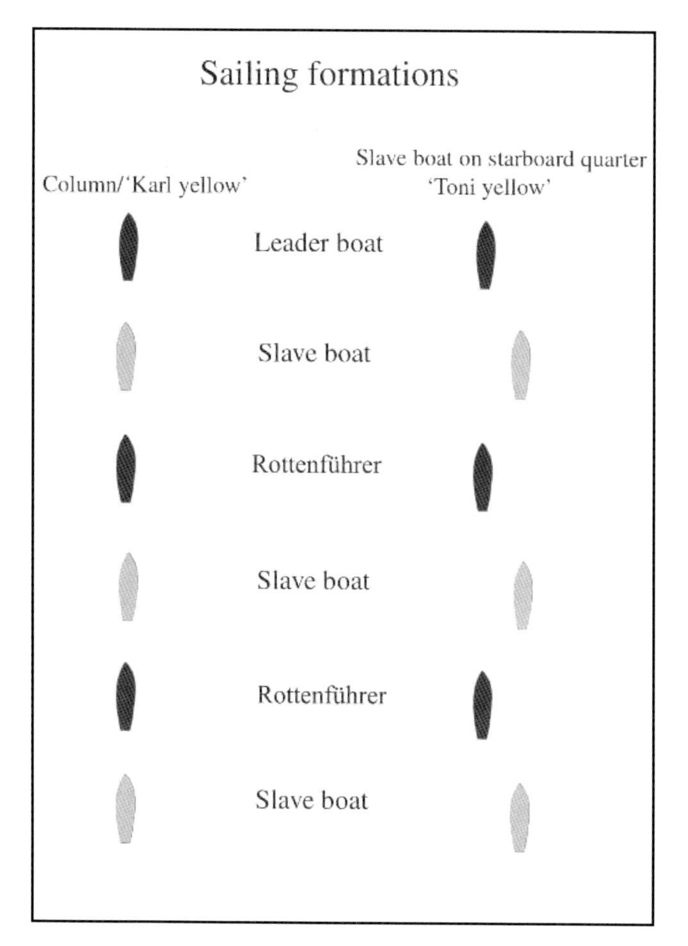

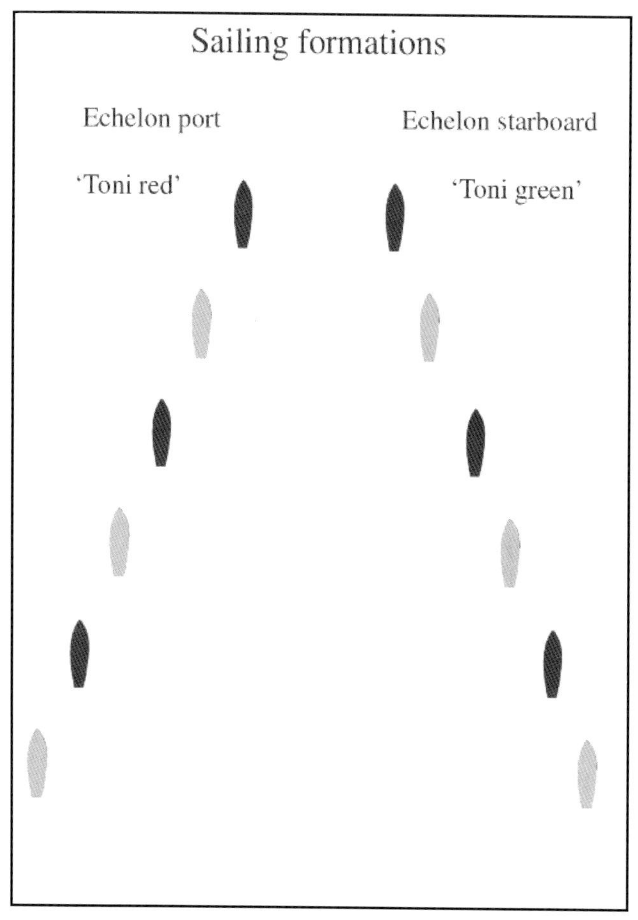

For this programme, twenty training days at sea were set aside, so that the various sections overlapped. As a rule, fifteen hours per day were spent at sea, not counting preparations to sail and shipping torpedoes and fuel in port. At this time, the training base was usually Neufahrwasser, in Danzig Bay.[4]

Meanwhile in the Channel the first losses had occurred, so that not only had new boats to be commissioned, but also replacement crews put at readiness. The loss of commanders caused particular concern. When 2.SFltl. at Boulogne lost Oberleutnant zur See Kecke, S 35, dead and Oberleutnant zur See Zimmermann, S 30, seriously wounded, to air attack, Personnel Reserve had no replacement to send and two officers from the T-boat Arm with no experience of S-boats (Oberleutnant zur See Meentzen and Oberleutnant zur See Feldt) had to be transferred in.

The problem of recruitment was ever present throughout the war for the S-boat Arm. For long, the U-boat Arm had unquestioned priority in securing young watchkeeping officers. Serving aboard S-boats at high speed by night and in formation made great physical and mental demands comparable to those for a high-achievement sport. In the Channel especially, British fighter and shipborne radar superiority was such that a clash with enemy forces had to be expected on each mission. Weak commanders could not handle this.[5] For flotilla commanders and the Arm as a whole there was always a dilemma whether to replace a weak commander or weaken the fighting strength of the flotilla by keeping him and inviting a greater risk to other boats on subsequent missions. The FdT understood this and therefore warned the T-boat Arm, too, not to allow the demands of war to become excessive. After the loss of S 53 (Oberleutnant zur See Block), he wanted to make it clear 'that a young naval officer, a recent entry of average ability, needs from one to two years' training in peacetime to learn the trade to the extent that he can handle all situations likely to crop up along the English south-east coast'.[6] He also requested Personnel Division to send him only proven officers with quality time on destroyers and torpedo boats for the responsible position of S-boat commanders. Such a request could not be met, because of the pressures exerted by the U-boat Arm. 'We cannot just send you only the most suitable officers,' the Personnel Office decided.[7] Flotilla commander Kapitänleutnant Feldt made the bitter observation that he had been aware of the weaknesses of Oberleutnant zur See Block when he sailed with him as instructor, but had always been obliged to bow to the exigencies of operations.[8]

Meanwhile, new boats had become available in quick succession and the following new flotillas were formed: 4.SFltl. (1 October 1940), 6.SFltl. (1 March 1941), 5.SFltl. (15 July 1941), 7.SFltl. (1 October 1941) and 8.SFltl. (1 November 1941). All trained their crews along the lines described, as well as replacements for men lost or wounded. In order to systematise and, most importantly, incorporate experience gained at the front, it was decided next that a training flotilla should be formed.

The S-boat Training Flotilla (Schnellbootsschulflottille)

In July 1942, the new flotilla was set up at Swinemünde in the Baltic using old boats withdrawn from active duty at the front. Veteran personnel, proven on operations, were brought together under the leadership of Kapitänleutnant Opdenhoff[9] as flotilla commander. The priority was the training of commanders and replacement personnel, rather than welding together whole crews. Up to sixteen old boats, all no strangers to engine breakdowns, were made available, together with three depot ship.[10]

For future commanders, the best career path had been identified as: time as cadet and midshipman served aboard S-boats; after passing out as a naval officer, up to about the age of 23, service as watchkeeping officer aboard torpedo boats; then after six months in the S-boat Training Flotilla, commander in a frontline flotilla. The need for the training facility expanded as the supply of new boats and human casualties increased in all theatres of war.

As a rule, the boats sailed to the following bridge orders:
Minimum revs – 8 knots
Slow ahead – 12 knots
Half ahead – 15 knots
Twice half ahead – 20 knots
Full ahead (*Grosse Fahrt*) – 24 knots
Twice full ahead – 28 knots
All ahead – 34 knots
Twice all ahead – 38 knots
Maximum ahead (*Äusserste Kraft*) – 40 knots
Thrice maximum ahead – everything the engines could give

Orders by Signal

By Day

Increase speed – wagging yellow flags upright
Reduce speed – holding up yellow flag by staff, extend corner of flag
Stop – yellow flag held over side, both sides
Go astern – wagging yellow flags over side
Course change – flag signal, then wagging red flag (port) or green flag (starboard)

By Night

Increase speed – hand searchlight or Aldis-type lamp, short flash
Reduce speed – lamp, three long flashes
Engine speeds – minimum revs, three long flashes; half ahead, short white flash; full ahead, long green flash; all ahead, short green flash
Course changes were passed by morse; when last boat showed clear, signalled with long flash[11]

In November 1943, the FdS drew up a balance sheet: compared with the losses of boats in the previous years (1940, four boats; 1941, three boats; 1942, five boats), after eleven months of 1943, twenty boats had reported substantially increased losses amongst personnel. The planned building programme was aimed at increasing the output of new boats from three monthly to, at first, twelve and, later, seventeen, with a final target of twenty-five boats per month. To achieve this, the production of engines, which had been the bottleneck until then, would be intensified and a third supplier, Danziger Waggonfabrik, added. In a realistic assessment of the possibilities, the FdS pointed out that this was an increase of only six boats per month but, even so, the training organisation had to be adjusted and expanded.[12]

Semaphore ordering decrease in speed.

The S-boat Instruction Division (Schnellbootslehrdivision – SLD)

With effect from 1 November 1943, SLD began its task under the former head of the 1st S-boat Training Flotilla, now Korvettenkapitän Opdenhoff. At the same time a section was set up at Swinemünde-Eichstaden under Kapitänleutnant Meyering to train deck personnel, while the 1st Training Flotilla passed to Kapitänleutnant Wilcke. A second section for engine room personnel was established in June 1944 at Kaseburg under Korvettenkapitän (Ing) Paasch. Two other training flotillas, the 2nd Flotilla under Kapitänleutnant Klose, and the 3rd Flotilla under Kapitänleutnant Siems, were founded in April and June 1944 respectively.[13] In February 1944, Korvettenkapitän Feldt, former commander of 5.SFltl., took over SLD from Opdenhoff to add recent fresh experience to the training programme.

Despite this expansion in the training flotillas, it remained policy that newly formed flotillas, or those equipped with new-type boats, carried out their own training. This was done in collaboration with SLD, while it remained competent for the training of commanders and replacements. The flow of new commanders remained a problem, even though Dönitz had ruled that 'the S-boat Arm in its expansion is to be afforded in every respect the same priorities as the U-boat Arm'.[14] As an emergency measure, the FdS had already begun to use especially competent coxswains as commanders, although he continued to trawl for a larger intake of naval officer applicants within the service, and midshipmen, who could later be clawed back to the S-boat Arm as senior midshipmen or officers.

The SLD chief had special responsibility in deciding whether to qualify aspiring commanders or to reject a man in cases of doubt. The fact that the final assessment was not made until after the first voyages with a front-line flotilla did not mitigate the difficulty of making the decision.[15] If operations and front deployments permitted, the new commander aspirants would sail a couple of

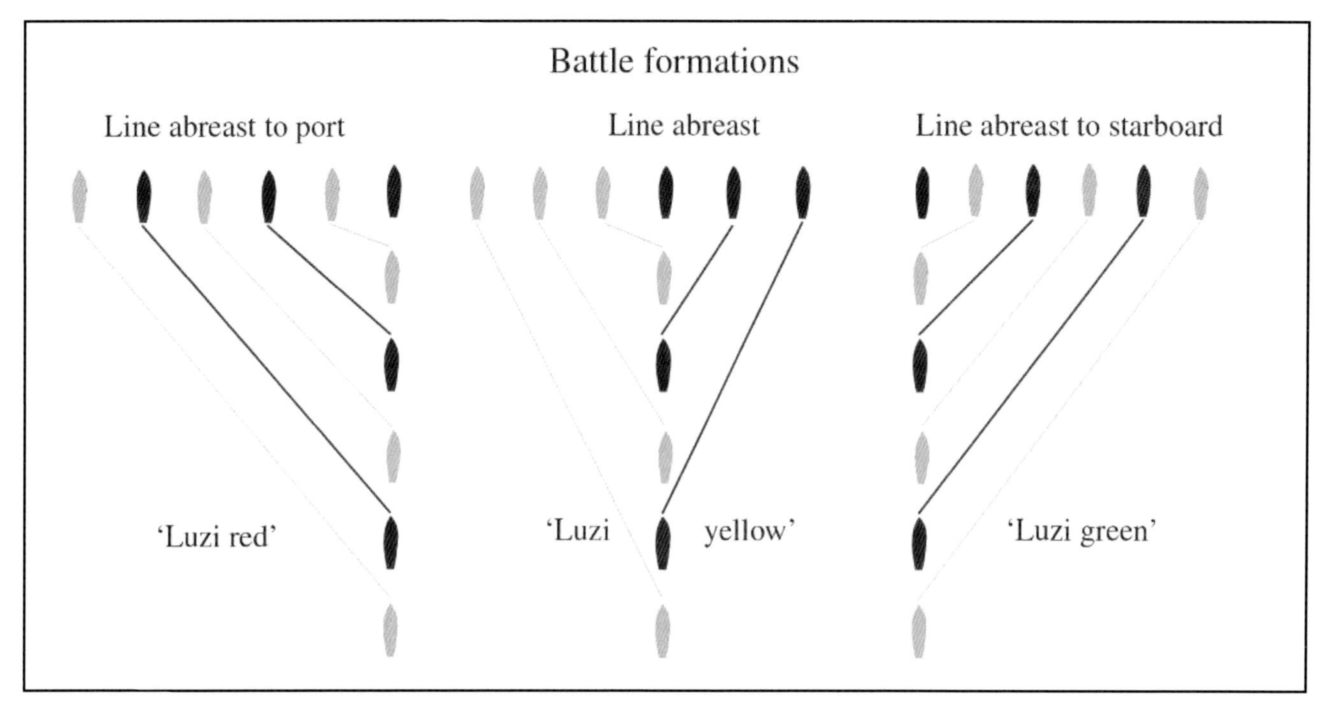

Battle formations.

night exercises with a veteran commander, nicknamed 'Ärger Karl' ('*ärger*' meaning 'fed up with it'), and if these were satisfactory, he would then sail with an experienced commander in the third or fourth *Rotte*. After that, the decisions would be taken to approve or reject the man as commander.[16]

On operations, the new commanders were generally monitored by the flotilla chief sailing in command of the leader boat. This was good practice in peacetime, for the 'Junior Karl' could learn from the flotilla chief, and so obtain his 'last coat of varnish'.[17] In wartime, however, it would have been a more reasonable procedure to have relieved the flotilla commander of the job of supervising his young captains and let an experienced shipboard adviser represent him alongside the new man. This could not be done because of the lack of adequate intake, despite endless requests from the front flotillas. Even after the training programme had been systematised, the basic problem remained that too many young officers were needed for S-boat operations stretching from the North Cape to the Sea of Azov, while a well-qualified intake was also being demanded by the U-boat Arm and all other classes of warship from battleships to patrol boats. Moreover this was a navy that had swelled from its original complement of 15,000 in 1919 to 800,000 men.

A lack of foresight and maritime experience could no longer be compensated for – as might be usual in peacetime – by long intensive training. This was the dilemma of a nation that saw itself as a continental power caught up in a major war with a sea power. In Germany the crews had to become accustomed to the elements, while Great Britain's coastal forces, which by the end of the war numbered well over 1,000 boats, were manned by naval reservists who knew the sea.[18]

What Germany had to do was teach the ground rules of mastering boat and armament and hope that the sea legs would come of their own accord. To school men to sail in waters of tide and current such as the North Sea and English Channel, at night, in poor visibility and in formation, was something that could be passed on only to a limited degree. Training remained patchwork and those in positions of responsibility knew this; but in wartime it could not be helped:[19]

An essential signalling function: the 'indicators'.

> The 3.SFltl. training programme was wishful thinking. We could not exercise the guns because we had no target tugs. We had only two periods by day, and two by night, for torpedo practice. After ten weeks I was already at the front with 4.SFltl. That was the general picture in the last years of the war.[20]

The personnel situation below commander level was generally satisfactory 'thanks to the understanding and co-operation with 2AdO [2nd Admiral Baltic], who made available to the SLD the requirement in personnel in adequate numbers, and even gave us a certain freedom of choice'.[21] Nevertheless the problem persisted even here that the men had too little time to get their sea legs.

Towards the End

The long-term aim of bringing all three training flotillas up to sixteen boats fell away in 1944 because of the decrease in new boat deliveries and rising losses in the Channel, defending against the invasion. Planned detachments to Romania and Finland also had to be fulfilled, as well as replacements for the front-line flotillas. On 1 August 1944, the training flotillas had twenty-five boats (1st Flotilla – 13, 2nd Flotilla – 7, 3rd Flotilla – 5), each flotilla having a depot ship (*Adolf Lüderitz*, *Tsingtau* and *Carl Peters*).22 Compared to the front-line flotillas, this was a large stock, but the boats and engines were old and clapped out, and only a few were ever serviceable at a time.

The FdS was now hoping for an increase in new boats, allowing the old boats of 5. and 6.SFltl. to be transferred into the SLD. This was done only partially, for the approaching end gradually forced the training flotillas ever closer to the actual fighting. Thus in September 1944, the 2nd Training Flotilla was surprised at being sent to assist the Army at Kurland. From December 1944, the 1st Training Flotilla took over convoy escort work at Egersund on the Norwegian coast, and at the beginning of 1945, the 3rd Training Flotilla and SLD transferred to Svendborg.

At the conclusion of hostilities, the 2nd and 3rd Training Flotillas, with twenty-eight boats and the depot ships *Tsingtau* and *Carl Peters*,[23] were in Geltinger Bay. The 1st Training Flotilla, with five boats and the depot ship *Adolf Lüderitz*, was at Egersund.[24]

16
The S-Boat and Its Armament

At the outbreak of war, the two S-boat flotillas in service had either Type S 10 or the two-metre longer, but outwardly similar, Type S 14. Boats S 18 to S 25 were of Type S 14 construction but fitted with Daimler-Benz MB 501 motors, 2,000hp, 20 cylinders, providing a top speed of 39.5 knots.[1] Armament consisted of two torpedo tubes, a single 2cm flak, smoke canisters and depth charges. The complement was twenty men:

commander
boatswain ('No. 1')
5 seaman ratings
engine-room warrant officer
3 engine room NCOs
6 stokers
2 radio operators
torpedo mechanic/cook

	S 10–13	S 14–17
Dimensions (metres)	length 32.3 beam 4.9 draught 1.4	length 34.6 beam 5.1 draught 1.4
Operational displacement (tonnes)	95	115
Speed (knots)	30 cruising 35 max	35 cruising 37 max
Range (nm)	600 at 30 knots	600 at 30 knots
Engines	3 MB 502 diesels 1,320hp 16 cylinders 3 shafts 3 propellers fuel 13 tonnes	3 MAN diesels 2,050hp 24 cylinders 3 shafts 3 propellers fuel 16.4 tonnes

Technical specifications – Types S 10 and S 14.

At the end of 1939, the first Type S 30 boats (S 30 to S 37) were commissioned, and those boats fitted with the unreliable MAN diesels were put into reserve. The Type S 30s had been under construction for China but were impounded at the outbreak of war and completed for the Kriegsmarine. In dimension they were similar to the S 10–13 boats and had Daimler-Benz MB 502 diesels. Because the manufacturer – the sole supplier of S-boat motors – was experiencing difficulties with the crank casings for the MB 501, boats S 54 to S 61 were finished as Type S 30. This type could negotiate the locks of the Rhine–Rhône Canal and were later formed

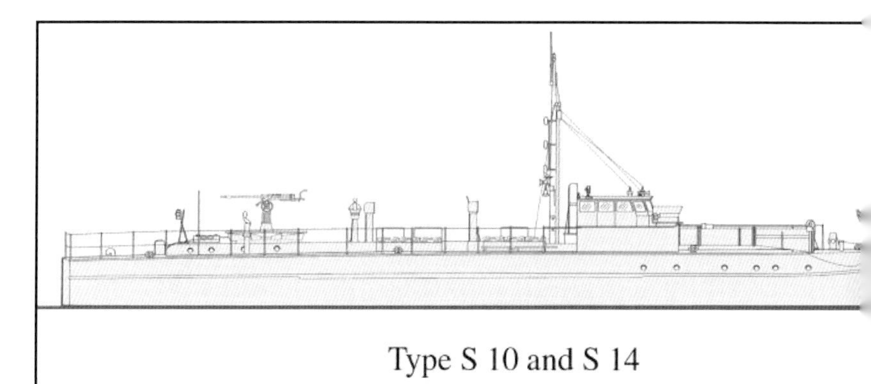

Type S 10/S 14 boat with command position forward of wheelhouse.

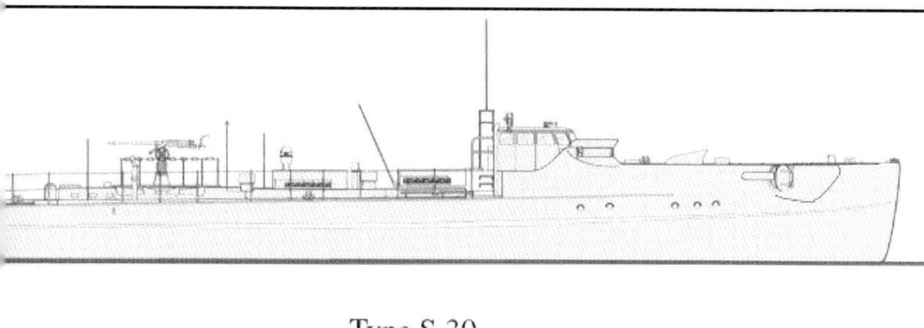

Type S 30.

into the 3rd S-boat Flotilla in the Mediterranean.

In contrast to the boats of Type S 10–14, the foredeck was enclosed, the torpedo tubes built in and the sea-keeping qualities better. The command position located forward of the wheelhouse shipped a lot of spray in heavy weather. Constantly wet binoculars and the low line of sight affected visibility considerably.

The 35–6 knots' top speed was not reached in the Mediterranean; occasionally it would fall below 30 knots, but usually it was a little above.[2] Forty-four S-boats were scheduled under the 1936 shipbuilding programme. This was raised to seventy-five boats by 1947 in the Z-Plan of 9 February 1939. The interim target was forty-eight boats by the end of 1943.[3] At the outbreak of war, SKL wanted to reduce the surface forces in favour of the U-boat programme and so aimed for a minimum of forty to fifty S-boats and then a yearly replacement production figure of sixteen.[4] It was estimated that this figure would cover the expected losses. In the framework of this building programme, new boats began to come off the slip from the beginning of 1941. As new crews were available on only a limited basis, the older and less reliable boats were to be decommissioned. Based on the Type S 14, the new units received an enclosed forecastle tried and tested aboard the Type S 30. These boats had the command position situated on the wheelhouse roof, which now became a true 'bridge'.[5]

The boats of this series were built by Lürssen and Schlichting at Travemünde. Lürssen delivered S 26–9, S 38–53 and S 62–100, Schlichting Werft S 101–33. Although the series began with S 26, it was generally known as Type 38. Its equipment included a magnetic compass, a high-frequency transmitter/receiver (40/70W[6]) and a radio-telephone set (1W[7]).

The boats were painted brilliant white, a livery said later to have been the key to their initial successes, as the contours merged completely into the night.[8] Only at the time of Operation Barbarossa in the Finnish skerries was a grey-green/blue wave-form dazzle pattern on a white background chosen.

As with their predecessors, these boats were fitted with adjustable rudders to achieve the so-called 'Lürssen effect'. The two smaller outer rudders, normally coupled to the main rudder by means of a rod, could be angled off the fore-and-aft line. At about twenty degrees, the streaming was affected such that the stern rose a little, providing two extra knots. Tactically, this was generally used only over longer cruising distances on a straight course and at constant speed.[9]

Looking forward from the command position.

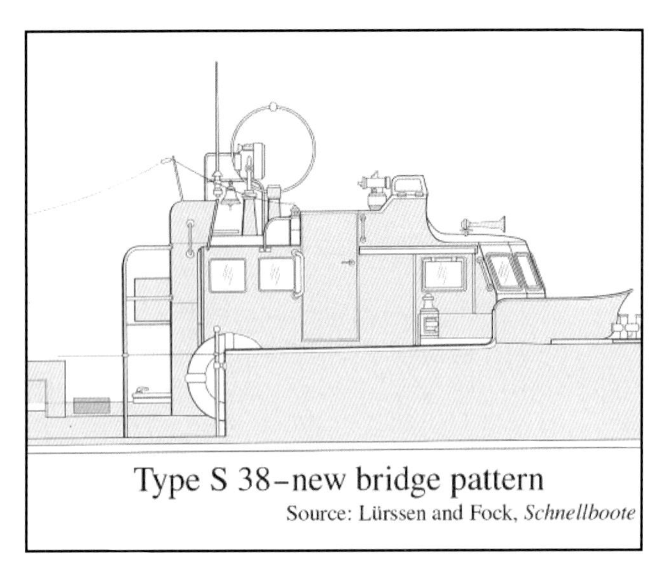

Type S 38–new bridge pattern
Source: Lürssen and Fock, *Schnellboote*

Type S 38.

The method of boat construction, light metal on double carvel planking, was retained. After long years of logical development, the standard S-boat of the German Navy had been achieved. Improvements over subsequent years were in details only, such as the new bridge tried out on S 67 in March 1942. This was plastic, similar to the later cupola bridge, the idea being further to reduce the boat's silhouette. Because it reflected light in all directions, the glass parts were painted over white before sailing.[10]

As air attacks increased, with their attendant personnel losses, the FdS asked for bridge armour. After experiments with in-built armour plating on S 50 and S 63, Lürssen developed an armoured cupola, similar in design to the plastic experiment aboard S 67, and this was introduced generally from the spring of 1943.[11] Previously, new boats had been fitted with a cupola over the bridge, but of light construction only.[12]

The carvel planking was reinforced. The MB 511 motors now provided 2,500hp and a top speed of up to forty-two knots. The improved MB 518 version with 3,000hp was installed experimentally on S 170 and S 208 only, S 170 achieving forty-three knots.[13] From the spring of 1942, an echo-sounder was fitted and an improved direction-finder with folding frame followed.[14]

It had become clear early on that the single 2cm flak gun was neither a deterrent to enemy aircraft nor much use in naval combat. In December 1940, the FdT had requested a 2cm cannon for the foredeck to provide a field of fire ahead. This was installed in a well from the summer of 1941 and proved highly successful. This model gun was also fitted to Type S 30 boats later in the Mediterranean. The FdT, and later the FdS, next requested a 4cm cannon to engage the well-armed MGBs from aft, this weapon being fitted from the late summer of 1942.[15] At the same time, a flak gun with fast rate of fire was needed. The ideal model was the 3cm gun used aboard Luftwaffe

Dimensions (metres)	length 34.9 beam 5.1 draught 1.85
Operational displacement (tonnes)	108
Speed (knots)	35 cruising 39.5 max
Range (nm)	750 at 35 knots
Engines	3 Daimler-Benz MB 501 diesels 2,000hp 20 cylinders 3 shafts 3 propellers fuel 16.4 tonnes
Complement	20
Armament	2 torpedo tubes (plus 2 reload torpedoes) 1 × 2cm flak (MG C38) 2 or 3 MG 08 machine guns 6–8 depth charges or dummies 2 smoke canisters 6 mines or defensive buoys (but then no depth charges or torpedoes)

Technical specifications – Type 38.

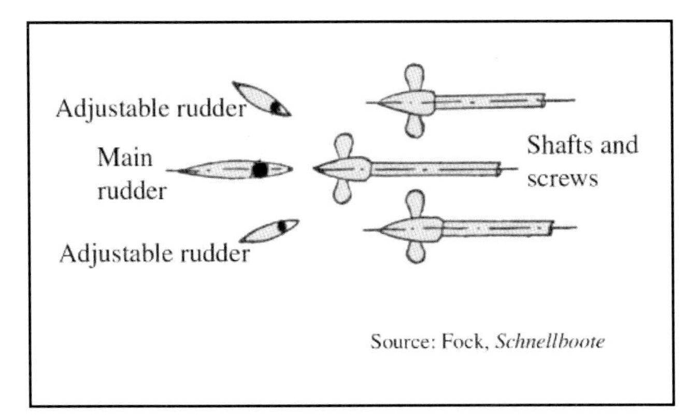

The Lürssen Effect.

aircraft, but this was not ready for naval use until close to the end of the war. Instead, some boats received a fully automatic 3.7cm gun or a 2cm quadruple. Some of these weapons were fitted with shields. Neither full armour protection nor an armoured S-boat with heavy armament ever entered the design stage.[16]

Amidships on nearly all boats, an extra twin MG gun was installed on a pedestal, and up to three MGs either side of the bridge. These additional weapons required an increase in the complement to twenty-eight on operations. A mix of weapons was preferred, so that ideally a *Rotte* would consist of one boat with a 4cm cannon, the other carrying a powerful flak armament.

The torpedoes were discharged through two fixed, built-in tubes for one torpedo each, the reloads being kept on a bed of ball bearings for ease of movement. For reasons of weight, the reserve torpedoes were landed before mining operations. Boats from S 701 upwards were fitted with two stern tubes. Since this precluded the carrying of mines, it was a development criticised by S-boat Command.[17] From the autumn of 1942, the GA-director was mounted. This allowed torpedoes to be fired on a bearing relative to the fore-and-aft line instead of aiming the nose at the target.[18] The G7a torpedo was used to the end of the war, because the electric drive of the more advanced G7e was found too slow for combat use. The same applied to the T5 Zaunkönig, which homed in on propeller noise.[19]

The boat catering for all these changes, less the stern tubes, was designated S 100, although its dimensions were similar to Type 38. The first model of the new type was commissioned on 5 May 1943. By the end of December, the first boat of a short series of eight was completed at the Gusto Werft, Schiedam in Holland. Originally planned for use in Dutch waters, they were based on an old Lürssen design, entered service as S 151–8 and were sent to the Mediterranean to reinforce 7.SFltl. Twenty-eight metres long and displacing 66 tonnes, they were considerably smaller than the other boats. Top speed was 32–3 knots, provided by three MB 500 12-cylinder engines each having a thrust of 950hp. The boats proved to be poor sea-keepers and suffered frequent engine breakdowns.

S 67 with plastic cupola over the bridge.

When Dönitz took command of the Kriegsmarine at the end of January 1943, he considered carefully the building programme for the fleet. Along with the question of decommissioning the heavy units, his main concern was to prioritise U-boat construction. He also emphasised the need for the S-boat Arm: 'It can account for an important element in the tonnage

A Type S 38 boat with no foredeck gun.

war against British convoy traffic close to their coast.'[20] For that purpose, he proposed raising the monthly production immediately from three to six boats. In the conference at Führer HQ on 11 April 1943, Hitler approved this revised naval building plan. The argument in favour went:

> Against the constantly improving enemy defences, the S-boat can only remain effective if it continues to operate as a sufficiently large force. Single-boat successes achieved by surprise are incidental, due to effective radar detection and the size of the defences. The development of S-boat tactics therefore follows the same path as U-boat tactics. In the Channel the boats are now used only in packs. The current rate of building of only three S-boats monthly merely replaces the losses. With fewer S-boat operations being sailed, it will become possible for the enemy to step up attacks on our own sea communications, especially in the Hoofden.[21] Unburdened of his worries along the English coast, he can make the situation for our own coastal convoys extremely difficult by his own numerous escort craft. The tally of S-boats in the Channel does not correspond in any way to the prospects for success or their significance for German naval policy. The least rate of building must be set at six boats per month.[22]

The final fleet building programme, signed by Dönitz on 7 June 1943, allowed for 108 new boats yearly, equating to nine per month.[23] Danzig Waggonfabrik was drawn into the programme, together with Lürssen and Schlichting. Production failed to meet the target. In 1943, on average Lürssen turned out two to three boats monthly, and Schlichting one. In 1944, Lürssen delivered 39 boats, Schlichting 15 and Danzig Waggon 8, an output of 5 boats per month, well short of the expected 9.

By August 1944, Lürssen had increased monthly production to six boats, but after heavy air raids on the yards and suppliers, particularly the engine factories, the numbers dropped rapidly: the three yards managed only two boats between them in November 1944 and four in December. After that, the Danzig factory closed as the Soviets advanced.[24] In October 1944, a warship building programme for 1945 was drawn up, followed in February 1945 by an emergency programme in which nineteen S-boats were planned for. In view of the approaching end, this was simply window dressing.[25] In 1945, Lürssen turned out eight boats and Schlichting three.

From the beginning, S-boats were supported logistically by the depot ship attached to each flotilla. They provided accommodation for the crews and had weapons, ammunition and fuel aboard, and facilities

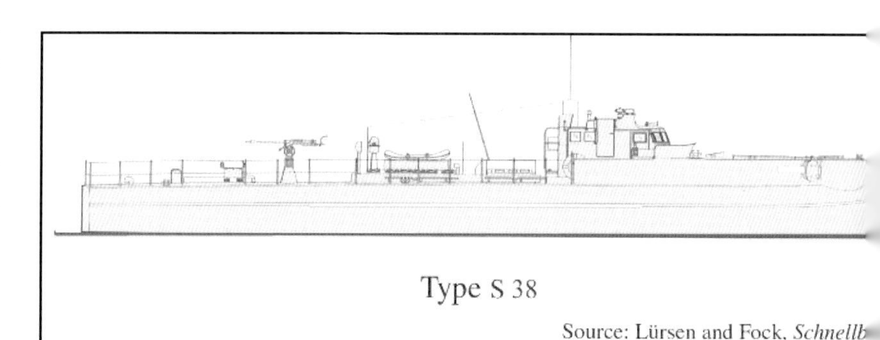

Type S 38.

Taking torpedoes aboard a Type S 38.

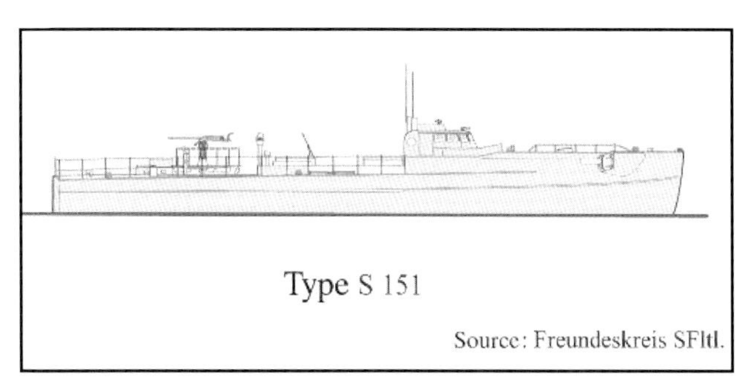

Optic for GA torpedo director.

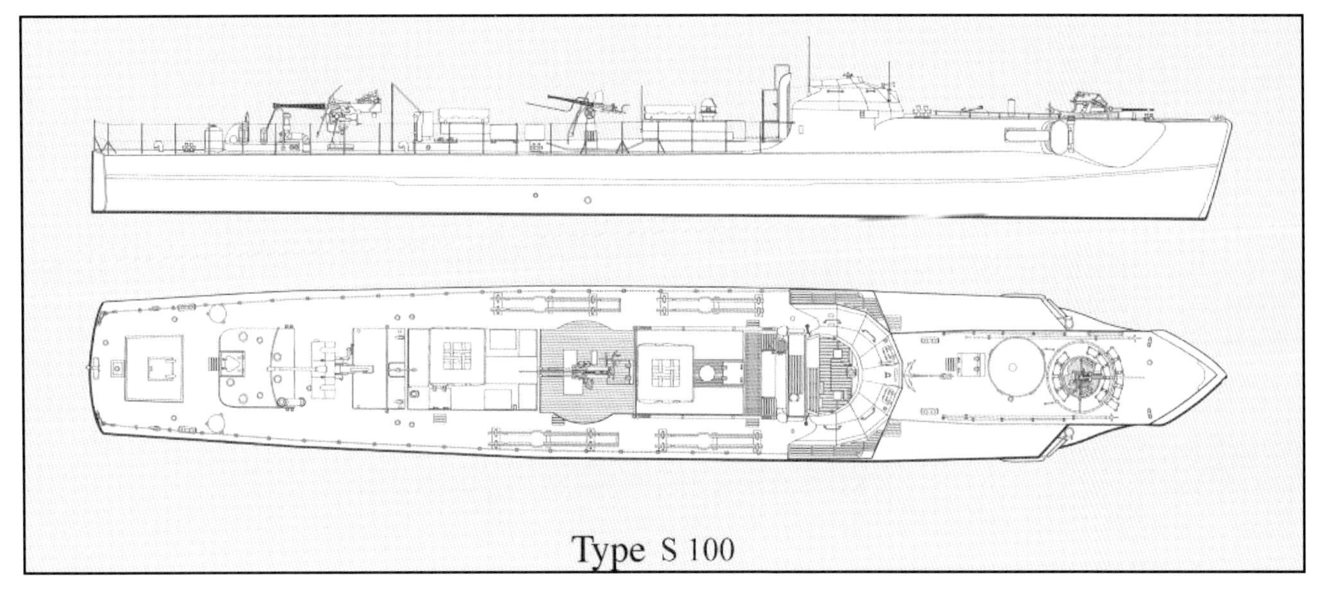

Type S 100.

Boats in the bunker laden with mines.

Depth charges and smoke canisters at the stern.

Upgraded armament: a 2cm twin and a 3.7cm cannon.

for engine maintenance and repair. From the end of 1940, they were withdrawn from the Channel ports because of increasing air attacks. Only in the Norwegian Sea and Baltic did they accompany the flotillas into the operational areas. In the Black Sea, the steamer *Romania*, and in the Mediterranean the *Bengazi* were converted to depot ships, but the local situation prevented their use in the role.

In place of depot ships, in the west from the summer of 1941 S-boat bunkers were constructed,

The torpedo mechanic was responsible for the torpedoes, smoke-making equipment and the galley.

Coffee for the bridge, an important job on every S-boat.

The torpedo mechanic/cook in his galley.

Bridge designs.
Left above: Type S 38.
Left below: Type S 100.
Above: Type S30.

first at Boulogne and Ostend, later at Rotterdam, Cherbourg and Ijmuiden. An extension of the bunker complexes requested by the FdS in the summer of 1942, with reference to the planned expansion of the S-boat Arm, was agreed in part. The Ijmuiden bunker, with eighteen boats on moorings and numerous installations for overhaul and repair, was only two-thirds complete by the end of 1944. Other planned developments at Cherbourg and Ivan Baba (Black Sea) were abandoned because of the strategic situation or the lack of materials and labour. Thus, at Cherbourg only one of the two S-boat flotillas there (5. or 9.) could have bunker protection at any one time. After the invasion, unlike the U-boat bunkers, which had a far

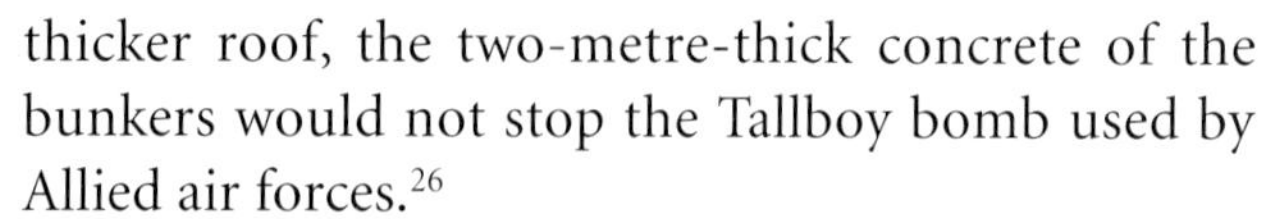

thicker roof, the two-metre-thick concrete of the bunkers would not stop the Tallboy bomb used by Allied air forces.[26]

To the end, new boats were still being commissioned. Here, one is seen leaving the shipyard.

Engine overhauls were carried out in these bunkers. Initially, these were scheduled after 250 hours' use, a period that increased during the war to 300 and later 500 hours, as a result of improvements in engine construction. The overhaul involved removal of cylinders, cleaning pistons and rings, checking burners and cleaning jets, removing cylinder cooling jackets, checking oil and mechanisms, removal of air cooling system, cleaning lubricant and fuel filters, cleaning propeller bearings and checking the cooling-water circulating system. This was normally completed with the assistance of the boat's crew within seven days.[27]

Depot ship *Tanga* with S-boat.

After initially 500 and later 1,000 hours, the engines would be exchanged. Shipyard help was needed for this because other structural repairs would be carried out, as a rule requiring three weeks. Once air attacks began seriously to hamper the production of marine engines, the provision of reserve motors became a problem. The long supply line from Germany to the Mediterranean and Black Sea increased the reconditioning periods considerably. The planning and production of reserve motors was 'the most difficult problem for maintaining operational readiness under the given circumstances'.[28]

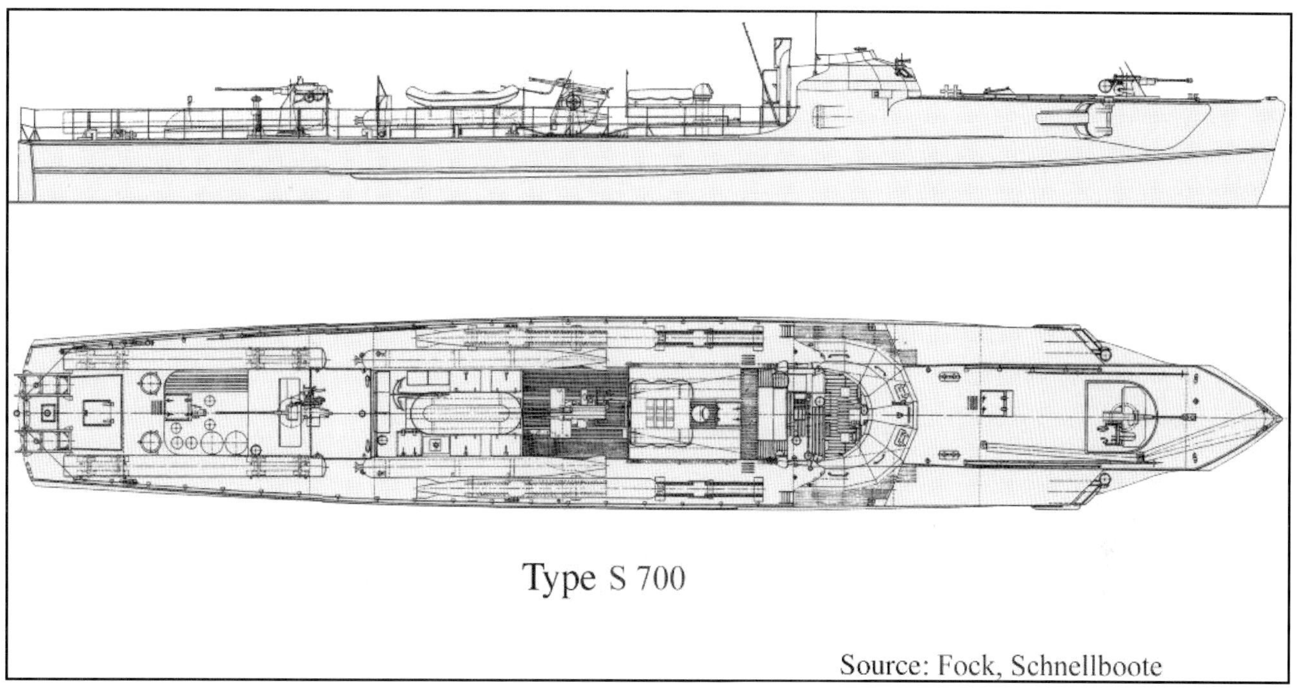

Type S 700 – the last and most modern S-boat.

Boats in the Cherbourg bunker.

During engine overhaul.

FdS inspecting a 'Stalin organ' rocket launcher in use.

S-boats with supply ship in Finland. Note dazzle pattern unique to Finnish theatre during Barbarossa.

Change of engine at the Palermo yard.

Control room NCO at the main engine.

17
The Commodore

On 20 April 1942, the post of Führer der Schnellboote (FdS) was created and 36-year-old Korvettenkapitän Rudolf Petersen given the role. This was an unusual appointment, for comparable command positions were generally filled by a man of higher rank. The decision of the Kriegsmarine to place at the head of the S-boat Arm an officer from within its own corps would prove to be the correct and wise choice.

Petersen was born the son of a pastor on 15 June 1905 at Atzerballig on the island of Alsen. With four other children of the family, he grew up on the island, then a part of the Kaiserreich, and attended the local municipal school and later the college at Hadersleben. When Northern Schleswig was ceded to Denmark after the First World War, his father was not in favour of becoming a Dane nor entering its Lutheran Church. The family moved to the capital, where his father joined the community of the Berlin-Brandenburg Church at Berlin-Lichterfelde. Here Petersen passed his final examinations in 1920.

On 1 April 1925, Rudolf Petersen entered the Reichsmarine as a naval cadet. After the usual infantry and sea training, he obtained his commission on 1 October 1929 and served in torpedo boats, then aboard a light cruiser showing the flag overseas. He spent two years in the naval oceanographic service, following which he was appointed a platoon commander at a recruiting depot and then adjutant to the commander of a T-boat flotilla. He made Oberleutnant zur See on 1 October 1931 and Kapitänleutnant on 1 September 1935. On 1 October 1935, he joined the S-boat Arm and was given a command. In parallel with this position, he commanded a training company for officer cadets and in August 1938, after completing his Admiralty staff training at the Naval Academy, was given the 2nd S-boat Flotilla to command. He headed this flotilla in its first operations in the North Sea and Baltic, for the occupation of Norway and finally the attack on the Soviet Union from Baltic waters. During this period as flotilla commander, Petersen was awarded the Iron Cross Second and First Class (10 April 1940 and 31 May 1941 respectively), and Knight's Cross on 4 August 1940.

As the result of a car accident in 1941 he was classified unfit for shipboard service and served as Admiralty staff officer with the Führer der Torpedoboote (FdT), to whom the S-boat Arm was subordinate at that time. All official assessments provide the image of a very open man with wide interests and a high and serious view towards life and his naval career. He was considered more suited to being a front-line officer rather than an administrator. He realised this himself, for when a former comrade-in-arms revealed that he was going to make a study of the 2.SFltl. War Diaries, Petersen told him, 'Well, good luck with that . . . but from my time there you will not find very much, I fear; I was always very much averse to writing.'[1] There was another side to it, for an earlier assessment reads: 'especially interested in Church questions, since his father is active as a pastor in the Bekenntnis-Church in Berlin.'[2]

His interest in history, his profound analysis of naval history and his ability to form a realistic appreciation of a situation, devoid of ideological colour and fanaticism, led Petersen to suspect at the outbreak of war what Germany's fate was to be. Mooring at Heligoland after a voyage in which he learned of the British declaration of war on his country, he told his officers, 'This is the Second World War. It will last longer than the First, but we can only lose it, for it is a naval war.'[3] He never repeated this statement, but his idea that the naval war was one of attrition, having nothing to do with spectacular successes but rather striking at the British lines of supply with the available forces whenever and wherever possible, dominated his thinking both as flotilla commander and also FdS. For this reason,

Petersen in the Situation Room.

Petersen placed great value on using his boats and flotillas sparingly, for only with the maximum available fleet could permanent pressure be applied to the enemy. It also explains why he considered it his duty to ensure the safety and protection of the men committed to his care. In the course of the war, he was criticised by his superiors as lacking enthusiasm for operations. This did not change or influence significantly his outlook or manner of proceeding. His attitude was condemned by Kapitän zur See Bütow, FdT, in June 1940, when Petersen committed all his flotilla, instead of a small group from it, to protecting the mine-damaged S 23 during the tow home.[4]

At the end of April 1941, he was removed temporarily from command of the flotilla to work with flotilla engineer Kapitänleutnant Gördes on preparations for Operation Barbarossa in the Baltic. 'These two officers are distinguished by their very well-executed measures, worked out under great difficulty and in the fullest secrecy,' the FdT enthused after the operations had concluded.[5] During his enforced stay with FdT staff when unfit for sea service, Petersen was awarded another special task: the formation of 8.SFltl. at short notice and making the necessary organisational and logistical preparations for service in the Arctic. His foresight and precision, together with his technical and service achievements, confirmed his organisational ability and he therefore became the prime choice for the newly created office of Führer der Schnellboote (FdS).

Petersen met the demands of the post unspectacularly, but with a clear vision of what it entailed. The job underlined the importance of the S-boat Arm, now recognised officially by Naval Command. He was not a man alone, making lonely decisions, but a team officer who worked with his staff and combined knowledge and expertise into a uniform picture. He was quick to grasp a situation, to see its essentials, to react appropriately. His honesty commended him to all his subordinates and, despite coming from the farthest north of Germany, he had the gift of getting all to fall in behind him. He was tolerant to all and therefore tolerated; his weaknesses, which he worked selflessly and unobtrusively to redress, were allowed for.[6]

Under Petersen's leadership, the S-boat Arm developed into an effective weapon of attack, and by the end of the war was the only offensive naval arm on the coasts of occupied Europe, its main focus of operations throughout the war having been in the Channel. Unblinkered by ideology or ultra-conservative thinking, Petersen took advantage of all the modern technologies available, particularly radio monitoring. He improved boats and armaments and fought tirelessly, though in vain, to overcome the enemy's superiority in radar. Wrestling endlessly with the formidable Allied coastal and convoy defences, he mastered the tactical operational principles of mine and torpedo.

Petersen's basic premise that the war was one of attrition never changed. On the contrary, the longer the war went on, the clearer it became that successes could not be forced; chances to score had to be created by probing the enemy's weak spots. His method was to strike quickly and with full commitment. Higher

Petersen at a flotilla parade, 1944.

command did not always see this as the correct path. Generaladmiral Marschall, C-in-C Group West, reprimanded the FdS in 1943 for committing all his available forces to search for a missing boat and ordered that in future he must first obtain the approval of Group West. Petersen responded,

> Despite the overall defensive situation in the West and the defensive attitudes of the circles of command, I have always made the effort, so far as possible, to keep the S-boats in a state of constant offensive readiness and to that end have made all my arrangements. The need to use the fighting strength of the S-boats on every occasion that presents itself for an offensive operation appeals to me especially.[7]

Moreover, he requested a personal interview with Marschall. On his return from Paris, Petersen told his circle of confidantes, 'They think we are cowards.'[8] All the same, Marschall confirmed his confidence in Petersen in a letter, while complaining about his 'distrust and sensitivity'.

In 1944, Admiral Krancke, as Marschall's successor, repeated the censure in connection with the invasion of Normandy, when he bemoaned the few successes of the S-boat Arm and demanded more tenacity and ruthlessness in combat.[9] In the final months of the war, the C-in-C Kriegsmarine made the same criticism. Dönitz raised the point initially as a question, later directly in writing, to the effect that sparing one's own forces and avoiding great risks led to too great a reflection on the dangers, and he too called for more ruthlessness in action.[10]

Petersen discussed these admonitions and his possible responses to them with only his closest circle. Flotilla commanders and boat captains knew nothing of them. When asked after the war, many reacted with a shake of the head, while others were surprised or astonished. The cool objectivity that Petersen and his staff displayed during these disagreements can be seen underlying all the opinions, initiatives and memoranda by which the FdS depicted the situation in the various operational zones throughout the war. So objective and logical were they, in fact, that the command structure to the very top accepted his point of view as a rule and went along with his suggestions. There was accordingly never an attempt to unseat Petersen. On 1 April 1943 he was promoted to Fregattenkapitän, on 1 April 1944 to Kapitän zur See and finally to Kommodore on 1 October 1944.[11] He received the Oak Leaves to his Knight's Cross on 11 July 1944.[12]

To his inner circle, Petersen did not disguise his aversion to National Socialism. As the son of a Berlin Bekenntnis Church pastor who had occasionally seen the inside of a Gestapo jail, he dismissed the National Socialist world view as a kind of pseudo-religion harmful to the being of the German people. After meetings with party bosses in connection with visits and conferences, he had very negative opinions of

Petersen, Krancke and Feldt, 1944.

them. Nevertheless, he was not a Resistance kind of person. He was much opposed to assassinating the head of state. When, in July 1944, Petersen reported to Obersalzberg to receive the Oak Leaves to his Knight's Cross, he took pains to have himself well briefed on those matters he intended to broach with the Führer. He would certainly have spoken out frankly. Upon his return, he was very deeply impressed by Hitler's compassion and his astonishingly detailed knowledge of the shortages in the S-boat Arm. Petersen's close circle watched his long struggle to cast off Hitler's demonic power and the spell he cast. Later, he would recall how, during the conversation, his cap had slipped from his knees to the floor, at which Hitler had bent down spontaneously, picked it up, dusted off the crown and politely returned it.[13]

Together with a clear military attitude, Petersen felt directly responsible for the crews. This had its roots in his Christian beliefs, but his internal struggle between his handing down operational orders that brought death and destruction, and the Christian requirements of love for one's neighbour and respect for human life, was seen by only his closest circle. He took personnel losses very much to heart and could not conceal his sympathy and personal grief, and it was seen that the deaths pained him deeply, particularly since the sacrifice was for an ideology he did not share. This was most evident in the case of Opdenhoff, whom he had known for many years, and who fell in the last days of the war as commander of 2.SFltl., a victim to British aircraft in Dutch waters. When the loss was confirmed, Petersen left the situation room with tears in his eyes, unable to speak.[14]

Only seldom did this inner conflict flare. At Christmas 1944 in the ruined bunker of Ijmuiden, the remnants of 8.SFltl. were assembled. A Christmas tree had been mounted on the rear gun of S 199, the crew sang, the commander read out a goodwill message from the homeland. Suddenly, Kommodore Petersen appeared and shouted harshly, 'Are you mad? A Christmas tree on a gun? The symbol of peace on the tool of war? This cannot be allowed, the contradiction is too stark.' Quietly but firmly, he continued, 'It cannot be allowed. It can only be permitted in the sign of the Cross, in the sign of the Love which died for peace with God. Only then will there be peace on Earth.' The crew was amazed but stirred by the truth of what he said. Then the commodore went aboard and, contrary to orders, 'shared at this Christmastide in their mutual suffering and anxiety, and their hopes for peace'.[15]

At the termination of the conflict, the major part of the surviving S-boat fleet gathered with its depot ships in Geltinger Bight for surrender to the British. On 11 May 1945, the crews paraded to hear a short address by Petersen before the war flag was lowered for the last time. For Petersen this was not the end, however. As a court-martial judge, he had confirmed the sentence of death passed by the S-boat Arm war court on three deserters. The sentence had been carried out the previous day.

In the three trials over the next eight years[16] in which he stood accused, many reasons have been suggested for his decision to confirm the sentence. Undoubtedly the intensive talks with Dönitz, as acting head of state, and von Friedeburg, the last Kriegsmarine C-in-C, had a major influence.[17] Eventually he was acquitted. Nevertheless, there is a piece missing from the image of the man, who for years led his flotillas cleverly and cautiously, aware of his responsibilities and imbued with a special feeling for the anxieties and needs of his crews.

So far as can be determined from the court-martial files, until then he had never confirmed a death sentence. Petersen made no attempt to explain or shift the responsibility, but accepted it fully. It was a heavy burden. Haggard from years in prison, serious illness and a long period of unemployment, he lived a quiet existence in Flensburg after marrying his long-term fiancée.[18] For several years, he worked as head of the yachting school at Glücksburg before losing his life tragically at New Year 1983.[19] Although many of his close collaborators rose to high rank and honours in the Bundesmarine and often invited him to look over the new German S-boat Arm, he always declined; the Bundesmarine should not be burdened with a 'war criminal'.[20] He had the companionship of good and loyal friends, who remained warmly devoted to the commodore, to the end of his life.

Epilogue

When the war began, there were two S-boat flotillas, with a total of fifteen boats. These operated in the German Bight and central Baltic. At the conclusion of hostilities, ninety-one boats remained afloat, being divided into nine flotillas, three training flotillas and one S-boat Division strewn from the Adriatic to the North Sea and Baltic, and to southern Norway. In the intervening period, S-boats had operated from North Cape to Kronstadt, off the Caucasus coast, to Mersa Matruh in North Africa and as far west as Land's End. A total of 216 boats were built and 140 lost. The casualties were 767 dead, 620 wounded and 322 PoWs.[1] This is the sober debit balance. To attempt to evaluate efficiency by listing the enemy vessels sunk or damaged – as with U-boats – seems pointless. The operational conditions were basically too divergent.

U-boats pursued war on seaborne commerce relentlessly and aimed at the maritime potential of the Allies. On political instructions, in the Arctic north, S-boats languished for many months unused, contrary to the will of S-boat Command. In the first phase of the 1941 Baltic operations, they assisted in the bottling-up of the Soviet fleet. This occurred again in the first half of 1944. Then, after the collapse of the land front, naval protection duty, support of the beleaguered Army ashore and rescue operations determined the nature of their work.

In the Black Sea, their primary role was to support the fighting ashore. They moved here and there, back and forth, until finally, still without a proper operational base, they were forced to scuttle.

In the Mediterranean, their original purpose was to blockade Malta. When North Africa was lost in May 1943, they were driven back northwards, gradually being deprived of freedom of movement until, in the last days, surrender offered the only salvation against the wrath of the partisans.

Only in the Channel (with the exception of the fight to repel the invasion in mid-summer 1944) did the operational aims remain unchanged. Here, S-boats and U-boats shared the same goal, the cutting-off of the imports necessary for Britain's survival. U-boats sought the convoys on the oceans while the S-boats tackled the enemy close to his own shore.

Since World War I, the U-boat Arm had been a feared naval branch with its own independent chain of command and a proven weapons system. The S-boats on the other hand were seen initially as a weapon of opportunity without special value and had to struggle to establish their place and show what they could achieve. In Kapitän zur See Bütow, they found a competent FdT who set about his task energetically and with great operational understanding. Later, after the early successes in the Channel, the Kriegsmarine knew what could be expected from the new weapon and the demand followed.

As the conflict expanded into other theatres, with its simultaneous increase in losses, the available S-boat fleet was no longer sufficient in numbers. They were ordered to the Arctic, Mediterranean and Black Sea when the English Channel was the only correct choice. Here they could still get through defences and score successes that would certainly have been greater had the force committed been that much larger. But time was against them, for the British erected a strong system of coastal stations, minesweepers, gunboats, destroyers and aircraft, and they all worked together pragmatically, without rivalries or claims for independence. All were devoted to the common goal: to protect the life arteries of the nation.

With the appointment of the first FdS in April

1942, the S-boat Arm had finally become established in the German Navy. The boat itself had evolved and could demonstrate its superiority in sea-keeping, weaponry and tactics in many skirmishes. After the visible end of the German heavy-ship era with the loss of the *Bismarck*, it became a war of the senior lieutenants and their men. On U-boats, S-boats and coastal craft, continually operational, they fought wind and sea against an enemy becoming ever more dominant. In this day-to-day environment, they learned how best to use boat and sea to their advantage and in this respect, in contrast to the large units, were the equal of the maritime British.[2]

The zenith of the S-boat, and the U-boat in the Atlantic, was reached in 1943. Petersen, who from Korvettenkapitän to Kommodore led the Arm as the first and only FdS, saw this more clearly than anybody, for the enemy defences were becoming ever stronger and more effective. He had a good feel for tactics and devised new ideas that ranged from lurking near the convoy routes to lightning attacks at full speed, but in the end was forced to admit failure before the numerical and technological superiority of the enemy. Although the S-boat and its weapons were being improved constantly, with more powerful engines, armoured bridges, echo sounders, directed torpedo firing and improved shipboard armament, the decisive ability to oversee the situation on the battleground – radar – was missing. The dominance of the enemy air forces was also a decisive factor. Any S-boat spotted at sea by day was generally lost. 'While the enemy sees, we are like a blind man, limited to the sense of sound,' the FdS complained. Lacking support from the Luftwaffe and the heavy units, his only hope to surprise the enemy was to vary tactics between mine and torpedo, and strike at different locations.

In the long run, that had no hope of paying off, and it did not. The losses continued to rise and successes became less frequent. With the invasion, the harbours no longer afforded cover. The devastating attack on Le Havre reduced the S-boat Arm in the west by more than a third. A little later, massive bombs penetrated the bunkers that until then had been safe. Slowly but surely, the force was finally squeezed by the contracting land front to a small operational base from which it had no further opportunity to operate against an enemy superior in the air and at sea.

That S-boat operations continued into the last days of the war speaks volumes for the unbroken spirit in the flotillas and aboard the boats. It also reflects a certain desperation in a total war in which the men had seen their homeland bombed to rubble, and watched with horror at what was approaching them from the east. It had become a war with no way out, in which all that remained to be done was their duty, and not to fail their comrades. Not until later would they recognise how they had been misled by a criminal political leadership, but this does not in any way lessen the respect one should have for their achievements.

Appendices

I
The S-Boat Flotillas

1st S-boat Flotilla

Operated in Baltic, Norway (*Weserübung*), Channel, Baltic (Barbarossa), 1942–4 Black Sea, after reformation to end 1944 Baltic.

Commanding Officers:

Kapitänleutnant Sturm	March 1938–November 1939
Kapitänleutnant Birnbacher	November 1939–September 1942
Kapitänleutnant Christiansen	September 1942–September 1943
Kapitänleutnant Büchting	September 1943–end

2nd S-boat Flotilla

Operated in North Sea and Baltic, Norway (*Weserübung*), Channel, Baltic (Barbarossa), Channel.

Commanding Officers:

Kapitänleutnant Petersen	August 1938–October 1941
Kapitänleutnant Feldt	October 1941–February 1944
Korvettenkapitän Opdenhoff	February 1944–February 1945
Kapitänleutnant Wendler	February 1945–end

3rd S-boat Flotilla

Operated in Channel, Baltic (Barbarossa), Mediterranean.

Commanding Officers:

Kapitänleutnant Kemnade	May 1940–July 1943
Korvettenkapitän Schultz, H-M	July 1943–September 1944
Kapitänleutnant Müller, A	September 1944–October 1944
Kapitänleutnant Schulz, G	October 1944–end

4th S-boat Flotilla

Operated in Channel until 1945, then to Norway.

Commanding Officers:

Kapitänleutnant Bätge	October 1940–March 1943
Korvettenkapitän Lützow	March 1943–October 1943
Kapitänleutnant Fimmen	November 1943–end

5th S-boat Flotilla

Operated in Baltic (Barbarossa), Channel, 1944 Baltic, Channel, 1945 Baltic.

Commanding Officers:

Kapitänleutnant Klug	July 1941–June 1944
Kapitänleutnant Johannsen	June 1944
Kapitänleutnant Holzapfel	July 1944–end

6th S-boat Flotilla

Operated in Channel, Norway, Channel, Baltic, Channel.

Commanding Officers:

Korvettenkapitän Obermeier	March 1941–July 1944
Kapitänleutnant Matzen	July 1944–end

7th S-boat Flotilla

Operated in Mediterranean.

Commanding Officers:

Kapitänleutnant Trummer	June 1942–July 1944
Kapitänleutnant Schulz, G	July 1944–October 1944

(then transferred to 3rd S-Boat Flotilla)

8th S-boat Flotilla

Operated Norway and Channel.

Commanding Officers:

Kapitänleutnant Christiansen	November 1941–July 1942
Kapitänleutnant Zymalkowski	December 1942–end

(Flotilla was disbanded after Norwegian operations in July 1942 and re-formed in December 1942.)

9th S-boat Flotilla

Operated in Channel.

Commanding Officers:

Kapitänleutnant von Mirbach	April 1943–end

10th S-boat Flotilla

Operated in Channel.

Commanding Officers:

Kapitänleutnant Müller, K	March 1944–September 1944
Kapitänleutnant Bludau	September 1944–end

11th S-boat Flotilla

Operated in Black Sea.

Commanding Officers:

Kapitänleutnant Meyer, H-J	June 1943–September 1943
(Composed of former Italian MAS-boats. Flotilla was re-formed in Baltic in 1944 but received none of boats assigned.)	
Kapitänleutnant von Stempel	December 1944–April 1945

21st S-boat Flotilla

Operated in Aegean.

Commanding Officers:

Kapitänleutnant Wuppermann	September 1943–February 1944
Kapitänleutnant Graser	March 1944–October 1944

(Composed of LS-boats.)

22nd S-boat Flotilla

Transferred in the Adriatic to Croatia.

Commanding Officers:

Kapitänleutnant Wuppermann	December 1943–February 1944
Kapitänleutnant Hüsing	March 1944–October 1944

(Composed of KS-boats.)

24th S-boat Flotilla

Operated in Aegean and Adriatic.

Commanding Officers:

Kapitänleutnant Meyer, H-J November 1943–October 1944 (then transferred to 3rd S-Boat Flotilla)

(Composed of former Italian boats.)

1st S-boat Division

Operated in Mediterranean.

Commanding Officers:

Fregattenkapitän Schultz, H-M	July 1943–March 1945
Kapitänleutnant Wuppermann	March 1945–end

(commanded 3rd, 7th, 21st, 22nd and 24th S-Boat Flotillas.)

S-boat Training Flotilla (Schnellbootsschulflottille)

Commanding Officers:

Kapitänleutnant Opdenhoff	July 1942–October 1943

Unit then renamed:

S-boat Experimental Division (Schnellbootslehrdivision)

Commanding Officers:

Kapitänleutnant Opdenhoff	November 1943–February 1944
Korvettenkapitän Feldt	February 1944–end

1st S-boat Training Flotilla (1.Schnellbootsschulflottille)

Operated in Norway.

Commanding Officers:

Kapitänleutnant Wilcke	November 1943–end

2nd S-boat Training Flotilla

Operated in North Sea.

Commanding Officers:

Kapitänleutnant Klose, H H	November 1943–end

3rd S-boat Training Flotilla

Commanding Officers:

Kapitänleutnant Siems	June 1944–January 1945
Kapitänleutnant Detlefsen	January 1945–end

Source: FdT and FdS War Diaries

II
Flotilla Insignia

The following flotilla insignia details originate from photographs and descriptions provided by former crewmen. Each flotilla had a different insignia. Often the commander's initials in large capitals, or abbreviations, would be used. Another logo was a shooting star.

Uniform shields occurred as follows:

3.SFltl. used images of denizens of the sea.

2.SFltl. was identified by a common shield. Each boat had a single identifying card on the bridge coaming.

4.SFltl. A black panther painted on the forecastle at the level of the bridge.

6.SFltl. A shield device at the bow.

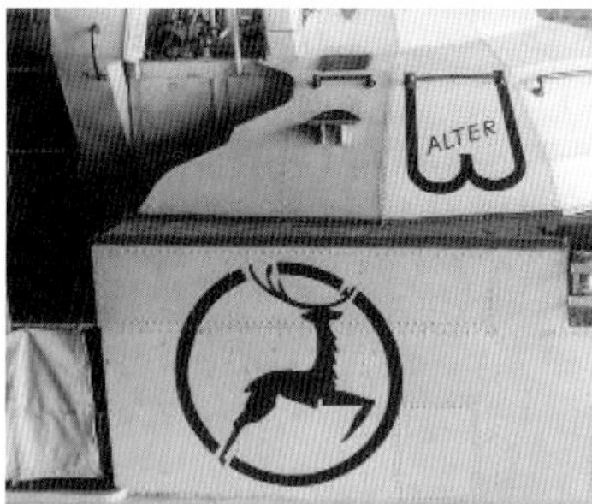

8.SFltl. Recalling its operations in the Arctic, a black reindeer within a circle.

9.SFltl. Elongated shield surmounted by black cross on the forecastle at the level of the bridge either side.

III

Naval Square Chart

The exact location was described in four stages:

1. General sea area – two letters, eg AN
2. Large square – 54 x 54 nautical miles, eg 41
3. One of nine small squares within large square – 18 x 18 nautical miles, eg 7
4. One of nine squares – 6 x 6 nautical miles within (3) above, eg 4

To narrow down the locations further, more information might be given, such as 'lK' ('*linke Kante*' = 'left side'). In the example, the island of Heligoland has the position AN9566 rK ('*rechte Kante*' = 'right side').

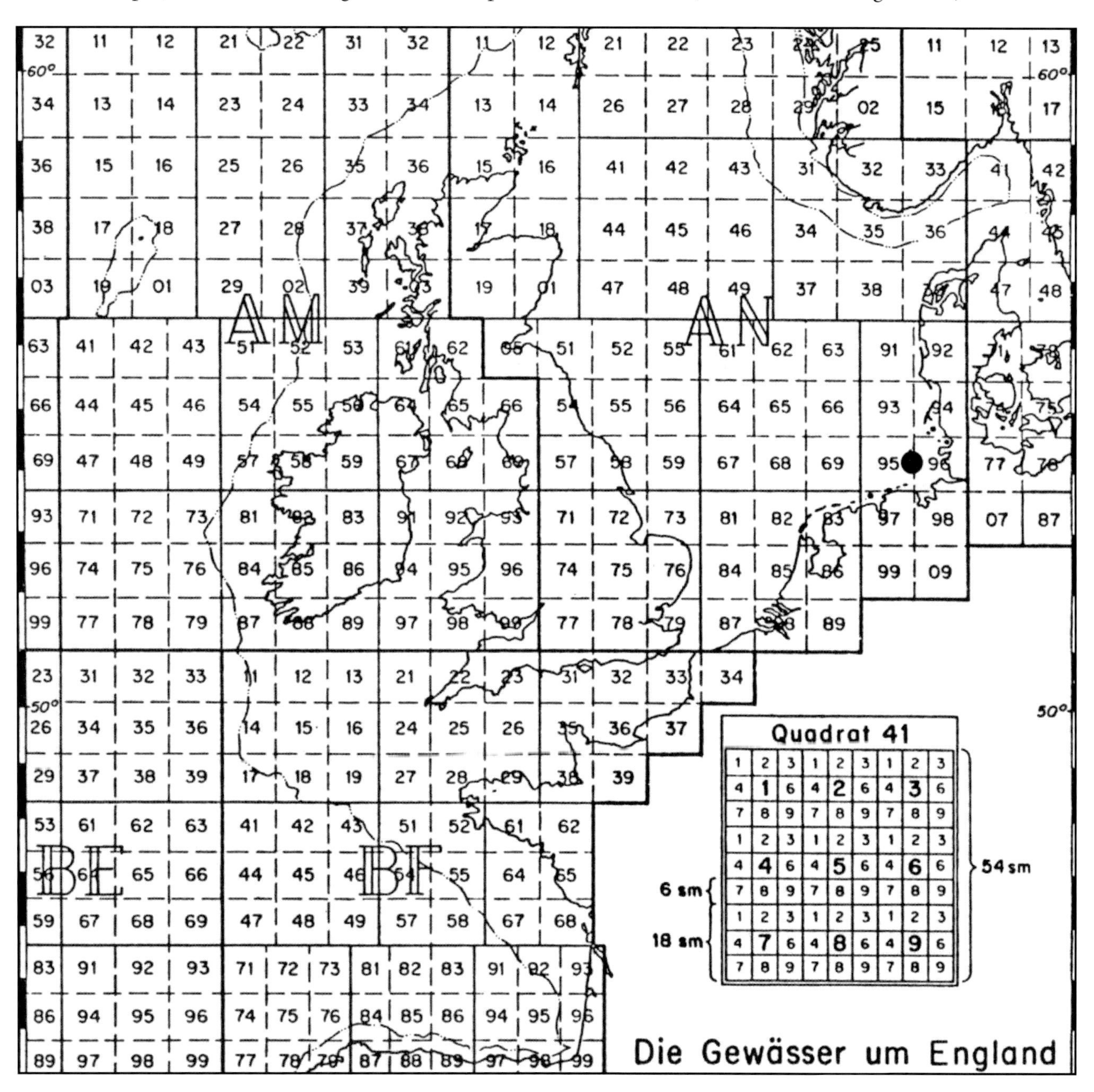

IV
Torpedoes and Mines

Torpedoes Used by S-Boats

Mark	Type	Length (m)	Diameter (cm)	Propulsion	Warhead (kg)	Speed (knots)	Range (nm)	Detonator
T I	G7a	7.17	53.3	4-cylinder motor	300	30 40 44	6.7 4.3 3.2	contact/ magnetic
T II	G7e	7.17	53.4	electric motor	300	30	2.7	contact/ magnetic
TV Zaunkönig	G7es	7.17	53.4	electric motor	274	24.5	3	contact/ magnetic
T IIId Dackel*	G7e	c10	53.4	electric	300	9	c32	contact

* The Dackel comprised two G7e torpedoes; the head therefore projected out of the open torpedo tube door. The missile ran 16 nautical miles straight and then a further 16 nautical miles in an LUT search pattern. Total running time was about 3.5 hours.

Steered-Torpedo Programme

FAT I: Surface-search G7a torpedo, distance version (30 kts). After a short preliminary run (selection available in 500m stages), made short or long zig-zags (choice between 1,200m or 1,900m), beginning either left or right, and then FAT course took over. Selections were made using hand crank at the FAT selector box fitted to the torpedo tube.

FAT II: Same programme for G7e.

LUT I: Course-independent torpedo for G7a and G7e. In addition to FAT programme, the course of the preliminary run and the mean course of the zig-zags – the LUT course – could be preselected.

Acoustic Self-steering: Target-seeking steering for G7es, in which torpedo homed in on screw noise.

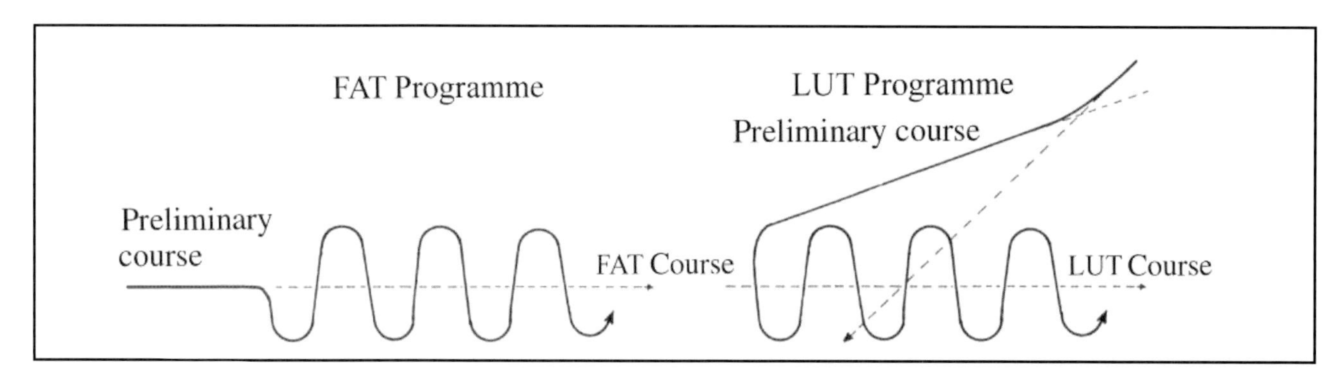

Mines Laid by S-Boats

Type	EMC	UMA	UMB	LMB	LMF	TMA
Name	General Issue Type C	U-boat Mine Type A	U-boat Mine Type B	Aerial Mine Type B	Aerial Mine Type F	Torpedo Tube Mine Type A
Mine type	anchor and cable	anchor and cable	anchor and cable	ground mine	anchor and cable	anchor and cable
Detonator type	contact	contact	contact	remote	contact	contact
Weight (kg)	1,135	812	634	950	1,050	800
Charge (kg)	250	30	40	680	290	230
Safe distance (m)	100–30	30	35	no information	no information	130
Maximum depth (m)	230	50	150	35	300	270
Minimum depth (m)	7	5	7	no information	50	50
Max. drop speed (kts)	25	25	25	no limit	no limit	no limit

Most important switching and detonation fittings:
M 1–3: magnetic detonator
A 1–3: acoustic detonator (some also designated AA 1–3)
MA 1–3: combined magnetic-acoustic detonator
D 1: pressure detonator (some also designated DM 1)
PU (*Pausenuhr*): activated mine at set time within 24 hours of laying
VW (*Verzögerungswerk*): mechanism-delayed activation
ZE (*Zeiteinrichtung*): time-switch deactivated mine
ZK (*Zählkontakt*): mine detonated after preset number of contacts
UES (*Uhrwerkschalter*): mine activated at set time between 6 hours and 6 days

Mines might be painted a particular colour to identify the kind of detonation device; eg 'LMB green' was an aerial mine Type B with acoustic detonator.

Minefield Protection Buoys
SprB: *Sprengboje* (explosive buoy), 200 kg total weight; would damage or destroy minesweepers and minesweeping gear.
RB: *Reißboje* = drag-buoy, 877kg total weight; would rip towlines off minesweeping gear.

Sources: Günther, *Entwicklung der Seemine*; Ledebur, *Seemine*; Seekriegsanleitung, Teil III, Heft c, Sperrwaffen; MDv Nr 175, *Minenbedienvorschrift*; War Diary FdT and FdS.

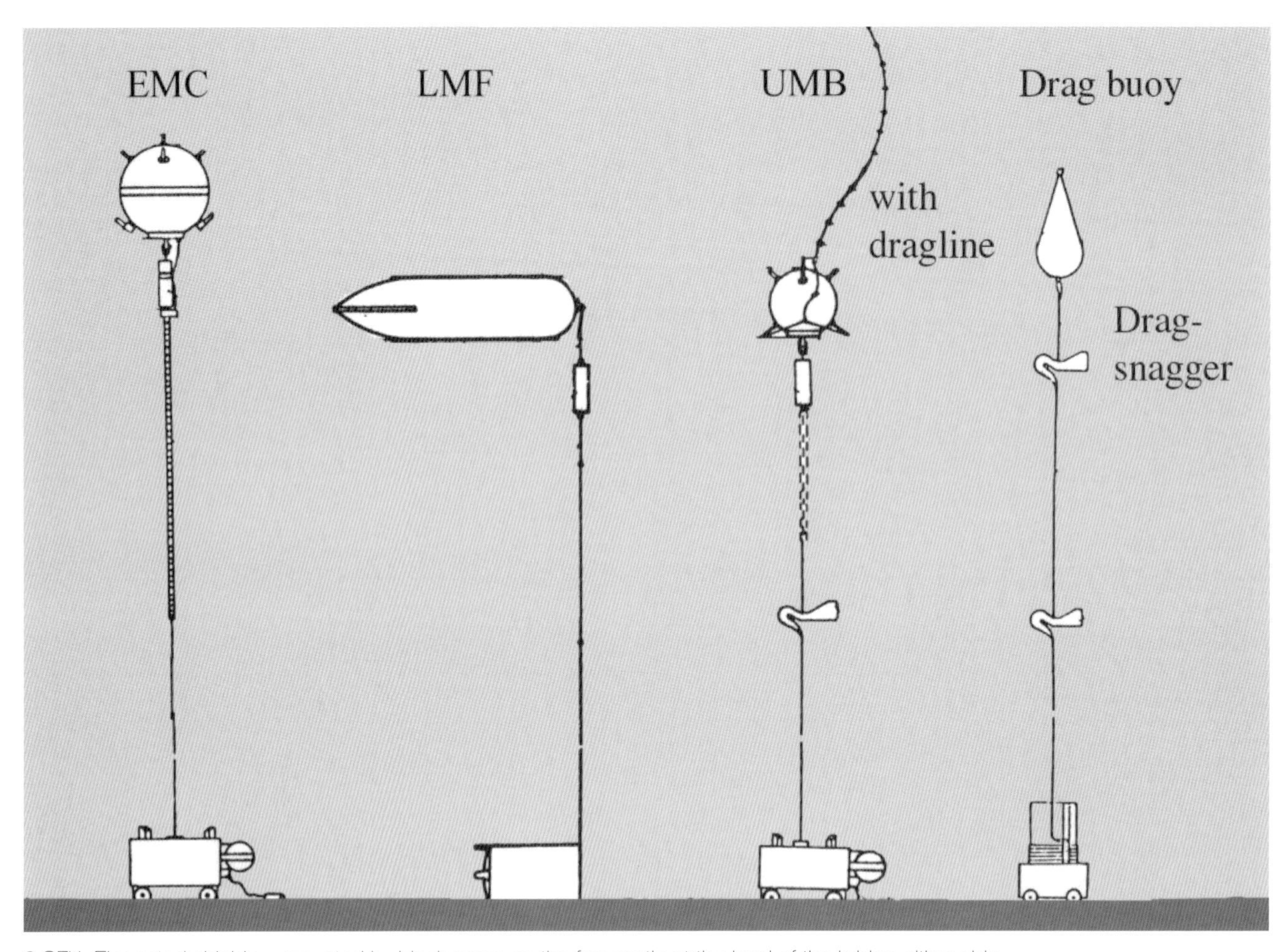

9.SFltl. Elongated shield surmounted by black cross on the forecastle at the level of the bridge either side.

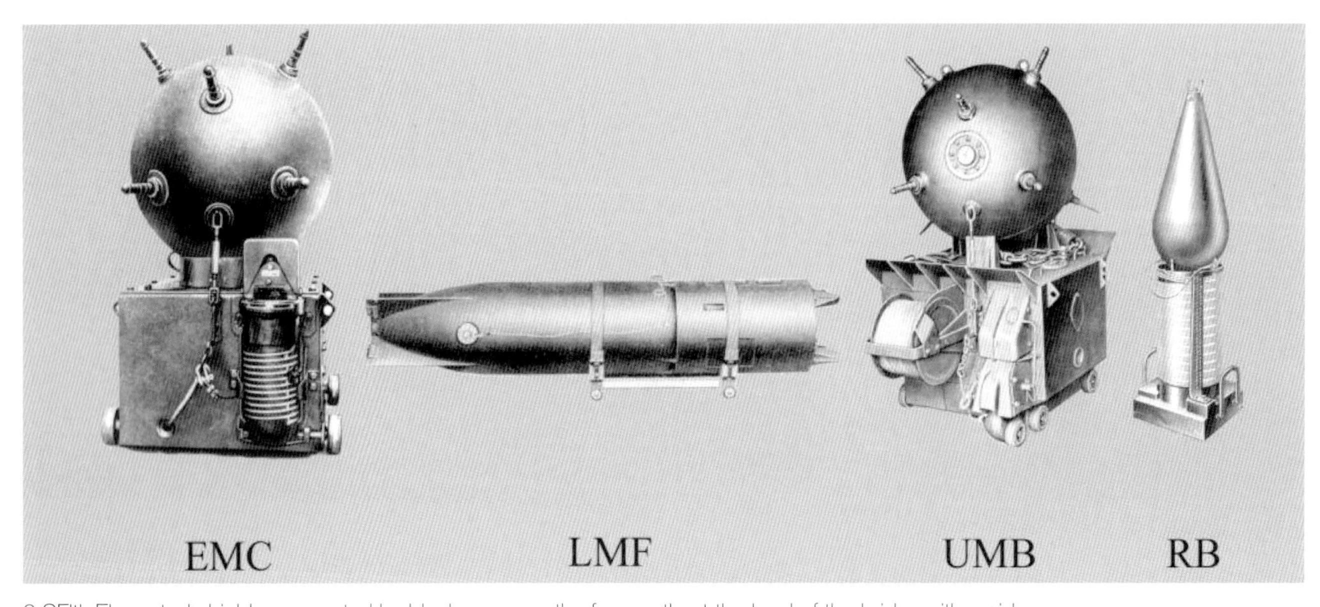

9.SFltl. Elongated shield surmounted by black cross on the forecastle at the level of the bridge either side.

Report on Torpedo Fired

Every torpedo fired had to be reported on the appropriate form. Shown below, and on page 174 is the report of Oberleutnant zur See Klose, commander S 70, after an engagement at 0118 hrs on 9 July 1942 in Lyme Bay, naval square AN2391, in which a fan of two torpedoes was fired at a 3,000-ton freighter. After 2 minutes 29 seconds, a hit was observed astern, with a cloud of smoke at the detonation point. A sinking could not be claimed because S 70 was forced to turn away by a convoy escort.

Block-Nr. 6391 **Schußmeldung für Überwasserstreitkräfte und U-Boote** Seite 16

"S 70" (Schießendes Fahrzeug) **Geheim!** Oblt. z.S. Klose Kmdt. (Dienstgrad, Name und Dienststellung des Schützen)

Datum: 9.7.42. Ort: □ 2391 Uhrzeit des Schusses: 01h 18m 30s

Wassertiefe: 60 m Wetter: 0 Sicht: 15 h m Wind: 4

Seegang: 3 Dünung: Richtung u. Stärke lang West

Ziel: Frachter 2519 (Name) 3000 t (Größe) 65 m (Länge) 4 m (Tiefgang)

Beladezustand u. Ladung:

Erfolg: Treffer 1 Fehlschuß Angriffsschuß 2 Fangschuß (auf gestoppt liegendes Ziel)

Lfd. Nr.		Einzelschuß, Mehrfach- oder Fächerschuß	1	2	3	4
1		Zeittakt in sec und Streuwinkel in Graden	3/2			
2	Torpedo	Art, Nummer, Aptierung G 7 a	7794	1905		
3	Torpedo	V_t und eingestellte Laufstrecke	40 sm	/ 170 hm		
4	Torpedo	Eingestellte Tiefe	2	2½		
5	Pi	Nummer, Art der Aptierung G 7 H	27073	25518		
6	Pi	Z-Einstellring				
7	Pi	S-Einstellring				
8	Rohr	Bezeichnung				
9	Rohr	Ausstoßart	Luft			
10	Beim Schuß	Eigene Fahrt	7 sm / h			
11	Beim Schuß	Eigener Kurs	0°			
12	Beim Schuß	Schiffspeilung	352°			
13	Beim Schuß	Schußwinkel	0°			
14		Zielstelle, Ziel- und Rechengerät	Brücke, RZA			
15		Abkommpunkt	Mitte Schornstein			
16		Torpedokurs	0°	2°		
17		Eingestellte Schußunterlagen V_g = 7 sm/h		γ-gr. 18°	9°	
18		Tauchtiefe beim Schuß (nur bei U-Booten)				
19		Lastigkeit beim Schuß (bei Schiffen usw. Krängung beim Schuß)				
20		Entfernung beim Schuß u. beob. Laufzeit	3000m	2m 29s		
21		Torpedoniedergang und Lauf	+ 2			
22		Schuß im Abdrehen oder auf geraden Kurs	Im Abdrehen			
23		Eingestellter Winkel nach Farbe u. Graden				
24		Bei G7e und Schußweite über 3000 m: a) letzte Nachladung vor dem Schuß: b) letzte Heizung vor dem Schuß:				

I.V.A.

Anlaufskizze mit Schußbild. Wie sind Schußunterlagen erworben? Besondere Beobachtungen, Abwehr, Erklärung für Fehlschuß:

γ = 110°
β = 9°

Wirkung am Ziel, Höhe und Aussehen der Sprengsäule, Zeit bis zum vollkommenen Untergang. Wahrnehmungen im eigenen Boot:

Nach 2m 29s Laufzeit Treffer im Achterschiff mit beobachteter Detonationswolke. Ein Sinken konnte auf Grund von Abdrängen des Bootes vom Geleit durch den Schußbewacher nicht beobachtet werden.

gez. Klose
Oblt. z.S.u. Kmdt.
11/7.

Unterschrift des Schützen – Unterschrift des Kmdten. – gegebf. beglaubigt.

Stellungnahme, Gutachten und Entscheidung:

Zweierfächer durch Abkommpunktverlegung

Treffer Angriffsschuß

gez. Junker

(Unterschrift – Datum)

V
S-Boat Awards and Badges

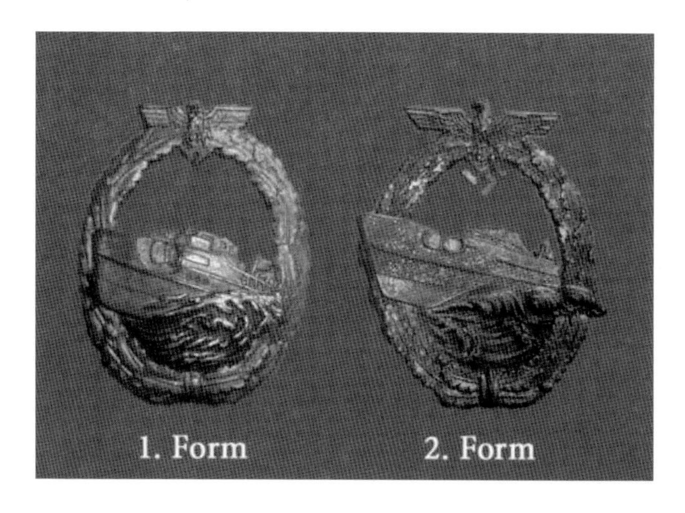

After Operation *Weserübung*, in which ten destroyers were sunk at Narvik, on 4 June 1940 C-in-C Grandadmiral Raeder ordered the introduction of a destroyer war badge. On 12 August 1940, he enlarged the circle of those entitled to wear it to S-boat crews who had distinguished themselves in the attack role. The FdT was responsible for deciding who should receive the award.

By virtue of the increasing importance of the S-boat Arm, on 30 May 1941 Raeder authorised the S-boat war badge, to be awarded after twelve offensive missions, for an especially successful operation, individual acts of bravery, loss of the boat due to enemy action or after a wound in action. Initially the FdT handled the awards; later the responsibility passed to the FdS.

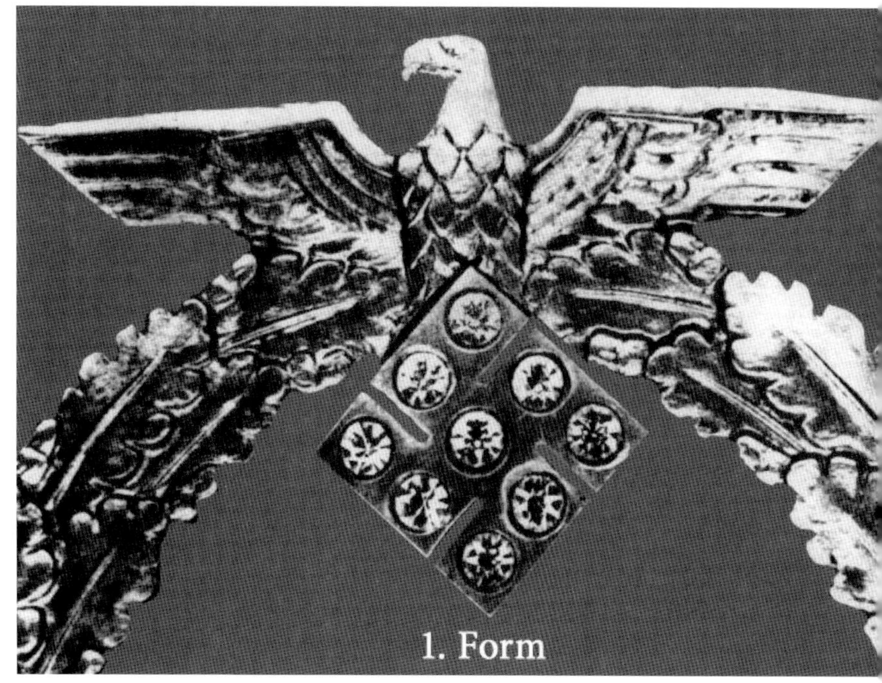

From 28 January 1943, the design of the badge was changed so that now the forepeak of an S-boat projected beyond the wreath of oak leaves. As the war progressed, it became the practice to reward servicemen by the war badge of their arm of service with diamonds after receiving the Oak Leaves to the Knight's Cross. No standing order existed. The first S-boat War Badge with Diamonds was awarded by Grandadmiral Raeder on 16 February 1942 to Kapitänleutnant Töniges as the most successful commander. It was apparently a provisional design; those awarded later had a swastika of finer definition and open torpedo tubes. In the autumn of 1944, the FdS was authorised to award the War Badge with Diamonds together with a certificate, which had not been usual with the earlier awards.

There is no complete list of recipients of the War Badge with Diamonds. Besides Töniges, FdS Petersen, and flotilla heads Feldt, Kemnade, Christiansen, Klug, von Mirbach and Wuppermann received the award.

Notes

Chapter 1

1. Docter, *Anfänge*, p 325f; also Fock, *Schnellboote*, vol 1, p 9ff, 22ff and 30ff
2. Fock, *Schnellboote*, p 60ff; also Güth, *Revolution*, p 162
3. Docter, *Anfänge*, p 325f
4. For Lohmann's activities, see Rahn, *Reichsmarine*, p 219ff. In all, forty-six trainees obtained a Certificate of Competence for the Nautical and Technical Handling of Motor Boats (Rahn, *Reichsmarine*, p 220).
5. Fock, *Schnellboote*, vol 1, p 133f
6. For the full history, see Docter, *Anfänge*, p 374f; Conrady, *Motortorpedoschnellboote*, p 356f; Fock, *Schnellboote*, vol 1, p 131ff and MGFA, *Militärgeschichte*, vol 5, p 316ff.
7. Instructions of Head of Admiralty, 10 February 1932, reproduced in Fock, *Schnellboote*, vol I, p 140.
8. See Treue, *Marinerüstung*, p 134
9. Treue, *Marinerüstung*, p 134
10. *Tsingtau* was commissioned as a fleet tender in 1934. Length 87 metres, displacement 2,500 tonnes, speed 17 knots (Gröner, *Kriegsschiffe*, vol 4, p 69f).
11. *Tanga* had been ordered as a mother ship for Chinese boats, but was bought while still on the stocks and completed in 1938. Commissioned 21 January 1939. Length 96 metres, displacement 2,600 tonnes, speed 17 knots (Gröner, *Kriegsschiffe*).
12. Gröner, *Kriegsschiffe*, p 136
13. The Z-Plan was based on the SKL memorandum 'Naval War Policy against England and the Requirements Arising therefrom for the Strategic Aims and Expansion of the Kriegsmarine', dated 25 December 1938, reproduced in Salewski, *Seekriegsleitung*, vol 3, p 27ff. In appendix III ('S-boats'), the same numbers are set out as appeared later in the Z-Plan (Salewski, *Seekriegsleitung*, vol 3, p 63). For the Z-Plan, see Schulze-Wegener, *Kriegsmarine-Rüstung*, p 13.
14. Treu, *Marinerüstung*, p 137
15. Work to lay the Westwall minefield began on 3 September 1939 and extended into 1940. See MGFA, *Das Deutsche Reich und der Zweite Weltkrieg*, vol 2, p 163.
16. Marineleitung, *Schnellbootstaktik*, para 145
17. Marineleitung, *Schnellbootstaktik*, para 147

Chapter 2

1. For the run-up to the occupation of Denmark and Norway see Ottmer, *Weserübung*, p 3ff. At the outbreak of war, Raeder spoke of 'knowing how to die with honour' (Salewski, *Seekriegsleitung*, vol 1, p 91). 'The dead North Sea' is the nucleus of the reflections on naval strategy in Wegener, *Seestrategie*.
2. Hubatsch, *Weisungen*, p 55
3. Ottmer, *Weserübung*, p 54ff
4. Salewski, *Seekriegsleitung*, vol 1, p 181f
5. The naval oiler *Altmark* was boarded in Norwegian territorial waters on 16 February 1940 by the British destroyer *Cossack* to liberate Merchant Navy prisoners held aboard the ship. Seven *Altmark* crew were killed (Hubatsch, *Weisungen*, p 35).
6. Ottmer, *Weserübung*, p 24ff; also Hubatsch, *Weisungen*, p 31ff
7. Hubatsch, *Weisungen*, p 57
8. See chapter 15
9. For the operational plans 'Wilfred' (minelaying) and 'R4' (landings), see Roskill, *War at Sea*, vol I, p 157f.
10. *Carl Peters* was commissioned on 6 January 1940 and allotted to 1.SFltl. Length 114 metres, displacement 3,600 tonnes, speed 23 knots (Gröner, *Kriegsschiffe*, vol 4, p 69f).
11. The War Diaries for both flotillas for the period of the Norwegian operation are missing; therefore events are based on the other available war diaries and published literature.
12. War Diary SKL(A), vol 8, 23 April 1940, p 248f
13. War Diary FdT (Führer der Torpedoboote), 30 April 1940, folio 40
14. Torpedo boat *Leopard* was rammed and sunk by the minelayer *Preussen* on 30 April 1940.
15. War Diary SKL(A), vol 9, 9 May 1940, p 90
16. War Diary SKL(A), vol 8, 21 April 1940, p 225

Chapter 3

1. For the story of the operational planning in the west, Frieser, *Blitzkrieg-Legende*, and MGFA, *Das Deutsche Reich und der Zweite Weltkrieg*, vol 2, p 244ff.
2. Wagner, *Lagevorträge*, p 44
3. See chapter 2.
4. War Diary SKL(A), vol 9, 14 May 1940, p 139
5. War Diary FdT, 21 May 1940, folio 46
6. From Kiel, the FdT had equipped one receiving and one transmitting van with the following: two short-wave transmitters, one all-frequency receiver, one small-ship receiver, one portable German telex apparatus and field telephone installations with cables and accessories (War Diary FdT, 30 May 1940, folio 60).

7. For details of the order holding back the armour, Frieser, *Blitzkrieg-Legende*, p 363ff.
8. During the war, the British believed that S 34 had fired. Not until the 1980s was the incident clarified at the instigation of the former S 34 commander, Obermaier, then Vizeadmiral and latterly NATO commander, Baltic Approaches (BALTAP) (Hümmelchen, *Schnellboote*, p 26, and exchange of correspondence between Obermaier and the author).
9. War Diary FdT, 1 June 1940, folio 68
10. War Diary FdT, Annexe, 1–15 June 1940, folio 105f
11. See note 10.
12. Exact details in Roskill, *War at Sea*, vol I, p 603, appendix L. Operation Dynamo is covered extensively on p 216ff.
13. War Diary SKL(A) 31 May 1940, p 323
14. Bonatz, *Seekrieg im Äther*, p 128f
15. Roskill, *War at Sea*, vol I, pp 93ff and 598
16. For the torpedo crisis, Rössler, *Torpedoes*, p 84ff
17. War Diary Group West, 5 July 1940, folio 20
18. War Diary FdT, 11 June 1940, folio 93
19. Report of FdT to Raeder, 19 June 1940, on occasion of latter's visit to Boulogne. Raeder decided 'that the construction of concrete shelters for the boat is not approved and only camouflaged anchorages are to be built, provided this can be done quickly' (War Diary FdT, 19 June 1940, folio 99).
20. Missions are comprehensively described in Ruge, *Küstenvorfeld*, p 52ff.
21. War Diary FdT, 30 June 1940, folio 44f
22. For basic Luftwaffe/Kriegsmarine co-operation, see Neitzel, *Einsatz der deutschen Luftwaffe*.
23. For presentation of co-operation see War Diary FdT, 15 July 1940, folio 190f.
24. War Diary Group West, 15 July 1940, folio 58. Similar criticism one week later: 'FdT has been instructed again that "no reports of steamers" is not a reason for not sailing a mission' (War Diary Group West, 23 July 1940, folio 122).
25. War Diary Group West, 25 July 1940, folios 130 and 132; also War Diary FdT, 25 July 1940, folio 232f
26. Roskill, *War at Sea*, vol I, p 323ff
27. War Diary FdT, 3 July 1940, folio 158
28. For details of individual types of mine, see Ledebur, *Seemine*.
29. War Diary FdT, 12 July 1940, folio 181
30. For the types, see chapter 16.
31. Information, files submarine *Sark*, War Diary SKL(A), vol 12, 12 August 1940, p 142
32. Raeder had been approached on this subject during his visit to the S-flotillas in August. SKL expressed subsequently in a letter to the FdT and flotillas its special recognition for their unheralded mining activities. War Diary SKL(A), vol 12, 13 August 1940, p 155. These letters cannot be found in the war diaries of Group West of the FdT.
33. For the history and planning of Operation *Seelöwe*, see MGFA. *Das Deutsche Reich und der Zweite Weltkrieg*, vol 2, p 368ff; also Potter and Nimitz, *Seemacht*, p 500ff.
34. War Diary SKL(A), vol 13, 17 September 1940, p 228
35. War Diary Group West, 13 August 1940, folio 8
36. Mining orders as Annexe to War Diary Group West, 10 September 1940, folios 103 and 175ff
37. For example on the night of 15 September 1940, operations by the 2nd Torpedo Boat Flotilla mining the Strait of Dover, the 4th R-boat Flotilla sweeping path of S-boats and 2.SFltl. securing area for R-boats, were planned to coincide, but in the event only the torpedo boats put out because of the weather.
38. War Diary SKL(A), vol 14, 14 October 1940, p 149
39. Instruction 1.SKL. op 2270/40g.kdosChefs, 14 October 1940, set out in War Diary FdT, 19 October 1940, folio 99. War Diary Group West does not mention it until 21 October 1940 (War Diary Group West, 21 October 1940, folio 159ff).
40. War Diary FdT, 19 October 1940, folio 102
41. The dispute between SKL and Group West over operational zones for surface forces simmered for some time (Salewski, *Seekriegsleitung*, vol I, p 268f). For the primary indications, see War Diary SKL(A), vol 14, 12 October 1940, p 132, 16 October 1940, p 182 and 17 October 1940, p 194ff.
42. War Diary SKL(A), vol 14, 25 October 1940, p 298
43. The former BSO, Vizeadmiral Mootz, as C-in-C Naval Security West, took over the duties of Naval Commander West. His headquarters remained at Trouville. He had under him C-in-C Minelayers, FdM West and FdV West (War Diary SKL(A), vol 14, 26 October 1940, p 317).
44. New boundary from (a) English coast at 53°45'N to (b) 53°45'N 02°30E to (c) Dutch coast 53°N (War Diary SKL(A) 2 November 1940, p 20).
45. War Diary FdT, 25 October 1940, folio 108f
46. War Diary FdT, 8 November 1940, folio 134
47. War Diary FdT, Annexe, 1–15 November 1940, folio 147
48. War Diary SKL(A), vol 14, 30 October 1940, p 361
49. See Roskill, *War at Sea*, vol I, p 327.
50. The boat had just been commissioned and, coming from Germany, had aboard the entire set for 1.SFltl., and not only the code of the day. See Diary FdT, 22 November 1940, folio 164. The Instruction of Fleet Command (2.Adm.Fleet 30 January 1941) is at War Diary FdT, Annexe, 15–30 November 1940, folio 182.
51. 'Installation of a 2cm gun on the foredeck, set into the forecastle in such a way that the weapon projects only slightly above the deck, gimbal-mounted suspension and operated in a well by one man' (War Diary FdT, 3 December 1940, folio 195).
57. War Diary FdT, 4 May 1940, folio 100
58. Order by FdT, 5 May 1940 in War Diary FdT, folio 109

Chapter 4

1. See chapter 5.
2. War Diary FdT, 5 May 1941, folio 109
3. War Diary FdT, 16 May 1941, folio 114
4. This was the dummy *Mamari*; see Hümmelchen, *Schnellboote*, p 564f and *Lloyd's War Losses*, p 262; Lenton and Colledge, *Warship*, p 309. The reference to this ship's having been sunk by U-73 in the Atlantic appears incorrect.

5. See chapter 3.
6. See also the comprehensive treatment of the expansion of the Coastal Forces in Jefferson, *Coastal Forces.*
7. Displacement 32–4 tons, length 21.3m, speed 35–8 kts, armament – one 3.7cm cannon, two twin 12.7mm machine guns either side of the bridge (North, *Coastal Forces*, p 42).
8. Displacement 60 tons, length 33.5m, speed 22–5 kts, armament – one 4cm cannon, three twin 12.7mm machine guns (North, *Coastal Forces*, p 53).
9. The commander of MTB 31, who had sailed with other boats in search of survivors, described how a German aircraft flew low over the boats to indicate the direction in which the men would be found (Jefferson, *Coastal Forces*, p 114). This was minefield SW1, laid at the beginning of August (War Diary SKL(A), vol 13, 1 September 1940, p 3).
10. For the differences between the Luftwaffe and Kriegsmarine High Commands on aerial minelaying see Neitzel, *Einsatz der deutschen Luftwaffe*, pp 33, 70, 133; also Salewski, *Seekriegsleitung*, vol 1, p 141ff.
11. Roskill, *War at Sea*, vol I, p 328; Jefferson, *Coastal Forces*, p 114 gives the figure for Nore between the outbreak of war and December 1940 as 179 ships.
12. Roskill, *War at Sea*, vol I, pp 329, 498, 616
13. Twin-engined torpedo-bomber/reconnaissance aircraft, entered service in December 1939; armament – four 7.6mm machine guns, up to 900kg of bombs or mines, or one torpedo (Munson, *Flugzeuge*, p 59).
14. Twin-engined bomber, entered service 1936; armament – five 7.6mm machine guns, 540kg of bombs (Munson, *Flugzeuge*, p 60).
15. Goulter, *Forgotten Offensive*, p 348
16. War Diary FdT, 21 June 1941, folio 138. Despite his Barbarossa duties, the FdT kept his eye on operations in the west and commented on them in the War Diary.
17. See chapter 3; also Neitzel, *Verbunkerte Frontstützpunkte*, p 32. Ostend was ready on 10 June 1941, Boulogne 21 June 1941, both with four pens. War Diary FdT, 10 June 1941, folio 128f and 30 June 1941, folio 145.
18. In 1941, destroyers and torpedo boats carried out three minelaying missions, on 7 January, 23 January and 5 March (Rohwer-Hümmelchen, *Chronology of the War*, vol 1). In April 1941, the Luftwaffe laid eleven mines off the ports, in May twenty-eight and in June one (Neitzel, *Luftwaffe*, p 258).
19. Giessler, *Marine-Nachrichten-und Ortungsdienst*, p 70
20. In the operation of 6 August 1941, hits were observed but no sinkings confirmed. On 10 August 1941, the freighter *Sir Russell* was sunk.
21. War Diary SKL(A), vol 23, 20 July 1941, p 410f
22. War Diary SKL(A), vol 24, 5 August 1941, p 66
23. War Diary FdT, 15 September 1941, folio 191
24. At this time the staff was headed by No. 1 Admiralty Staff Officer Korvettenkapitän Herbert-Max Schultz, who also signed the War Diary. Kapitän zur See Bütow resumed command personally on 11 November 1941.
25. War Diary 2.SFltl., 13 October 1941, folio 202

Chapter 5

1. For the run-up to the war against the Soviet Union, MGFA, *Das Deutsche Reich und der Zweite Weltkrieg*, vol 4, p 3ff.
2. Hillgruber, *Strategie*, p 211
3. Atlantic operations: armoured ships *Admiral Graf Spee* and *Deutschland*, September–December 1939; heavy cruiser *Admiral Scheer*, October 1940–April 1941; heavy cruiser *Admiral Hipper* November–December 1940; battleships *Scharnhorst* and *Gneisenau*, January–March 1941; heavy cruiser *Admiral Hipper*, February 1941; battleship *Bismarck* and heavy cruiser *Prinz Eugen*, May 1941.
4. For the basic planning and deliberations of the Kriegsmarine, Salewski, *Seekriegsleitung*, vol I, p 354f; also Ruge, *Sowjetflotte als Gegner*, p 21f.
5. Hubatsch, *Weisungen*, p 97
6. War Diary SKL(A), vol 17, 30 January 1941, p 401ff
7. The grouping-up was dissolved shortly afterwards, the boats returning to their original flotillas. 5.SFltl. was formed officially on 15 July 1941.
8. War Diary SKL(A), vol 18, 5 February 1941, p 82fl; MGFA, *Das Deutsche Reich und der Zweite Weltkrieg*, vol 4, p 323f; Lohmann-Hildebrand, *Kriegsmarine*, vol I, p 62–3 and 62-12.
9. Three mineships sank in the minefield on 9 July 1941, not having received prior warning. See MGFA, *Das Deutsche Reich und Der Zweite Weltkrieg*, vol 4, p 650.
10. War Diary SKL(A), vol 22, 17 June 1941, p 188f
11. Especially Operations Regenbogen (*Hipper* and *Lützow*) and Ostfront (*Scharnhorst*) (Salewski, *Seekriegsleitung*, vol II, pp 196ff and 335ff).
12. War Diary FdT Helsinki, 21 June 1941, folio 24
13. War Diary FdT Helsinki, 21 June 1941, folio 24
14. After the 1939/40 Winter War, in the peace agreement signed in Moscow on 13 March 1940, the Finns were obliged to cede the isthmus with the port of Hangö to the Soviet Union for thirty years, and a Soviet naval base had been built there subsequently.
15. These were the first prisoners brought ashore: 2.SFltl. – fifteen crew from Estonian freighter *Liisa*; 3.SFltl. – two men from Latvian steamer *Gaisma*, and four from Soviet steamer *Shuka*.
16. Metal shavings were repeatedly found in the oil. Problems with roller bearings led to their replacement by slide bearings. As a rule, motor overhauls and engine changes had to be carried out in German yards, as other bases were not suitably equipped.
17. Directive of BdK in War Diary FdT Helsinki, 24 June 1941, folio 53
18. War Diary FdT, Helsinki, 29 June 1941, folio 91
19. As the laying of EMC mines by S-boats had not been discussed in the preparations for Barbarossa, the BdK had decided against S-boats carrying the appropriate EMC-mine rails; see War Diary FdT, Helsinki, folio 46.
20. War Diary SKL(A), vol 24, 7 August 1941, p 110f; also chapter 4
21. Details on this operation: Melzer, *Baltische Inseln*, p 39ff
22. War Diary SKL(A), vol 25, 20 September 1941, p 339f

Chapter 6

1. Scott, *Battle*, p 36
2. Hümmelchen, *Schnellboote*, p 61. Roskill, *War at Sea*, vol I, pp 328 and 498 states that nineteen ships of 63,853 gross tons were sunk in the Nore area in December 1941.
3. See chapter 14.
4. Bonatz, *Seekrieg im Äther*, p 139. The loss gave rise to bitter controversy about the selection of commanders. See chapter 15.
5. See chapter 7.
6. Opinion of Group West on FdT War Diary entries 16–28 February 1942, folio 147.
7. According to SKL Qu AII 35/42 g.Kdos, v.7.7.42, quoted in FdT War Diary, 20 April 1942, folio 289.
8. FdT War Diary, 28 March 1942, folio 257
9. The lack of availability of boats was due to commander changes, with resultant delays for training in Germany, while other boats were in the yards for refit, repair or replacement engines.
10. FdS War Diary, 8 July 1942, folio 168f
11. The official British record after the war continued to show MGB 335 as sunk. See *Statement of Losses*, 1947.
12. MGB 335 was a Fairmile C type boat; armoured bridge, speed 26 knots max, armament – two single 3-pdr (*c*4cm), two twin 12.7mm Lewis guns and 4 machine guns (North, *Coastal Forces*, p 65f).
13. FdS War Diary, 11 September1942, folio 34
14. Roskill, *War at Sea*, vol II, p 255f
15. FdS War Diary, 14 October 1942, folio 105ff
16. FdS War Diary, 9 March 1943, folio 26
17. FdS War Diary, 29 May 1943, folio 22
18. See chapter 16.
19. FdS War Diary, 18 September 1943, folio 22f
20. FdS War Diary, 10 October 1943, folio 21
21. Roskill, *War at Sea*, vol III, part I, p 97f
22. 2.SFltl. War Diary, 5 November 1943, folio 48
23. FdS War Diary, 5 November 1943, folio 35
24. Roskill, *War at Sea*, vol II, p 485f and vol III, part I, p 389
25. Roskill, *War at Sea*, speaks of 'going on to the offensive after a period of balance' (vol II and vol III, part I). For FdS, see FdS War Diary, 30 November 1943, folio 212.

Chapter 7

1. In German files at Drontheim.
2. See chapter 5.
3. For the general development of the Polar Front, see MGFA, *Das Deutsche Reich im Zweiten Weltkrieg*, vol 4, pp 378ff and 810ff, vol 6, p 404ff; also Potter and Nimitz, *Seemacht*, p 642ff.
4. Hitler's War Directive No. 36, 22 September 1941, reproduced in Hubatsch, *Weisungen*, p 179
5. Hubatsch, *Weisungen*, p 150
6. Hubatsch, *Weisungen*, p 188
7. Wagner, *Lagevorträge*, p 336
8. He was subordinate to Commanding Admiral Norway, and in turn Admiral Polar Coast was subordinate to him in operational matters.
9. War Diary 8.SFltl., 23 January 1942, p 83f
10. War Diary 8.SFltl., 31 January 1942, p 94
11. Wagner, *Lagevorträge*, p 347f; for 'Zone of destiny', see Salewski, *Seekriegsleitung 1935–1945*, vol 2, p 22ff.
12. War Diary 8.SFltl., 15 March 1942, p 130
13. War Diary 8.SFltl., 15 April 1942, p 146
14. War Diary 8.SFltl., 15 April 1942, p 153
15. War Diary 8.SFltl., 15 April 1942, p 156
16. S 113 was in dock at Trondheim for a long period with bottom damage.
17. Wagner, *Lagevorträge*, p 427
18. These boats were S 10, S 11, S 15 and S 16. See War Diary SKL(A), vol 40, 4 December 1942, p 104 and 14 December 1942, p 302; also vol 41, 20 January 1943, p 356 and vol 43, 21 March 1943, p 417.
19. See chapter 3.
20. War Diary SKL(A), vol 43, 21 March 1943, p 417
21. War Diary SKL(A), vol 45, 23 May 1943, p 398
22. On 1 December 1943, the office of Commanding Admiral Norway was redesignated Naval High Command Norway (Lohmann-Hildebrand, *Kriegsmarine*, vol II, p 121).
23. War Diary SKL(A), vol 48, 24 August 1943, p 443
24. War Diary SKL(A), vol 62/II, 18 October 1944, p 431f
25. See chapter 12.
26. One seeks in vain for mention of S-boats in polar Norway in Roskill, Potter and Nimitz, and in all other literature of the Allied side. Even Ruge, *Sowjetflotte als Gegner*, is silent on the matter.

Chapter 8

1. For the political and military developments in the Mediterranean and the Balkans, see MGFA, *Das Deutsche Reich und der Zweite Weltkrieg*, vol III, '*Das Mittelmeer und Südosteuropa*'.
2. Hubatsch, *Weisungen*, p 152
3. Wagner, *Lagevorträge*, p 272
4. Wagner, *Lagevorträge*, pp 282 and 289. For the political infighting respecting the Mediterranean, see also Salewski, *Seekriegsleitung*, vol I, p 470ff
5. Kemnade, *Afrika-Flotille*, p 133f
6. Roskill, *War at Sea*, vol II, p 61
7. Because the engagement was from the land, the sinking could not be confirmed. The next morning, Me 109 fighters sighted the drifting boat and sank it with cannon-fire.
8. Playfair, *Mediterranean*, vol III, p 293
9. For the wrangling about 'Hercules', see Reuth, *Entscheidung*, p 171f.
10. For the Inshore Squadron, see Roskill, *War at Sea*, vol II, p 43f.
11. Tobruk was surrendered at 1844 hrs on 20 June 1942 but news did not reach the flotilla commander until 2255 hrs (War Diary 3.SFltl., vol 6, folio 906).
12. Comparisons between the statements in the literature (eg

Ufficio Storico, *Lloyd's War Losses* and Hümmelchen, *Schnellboote*) throw up major differences regarding positions and times. The battle report (Syfret, Report, p 4503ff) does not coincide with the 3.SFltl. War Diary and considers that S 30 sank *Almeria Lykes* and *Wairangi*, S 36 *Santa Eliza* and S 59 *Glenorchy*.
13. For Operation Pedestal, see Syfret, Report, p 4503ff, Shankland, *Durchbruch* and Roskill, *War at Sea*, vol II, p 302ff.
14. Because of the 3.SFltl. losses and the growing demands for S-boats, on 10 July 1942 SKL decided to send S-boats S 151–8 to the Mediterranean. The transfer was scheduled for autumn (War Diary SKL(A), vol 33, 23 May 1942, p 437f and vol 35, 10 July 1942, p 203). The boats began leaving on 15 September, reached La Spezia on 8 October and ran into Augusta on 15 December 1942.
15. War Diary SKL(A), vol 39 I, 6 November 1942, p 119
16. For the occupation of France, see MGFA, *Das Deutsche Reich und der Zweite Weltkrieg*, vol 6, p 740f.
17. These were T 121, T 122 and T 123, together with the submarines *Dauphin, Saphir, Phogue, Requin, Calypso* and *Espordes* (War Diary 3.SFltl., 8 December 1942, folio 72).
18. For the significance of Tunis and the role of the 'new' C-in-C Kriegsmarine, Dönitz, see Salewski, *Seekriegsleitung*, vol II, p 245ff.
19. At this time the Luftwaffe had only twenty-five Ju 88 long-range reconnaissance aircraft for the entire Mediterranean region. For this reason, flights over the Bone region were abandoned until further notice by Fliegerführer Tunesien (3.SFltl. War Diary, 1 December 1942, folio 1081); see also Felmy, *Luftwaffe*.
20. When the boats returned, it was noticed that S 35 was missing. As no radio contact could be established, the other boats put to sea, but found only wreckage, leading to the conclusion that S 35 had been mined and sunk.
21. HMS *Lightning* belonged to Force Q operating from Bone with four cruisers and four destroyers, while Force K was based at Malta with three cruisers and four destroyers. The Polish destroyer *Blyskawica* entered the Mediterranean to replace *Lightning* (Roskill, *War at Sea*, vol II, pp 431 and 439).
22. S 56 was later raised and towed to Toulon, where she suffered more heavy damage during an air raid on 20 November 1943. The boat was scrapped without having re-entered commission. After Palermo, therefore, she is not counted amongst the number of available S-boats.

Chapter 9

1. War Diary SKL(A), vol 46, 15 June 1943, p 32f
2. In this action, the US destroyers *Roe* and *Swanson*, which had not been advised about *Ordronaux*, collided and received damage while attempting to engage the latter and avoid the minefields off Porto Empedocle at the same time (Morrison, *History*, vol IX, p 78f).
3. War Diary 3.SFltl., 10 July 1943, folio 1372
4. Roskill, *War at Sea*, vol III-I, p 121
5. War Diary SKL(A), vol 47, 14 July 1943, pp 280 and 299f
6. A few days before the Sicily landings, Kemnade was hurt in a car accident and Oberleutnant zur See Albert Müller deputised for him as flotilla commander.
7. Schramm, *OKW War Diary*, vol 6, 6 September 1943, p 1061f
8. In the Mediterranean at this time, the British had 16 MLs, 13 MGBs and 39 MTBs, the Americans 42 MTBs (Roskill, *War at Sea*, vol III-I, p 377; also Bulkley, *PT Boats*, p 449f).
9. War Diary, SKL(A), vol 50, 21 October 1943, p 422f
10. War Diary, SKL(A), vol 50, 27 October 1943, p 561ff
11. War Diary, SKL(A), vol 51, 2 November 1943, p 32f; 12 November 1943, p 285f; and 17 November 1943, p 389
12. For transportation – as for boats to the Black Sea – all engines and armament were removed and the boats' hulls carried by the so-called Kuhlemeyer special transporter.
13. The KS-boats (*Küsten-S-Boote*) of 22.SFltl. were 16 metres in length, displaced barely 20 tonnes and had a speed of 30–2 knots when armed with two stern torpedoes. The LS-boats (*Leichte S-Boote*) of 21.SFltl. were 12.5 metres long, displaced 12 tonnes and could make 38–40 knots carrying two stern torpedoes (Gröner, *Kriegsschiffe*, vol 2, p 140ff). Gröner puts the LS-boats in 24.SFltl., but this does not conform to the War Diaries.
14. Schenk, *Ägäis*, p 116f; also Hümmelchen, *Schnellboote*, p 118f
15. War Diary, SKL(A), vol 56, 2 April 1944, p 27f
16. The Italian files show Kotor as Cattaro.

Chapter 10

1. MGFA, *Das Deutsche Reich und der Zweite Weltkrieg*, vol 4, p 508ff
2. Potter and Nimitz, *Seemacht*, p 626ff
3. War Diary SKL(A), vol 28, 16 December 1941, p 256; vol 29, 6 January 1942, p 76; 9 January 1942, p 130
4. See chapter 5.
5. Kopp, *Teufelsschiff*
6. This period was increased to 500 hours in due course.
7. Also found on the mountain were other Soviet weapons, including three 13cm with a coastal defence rangefinder and four 7.5cm guns.
8. Kapitänleutnant Georg-Stuhr Christiansen took over the flotilla on 1 September 1942.
9. For the Army operations, see MGFA, *Das Deutsche Reich und der Zweite Weltkrieg*, vol 6, p 930ff.
10. The boats were transferred in from the end of June to the beginning of August.
11. War Diary SKL(A), vol 36, 21 August 1942, p 439; 22 August 1942, p 455; 26 August 1942, p 522; vol 42, 5 February 1943, p 75
12. Dönitz was appointed successor to Raeder as C-in-C Kriegsmarine on 31 January 1943.
13. KTB SKL(A), vol 42, 13 February 1943, p 22f. The Directive is dated 9 February 1943.
14. War Diary 1.SFltl., folios 84 and 101
15. This captured gun was nicknamed 'ratch-boom' for its

distinctive mechanism and flight of shell.

16. For the 'castling' and its effect on the Caucasus Front, see Roth, *Operation Denken*, p 295ff.
17. Vizeadmiral Kieseritzky was killed in an air raid on the Crimea, 19 November 1943. He was succeeded by Vizeadmiral Brinkmann.
18. Length 18.7m, beam 4.7m, displacement 29.7 tonnes, armament – two torpedoes, one 2cm gun, depth charges with hydrophone installation. As escort vessels they were not particularly seaworthy, the petrol engines were very prone to breakdown, spare parts were often difficult to obtain and maintenance work was complicated (Gröner, *Kriegsschiffe*, vol 2, p 147f).
19. The 'Zieten' plan is described in War Diary 1.SFltl., appendix 3, 15 June 1943, folio 20.
20. War Diary SKL(A), vol 48, 28 August 1943, p 517
21. Kapitänleutnant Hermann Büchting took over the flotilla in mid-September and commanded it to the end.
22. Potter and Nimitz, *Seemacht*, p 638
23. Three boats were decommissioned immediately, the other four towed via Constanta to Linz for a full refit but were decommissioned there later.
24. Oral instructions of Admiral Black Sea, War Diary 1.SFltl., 21 October 1943, folio 172.
25. War Diary 1.SFltl., 1 November 1943, folio 192
26. For 'Holding the Crimea' and Dönitz's role, see Salewski, *Seekriegsleitung*, B2, p 387ff.
27. Meister, *Seekrieg*, p 272
28. War Diary SKL(A), vol 51, 8 November 1943, p 210; 11 November 1943, p 264
29. Adler was a detailed evacuation plan drawn up by the Commandant for the Sea Defence of the Crimea and provided for an effective defence until the evacuation by air and sea was completed (War Diary 1.SFltl., appendix, April 1944, folio 98).
30. War Diary SKL(A), vol 56, 10 April 1944, p 217
31. War Diary SKL(A), vol 56, 13 April 1944, p 278ff
32. War Diary SKL(A), vol 56, 20 April 1944, p 440
33. War Diary SKL(A), vol 57, 1 May 1944, p 1f
34. War Diary 1.SFltl., appendix 4, 1–15 May 1944, folio 147
35. War Diary SKL(A), vol 60/II, 29 August 1944, p 767f
36. Transfer Report, S 86 and S 89, 22 September 1944

Chapter 11

1. For the various assessments on the Allied side, Weinberg, *Welt in Waffen*, p 651ff.
2. Details of the Allied preparations, from Potter and Nimitz, *Seemacht*, pp 738–41.
3. For assessment of the situation on 20 November 1943, see Salewski, *Seekriegsleitung*, vol 3, p 377.
4. Hitler's Directive for Conduct of the War No. 51, 3 November 1943, in Hubatsch, *Weisungen*, p 270f; also Thamer, *Entscheidung im Westen*, p 3ff.
5. Foundations of the leadership relationships on German side in Wegmüller, *Abwehr der Invasion*; also Ose, *Entscheidung im Westen*.
6. For the panzer controversy, see Wegmüller, *Abwehr der Invasion*, p 130ff; also Ose, *Entscheidung im Westen*, p 52.
7. Wegmüller, *Abwehr der Invasion*, p 113ff
8. The so-called Milch-Plan, quoted in Dahms, *Geschichte*, p 495.
9. War Diary Group West, 3 May 1944, folio 241
10. For preparations on German side, see Krancke, *Invasionsabwehrmassnahmen*, p 170ff; also contains extensive coverage of the KMA (Coastal Mine A).
11. In all, more than ten million cubic metres of reinforced concrete were used in the building of the so-called Atlantic Wall. The project employed 260,000 workers, 10 per cent of them German. (Dahms, *Geschichte*, p 496).
12. Wegener, *Normandie-Invasion*, p 162; Wegener was a former head of the Group West Command Staff.
13. War Diary Group West, 24 and 25 April 1944, folios 202 and 204. A destroyer, two LCIs and three LCTs sank on these mines (Potter and Nimitz, *Seemacht*, p 747).
14. War Diary Group West, 12 April 1944, folio 177
15. War Diary Group West, 28 May 1944, folio 296. On 14 May 1944, they had already noted that 'the participation of the Luftwaffe remains uncertain' (folio 262).
16. Potter and Nimitz, *Seemacht*, p 737
17. Potter and Nimitz, *Seemacht*, p 738
18. It is strange that, although the Germans must have understood these conditions from their planning for *Seelöwe* in 1940, since they applied equally to landings on British shores, they were apparently never taken into consideration.
19. Vogel, *Kriegsführung*, p 133f; also War Diary Group West, 14, 22 and 30 May 1944, folios 261f and 300
20. Morrison, *History*, vol XI, p 83
21. Morrison, *History*, vol XI, p 49
22. Wegmüller, *Abwehr der Invasion*, p 220
23. Ryan, *Längster Tag*, pp 113 and 124
24. Wegmüller, *Abwehr der Invasion*, p 221f. The FdS received the order for immediate readiness by telephone shortly before 0300. He had been alarmed to see similar orders being issued to the 2nd Security Division and had already put 4., 5. and 9.SFltl. at immediate readiness (War Diary FdS, 6 April 1944, folio 7).
25. War Diary SKL(A), vol 58 I, 6 June 1944, p 93
26. Translator's note: Wretchedly inaccurate naval gunnery and aerial bombing left the German defences immediately behind Omaha beach intact. An estimated 3,000 American troops lost their lives in the water. Omaha beach was eventually taken by American land forces arriving from adjacent Utah beach during the afternoon of 6 June (Keusgen, *Stützpunkt WN 62*; Severloh, *WN 62*).
27. Ose, *Entscheidung im Westen*, p 119; also Hillgruber, Hümmelchen, *Chronik*, p 248f.
28. Morrison, *History*, vol IX, pp 155f and 199
29. War Diary, Group West, 7 June 1944, folio 15f
30. War Diary, Group West, 7 June 1944, folio 17f
31. War Diary FdS, 8 June 1944, folio 34

32. See chapter 14.
33. PRO London, OIC-SIS, p 105f
34. War Diary FdS, 10 June 1944, folio 55
35. Artillery lighters or 'prams' usually had an armament of two 8.8cm, one 3.7cm and ten 2cm guns (Breyer, *Kriegsmarine*, vol 2, p 142).
36. War Diary Group West, 12 June 1944, folio 23f
37. PRO London, OIC-SIS, p 126. The Germans' first receipt of advice was a report from U-'Siedler' (translator's note: the author does not provide more information respecting who this source was) stating, 'Traffic by night stopped.' War Diary Group West, 5 July 1944, folio 27 stated, 'This report comes as a surprise to Group.'
38. PRO London, OIC-SIS, folio 136
39. War Diary FdS, 13 June 1944, folio 86f
40. For the background to the attack and its aftermath, Tent, *E-boat Alert*, p 156ff.
41. The following boats were sunk: S 84, S 100, S 138, S 142, S 143, S 144, S 146, S 150, S 169, S 171, S 172, S 173, S 187, S 188.
42. 2.SFltl., Boulogne, four boats; 4.SFltl., Boulogne, two boats; 8.SFltl., Ostend, three boats; 9.SFltl., Le Havre, one boat, Cherbourg, three boats.
43. Tallboy bombs, total weight 5.5 tons, first used at beginning of June in Normandy (Tent, *E-boat Alert*, p 107).
44. Note on B-Dienst report respecting speed reductions for Allied shipping due to danger from mines (in 7.5 fathoms, 5 knots; in 10 fathoms, 11 knots; in 15 fathoms, 14 knots), War Diary Group West, 3 July 1944, folio 19.
45. War Diary Group West, 25 June 1944, folio 48
46. War Diary Group West, 28 June 1944, folio 50f
47. Morrison, *History*, vol XI, p 163
48. Wegmüller, *Abwehr der Invasion*, pp 236 and 246
49. Ose, *Entscheidung im Westen*, p 157
50. War Diary OKW, vol IV, p 1572f; also Speidel, *Invasion*, p 139
51. For the Kriegsmarine, see Salewski, *Seekriegsleitung*, vol 2, p 432ff.
52. See chapter 12.
53. War Diary Group West, Review of Month, July 1944, folio 78
54. The torpedo had a length of 10 metres. Its speed was 9 knots, range 57 kilometres, running time about 3.5 hours (War Diary Group West, 8 July 1944, folio 51).
55. War Diary SKL(A), vol 60 II, 16 August 1944, p 390f
56. Morrison, *History*, vol XI, p 192 speaks of the cruiser HMS *Frobisher*'s being sunk, two destroyers and a repair ship damaged.
57. War Diary FdS, 5 September 1944, folio 149

Chapter 12

1. For the general political, military and economic situation of Germany, see Schramm, *War Diary*, vol 7, 1944–5, Introduction, p 3ff. Schramm speaks here also of the overextended Army, condemned to 'burn itself out from within' (p 22), an evaluation surely pertinent to the other Wehrmacht branches.
2. Romania dropped out on 23 August 1944, Bulgaria was occupied on 5 September 1944, and the Soviet–Finnish armistice came into force on 19 September 1944. Italy had already capitulated on 8 August 1943.
3. Foerster, *Ardennenoffensive*
4. The Group Commands were disbanded in the autumn of 1944, since there was no overall command of the naval forces, and area commands of an individual nature were developing in the Baltic, North Sea and Norway to the extent that a co-ordinated command structure appeared inappropriate. (Group North disbanded 31 July 1944, Group West 20 October 1944, Group South December 1944.) Leadership was taken over by the Naval High Commands North Sea, Baltic, South and West, in which West was responsible for the coasts but had no naval forces to command (Lohmann-Hildebrand, *Kriegsmarine*, vol I, p 3-1, 3-15, 40-3 and 40-6; vol II, p 81-1, 91-11 and 161-1; also Ehrensburger, *Organisation*, pp 47 and 53f).
5. After the loss of Z-24 and T-24 off the French coast on 25 August 1944, SKL noted, 'That is the end of destroyer and torpedo boat operations along the Atlantic coast' (War Diary, SKL(A), vol 60/II, 25 August 1944, p 657).
6. Neitzel, *Einsatz der deutschen Luftwaffe*
7. War Diary SKL(A), vol 63/II, 26 November 1944, p 594
8. See chapter 7.
9. The artificial harbour was still being used for supplies into December, which explains the supply problems encountered by the Allies, slowing their progress in the west (Greiner, *Abwehr*; Tent, *E-boat Alert*, p 214).
10. Regarding the strengthened defences, including technological developments, see Roskill, *War at Sea*, vol III, part II, p 138 (destroyer–MGB collaboration) and p 268f; and Whitley, *German Naval Forces*, p 758.
11. Roskill, *War at Sea*, vol III, part II, pp 139 and 287. Regarding the actual numbers of MGBs and MTBs, the statistics are not unequivocal. The figures given here are for September 1943 (Roskill, *War at Sea*, vol III, part I, p 97). However, the total number must have been higher (Roskill, *War at Sea*, vol III, part II, p 437).
12. See Roskill, *War at Sea*, vol III, part II, pp 268 and 277.
13. Bonatz, *Seekrieg im Äther*, pp 37f and 371. For monitoring German radio from the British side, see comprehensive files of PRO under reference ADM 223 and DEFE 3.
14. The main purpose of this operation was not supply, but the capture of Generalleutnant von Kluge and, on Hitler's order in connection with the 20 July 1944 plot, to place him in *Sippenhaft* – detention without trial as the close relative of a suspected traitor (Rebensburg, *Erinnerungen*, p 56).
15. Müller was exchanged for Captain Michael Foot, the later Minister of Labour and a Labour Party leader. The FdS forwarded Müller's report to OKM on 23 December 1944 (BA/MA RM 7/131, folios 60.78).
16. War Diary SKL(A), vol 64/I, 15 December 1944, p 368. The decision for an air attack was made by the SHAEF meeting on 5 December in order to destroy the S-boat threat. Results of the

raids could not be confirmed because of bad weather, and the Allies were therefore surprised by the S-boat operations of 22 and 24 December. On Christmas Day 1944, CINC NORE SHAEF requested an immediate resumption of air attacks (Tent, *E-boat Alert*, p 212).
17. War Diary, SKL(A), vol 64/II, 16 December 1944, p 394ff
18. War Diary SKL(A), vol 64/II, 17 December 1944, p 419
19. In weighing up various possibilities to strengthen the operation in the west, Petersen decided to equip 4.SFltl. urgently with modern boats fitted with anti-radar devices, and to employ very experienced crews. The 5th S-boat Flotilla also had veteran crews but the boats were clapped out, and he decided that these should be exchanged for the newer boats, some anti-radar equipped, with which the 1st S-boat Training Flotilla was training. The latter flotilla took over the strongest fighting boats of 5.SFltl. and, with the addition of two former Black Sea boats, then transferred to Norway to replace 4.SFltl.
20. War Diary SKL(A), vol 64/II, 26 December 1944, p 617f
21. War Diary, SKL(A), vol 64/II, 31 December 1944, pp 695f and 708
22. War Diary SKL(A), vol 65, 5 January 1945, p 70
23. Wagner, *Lagevorträge*, p 630
24. 2. and 6.SFltl. arrived at Den Helder and Rotterdam respectively on 19 December 1944, 4.SFltl. at Rotterdam on 28 December 1944 and 5.SFltl. at Den Helder on 10 January 1945.
25. War Diary SKL(A), vol 65, 16 January 1945, p 277
26. Letter SKL (1/SKL1a 95/94, 16 January 1945) and reply by FdS (telex, 20 January 1945) in BA/MA RM 7/158, pp 233f and 241
27. War Diary SKL(A), vol 65, 20 January 1945, p 362
28. War Diary SKL(A), 24 January 1945, p 435
29. Letter, ObdM B.Nr. 1/SKL. 7Schn 2538/45 g.Kdos 31 January 45 in BA/MA RM7/261, p 161f. Letter was ordered by Dönitz on 24 January 1945, completed and approved on 1 February 1945. War Diary SKL(A), vol 65, 24 January 1945, p 435 and vol 66, 1 February 1945, p 9.
30. BA/MA RM 1/261, p 122f
31. Opinion, FdS, 15 February 1945 in BA/MA RM7/158, p 185ff; Hoops, *Einsatz*, p 285ff; also oral and written remarks by former operations officer, FdS Staff, Bernd Rebensburg to the author, especially as regards the attitude of Petersen and how deeply wounded he was by Dönitz's accusation; Tent, *E-boat Alert*, p 226ff
32. War Diary SKL(A), vol 66 12 February 1945, p 120ff
33. War Diary SKL(A), vol 66, 20 February 1945, p 209ff
34. The S-flotilla claimed to have sunk seven ships of 20,000 gross tons; the actual figure was three ships of 5,000 gross tons (Hümmelchen, *Die Schnellboote*, p 203).
35. War Diary SKL(A), vol 67, 25 March 1945, p 353; 26 March 1945, p 370
36. War Diary SKL(A), vol 66, 22 February 1945, p 249
37. War Diary SKL(A), vol 66, 24 February 1945, p 273
38. BA/MA RM7/158, p 166
39. BA/MA RM7/158, p 162
40. Battle report, BA/MA RM7/158, p 146f
41. BA/MA RM 7/158, p 31
42. War Diary SKL(A), vol 68, 6 April 1945, p 81; 10 April 1945, p 163
43. War Diary SKL(A), vol 68, 16 April 1945, p 81; 17 April 1945, p 266
44. For successes, see Roskill, *War at Sea*, vol III, part III, p 279. These S-boat successes are, however, understated, some being attributed to the K-Verband erroneously (eg the destroyer *La Combattante*); see Hümmelchen, *Schnellboote*, p 203. The S-boat losses were eleven sunk at sea, three in harbour by air attack and one total loss, S 701. Losses: S 167, S 176, S 177, S 180, S 181, S 199, S 202, S 220, S 223, S 703, S 193. Lost in air raid at Wilhelmshaven: S 186, S 194, S 224 (Hümmelchen, *Schnellboote*, p 254ff and Groener, *Kriegsschiffe*, vol 2, p 137ff).
45. Transfer Order according to War Diary SKL(A), vol 68, 5 May 1945, p 435-A, for the dissolution of the German naval forces, 12 and 15 May 1945; see Lohmann-Hildebrand, *Kriegsmarine*, vol I, p 20–7.

Chapter 13

1. War Diary SKL(A), vol 3, 31 January 1944, p 560; vol 54, 3 February 194, p 45; 7 February 1944, p 134
2. War Diary SKL(A), vol 58/I, 13 June 1944, p 361
3. These four boats had not been given to Finland by the time Finland abandoned the Axis.
4. On 8 August 1944, T 22, T 30 and T 32 of the 3rd S-boat Training Flotilla sank. T 23 escaped undamaged.
5. Salewski, *Seekriegsleitung*, vol 2, p 454ff
6. Krause-Traudes, *Einsätze*, p 231
7. Melzer, *Baltische Inseln*, p 180. The War Diary, Admiral Baltic, first mentions the Führer Directive on 22 October 194, p 465.
8. Details of a battle involving 5.SFltl. are portrayed in Krause-Traudes, *Einsätze*, p 231ff.
9. Four boats collided during operations on the night of 18 November 1944.
10. War Diary SKL(A), vol 65, 22 January 1945, p 403
11. Schön, *Ostsee*, p 405f
12. For the overall rescue operation see Schön, *Ostsee*; also Potter and Nimitz, *Seemacht*, p 618ff.

Chapter 14

1. See Reuter, *Funkmess*, which gives full coverage of radio direction finding and radar development. For the Battle of Britain, see MGFA, *Das Deutsche Reich und der Zweite Weltkrieg*, vol 2, p 382ff.
2. Roskill, *War at Sea*, vol II, p 160ff
3. Requested initially in FdT, '*Die S-Bootswaffe im Kampf gegen die britische Zufuhr*', Memorandum to C-in-C Kriegsmarine on the occasion of his visit to 2. and 4.SFltl., retained as appendix to 2.SFltl. War Diary, 31 December 1941.
4. For the equipment, see Giessler, *Marine-Nachrichten- und Ortungsdienst*, p 135ff.
5. Müller, *Ortung*, p 5
6. Müller, *Ortung*, p 4

7. Giessler, *Marine-Nachrichten- und Ortungsdienst*, pp 80 and 87
8. Reuter, *Funkmess*, p 241
9. Report on the trials appears in Naval Intelligence Division, 'Interrogation of the survivors of S 147 and S 141', June 1944, p 15.
10. See chapters 3 and 4.
11. Bonatz, *Seekrieg im Äther* for a comprehensive survey.
12. See chapter 3.
13. FdS War Diary, 25 September 1943, folio 17
14. Rahn, *Warnsignale* provides a short survey with the newest state of the art.
15. See chapter 11.
16. Regarding the substantial effects in the Mediterranean against the Italian navy, see Santoni, *Ultra*.
17. Z.B.1417/23/12 - U 74 again informed that 'our own MTBs will be operating during the night 23–24/12 in square 3491 [east of Malta] and to the southward of that position' (Naval Section, *ZPZ/ZG*, p 256).

Chapter 15

1. Oral statement Kapitänleutnant Rebensburg, formerly commander with 2.SFltl.; also Fock, *Schnellboote*, vol 1, p 138.
2. Kemnade, *Afrika-Flotille*, p 16f
3. Lohmann-Hildebrand, *Kriegsmarine*, vol II, p 180ff
4. Kemnade, *Afrika-Flotille*, p 27f
5. Rebensburg, *Erinnerungen*, p 22
6. War Diary, 2.SFltl., 20 February 1942, folio 68f
7. Rebensburg, *Erinnerungen*, p 24
8. Oral communication, Korvettenkapitän Feldt (ret'd) to author.
9. Opdenhoff, Hermann, b.1915, July 1939–June 1942, boat commander, 2.SFltl., first holder, Knight's Cross, S-boat Arm (awarded 16 May 1940); see chapter 2.
10. With effect from 1 October 1943, according to War Diary FdS, these were S 19–22, S 24, S 25, S 50, S 95, S 103, S 105, S 107–9, S 115, S 118, S 123, of which six were out of service; also *Tanga, Adolf Lüderitz* and *Carl Peters*.
11. Composition and sketches based on information supplied by former S-boat crewmen.
12. Memorandum FdS, 'The S-boat Arm at the Beginning of November 1943', War Diary FdS, Annexe, 16–30 November 1943, folio 225ff
13. Lohmann-Hildebrand, *Kriegsmarine*, p 55-10f
14. Quoted from Memorandum FdS, 'The S-boat Arm at the Beginning of November 1943', War Diary FdS, Annexe, 16–30 November 1943, folio 226.
15. Oral communication from Korvettenkapitän Feldt (ret'd) to the author.
16. This was how things were done according to information from Leutnant zur See Kohrt (ret'd) in a communication to the author on 27 April 2006.
17. Fregattenkapitän Wuppermann (ret'd), for example, speaks in a very positive manner about his apprenticeship as 'Junior Karl' in early 1939 under the then commander, 1.SFltl., Kapitänleutnant Sturm (communication from Wuppermann to the author).
18. Scott, *Narrow Seas*, opening and closing remarks.
19. Oral communication from Korvettenkapitän Feldt (ret'd) to the author.
20. Information from Leutnant zur See Kohrt (ret'd) to the author.
21. Memorandum, FdS, 'The S-boat Arm at the Beginning of November 1943', War Diary FdS, Annexe, 16–30 November 1943, folio 225
22. War Diary FdS, 1 August 1944
23. *Carl Peters* was mined and sunk in Geltinger Bay on 10 May 1945.
24. Disbandment of German naval forces May 1945, Lohmann-Hildebrand, *Kriegsmarine*, vol I, p 20-7f.

Chapter 16

1. Details per Fock, *Schnellboote*, vol I, p 143f and vol II, p 222. Operational displacement means a boat fully laden carrying weapons and ammunition.
2. On 20 July 1942, S 60 ran a measured mile at 29.8 knots. Reasons offered were 'clapped out boats' and 'old engines' (oral statement, Konteradmiral Kemnade to the author, 3 September 1975).
3. Schulze-Wegener, *Kriegsmarine-Rüstung*, p 12f; also chapter 1
4. SKL, 27 October 1939, quoted in Salewski, *Seekriegsleitung*, vol 2, p 606
5. The term 'bridge' originates from the time of the paddle-steamer, when a bridge was erected for the ship's officers between the paddle boxes.
6. Station Fu G VII with radio receiver (SW/LW), frequencies 50–100m/6,000–3,000kHz and 500–1000m/600–300kHz.
7. Low ultra-short, frequencies 6.55–7.22m/41.55–45.75mHz.
8. Petersen, *Erfahrungsbericht*, p 11
9. Fock, *Schnellboote*, vol 2, p 79
10. Information from former flotilla commander Korvettenkapitän Zymalkowski (ret'd) to the author, 16 February 1984.
11. Petersen, '*Die Schnellbootswaffe Anfang Oktober 1942*', War Diary FdS, Annexe, October 1942, folio 155
12. These new light-metal bridges were installed on Lürssen boats from S 68, and on Schlichting boats from S 118.
13. Hümmelchen, *Schnellboote*, p 222; Fock, *Schnellboote*, vol 2, p 222. Both assert on the other hand that boats S 301–7 also had MB 518 motors installed.
14. A Flachlot trial was carried out aboard S 112; the installation of the Atlas Kleinlot was scheduled for spring 1942. See opinion, FdT in War Diary 2.SFltl., February 1942, folio 70. Precise details for the introduction of the new DF cannot be found.
15. During the battle on 11 September 1942 when MGB 335 was captured, S 117 was the only boat with a 4cm cannon installed; see chapter 6.
16. For the deliberations on an armoured S-boat, see Schulze-Wegener, *Kriegsmarine-Rüstung*, p 167ff.
17. Petersen, *Erfahrungsbericht*, p 28f

18. GA = *Geradeauslauf-Apparat*. With continuous adjustments for data, the correct intercept course for the torpedo was computed by the apparatus.
19. See chapter 11.
20. Salewski, *Seekriegsleitung*, vol 2, p 278
21. In Kriegsmarine terminology, 'Hoofden' was the sea area between the Dutch west coast and the British east coast.
22. Wagner, *Lagevorträge*, p 483ff
23. Schulze-Wegener, *Kriegsmarine-Rüstung*, p 125
24. Schulze-Wegener, *Kriegsmarine-Rüstung*, p 173f; Hümmelchen, *Schnellboote* and Fock, *Schnellboote* differ as to the number somewhat, but the two paint the same picture.
25. Schulze-Wegener, *Kriegsmarine-Rüstung*, pp 200 and 205f
26. Neitzel, *Verbunkerte Frontstützpunkte*, p 32f
27. Petersen, *Erfahrungsbericht*, p 22f
28. Petersen, *Erfahrungsbericht*, p 25

Chapter 17

1. Letter from Petersen to Gördes, 8 January 1975, quoted in Rath, *Kommodore Petersen*, p 112
2. Assessment of 1 November 1937, Rath, *Kommodore Petersen*, p 113
3. Rebensburg, *Erinnerungen*, p 2
4. See Chapter 3
5. FdT War Diary, 22 June 1941, folio 141
6. Rebensburg, *Erinnerungen*, p 30
7. FdS War Diary, 21 February 1943, folio 18
8. Rebensburg, *Erinnerungen*, p 35
9. See chapter 11
10. See chapter 12
11. The office of Kommodore was introduced on 1 April 1939 for officers in the rank of Kapitän zur See. Kapitän zur See Bonte and his successor Kapitän zur See Bey as FdZ (destroyers), Kapitän zur See Dönitz as FdU (U-boats) and Kapitän zur See Ruge as FdM(W) (minesweepers, west), all qualified. A commodore wore the cap of an admiral and one broad ring on the lower sleeves of the uniform jacket, but the shoulder cords/epaulettes of a Kapitän zur See. The title was 'Kapitän zur See and Kommodore', the form of address 'Herr Kommodore'. The emblem of command was a white, square, swallow-tailed pennant with a black Iron Cross. From 1942, a commodore was authorised to fly from the yard of his flagship the *Führer-stander* (leader pennant). Ziener, *Marineuniform*, p 259, ch v. 1 December 1939, and MDv. Nr. 53, *Flaggen, Salut- und Besuchs-Ordnung für die Kriegsmarine*, v. 21 March 1932 (1941 impression).
12. The date 13 June 1944 is often mentioned; possibly this is the date on the certificate. Hitler presented the award at the Berghof on 11 July 1944 (Wagner, *Lagevorträge*, p 598).
13. See additionally the basic statements in Rath, *Kommodore Petersen*; also exchange of correspondence between Quistorp (below) and the author.
14. Rebensburg, *Erinnerungen*, p 50
15. From the sermon delivered by Pastor A Quistorp (formerly commander S 199) in October 1982 to the Vegesack community and former members of 8.SFltl.; see Rath, *Erinnerungen*, p 111.
16. The first trial, before the Jury Court at Hamburg in 1947/8, ended in acquittal. After revision by the Supreme Court for the British Zone at Cologne in 1948, the decision was overturned and remitted to the Jury Court for retrial, which led to Petersen's conviction and imprisonment in 1949. After an appeal in 1953, a second retrial found him not guilty (Rath, *Erinnerungen*, p 88ff). (Translator's note: The author has provided no particulars of the charge. If Petersen himself reviewed the sentence of a court martial at which he had been a trial judge, or authorised the executions knowing that the sentences had not been reviewed lawfully, the procedure would be flawed and the executions illegal. This would technically be murder on his part.)
17. Orth, *Kampfmoral*, p 143f; also Rath, *Erinnerungen*, p 65ff. (Translator's note: Most probably the reason is to be found in the third paragraph of Dönitz's Order of the Day to the Wehrmacht, 1 May 1945: 'The situation demands of you further unconditional service, from you who have already achieved such great historical deeds, and who now only yearn for an end to the war. I demand discipline and obedience. Only through the execution of my orders without reservation can chaos and utter disaster be avoided. That man is a coward and a traitor who now abandons his duty and thereby condemns German women and children in the East to slavery and death.' Speech reproduced in full in Lüdde-Neurath, *Regierung Dönitz*, Musterschmidt Verlag, 1948.)
18. In 1934, the Reichsmarine refused Petersen permission to marry because his intended bride was 'inappropriate', being a Kiel barmaid. Since his parents were also opposed to the marriage, Petersen held back until 1954, following their death and when his affairs were in order (Peter Petersen – nephew – in Rath, *Erinnerungen*, p 116).
19. On New Year's Eve 1982, while he was attempting to prevent hooligans causing a serious disturbance, a lighted firework was thrown at him. He collapsed unconscious and died of a brain haemorrhage in a Flensburg hospital on 2 January 1983 (statement by Dr Gillner, quoted in Rebensburg, *Erinnerungen*, p 62).
20. Per, amongst others, Vizeadmirals Klose, Meentzen and Obermaier, Konteradmirals Kemnade and Birnbacher, Flottillenadmirals Erdmann and Klug.

Epilogue

1. Hümmelchen, *Schnellboote*, p 223
2. See War Diary SKL(A), vol 53, 4 January 1944, p 54.

Sources and Bibliography

Primary Sources

Bundesarchiv/Militärarchiv = BAMA
KTB = War Diary
SKL = Seekriegsleitung

KTB SKL 1939–1945, Part A. commissioned by *Militärgeschichtliches Forschungsamt/BAMA/Marine-Offizier-Vereinigung*, publ Werner Rahn and Gerhard Schreiber in collaboration with Hansjoseph Maierhöfer, Vol 1–68, Herford, Bonn 1988–1997.

KTB, Führer der Torpedoboote (FdT), 30.11.1939–31.08.1940, BAMA RM 53/3; 01.09.1940–28.02.1941, BAMA RM 53/4; 01.03.1941–30.11.1941, BAMA RM 53/5; 01.12.1941–20.04.1942, BAMA RM 53/6.

KTB FdT Helsinki, June–October 1941, BAMA RM 53/13–53/18.

KTB, Führer der Schnellboote (FdS), 20.04.1942–31.12.1942, BAMA RM 55/1 and 55/2; 01.01.1943–15.06.1943, RM 55/29–55/39; 15.06.1943–30.06.1943, BAMA RM 55/4; 07.07.1943–31.10.1943, BAMA RM 55/40–RM 55/47; 01.11.1943–31.12.1943, BAMA III M(F) 51; 01.01.1944–31.01.1945, BAMA RM 55/7–55/12.

KTB, Marinegruppenkommando West, 01.07.1940–31.12.1940, BAMA RM 35/II 38–42; 01.01.1942–31.07.1944, BAMA RM 35/II 52–64; 01.08.1944–17.09.1944, BAMA RM 35/II 66–67.

KTB 1. Schnellbootsflottille, 01.10.1941–15.01.1945, BAMA RM 59/7–11. (In RM 59/10 01.–15.09.1943,in RM 59/11 01.08.–30.09.1944 and 16.10.–31.12.1944. periods missing.)

KTB 2.Schnellbootsflottille, 03.09.1939–15.10.1944, BAMA III M 362/1–8, (Period Weserübung, occupation of Norway, missing).

KTB 3.Schnellbootsflottille, 01.10.1941–30.09.1943, BAMA III M 363/5–8; 01.12.1944–31.01.1945, BAMA RM 59/30.

KTB 5.Schnellbootsflottille, 17.06.1941–15.12.1944, BAMA RM 59/43–50.

KTB 6.Schnellbootsflottille, 01.03.1941–15.10.1944, BAMA RM 59/51–52.

KTB 7.Schnellbootsflottille, 01.04.1942–12.10.1944, BAMA RM 59/53–56, (period 16.06.–16.07.1943 missing).

KTB 8.Schnellbootsflottille, 08.11.1941–10.07.1942, BAMA RM 59/57; 01.12.1942–30.06.1943, BAMA RM 59/58.

KTB 1.Schnellbootsdivision, 16.06.1944–15.11.1944 and 01.12.1944–31.12.1944, BAMA RM 59/1.

Deutsche Minenräumdienstleitung (publisher), *Deutsche Minenräumdienstvorschrift* Nr. 13, 1946.

Erfahrungsbericht über die Bewährung des Schnellboottyps S 38 in technischer und seemännisch-taktischer Hinsicht. (Report on the Performance of S-boat Type S-38 from the technical and nautical-tactical perspective - unpublished draft by the former FdS Staff, also known as the "Petersen-Report".)

HMSO, *Ships of the Royal Navy – Statement of Losses during the Second World War*, London 1947.

Marineleitung, Seekriegsanleitung, Part II, Issue 1, *Schnellbootstaktik*, Berlin 1934, unchanged reprint, 1937.

Müller, Erfahrungsbericht des ausgetauschten Kptl. Karl Müller, (Report of Exchanged Prisoner Karl Müller) BAMA RM 7/131 Sheet 60–78.

OKM (publisher), Seekriegsanleitung, Part III, Issue c, Sperrwaffen, Berlin 1940.

Public Record Office, London, Operational Intelligence Centre; Special Intelligence Summary, also ADM 223 and DEFE 3.

Sperrwaffeninspektion (publisher), M.Dv. Nr. 175 Minenbedienungsvorschrift,1944.

Report on Transfer of boats S 86 und S 8 from Linz to Crsova and back.

Books and Publications

Bachmann, Hans R, *Die deutsche Seekriegführung in der Ostsee nach Ausschaltung der polnischen Marine im Herbst 1939*, Marine-Rundschau 1971, p197 ff.

Behrens, Gerhard, *Die Geschichte der 1. Schnellbootsflottille 1931–1945*, Kiel 1986.

Bonatz, Heinz, *Die Deutsche Marine-Funkaufklärung 1914–1945*, Darmstadt 1970.

————, *Seekrieg im Äther: Die Leistungen derMarine-Funkaufklärung 1939–1945*, Herford 1981.

Breyer, Siegfried, *Die Deutsche Kriegsmarine 1939–1945*, Vol 2, Hanau 1986.

Bulkley, Robert J, *At Close Quarters, PT Boats in the United States Navy*, Washington 1962.

Conrady, H D v, "Die deutschen Motor-Torpedoschnellboote", in *Marine-Rundschau*
1962, p356 and 1963, p113.

Dahms, Hellmuth Günther, *Die Geschichte des Zweiten Weltkrieges*, Frankfurt/M 1989.

Dickens, Peter, *Night Action: MTB Flotilla at War*, London 1974.

Docter, H, "Die Anfänge des Marine-Schnellbootbaus", in *Wehrtechnische Monatshefte* 1963, p.325 and 374.

Ehrensberger, Konrad, *100 Jahre Organisation der deutschen Marine*, Bonn 1993.

Fechter, Helmut, and Hümmelchen, Gerhard, *Seekriegsatlas Mittelmeer – Schwarzes Meer 1940–1945*, Munich 1972.

Felmy, Hellmuth, *Die deutsche Luftwaffe auf dem Mittelmeerkriegsschauplatz*, unpublished study N.8 of the Führungsakademie der Bundeswehr, Führungslehre Luftwaffe, undated.

Fock, Harald, *Schnellboote*, Vol 1, *Von den Anfänge bis zum Ausbruch des 2. Weltkrieges*, Herford 1973; Vol 2, *Entwicklung und Einsatz im 2. Weltkrieg*, Herford 1974.

Foerster, Roland G, "Die Ardennen-Offensive 1944. Politisch-strategische Überlegungen und operative Konzepte auf deutscher Seite", in Ottmer, Hans-Martin (editor) *Ausgewählte Operationen und ihre militärhistorischen Grundlagen/im Auftrag des MGFA*, Herford 1993.

Frank, Hans, *Der Einsatz der 3.Schnellbootsflottille im Mittelmeer 1941 bis 1943*, Führungsakademie der Bundeswehr, Hamburg 1975.

Frieser, Karl-Heinz, *Blitzkrieg-Legende, Der Westfeldzug 1940*, Munich 1995.

Giermann, Christian, *Schnellbootseinsätze der Kriegsmarine im Westraum 1942/1943, eine Untersuchung von Taktik und Technik im Hinblick auf Schnellboote der Deutschen Marine*, Führungsakademie der Bundeswehr, Hamburg 1970.

Giessler, Helmuth, *Der Marine-Nachrichten- und Ortungsdienst*, Munich 1971.

Goulter, Christina J M, *A Forgotten Offensive, Royal Air Force Coastal Command's Anti-Shipping Campaign, 1940–1945*, London 1995.

Greiner, Christian, "Die Abwehr der deutschen Ardennen-Offensive", in Ottmer, Hans-Martin (editor) *Ausgewählte Operationen und ihre militärhistorischen Grundlagen/im Auftrag des MGFA*, Herford 1993.

Gröner, Erich, *Die Deutschen Kriegsschiffe 1815–1945*, Vol 2, *Torpedoboote, Zerstörer, Schnellboote, Minensuchboote, Minenräumboote*, Koblenz 1983, Vol 4, *Hilfsschiffe I: Werkstattschiffe, Tender und Begleitschiffe, Tanker und Versorger*, Koblenz 1986.

Günther, Albin, *Die Entwicklung der Seemine von 1777–1945*, Marinewaffenkommando (publisher),1958.

Güth, Rolf, *Von Revolution zu Revolution*, Herford1978.

Hamilton, Nigel, "D-Day: Gemeinsame Operationen und die Frage der Führung", in Groß, Gerhard P (editor), *Führungsdenken in europäischen und nordamerikanischen Streitkräften im 19. und 20. Jahrhundert/ for MGFA*, Hamburg 2001.

Hillgruber, Andreas, *Hitlers Strategie*, 3rd Edition, Bonn1993.

Hillgruber, Hümmelchen, *Chronik des zweiten Weltkrieges*, Düsseldorf 1978.

Hoops, Henning, "Der Einsatz von Schnellbooten 1945 im Kampf gegen den britischen Geleitverkehr im Kanal", in *Flottenkommando – 27, Historisch-Taktische Tagung der Flotte 1987*, Glücksburg 1987.

Hubatsch, Walther, *Weserübung*, Göttingen 1960.

————, *Hitlers Weisungen für die Kriegsführung 1939–1945*, DTV Dokumente, Munich 1965.

Hümmelchen, Gerhard, *Die Deutschen Schnellboote im Zweiten Weltkrieg*, Hamburg 1996.

Jefferson, David, *Coastal Forces at War*, Sparkford 1996.

Kemnade, Friedrich, Die *Afrika-Flottille*, Stuttgart1978.

Klietmann, Kurt-G, *Auszeichnungen des Deutschen Reiches 1936–1945*, 8th Edition, Stuttgart 1996.

Kopp, Georg, *Das Teufelsschiff und seine kleine Schwester*, Leipzig 1930.

Krancke, Theodor, "Die Invasionsabwehrmaßnahmen der Kriegsmarine im Kanalgebiet 1944", in *Marine- Rundschau 1969*, p170.

Krause-Traudes, Markus, "Einsätze der 5. Schnellbootflottille in der östlichen Ostsee im Herbst 1944", in *Flottenkommando – 27, Historisch-Taktische Tagung der Flotte 1987*, Glücksburg 1987.

Ledebur, Gerhard Frhr von, *Die Seemine*, Munich 1977.

Lenton, H T and Colledge, J J, *Warships of World War II*, 2nd Edition, London 1973.

Lloyds of London Press Ltd, *Lloyds War Losses*, Vol I, *British, Allied and Neutral Merchant Vessels sunk or Destroyed by War Causes*, London 1989.

Lohmann, Walter, und Hildebrand, Hans J, *Die Deutsche Kriegsmarine 1939–1945*, Vols I–III, Bad Nauheim 1956.

Lorenz, Hermann, "Die Ostsee-Kriegführung der Roten Flotte im 2. Weltkrieg", in *Das dt. Bild der russischen und sowj. Marine*, Supplement 7/8, Marine-Rundschau, Frankfurt/M. 1962.

Marineleitung, "Seekriegsanleitung", Part II, Issue 1, *Schnellbootstaktik*, Berlin 1934, unchanged reprint 1937.

Meister, Jürg, *Der Seekrieg in den osteuropäischen Gewässern 1941–45*, Munich 1958.

Melzer, Walther, *Kampf um die Baltischen Inseln 1917–1941–1944*, Neckargemünd 1960.

Militärgeschichtliches Forschungsamt (publisher), *Das Deutsche Reich und der Zweite Weltkrieg*: Vol 2, *Die Errichtung der Hegemonie auf dem europäischen Kontinent*, Stuttgart 1979; Vol 3, *Der Mittelmeerraum und Südosteuropa*, Stuttgart 1984; Vol 4, *Der Angriff auf die Sowjetunion*, Stuttgart 1983; Vol 6, *Der globale Krieg*, Stuttgart 1990.

Militärgeschichtliches Forschungsamt (publisher), *Deutsche Militärgeschichte 1648–1939*: Vol 5, *Deutsche Marinegeschichte der Neuzeit*, Munich 1983.

Militärgeschichtliches Forschungsamt (publisher), *Operationsgebiet Östliche Ostsee und der Finnisch-Baltische Raum 1944*, Stuttgart 1961.

Morison, Samuel Eliot, *History of United States Naval Operations in World War II*, Vol II, *Operations in North African Waters*, Boston 1957; Vol IX, *Sicily*

————, *Salerno–Anzio*, Boston 1954; Vol XI, *The Invasion of France and Germany*, Boston 1960.

Müller, Albert, *Erinnerungen 1941–1943*, unpublished.

Müller, Kptlt, "Die Schnellbootswaffe im Krieg mit der feindlichen Ortung", in *Fachvorträge über Schiffsortung beim Oberkommando der Kriegsmarine vom 09–10.03.1943*, publ. Ausschuss für Funkortung

Munson, Kenneth, *Die Weltkrieg II-Flugzeuge*, 12th Edition, Stuttgart 1983.

Neitzel, Sönke, *Der Einsatz der deutschen Luftwaffe über dem Atlantik und der Nordsee 1939–1945*, Bonn 1995.

Neitzel, Sönke, "Die verbunkerten Frontstützpunkte der U-Boot- und Schnellbootwaffe", in *Militärgeschichte*, Issue 2 (1994), p27.

Neitzel, Sönke, "Die Zusammenarbeit zwischen Schnellbooten und Luftwaffe", in *Militärgeschichte*, NF, Issue 4, Herford 1995, p55.

North, A J D, *Royal Naval Coastal Forces 1939–1945*, London 1972.

Orth, Kathrin, "Kampfmoral und Einsatzbereitschaft in der

Kriegsmarine 1945", in *Kriegsende 1945 in Deutschland*, published for *Militärgeschichtliches Forschungsamt* by Jörg Hillmann and John Zimmermann, Munich 2002.

Ose, Dieter, *Die Entscheidung im Westen*, Stuttgart 1982.

Ottmer, Hans-Martin, *Weserübung*, Munich 1994.

Patzwall, Klaus D, *Die Auszeichnungen der Kriegsmarine 1939–1945*, Norderstedt 1987.

Playfair, I S O, *The Mediterranean and the Middle East*, Vols I–III, London 1954.

Potter, Elmar B, Nimitz, Chester W, and Rohwer, Jürgen, *Seemacht. Von der Antike bis zur Gegenwart*, Munich 1982.

Rahn, Werner, *Reichsmarine und Landesverteidigung 1919–1928*, Munich 1976.

———-, "Warnsignale und Selbstgewissheit. Der deutsche Marine-Nachrichtendienst und die vermeintliche Sicherheit des Schlüssels M (Enigma)
1943/44", in *Militärgeschichtliche Zeitschrift*, No 61 (2002), Issue 1, p141.

Rath, Norbert, *Kommodore Rudolf Petersen*, unpublished biography, Kappeln 2000.

Rebensburg, Bernd, *Erinnerungen an den Schnellbootseinsatz im Westen 1940–1945*, Bonn 1999.

Reuter, Frank, *Funkmeß. Die Entwicklung und der Einsatz des Radar-Verfahrens in Deutschland bis zum Ende des Zweiten Weltkrieges*, Opladen 1971.

Reuth, Ralf Georg, *Entscheidung im Mittelmeer*, Koblenz 1985.

Rohwer, J, and Hümmelchen, G, *Chronology of the War at Sea 1939–1945*, Vol I, *1939–1942*, London 1972, Vol II, *1943–1945*, London 1974.

Roskill, S W, *The War At Sea 1939–1945*, Vol I, *The Defensive*, London 1954, Vol II, *The Period of Balance*, London 1956, Vol III/1 and III/2 *The Offensive*, London 1960 und 1961.

Rössler, Eberhard, *Die Torpedos der deutschen U-Boote*, Herford 1984.

Roth, Günther, "Operatives Denken bei Schlieffen und Manstein", in: Ottmer, Hans-Martin, and Ostertag, Heiger (editors), *Ausgewählte Operationen und ihre militärhistorischen Grundlagen*, Herford 1993.

Ruge, Friedrich, *Die Sowjetflotte als Gegner im Seekrieg 1941–1945*, Stuttgart 1981.

Ruge, Friedrich, *Im Küstenvorfeld*, Munich 1974.

Ryan, Cornelius, "Der längste Tag", in *Der Zweite Weltkrieg*, Vol 3, *Verlag Das Beste*, Stuttgart 1989.

Salewski, Michael, *Die deutsche Seekriegsleitung 1935–1945*, Vol I, *1935–1941*, Frankfurt/M. 1970, Vol 2, *1942–1945*, München 1975; Vol 3, *Denkschriften und Lagebeurteilungen*, Neustadt 1973.

Santoni, Alberto, *Ultra siegt im Mittelmeer*, Koblenz 1985.

Schenk, Peter, *Kampf um die Ägäis*, Hamburg 2000.

Schön, Heinz, *Ostsee 45*, 2nd Edition, Stuttgart 1984.

Schramm, Percy E, *KTB OKW*, Munich 1982.

Schulze-Wegener, Guntram, *Die deutsche Kriegsmarine-Rüstung*, Hamburg 1997.

Scott, Peter, *The Battle of the Narrow Seas*, London 1946.

Shankland, Peter, and Hunter, Anthony, *Malta Convoy*, London1961.

Speidel, Hans, *Invasion 1944*, Tübingen 1949.

Syfret, E N, "Report on Operation Pedestral", in *Supplement to the London Gazette*, 11.08.1948, p45001.

Tent, James Foster, *E-Boat Alert: Defending the Normandy Invasion Fleet*, Annapolis 1996.

Thamer, Hans-Ulrich, "Entscheidung im Westen", in Umbreit, Hans (editor), *Invasion 1944*, Hamburg 1998.

Treue, Wilhelm, *Deutsche Marinerüstung 1919–1942*, Herford 1992.

Ufficio Storico Della Marine Militare, *La Marine Italiana Nella Seconda Guerra Mondiale*, Vol II, *La Guerra Nel Mediterraneo, Vol 2*, Rome 1960, and Vol XVIII, *La Guerra Di Mine*, Rome 1966, also Dati Statistici, Rome 1950.

Umbreit, Hans, *Invasion 1944*, Hamburg 1998.

Vogel, Detlef , "Kriegführung in Westeuropa", in Umbreit, Hans, *Invasion 1944*, Bonn 1998.

Wagner, Gerhard, *Lagevorträge des Oberbefehlshabers der Kriegsmarine vor Hitler 1939–1945*, Munich 1972.

Wegener, Edward, "Die Normandie-Invasion und die Marine", in *Marine-Forum* 6/79, p161.

Wegener, Wolfgang, *Die Seestrategie des Weltkrieges*, Berlin 1929.

Wegmüller, Hans, *Die Abwehr der Invasion*, Freiburg 1979.

Weinberg, Gerhard L, *Eine Welt in Waffen: Die Globale Geschichte des Zweiten Weltkrieges*, Stuttgart 1995.

Whitley, Mike – Deutsche Seestreitkräfte 1939–1945, Stuttgart 1995.

Zienert, Josef, *Unsere Marineuniform*, Hamburg 1970.

Index